Agile Practices for Waterfall Projects

Shifting Processes for Competitive Advantage

Barbee Davis, PMP, PMI-ACP, PHR

J.ROSS
PUBLISHING

Copyright © 2013 by Barbee Davis

ISBN-13: 978-1-60427-083-9

Printed and bound in the U.S.A. Printed on acid-free paper.

10 9 8 7 6 5 4 3 2 1

Library of Congress Cataloging-in-Publication Data

Davis, Barbee.
    Agile practices for waterfall projects : shifting processes for
competitive advantage / by Barbee Davis.
        p. cm.
    Includes bibliographical references and index.
    ISBN 978-1-60427-083-9 (hbk. : alk. paper)   1. Project management.
    2. Teams in the workplace.   I. Title.
    HD69.P75D385 2012
    658.4'04—dc23

                                                        2012030919

Phone: (954) 727-9333 Ext. 5
Fax: (561) 892-0700
Web: www.jrosspub.com

CONTENTS

Preface ix
About the Author xi

Chapter 1: Why Agile Now? 1
    Three Current Project Questions 3
    Project Management Certifications 5
    The Genesis of Project Management 6
    The Need for Change 8
    References 10

Chapter 2: What Is Agile? 11
    "Big Agile" and "little agile" 11
    Iterative and Incremental Development by a Dedicated Team 13
    Embracing Change 14
    Working Closely with Your Customer 16
    References 17

Chapter 3: Where Did Agile Ideas Originate? 19
    Frederick Taylor 19
    Frank and Lillian Galbraith 21
    Henri Fayol 22
    Henry Ford 23
    Henry Gantt 24
    Winston Royce 25
    Peter Drucker 25
    Eliyahu Goldratt 26
    Abraham Maslow and Douglas McGregor 27
    James Reddin 29
    Hirotaka Takeuchi and Ikujiro Nonaka 29

Sakichi Toyoda, Kiichiro Toyoda, and Taiichi Ohno........................ 30
References 35

Chapter 4: What Are Agile Practices and How Do They Work? **37**
Find Errors Early 41
Prototyping 43
Early Customer Involvement 45
Agile vs. Waterfall 48
Plan, Do, Check, Act 49
References 53

Chapter 5: What Are Some More New Agile Concepts? **55**
Favor the Simple Over the Complex 55
Phase-to-Phase Relationships 58
The Non-Software Agile Process 59
User Stories 62
Progressive Elaboration 67
References 70

Chapter 6: Should My Projects Be Agile? **71**
Waterfall Process Candidates 74
Agile Candidates 75
The Agile Evaluator 77
Hybrid Products 80
The New Marketing Strategy 82
The Google Car 83
Hybrid Medical Devices 85
The New Product or Service Measurements of Quality 88
References 90

Chapter 7: How Does an Agile Team Get Started? **91**
Create Team Operating Rules 91
Select Techniques to Reach Consensus 93
Confirm Initiating Processes 95
Planning Agile Work 96
Iterative Development and Risk 97
The Agile-ish WBS 98
Moving User Stories Into Iterations 101

Chapter 8: How Do Agile Teams Estimate? **107**
Team Estimates 107
The Fibonacci Sequence 108

Planning Poker 111
Team Estimation Game 113
Dog Estimates 115
T-shirt Sizes 115
Selecting Tasks 115
Tracking Agile Progress 116
Daily Agile Stand-up Meetings 119
References 122

Chapter 9: What Agile Tools Are Important? 123
End-of-Iteration Practices 123
Velocity 124
Social Loafing 129
Interacting with Traditional Teams 132
Getting Started with Agile 133
Iteration Time Breakdown 136
References 138

Chapter 10: How Does Agile Scale to the Enterprise Level? 141
One Backlog—One Team 141
One Backlog—Mixed Teams 143
One Backlog—Many Teams 144
Multiple, Independent Product Backlogs 144
Separate, But Cooperating Teams 146
Collocated Teams 146

Chapter 11: How Do I Work With Distributed Teams? 151
Distributed Teams 151
Casual Conversations 154
Story Cards 155
Time Zones 156
Language 156
Communications Tools 158
Work Tracking Tools 160
Remote Daily Stand-ups 160
Travel 161
The Lone Expert 161
References 162

Chapter 12: What Do I Use for Agile Documentation? 163
Earned Value Method 163
Agile Earned Value 165

Software Documents 169
Burndown Chart with Scope Changes 171
Burnup Chart 174
Cumulative Flow Diagram 174
References 176

Chapter 13: What Needs to Change in My Own Skill Set? 177
Self-managed Teams 177
Collocated and Dedicated Teams 178
Facilitation Skills 179
Sales Skills 180
Coordination Skills 181
Collaboration Skills 181
Team Building Skills 182
Conflict Resolution Skills 182
Training Skills 184
Group Decision Making Skills 184
Social Styles Skills 185
Servant-Leader Skills 192
Millennium Management Skills 194
Process Tailoring Skills 199
References 200

Chapter 14: What Needs To Change In My Business Skill Sets? 201
Six Changes to Embrace 201
Cost of Failure 203
Aligning Projects to Strategic Objectives 205
Maximizing Revenue Streams and Flexibility 208
Handling Cancelled or Deferred Projects 211
Agile Budgeting and Forecasting 212
Actively Seeking New Technology 214
Documenting Team Authority 218
References 220

Chapter 15: What Shifts in Business Will Affect Me? 221
Common Team Workspaces 222
Design That Matters: Junkyard Incubators 225
Microsoft Research Division: Space Design 226
Steelcase, Inc.: Furnishings Design 226
Skype: Virtual Space Design 227
Explicit and Tacit Knowledge 228
References 231

Chapter 16: What Changes Are Needed in My Organization?................... **233**
Authorization 234
Resource Management... 235
Communications 236
Metrics... 236
Contracts... 237
High-level Involvement... 244
Cost Accounting and Other Reports 245
Team Member Reactions 247
Radical Management Shifts... 247
The Growing Importance of Intangible Assets 249
A Need for PMO Refocusing 249
A Change in Human Resources Practices... 252
References 254

Chapter 17: What Are Scrum, XP, and DSDM? **257**
Software Development... 257
Scrum 259
Extreme Programming... 264
Dynamic Systems Development Method 270
References 275

Chapter 18: What Are Lean, Kanban, Crystal, and Other
Agile Practices? **277**
Lean Manufacturing.. 277
Kanban 278
Toyota Production System... 283
Lean Software Development 284
Rational Unified Process 284
Crystal Methodologies.. 287
Feature Driven Development... 288
References 290

Chapter 19: How Do I Jumpstart Change?.. **293**
Choosing a Pilot Project 293
Train the Product Owner 294
Sell Up, Down, and Sideways... 294
Talk the Talk 297
Learn the Change Process 298
References 300

Chapter 20: Who Has Made Agile Work? **301**

CH2M Hill's Rocky Flats Project 301

Boeing's 787 Project 303

The Kauffman Performing Arts Center Project 307

AccuRev Agile Sales Team 308

GVK's Mumbai, India Airport Project 308

The Sydney Opera House Project 310

References 312

Chapter 21: Parting Advice **315**

Glossary **321**

Index **333**

PREFACE

As a project manager, I am aware that many organizations are facing a crisis, and they are looking to us in the project management profession for solutions. However, often the very creativity and innovation that we, and our teams, could bring to address these business challenges are suppressed with heavy documentation, rigid rules, and a disenfranchisement of us as true business partners.

As I traveled the world speaking on this topic, I witnessed the frustration that comes from project managers wanting to be able to help their organizations succeed, but not knowing how or where to start. I believe that answers to speed to market, employee retention, product innovation, and financial viability challenges will come when an Agile mindset is embraced throughout a business entity.

However, with the heavy emphasis on more traditional/Waterfall processes found in most modern corporate structures, it is difficult to find a thread to pull to unweave the blanket of excessive methodology that is weighing down our projects. Within these pages, I'd like to share with you what I know, and more importantly, what I have learned from hundreds of project professionals who successfully turned their companies around.

At the project level, we seldom believe that we have the power to transform the entire organization, and perhaps we can't. However, there are ways for you to start changing your own project teams and your own thought processes to have better success on a daily basis. In this book, I present both the concepts of Agile and detailed, practical ways that you can use them with a traditional team. Through an understanding of how Agile can help you and your team, you can garner increased results, which can then be used to get others in the organization interested in making a larger commitment to this paradigm shift.

I was a part of the PMI Agile pilot program when I was preparing to take my certification test and had trouble finding more than bits and pieces of information to use in my studies. So, contained within this book, I included a clear story of what Agile is, when it is appropriate to use it on your projects, and all of the terms and concepts you will need to understand to sit for your PMI-ACP certification. I have tried to make it realistic and fun to learn this new approach to old problems with the hope that Agile processes will help you prepare for the future shift in project management practices. I hope that you enjoy the read and take away ideas that get you started on your own innovative ways to add useful Agile practices to your own Waterfall projects.

Barbee Davis

ABOUT THE AUTHOR

Barbee Davis, MA, PMP, PMI-ACP, and PHR, heads Davis Consulting, a provider of project management guidance and services. Barbee also works for the Project Management Institute (PMI®). She is a R.E.P. Quality Reviewer for organizations who wish to be part of the PMI Registered Education Provider (R.E.P.) program. Ms. Davis leads special projects for PMI, such as the Students In Free Enterprise (SIFE) project that helps local PMI Chapters attract and educate college students about the project management field. She also created the PMI Intellectual Property Tutorial for R.E.P.s, which has been translated into eight languages. Over the past 5 years, Ms. Davis has written the semi-monthly column, *Quick Quizzes,* for the PMI *Community Post* that reached over 300,000 project managers worldwide. She also writes a similar feature, *Topic Teasers,* available through PMI Chapter newsletters.

Ms. Davis has designed and implemented projects in varied industries and managed large project rollouts for many large corporations. This ex-IBMer and former Wilson Learning facilitator is also proficient in online learning instructional design, having both written for and taught on Blackboard for universities and corporate clients. She has been on staff at the University of Nebraska at Omaha, Nebraska Wesleyan, and Bellevue University. As co-founder of ExecuTrain of Nebraska and Vice-President of Sales and Training, she has managed and provided technical training for solution developers and systems engineers, as well as offering end-user training on all platforms.

Besides holding the PMP certification, Barbee also has an Agile Practitioner Certification (PMI-ACP)®, a black belt in Microsoft Project, a Professional in Human Resources (PHR) accreditation, and an American Society of Training and

Development Training Certificate in instruction, facilitation, and instructional design. She is a popular and sought-after speaker around the world, especially on merging Agile practices with *PMBOK® Guide* processes to bridge the gap between the sometimes warring methodologies.

At J. Ross Publishing we are committed to providing today's professional with practical, hands-on tools that enhance the learning experience and give readers an opportunity to apply what they have learned. That is why we offer free ancillary materials available for download on this book and all participating Web Added Value™ publications. These online resources may include interactive versions of material that appears in the book or supplemental templates, worksheets, models, plans, case studies, proposals, spreadsheets and assessment tools, among other things. Whenever you see the WAV™ symbol in any of our publications, it means bonus materials accompany the book and are available from the Web Added Value Download Resource Center at www.jrosspub.com.

Downloads for *Agile Practices for Waterfall Projects: Shifting Processes for Competitive Advantage* consist of:

- An Agile Evaluator, Agile Evaluator Checklist, and Agile Evaluator sample results to help you decide if your projects are ready to move to Agile
- A Uganda Coffee website team exercise to get you started with Agile practices to plan a project
- Agile templates such as Planning Poker cards and Story Cards
- A PMI-ACP® Practice Exam to help you prepare for the certification test

Why Agile Now?

Project managers are like sharks. We have to keep swimming to keep alive and employable in a constantly evolving workplace. Despite our occupation's solidified need to brace ourselves and our teams to avoid unnecessary changes, the reality of the future looms clearly: projects will be managed with a hybrid process of Agile (flexible) and formal (traditional) practices. So, we need to think about how to evolve our approach to managing projects. The project managers who are visionary and practical enough to learn how to do this will have a huge career advantage over those who lag behind.

To understand how to update our own skills in the most efficient matter, we will need to consider these five questions:

1. Why change our project culture now?
2. How do we blend new Agile ideas into familiar, traditional project management processes?
3. What additional skills do we need as project managers if we make these changes?
4. What background information and sales techniques do we need to convince those above, below, and next to us in the organizational hierarchy to support an evolution to Agile?
5. What changes need to happen in our organization to allow Agile and traditional approaches to merge?

Why now? The answer is obvious if you look around to see the challenges that organizations are facing in today's economy. First, there is a tremendous push to accelerate the time to market. Second, we have to enhance our own ability, and that of our team, to manage quickly changing priorities and requirements. The world has changed dramatically, and there is too much competition to succeed by merely producing things faster and cheaper. We need to focus on adding innovation and creativity to our products and services.

Adding to these challenges is globalization, when in order to expand markets our organizations are opening branches all over the world, or perhaps adding remote teams in an attempt to reduce costs. These realities add the burden of managing projects and project teams within cultures foreign to our own, adding more layers to the stack of issues we already juggle on a daily basis.

Companies also face new issues of employee retention and engagement. Currently, with unemployment rates high in many parts of the world, people are staying put. But recent surveys estimate that about 60% of employees plan to look around once the economy stabilizes. Since these team members may not be invested in the company long term, it stands to reason that they may not be fully engaged and productive.

An additional consideration is the need to plan for New Millennium, or Generation Y, people coming into the workforce. When surveyed, their "work ethic" is self-fulfillment; they like collaborative leadership, and they view change as inevitable and increasing. This new generation of workers is already bringing a mindset tuned to Agile values with them. Rather than needing to educate and convince them to adopt Agile principles, the focus will shift to convincing them that our organization operates in harmony with a belief system that they already have.

The reason that we, as project managers, need to make our project processes more Agile, is not because it is the "flavor of the month," but because it allows us to:

- Drive business agility,
- Respond to a fast-changing business environment,
- Increase alignment of projects to business strategies to create the best return on investment, and
- Impact employee hiring and retention issues.

We achieve these goals by becoming more flexible in the way that we manage projects. Do not be concerned that the word "Agile" has become connected to the software industry. In its pure form, the one we will use, it means to be more versatile and able to adjust quickly to change. Some organizations have been using Agile approaches for over 10 years with amazing success.

John P. Kotter, a professor at Harvard Business School, who is regarded as an authority on leadership and change, and James L. Heskett, professor emeritus of Harvard University, wrote *Corporate Culture and Performance*. They examined more than 200 organizations, including Hewlett-Packard, Xerox, the Investment Company Institute (ICI), and Nissan. They found that in companies with a strong and adaptive Agile culture:

- Revenue grew more than 4 times faster,
- The rate of job creation was 7 times higher,
- Stock profits grew 12 times faster, and
- Profit performance was (take a moment and get a number in your mind, then read on) 750 times higher than those companies who were less nimble.[1] Would you guess even close to that number?

Thus, what we need to discover is a way to *add* Agile to organizations, but not wipe out the traditional processes sometimes known as "Waterfall" and replace them entirely, due to the huge investment we have in our current processes, training, and certifications. We can add the most appropriate parts of the Agile philosophy to specifically address some of the major problems facing our employers and ourselves, not only for software developers, but in all parts of the organization.

In recent years, there has been a heated debate between the Agile and Waterfall proponents, which often became quite passionate. On the one hand, the software development world has found a much needed solution to their woes in an Agile methodology, but other departments in the company may feel it is not robust enough to meet their needs. It is true, at first glance, that Agile and Waterfall may appear to be two competing, or even warring, project management approaches that would seem an unlikely mix. But when you know the evolutionary history of project management and the business theory on which it is based, it is easy to see that both Agile and Waterfall are more like loving siblings who come from the same hearty stock.

How do you justify moving to a more Agile technique when your company or industry is more heavily invested in a traditional project management approach? We need to remember that one of the most important focuses for all of us as project managers in today's world is to be innovative. We all want to explore new ideas and find different ways to support our executive management and teams, and to find better ways to do projects. So what are the big project problems that Agile solves?

Three Current Project Questions

There are three big questions to ask about your current projects. Be honest! First, have you ever had a project finish pretty much on time and pretty close to budget, but after it was all over, the customer was not thrilled with what you delivered? With the Agile methodology, your customer is involved, sitting next to you, being a part of meetings from the beginning of the project to the end. The customer approves a few features and functions every 1 to 2 weeks. So, you are confident that you know exactly what they want before you build it. If they are unhappy or not totally pleased along the way, you know it immediately—in plenty of time to fix the problem.

Here's the second question. Have you ever run out of time and money, but the project was not complete? If you answered yes, you are in the same situation as the majority of project managers. With Agile, you are working first on the features and functions that bring the most business value and are the most important to the customer. If you run out of time and money, and don't get finished with the entire list of requirements that may appear to be ideal, at least you have a working product or service that includes the most valuable parts: finished, tested, and useable or sellable.

The third question: Did you ever feel you could solve a project problem better than your boss, but your corporate roles have such ironclad boundaries that you are not asked or allowed to be a part of solving problems or making suggestions? With Agile, you are part of a dedicated, self-organizing, self-directed, cross-functional team that is authorized and empowered to run the project. The idea is that the people actually doing the work know the best way to solve problems that arise. Your boss, or even you as the project manager, have new roles—to remove obstacles and roadblocks to success for the project team. Most people are more motivated by achievement, by being appreciated and valued, and being free to work on interesting things, than by money. Today's teams are made up of smart people. You do not need to hand out work to them one tiny bit at a time. For the most part, teams are capable, willing, and able to know what to do and do what it takes to get the work of the project completed. They can find solutions to hard problems on their own.

If you answered "Yes" to any of the three questions, you are an honest project manager. We have all had these things happen if we've spent any time actively working in the profession. If you have had any of those problems, you should consider adding Agile to your projects to create a hybrid approach. In fact, Agile is addressing and solving quite a few common project management issues. As you read further, you will probably see that many of your own or your team's day-to-day frustrations can be solved, or even avoided in the first place, with a more Agile process.

Agile has been around for more than a decade, and most project managers have at least heard about it. Agile teams on average provide products and services faster, at a higher level of quality, at a lower price, and with more satisfied customers. And the people who work on these teams are happier and stay with the organization longer.

Agile simply means that you are more flexible in your approach to doing projects. You are able to adapt and change your project quickly when your project team, or your customer, finds it necessary. In 2008, the research group QSM Associates assessed the performance of 29 Agile development projects against

8,000 plan-based or Waterfall averages in three key areas: productivity, time to market, and quality. They found that the Agile projects were:

- 37% to 50% faster in delivering software to market,
- 16% to 35% more productive as a team, and
- Able to maintain normal defect counts despite significantly shorter schedules to complete the work of the project.[2]

Statistics such as these have captured the attention of management level decision makers around the world.

Project Management Certifications

Project management in a traditional fashion has been around in one form or another for over 100 years. You might hold a certification such as PMP® (Project Management Professional), CAPM® (Certified Associate in Project Management), PgMP® (Program Management Professional), PMI-SP® (Project Management Institute Scheduling Professional), or PMI-RMP® (Project Management Institute Risk Management Professional).

If you are European, you might be a PRINCE2® (Projects IN Controlled Environments 2) Registered Practitioner. There are hundreds of thousands of certified individuals who have had to work hard to learn PMI or PRINCE2 processes. They scheduled, took, and passed rigorous tests (perhaps after several tries). They worked to get additional training and experience to maintain their status, and most importantly, they used the principles successfully, for the most part, for a number of years.

A newer certification is the PMI-ACP® (Project Management Institute Agile Certified Practitioner). The *Project Management Body of Knowledge—Fifth Edition* includes Agile in a more integrated way than earlier editions. Just as there is a PMI Construction Standard, Government Extension, and Project and Portfolio Standard, to mention a few, you may see an Agile body of knowledge standard at some point to support the new PMI-ACP certification.

Be aware that among other criteria, the PMI-ACP requires experience working on projects using an Agile approach, or time spent on an Agile project team within the last three years, in order to qualify to take the exam. When you begin to include some of the new ideas in this book with your team, be sure to record those hours spent in order to meet the exam qualification requirement. You can view the other requirements at www.pmi.org.

Part of earning the PMI-ACP certification is a three-hour test, and once you pass it you need 30 Professional Development Units (PDUs) from training, or other experiential activities, to keep your certification active, rather than the 60

PDUs required by some of the other PMI certifications. If you are already a PMP certificant, the good news is that PMI-ACP PDU hours and PMP PDU hours can overlap. In other words, you can count the same hours toward recertification for both, as long as the subject matter of the training is appropriate.

So, that is the PMI-ACP certification, but what is Agile itself? Agile means that your team is more pliable. You are able to adapt and change the project quickly when the project team, the product owner, or the customer finds it desirable. The information technology world, in particular, is moving toward a more flexible approach to project management with fewer formal documents and less administrative overhead, while other parts of the organization may still use the more familiar, traditional project management processes.

Agile is in all of our futures. Even the most traditional project managers and organizations who insist on abiding by only the processes distributed by PMI will need to be ready to adjust their day-to-day actions. Agile is becoming mainstream, and all departments and industries are being touched. What can we learn from these new, Agile processes being used successfully by software developers? Is there a way that we can blend their new approaches into the more traditional project plans, which we as project managers must have to manage our own projects, to give us faster and more measurable results? How can we mix Agile ideas and processes into our more traditional Waterfall team's current way of doing things?

One of the first concerns to surface when considering Agile is that organizations have spent a lot of time and money accepting, training, and implementing their current project management processes. So, they are going to be less than anxious to dump that all overboard and start fresh. Our goal is to keep what works about the traditional processes and augment what does not, ending up with a hybrid approach that uses the best ideas from each practice.

Scrum advocates need not be concerned that we are speaking heresy. Scrum, which is an excellent and successful approach to project management and software development, is covered in Chapter 17, "What Are Scrum, XP, and DSDM?" Be assured that the hybrid approach that we will be discussing will not alter or infringe on Agile software development methodologies, but rather lead us to understand, support, and work in harmony with them throughout the other parts of the business environment.

The Genesis of Project Management

The traditional project management approach has been in place to some extent for a long, long, long time. As far back as 5,000 years ago, when the Egyptian pyramids were being built, there were unskilled day laborers doing the physical construction work who needed to be managed. Actually, most were farmers who owed annual taxes to the Pharaoh. The tangible items of value or agricultural products used as payment were of some interest to the crown. But that payment form really did not work to fulfill the Pharaoh's main vision: an elaborate and impressive tomb to ensure that his spirit would be safely transported to the next world.

A better solution to the tax issue was to have the farmers pay their obligation in the form of a certain number of days of labor, giving the Pharaoh the workforce needed for his construction projects. They probably had architectural drawings back then, and you have to imagine that someone smart had figured out the sequence in which tasks should be done, planned the materials, and then listed the jobs to be done on a daily basis. There were also the challenges of managing a large, uneducated, unmotivated, and disengaged workforce.

If we really knew what happened with project managers in ancient Egypt, we might wonder if the pyramids originally started out to be a rectangular tower, just like the architect's drawings showed on the papyrus scroll, accompanied by his technical and functional requirements written in colorful hieroglyphics. Like on our projects today, constraints and resource problems probably came up somewhere around the mid-point of the endeavor.

You can easily imagine the Egyptian project manager ranting to his construction foreman, "I *knew* we didn't have enough stones for this project, but the Pharaoh just wouldn't listen." So, instead of building a tower like the architect planned on the original drawings, he ended up working with what they had and redesigned the project "on the fly" to end up with a pyramid-shaped deliverable. The results have lasted until the present time, so this project management approach cannot be called a failure. But still today many modern projects are not completed to match the original vision.

Unfortunately, in some organizations, today's project management practices have not changed that much from historic times, although the situations and type of employees whom we work with are very different. It is those differences that further motivate us to evolve our practices. At first, Agile and Waterfall may seem like an odd mix to consider, but combining the two is becoming more prevalent. It is important to consider your own current project culture, and your own personal project management practices, to decide how they will need to change to prepare for the future.

If you are not a *Star Trek* fan, the long-running TV show and series of movies based on space travel and exploring new galaxies, you might not recognize the name of the Borg. The Borg was a fictional race of powerful cybernetic organisms. Individual Borg rarely spoke. Instead, they sent a collective audio message to their targets stating, "Resistance is futile," followed by a declaration that the human target in question would be assimilated, and its biological and technological distinctiveness would be added to their own, collective Borg presence. Similarly, we can say to project managers, "Resistance to Agile is futile. You will be assimilated!"

Projects right now are being managed with hybrid processes, and the project managers who step up and learn how to do this will be in great demand. Companies are already on the search and offering high salaries for people with an understanding of both approaches and how these skill sets can be merged for competitive, corporate advantage.

However, the reality is that current project management practices are well-ingrained into our culture. Your organization no doubt has many layers of protocols, templates, and regulations around how projects are authorized, assigned, staffed, completed, reported, archived, and evaluated. They may have internal training classes to prepare you in their proprietary methodology, or have invested large dollar amounts to send masses of employees to external training.

Perhaps, the organization funds the cost of certifications, certification testing, training to maintain the designations, and memberships in local and national project management related organizations. Project management offices (PMOs) may have been created and staffed with the mandate to coordinate and govern a single approach to projects, companywide. Suggesting that this should all be tossed away overnight to embrace a new philosophy will be futile.

The Need for Change

The answer to the question "Why Agile now?" comes from the need for change. Due to the economic downturn in world markets since 2008 and a speed-driven economy, most of us are being asked to bring products faster to market before the competition steals market share or creates a similar product with more and better features.

Apple® uses Agile methods to create and produce their iPad® products. That allows higher quality, more innovation, and a faster time to market. In contrast, Hewlett-Packard Company (HP) was forced to pull their TouchPads off the market and get out of the tablet business altogether. This action by HP was not due to a bad product; they were just too late to market and none of their features could quite measure up to those of their Apple competitor, which had an earlier release date. It would be interesting to know if their project management processes were a factor.

We currently manage projects with an assumption of stability that does not exist. Companies, products, and methods are constantly being replaced by more effective alternatives. The market has changed, and if we push faster to keep up, we may be tempted to cut out testing and cut out quality. We can also burn people out. **Agile** *is a technique to bring high quality products, services, and software to market more quickly, and get business value or revenue from them faster, while protecting and motivating the people on the team.*

Another big challenge is to adapt products and services more quickly, so that we can retain customers if there is something they do not like or a have a need that is not being met. Through social media outlets, such as Facebook, Twitter, Amazon.com reviews, and YouTube videos, buyers can promote a product, leading to a swell of acceptance and demand. Or, customers can use the Internet to say your product is terrible and ruin your business just as quickly unless you can correct, or add, what the customers tell you in their feedback they want adjusted.

When we say Agile, we need to move away from thinking it is a method only for software development and start to think about it as a way to adapt quickly to changing requirements or customer demands. It is all about flexibility, ability to respond to change, and building a corporate culture where knowledge workers are encouraged to collaborate and work to their highest level. An Agile approach addresses quality and customer acceptance in a fast and open way, while acknowledging and capitalizing on the value of the people on the team.

Despite the positive growth that Agile organizations show in important corporate metrics compared to those with a more traditional approach, project managers can read between the lines. "More flexible" means they are going to change things on you, which currently means:

- change requests,
- meeting changes,
- redoing requirements documents,
- redoing assignments,
- reworking Microsoft Project files, and
- reassigning people.

That is, more work!

Plus, since you are human, you are subject to a thought process that we all share called homeostasis. **Homeostasis** is *the process used by the body to maintain a stable environment*. We seek balance in our lives, so when things are at an imbalance, it tends to cause problems. One positive impact that homeostasis has on us psychologically is to keep us from being too discontent about our lives. Our mind tells us, "You know, what I have is exactly what I need... and since I have what I need... there is no need to change anything." Therefore, people will naturally resist anyone who tries to upset their homeostasis by telling them to do things differently.

We all will need to overcome nature's ingrained mental balancing act in ourselves and our teams in order to be successful. Change is hard. As stated earlier, we have already spent a lot of time and effort in getting a PMP or other certifications. The organization has spent thousands of dollars in training, setting up a PMO, and working to standardize documentation. Yet, we have to upset that homeostatic balance before we can be open to new things.

Change happens most easily when people are gently exposed to new ideas, not when we are force-fed them. Remember, as you try to introduce Agile at your own organization, add opportunities for people to learn. Then, let people form their own ideas, rather than trying to push them into excessive and immediate change. Do it in the same way that skilled marketers get us to buy a new car or watch a new TV show. They give us a little taste of what it looks like and what it can do for us, and then allow us to take a no-pressure test drive. Once we feel the power or experience new features, we want it. But be warned, if you want to continue to be successful as a project manager, you will have to change.

Paradigm Learning has an ad for training classes. It shows cavemen attending a class called "How to Not Get Eaten by Dinosaurs." The strategy being taught was to spread out and run as fast as you can in all directions at the first sound of the creatures. The cavemen attend the three-day class, and like classes today, some do not pay attention, even falling asleep. As luck would have it, as they emerge from the cave, sure enough—they encounter a dinosaur. Those who were not paying attention and did not learn the new "divide and run for your life" strategy were surely eaten. But those who were able to unlearn their old "freeze in fear" response and exhibit the new behavior lived. The caption reads, "In business, they eat the slow ones first."

This is an accurate metaphor for what we face today as project managers. Knowledge and success are no longer only about learning new things; they are about the ability to learn, unlearn, and re-learn. This ability to evolve is what will keep us current and highly employable. So, when we think about Agile, think of a "more adjustable," easily alterable process in which teams can quickly adapt to the shifts around them. The team members are able to respond to changes in the project requirements, business environment, and organizational ecosystem more quickly.

References

[1]Kotter, J. P., & Heskett, J. L. 2011. *Corporate Culture and Performance*. New York, NY: Simon & Schuster/Free Press, 2011.

[2]QSM Associates. May 2008. *The Agile Impact Report: Proven Performance Metrics from the Agile Enterprise.*

What Is Agile?

"Big Agile" and "little agile"

There are two types of Agile, "Big Agile" and "little agile." Big Agile is the philosophy; the business theory and perspective of how we want to work with others that supports why we would make this process change. If you truly intend to alter the way you think about *why* you do projects and *how* you do them, you cannot merely buy a toolkit, stick up a few Agile posters, or pay for an Agile course, and then automatically have an Agile team. What makes the things you do truly Agile is the *way* you do things and the *reasons* you have for doing them that way. In other words, you cannot "do" Agile, you have to "be" Agile.

Calling Agile "Big" and "little" is in no way related to relative value or success when used within a project. It is taken from the image that a large umbrella encompasses the philosophy and principles of Big Agile, which are more general and less decomposed into tools and techniques. Little agile refers to various approaches that are more specific to certain types of projects and industries, but which are still formed to fit under the big, overriding ideas.

So, Big Agile is the philosophy. Since Agile is intended to be modified and customized for each industry, organization, and small team need, we will never see a time where all the processes are the same and we can memorize them in clear steps, like we do now when studying for the PMP exam.

The group of practices that we call "little agile," on the other hand, do embrace a specific methodology to improve the success and quality of project outputs. These are the tools, techniques, and activities that people use to implement the big ideas. They are sometimes also referred to as "productized" processes. There are books written about the specific practices and the cyclical steps to take, for-profit classes that prepare you for certifications and carefully differentiated roles, and websites, associations, blogs, and webinars dedicated to this particular brand of little agile. The little agile process has become a product in and of itself.

Productized process sets are most frequently found in both software development and web development areas, although there are also specific techniques that have been adopted and customized through experience for manufacturing, as well as other more product-oriented industries. These approaches still provide for increased team flexibility, but within a standardized, repeatable set of guidelines that are driven under the hood by the Big Agile philosophy. Remember, despite the customization, the intent is that what you do on a daily basis is not as important as the changes in your thinking that drive the *why* of what you are doing.

With little agile, it is important to follow *all* of the steps, for example, the steps of a Scrum software development process. Picking and choosing only a part of the Scrum plan will negate the outstanding value that organizations using Scrum are gaining.

For now, let's discuss and understand the Big Agile concepts. Later, there is an overview of some of the little agile tools and practices you might encounter like SCRUM, Extreme Programming (XP), Dynamic Systems Development Method (DSDM) which is especially popular in Europe, Lean Manufacturing, Kanban, Crystal, TPS, Lean Software Development, Rational Unified Process (RUP), and Feature Driven Development (FDD), where there is great value to doing specific things in a cyclical order.

Since our goal is to find ways to integrate the best of the attitude shifts of Agile in our non-IT type projects, we will focus on the ideas that are encompassed in Big Agile, and then look at what we can borrow from the little agile skill sets to enhance our own projects.

So, when we talk about Agile, think about synonyms like "more flexible," "adjustable," "adaptable," "changeable", "quick", and "resourceful." The word Agile should evoke the image of an easily alterable process in which teams can quickly respond to change. They are able to adjust to changes in the project requirements, business environment, or regulatory changes, whether in the organization or in a merger environment. Today's teams need to provide fast responses to shifts, whether in customer fads or unexpected stock market adjustments.

When asked about the benefits of implementing Agile in a State of Agile Survey from VersionOne (2011), 84% of respondents said the number one advantage was the ability to manage changing priorities. The next most highly ranked value was in improved project visibility (77%), followed by 75% of those surveyed who found increased productivity was important to them. Improved team morale was reported by 72% of the respondents, while 71% said they saw a faster time to market as a result of changing to Agile. And, 68% found it gave them a better alignment between the project and its business objectives.[1] Granted, these were software development implementations, but if these positive and enviable changes were found in this area of the organization, there have to be similar benefits in some amount for non-IT projects, too.

Project managers are chasing a shifting target due to constant changes in today's business environment. If any of you are hunters, servicemen or women, archers, or even if you only have the Paper Toss app on your iPhone where you try to toss a wadded up paper into a wastebasket, you know about trajectories. If you are trying to hit a moving target, whether with a bullet, an arrow, or a wadded up piece of electronic paper, you cannot aim straight in front of you where the target is now. You must adjust for the wind, and the speed of the target if it is moving, and aim your throw ahead to where it will be in the future.

Our job today is to point ourselves and our projects toward where we need to be in the future in order to hit the business targets. Not only do we have to change where we are headed, we have to *lead* the change. One change, most definitely, is toward a more flexible process to manage projects. We need to embrace the Agile philosophy and principles regardless of the department in the company where we lead projects.

Iterative and Incremental Development by a Dedicated Team

There are three key features to Big Agile. The first is iterative and incremental development by a dedicated team. This idea is fairly simple: **iterative** means that you have *a process you repeat periodically, perhaps every 1 to 2 weeks*. The one to two week work period is an iteration. In practice, it can be two, three, or even four weeks. The idea is that you are forming short, consistent periods of time within which the team will work. If you choose two weeks as your iteration length, for example, each iteration of the project will be that same two week duration. This way, the team and all other supporting stakeholders can get into a short-term rhythm cycle, rather than waiting three months or longer before the project is expected to produce a finished portion of the final product.

Incremental means that you *do one piece, or chunk, of the work at a time*. In the next iteration, you do another piece of the work. At the end of each iteration, you have a small portion of the end product or service that you can show to the customer to obtain early feedback and, if necessary, to deploy, distribute, use, or sell to bring some return on the investment dollars that were spent to create it. This gives the organization something of value should the project be deliberately delayed, temporarily suspended, or even cancelled due to changing business needs. Then, in the next iteration, you create another portion of the vision, and so on.

A **dedicated team** means that *people focus on this one project full-time*, rather than trying to do little bits and pieces on many projects at once. In a traditional project management environment, when you consider that there are always multiple projects being estimated for feasibility, gearing up in queue, in full progress, and others that are winding down, it is not uncommon for someone to be working on 6 to 15 projects in varying stages at any one time.

You are still going to break the work into manageable pieces, but the process differs from creating a work breakdown structure (WBS), and then sequencing the resulting activities, in that the work of an Agile project remains grouped into pieces of useable product and then those pieces are prioritized. The ones that are most important and valuable to the customer or the business are done first, and the customer makes that judgment of importance, not the project team or the project manager. By customer, we mean people like an internal manager, an internal user, an external third-party vendor for whom you provide product, or even an external customer to whom you market and sell directly. The customer, or a representative of the customer, makes the judgment of importance that drives the prioritization process, not the project manager or the project team.

So, the first key concept of Big Agile is easy to understand if you think of Agile as iterative (repeating, consistent timeboxes of a few weeks) and incremental (pieces or chunks of the software, product, or services built within each timebox), designed so that you always have something with business value to show at the end of each iteration. In the first time period, or iteration, you do the activities that the customer decides are most important first, and then add things in the order that they are prioritized (incremental), and then repeat the process with another small chunk during the next time period (iterative or repeating). This is done by a dedicated team, a team that works exclusively on this one project.

Embracing Change

The second key concept of Big Agile is to embrace change rather than try to prevent or avoid it. Currently, when we focus on change, it is often change management, or change control. For example, we enforce change request documents. We keep change logs, and insist that Change Control Boards inspect, ponder, and rule on any change to the work of the project once it is underway.

The overriding idea in Waterfall projects is to *prevent* change, or at least make it so difficult that all of the stakeholders need to go through multiple hoops in order to adjust the requirements of the project, since it may alter the schedule and cost of the project, and cause contractual problems with third-party customers. An identifying concept of a more Agile team is that they are OK with change; perhaps they even welcome or instigate it themselves. This may make us shudder as project managers, particularly if you are working in construction or engineering, where a major structural change cannot be taken lightly.

And this aversion to change makes sense within the existing way that we initiate, plan, and execute projects. If the requirements are set ahead of time and detailed contracts are signed that outline not only what will be done, but the penalties if it is not done as written, the emphasis naturally falls to doing exactly what exists in the paperwork. The overriding obsession with preventing change is also natural, since any changes may alter the schedule and the cost of the project, and cause contractual problems with third party suppliers. Plus, each and every variation from what was originally input into the automated software means the project manager must be sure that everything is re-entered to assure the detailed metrics of the project remain accurate.

But as organizations begin to acknowledge and live with the day-to-day reality of the massive, ongoing changes they face, they begin to realize that the ability to be more flexible with adjusting their projects quickly while in progress may mean the difference between survival and obsolescence. In order to compete, we must lead more Agile teams that are OK with change.

You can do this without concern, because you are working in a way that change is easy to blend or work into your project. We are not talking about big, earth-shattering changes such as starting to build a skyscraper and ending up building an underground subway station. We are talking about short-term responsiveness to the customer or the discoveries of the team as they move through the work of the project.

Regardless of the level of impact, being open to reasonable adjustments in the project has become a must, because one of the shifting business philosophies has to do with a new responsiveness to customers. Whether change erupts from customers changing their minds, or something that occurs in the competitive marketplace, change has become the new constant.

Stephen Johnson puts it succinctly in his 2010 best seller, *Where Good Ideas Come From*:

> We live in an age of technical acceleration; the new paradigms keep rolling in, and the intervals between them keep shortening. This acceleration reflects not only the flood of new products, but also our growing willingness to embrace these strange new devices, and put them to use. The waves roll in at ever-increasing frequencies, and more and more of us are becoming trained surfers, paddling out to meet them the second they start to crest.[2]

So, planning is still a key concept in Agile, but it focuses more on the *process* of planning, and the value of the interactions of the people involved, rather than the actual creation of a formal Project Plan document. The climate of the project encourages change, and it operates in an environment where plans can be easily changed at specific, periodic points throughout the project.

In return for being flexible in regard to change and accepting it as normal, in the Agile approach to projects you are *protected from any change during a short, timeboxed period,* the **iteration**. This is also called "being timeboxed". The customer has prioritized and selected the most important things to do this iteration and, in return for that privilege, has agreed to *no changes* during this time.

When planning begins for the following two weeks, the customer has the option to make comments about the work already completed, reprioritize the existing work, or introduce new and previously unseen changes to things *before* the team begins working on them. At this point, the team has no doubt done enough work on the project to see that there are some technical or infrastructure items that will need to be done for this project to be solid. They have the ability to add stories of their own at this same break in the process.

Working Closely with Your Customer

The third major concept in Big Agile is that rather than waiting until the end of the project to show the customer what you and your team have done, you will work more closely with customers throughout the project than you might have done in the past. Currently, a project team may never meet either the internal or external customer. They get a requirements document with functional and technical specifications, or they are assigned a list of tasks from a WBS prepared by the project manager. In the Agile environment, the customer is invited to all meetings and interacts directly with the project team. First, he or she will work with the project manager to create a way to convey what the project is about, and rather than describing it in terms of specifics, another way to start is to present the goals and work of the project to the team in the form of "user stories."

A **user story** *describes part of the work of a project in a way that helps the team understand the ultimate business goal for that feature.* For example, a user story might read, "When this shopping cart feature is complete on my Amazon website page, the user will be able to make a purchase using a credit card." The customer conveys what the end result will be, but the project team figures out the specifics of *how* this story will be developed and *how* the end goal of credit purchases will be made possible for Internet shoppers.

At the end of your first one or two week iteration, the customer will sit down with the team to touch, hold, or try the new feature. If it is exactly what the customer had in mind, great! You are ready to move on to the next user stories on the prioritized list. If not, you know early in the process the alterations your customer wants and can make these changes more easily. After all, you only have two weeks invested. This is the equivalent of saying, "Come in and look at the paint on the walls of the first suite we painted in your new office building. If you don't like the color, tell us *now* rather than after we have painted the other 199 offices."

To truly understand Big Agile, and little agile as well, we need to take a look back into history, see where these ideas came from, and notice how they came to influence today's projects. An overview of the history of these ideas is coming in Chapter 3. Pay attention to it, because if you become convinced that the Agile philosophy has merit for your project team, you will need to be able to tie it back to historic business practices that will resonate with upper management and other departments in your organization.

References

[1]State of Agile Survey. 2011. VersionOne. Retrieved from http://www.versionone.com/ state_of_agile_development_survey/10/.

[2]Johnson, S. 2010. *Where Good Ideas Come From*. Riverhead Books. New York.

Where Did Agile Ideas Originate?

A misconception continues that Agile was an approach created for software development, but it actually came from business theories that were first used in the manufacturing and construction industries. In a manufacturing plant during the early 19th century, there were unskilled day laborers working on a manufacturing assembly line. Someone figured out if we could look at each movement they made, and make sure each person did it just the same way, we could find the fastest way to make cars, sewing machines, or shoes.

If more of the same products were needed, we could send one person home after 8 or 10 hours, and replace him or her with another person doing exactly the same movements for the next 8 to 10 hours. As if they were interchangeable parts, interchangeable workers performed one set of actions after the other along a slow-moving assembly line. These types of manufacturing plants helped form our current, traditional project processes.

Starting in the same period, new thinkers began to emerge. Here are a few of the pioneers you should know about, along with their contributions to the project management profession (see Figure 3.1).

Frederick Taylor

Frederick Taylor was a mechanical engineer who did his most important work from 1890 to 1901. He was a consulting engineer to paper mills and the steel industry. Wanting to improve industrial efficiency, Taylor did *time studies* on

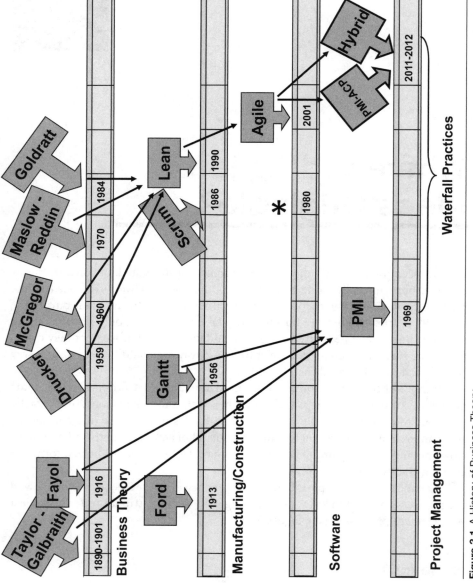

Figure 3.1 A History of Business Theory

shoveling coal into the furnaces at Bethlehem Steel to find the most efficient way to do it. Noting that they used the same shovel for all materials, and that the most effective load was 2.5 pounds, he designed shovels that would pick up exactly that amount with each scoop. Ultimately, he was the one who transferred the techniques that worked in steel and taught the manufacturing industry to count and replicate each and every movement on the assembly line for the greatest efficiency. Today, we know Taylor as the father of Scientific Management.[1]

Frank and Lillian Galbraith

While Taylor was doing time studies, a colleague, Frank Galbraith, did *motion studies* in the construction industry. For example, he noted the time and effort that went into a brick mason leaning over to pick up each individual brick from the ground, and found it wasted a lot of time and energy for the worker to reach clear down to his feet for each brick. So, Galbraith developed a scaffold to hold bricks at the waist level of bricklayers, removing the waste of effort and corresponding loss of seconds it took to lean over clear down to the pile of materials at ground level. This way the masons could work three times more quickly for longer stretches of time, since each brick took less effort.

You may already know about Frank Galbraith and not have even made the connection. Did you read the book *Cheaper by the Dozen*, or see the original 1950 movie, starring Myna Loy, Clifton Webb, and Jeannie Crain?[2] The story was based on the biographical book of the same name, written by two of Galbraith's children. There was also a less authentic version remake in 2003, starring Steve Martin and Bonnie Hunt. In that version, the only similarity was the title and the fact that the family had 12 children.

The father in the original movie was a characterization of the real Frank Galbraith. The title of the book came from a joke that he used frequently. The story goes that he would be out driving with his family and stop at a red light. Invariably, a passerby would shout, "Hey, mister. Why do you have so many kids?" Frank would consider the question studiously, and just as the light turned green, he would respond, "Well, they come cheaper by the dozen, you know," and speed off.

The story illustrates how Galbraith thought that having a dozen children was more efficient than stopping after one or two. If you read the book, you will see how he used his family as guinea pigs to prove his theories. One idea that Galbraith fervently believed was that with 12 children and only one bathroom, each person needed to be really efficient about how they bathed. So he taught his kids to start with their face and progress downward: Neck, left arm, under left arm, chest, right arm, under right arm, back, left leg and foot, right leg and foot, private parts….then get out of the way for the next kid.

Time and motion processes for the way children wash may seem extreme. But both Taylor and Galbraith emphasized finding the best processes to get work done the quickest way. They tried to get everyone to follow the same, efficient and standardized models, an idea that has carried through to today's workplaces as a management style. We all resent that approach when we are team members, but may emulate it ourselves if we are promoted to a managerial position. This is a model that Agile attempts to change.

Galbraith also invented process charts to focus attention on all of the processes that were done in the workflow, even ones that did not add value or occurred between the other elements. Neither Galbraith nor his colleague Taylor took into consideration the behavior of individual workers. It was Frank's wife, Lillian Galbraith, who realized that the motivation and attitudes of workers also had a substantial impact on the outcome of any process. By bringing new, psychological facets into the mix, she opened a fresh line of thinking regarding the best way to get work produced.

Henri Fayol

In 1916, about the same time that Frederick Taylor was publishing *Principles of Scientific Management*, another theorist, Henri Fayol, published one of the first books on general management theory, *General and Industrial Management*. He created the idea that there were five primary functions of management:

1. To forecast and plan.
2. To organize.
3. To command. (Note that this "command" is the start of a "command and control" approach to management.)
4. To coordinate.
5. To control. (Note that here is the "control" part.) Coming from his background as a mining engineer, Fayol meant *control* in the sense that we now refer to control processes in a quality environment, rather than a manager who is controlling the activities of subordinates. Feedback from quality checks in a manufacturing environment tells the operator whether or not a machine is functioning properly, or whether adjustments need to be made. Fayol believed that a manager must receive and interpret feedback from a process in order to make the necessary adjustments. However, *his original idea was that a manager would be open to feedback from the employees who were part of the process*.[3] In practice, the essence of his idea got twisted into the opposite idea—that managers should control those who reported to them.

If you are familiar with the Project Management Institute's (PMI)® *PMBOK® Guide* process groups: Initiating, Planning, Executing, Monitoring and Controlling, and Closing, you will recognize their roots. Note that both Fayol's functions and the *PMBOK® Guide* process groups are task oriented, rather than people oriented. Agile attempts to shift management practices away from "command and control" and into a more supportive managerial and project management role, often called the "servant leader," and to have the focus of the project be directed more toward people rather than to tasks.

Henry Ford

These early ideas of Taylor, Galbraith, and Fayol were the business theory in vogue even before they were published. In 1913, these theorists influenced Henry Ford when he was creating the Ford Motor Company. Most of us are familiar with Ford's innovative, game-changing, moving assembly line, which was used to manufacture the Model T car fondly known as the Tin Lizzie. By 1921, the Model T accounted for almost 57% of worldwide automobile production, and it was the best selling car of all time until 1972, when the Volkswagen Beetle overtook it.[4] Ford's famous quote about his car was, "You can have it in any color you want, as long as it's black." The underlying customer attitude was: we will decide what to make, and you as the customer will have to settle for that. His disinterest in customers' ideas was evidenced by his frequent comment, "If I had asked my customers what they wanted, they would have said a faster horse."

Many people do not realize that Model Ts were already in production before the moving assembly line innovation. And initially, Model Ts came in many colors, including red. But Ford found that black paint dried fastest on the assembly line, so black became the most expedient color, and ultimately the only choice that he gave to customers.

Ford also insisted that his suppliers send the parts that he purchased in wooden boxes with exact dimensions and wood types. He was the only game in town, so he could dictate the specific requirements to subcontractors. Once he removed the parts shipped within the containers to use in his production line, he then had the boxes pulled apart and used them for the wooden running boards on the cars. Free supplies! Perhaps that helped him keep his prices to the low, low purchase price of $295 per car. However, this practice highlights a relationship with suppliers that is less than a partnership.

Ford Motor Corporation is only one example of the era. It ran on the management philosophy that companies were only looking for the most organized, routine, and fastest way to make a product which they could then turn around and sell for the most money. This philosophy has remained as the foundation for modern project management as we know it. It is still a viable way to do projects that focus on time, cost, and quality as their defining metrics.

This sounds like our own traditional methodology, doesn't it? Break the final product into the smallest parts, sequence them, assign a few tasks to each worker, and you have the fastest and least expensive way to run an assembly line. However, today's customer insists on more than one choice of product style and one choice of color. We will soon see how this change in customer demands affected the thinking of business leaders.

Henry Gantt

Almost simultaneously to Ford's innovations during the 1910–1917 time period, Henry Gantt was creating a bar chart to visually show a project schedule. If you don't know what a Gantt chart looks like, picture the right side of a Microsoft Project screen. The *Gantt chart* proved its worth in 1931 when it was used by the construction industry to efficiently build Hoover Dam near Las Vegas, Nevada. The chart further earned its way into project management toolkits when it was successfully used to help build the United States interstate system of highways in the 1950s.

As a discipline, project management continued to evolve from several fields of application, including civil construction, engineering, manufacturing, and heavy federal government defense activities. The development of a submarine-launched Polaris missile in 1960 contributed to the familiar Program Evaluation and Review Technique (PERT), using a weighted formula method factoring in optimistic, expected, and pessimistic activity estimates to try to offset risk in project estimates.

Another essential tool, the Critical Path Method, was developed for managing plant maintenance projects. This method defines the longest path through the project, showing the shortest time in which the project can be completed, using activities that have the least possible amount of slack or float (the amount of time an activity can be delayed without delaying the project finish date).

All of these ideas, and more, flowed into the Project Management Institute (PMI), when it was created in 1969 as an organization based on the belief that the best practices of project management can be shared and utilized across multiple industries, and that international standards add value to the field. The PMI mission statement was, "To assist in improving the understanding and competency of experienced and new project management practitioners and customers worldwide."

Winston Royce

If you, or your colleagues, have any reluctance to adopt project management practices that come from software development practitioners, you will want to know about Winston Royce. The traditional project management processes now commonly called Waterfall were not "invented" by PMI, but came from a 1970 paper by Royce.

At the time, Royce worked for Lockheed Software Technology. His experience was primarily in developing software packages for spacecraft missions to enhance their planning, mission command, and post-flight analysis. In a paper describing his personal experiences, "Managing the Development of Large Software Systems," Royce had a type of project diagram that came to be characterized as Waterfall.

Royce did not call this diagram Waterfall; in fact, he did *not* even suggest that it was a good way to do projects. He specifically wrote, "The implementation described above is risky and invites failure." His son, Walker Royce, later recounted his father's comments regarding Waterfall, stating that the elder Winston thought that it would not work for any but the most straightforward projects. Walker stressed that his father always believed in iterative and incremental project development, as otherwise feedback showing problems in the project does not occur until too late in the process to take the appropriate steps to correct the problems.[5]

Unfortunately, the Department of Defense passed along the misconception that the elder Royce was recommending the alignment of project phases implemented as a one-pass approach, and soon, many government contractors were forced to use a rigid methodology that has since spread to most of the project management centered organizations.

Peter Drucker

The economy of the 1960s was becoming a more speed-driven, competitive market. As a result, as we are seeing today, this is the type of environment that leads to management philosophies evolving and changing. Peter Drucker, a well-known business guru, was already asking an Agile-type question, "What is the purpose of your business?" Many traditional CEOs of the time might have answered, "To make money, to make a profit." However, Drucker professed that the goal of a business should not be just to make money. It should be to create *value* for customers, because that is where the money companies make comes from.

Drucker also correctly stated that, in a sense, customers determine value by how much they will pay for a product. Without the customers buying products or services, the company would have no business. So, we should follow a "the customer is king" philosophy with the organizational goal to deliver the highest value to the customer as quickly as possible.

By 1974, putting the customer first was an accepted, mainstream business philosophy. Burger King® ran a successful series of radio, television, and print ads, inviting customers to: "Hold the pickles, hold the lettuce. Special orders don't upset us. All we ask is that you let us serve it your way!" They ended the ads with the phrase, "Have It Your Way, at Burger King." Putting Drucker's business philosophy into action, the obvious parallel was to allow customers to select the toppings they wanted on their hamburger, rather than having to order a pre-configured, standardized sandwich by menu number as they had to do at competitor's eateries. Sounds a little silly now that personal menu configurations are commonplace, but it was innovative and new at the time. And it was a huge success, as customers loved it.

Not only did Drucker have respect for customers who would buy products and services, he was instrumental in garnering a new respect for workers. After more than 60 years of the attitude toward workers still paralleling that of the old industrial manufacturing floor, with interchangeable workers making interchangeable contributions, Drucker coined the term, "knowledge workers." He forwarded the philosophical shift wherein organizations are short-sighted to not realize that people are an organization's most valuable resource. According to Drucker, we no longer have huge pools of uneducated workers to put in front of automated assembly lines and do repetitive tasks that take little or no training; we have educated, creative, and innovative employees who, when managed well, can help to solve many of the business's pressing problems.

Drucker, who was noted for spotting business trends, felt that a manager's job was to prepare and free people to perform and that knowledge worker productivity management would be the next great frontier of management. He believed that employees are assets, not liabilities, and that mangers who micromanage them are doing a disservice to the organization. These ideas are at the core of an Agile approach to projects.

Eliyahu Goldratt

Agile philosophies owe a debt of gratitude to Eliyahu Goldratt, best known for his **Theory of Constraints** (TOC), formulated in his 1984 novel, *The Goal*. Based on the idea that a chain is no stronger than its weakest link, Goldratt noted that an organization is often limited in how much it can achieve, and in its overall capacity, by a number of small constraints. The company may be limited by equipment, people, or a written or unwritten policy, to list a few examples. Goldratt proposed that every project has certain constraints. What we should do is *find the* *constraints and either remove them, or arrange the work of the project so that the constraints have the least effect on it.*

If we look at our own projects with an eye toward spotting problems, any time we hand off to another person or team, wait for a material resource to be delivered, or wait for approval from outside our team before we can move forward… those are constraints.

Keep constraints in mind as we look further at Agile. Adding Agile to your organization is really a culture shift in most places of business, and it focuses on a group of knowledge workers who know how to drive business value through the project flow as quickly as possible, as long as the project manager removes the constraints.

Abraham Maslow and Douglas McGregor

Abraham Maslow's *Hierarchy of Needs* is a visual representation that helps managers to understand what motivates employees. At the bottom of the hierarchy, usually drawn as pyramid, are basic needs for food, clothing, and shelter. Once those physical needs are met, people begin to look up the pyramid, seeking safety, a sense of belonging, and self-esteem. At the top of the hierarchy they look for self-actualization, and the opportunity to achieve all that they can to reach their full potential. Maslow's concept of motivation parallels the needs: once a lower level on the pyramid is met, physical and security needs for example, those needs are no longer a motivator and people move up to seek the next, adjacent level for fulfillment.

Piggy-backing on Maslow's work, Douglas McGregor, a professor at the Massachusetts Institute of Technology (MIT), came up with the concept of Theory X, to describe those whose management style might be more appropriate for working with those employees looking to meet lower order needs, and Theory Y, as a description of a style more successful when managing those employees wanting to achieve the higher order needs in the workplace.

In the early 1960s, McGregor described two very different views toward workforce motivation. He maintained that companies followed either one or the other approach, either a traditional view of people at work in terms of Theory X, or a more contemporary attitude toward employees, which he defined in terms of Theory Y. These two views made the following assumptions about workers:

- In Theory X, people are viewed as essentially lazy and unambitious, with little capacity or creativity for problem solving. Their motivation to work is based on fulfilling basic needs and security. Thus, people need to be closely controlled and coerced to work by their managers.

This makes sense as a management philosophy for uniform tasks and interchangeable workers.

- In Theory Y, workers are motivated by higher-order needs, tending to prefer self-control and self-direction. This view assumes that people have the capacity to problem-solve and are motivated by affiliation, self-esteem, and the possibility of self-actualization. The Theory Y manager moves away from the behaviors of someone running an assembly line with interchangeable workers, to one who thinks that people are knowledge workers who are smart and good; and who, if given a chance, will work together freely for the good of the company.

Theory Y managers are likely to cultivate a climate of trust. Important steps to developing a climate of trust include managers communicating openly with subordinates, minimizing differences between superior-subordinate relationships, and refining an environment that allows subordinates to thrive and realize their potential. This is a more appropriate management style for the highly skilled knowledge workers on today's teams, and you will see it reflected in Agile philosophies in regard to how people should be treated.

We have known about this managerial approach since the early 1960s, and we may learn it to take the PMP exam, but we do not always practice it along with a traditional approach to managing projects. For example, be honest, have you ever said, "Here, do these six tasks by Thursday and I'll check on you each day." This is Theory X, no matter how sweetly you say it, even if the worker is notified by e-mail or a Microsoft Project alert, rather than face-to-face.

However, Theory Y is the core of a manager's approach to Agile team members, so we should practice what is already known to be best. A new way to look at this is shown in Figure 3.2. Notice the X forms a figure that encloses Management and separates them from the staff. Things are pushed down from above. The workers at the bottom are enclosed and trapped. The Y forms an open area where management with a lowercase "m" is on the bottom, as the team's support, and the staff can pull up the information they need as they need it. People at the top, wanting to feel self-actualized and achieving their full potential, as Maslow predicted, are motivated to work together to create and innovate to solve problems or develop products that may not spring from a traditional workplace. Through self-directed teams, the needs of the customers are taken into foremost consideration.

If you think Maslow's idea are dated, the most successful commercial of all time, even long after it has stopped running, is The U.S. Army recruiting ad, "Be All That You Can Be. In The Army" It ran from 1980 to 2001, but even today it still expresses the heart of what people want and are looking for at work: self-actualization. The more the organization can provide an environment for employees to feel they are a part of things and vital to the success of projects, the more dedicated, engaged, and creative the team members will be. Think Agile!

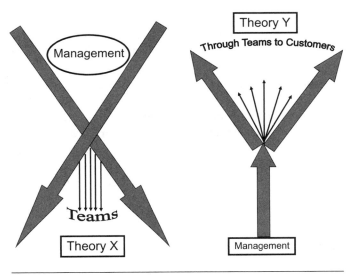

Figure 3.2 McGregor's Theory X and Theory Y Applied to Organizations

James Reddin

Another key contributor to Agile philosophy was James Reddin, known for his doctrine, the **3-D Theory of Management**. His premise was that there was no one, ideal management style. But there was only one important way to judge was whether or not the manager was effective. Reddin felt that managerial evaluations that checked off workplace behaviors on a list were not the way to measure the success of a manager. The three dimensions of a project are: manager, team, and final product, which all work together to produce the desired results. Reddin thought that *we should look at what the team produces. If they end up with a good product, the manager did a good job.*

Hirotaka Takeuchi and Ikujiro Nonaka

The term *Scrum*, which is a little agile methodology, came about in 1986 in a study published in the *Harvard Business Review*, "The New New Product Development Game."[6] It was written by Hirotaka Takeuchi and Ikujiro Nonaka, and described an approach to creating products with overlapping phases. In Scrum, the project teams were composed of small groups of workers with overlapping, or cross-functional, skill sets. Takeuchi and Nonaka compared these collaborative teams to a rugby formation, which is called a *scrum,* and forwarded the idea that rather than the old model industrial age assembly line, the way to create products should be like a rugby team's scrum formation.

In rugby, when a ball goes out of play and it is unclear which team should have possession, the opposing teams form a double line, put their arms on each other's shoulders, and, literally, put their heads together. Think of the players as the project team stepping forward together as one team, and the product owner or the customer as the other team, to work together in a cooperative way. The ball is introduced to the line at one end and all those involved work together to move it through the scrum line and out the other end, where it becomes introduced into open play.

Sakichi Toyoda, Kiichiro Toyoda, and Taiichi Ohno

The Scrum idea, coupled with Goldratt's philosophy of removing constraints, merged with other changing business ideas and came together within the automotive industry, as Toyota's Lean approach. The main idea of **Lean** is that *anything in the process that is not providing customer value is wasteful and should be removed.* This leaves the Agile team and the product owner/customer free to work together to move business value through the process flow as quickly as possible.

As a practice, Lean centers on *preserving value with less work.* You may hear it referred to as the "art of the work not done." The Lean management philosophy is derived mostly from the Toyota Production System (TPS), which focuses on manufacturing and logistics as well as interaction with supplier and customers.

Although it was almost 30 years in the making, Lean became prominent and was adopted by other manufacturers around 1975. Originally, it was called "just-in-time production", and it tries to design out overburden (*muri*), inconsistency (*mura*), and to eliminate waste (*muda*), while at the same time being as flexible as possible. The thought is that flexibility reduces stress or overburden to equipment or people, and that stress is one of the main causes of waste.

Just-in-time inventory control was originated by Sakichi Toyoda, the founder of Toyota, his son Kiichiro Toyoda, and engineer Taiichi Ohno. Ohno is said to have been inspired by American supermarkets that restock the shelves only when customers have purchased items. He transported the idea to the automotive industry with a system for defining how many of any given part to produce. For example, when Part X was needed for a car, a work center employee would go to the storage space and take the number of Part Xs needed for the number of Toyotas that were on the assembly line. The work center that produced Part X would then produce more of them, but just enough to fill the space left from the parts that had been removed for use in the cars already being assembled. You may hear this also called a **pull** system, or referred to by the Japanese term, **kanban**.

The result was low inventory levels, which translated into lower material and labor costs, less invested in storage space, and a reduction in the risks of theft, damage, or obsolescence of the parts. Others trying to adopt similar techniques made the error of only reducing inventory levels, without fully understanding the motivation and philosophy that was behind it. This exposes a real, parallel danger for those adopting Agile, in that it is not enough to change the outside face of team behavior if the team, the project manager, and the organization as a whole do not support the core philosophies that drive the changes.

The principles of the Toyota Way parallel many of the same principles from the Big Agile philosophy because Toyota was one originating source. A particularly influential one is the idea of continuous improvement: have a long-term vision and then constantly work to improve the process to meet your goals. **Kaizen** is *Japanese for "improvement" or "change for the better," and refers to philosophies and practices that that focus on continuous improvement.*

When William Deming, best known for his later work with the quality initiatives of the 1980s, worked with Japanese manufacturers after World War II to help them rebuild their economy, he brought the kaizen concept back to the United States with him. So, you may hear continuous improvement associated with his name.

Other Toyota principles are:

- Have respect for others,
- Try our best to understand each other,
- Take personal responsibility for your work, and
- Work in an environment to build mutual trust and encourage personal and professional growth through shared opportunities that maximize team performance.

One could be talking about an Agile team when looking at the Toyota Way, using a pull system to create only what is needed at the moment. This practice levels out the workload so that people are not overworked, stressed, or worn out, each of which can reduce a person's ability to think clearly and turn in a high level of performance. The principles also build a culture where you can stop to fix problems along the way, to get quality built in from the first. Visual controls are used to get the problems out in the open and the make the team progress easy to follow, while a corresponding intent is to grow leaders who understand the work, live the Toyota philosophy, and teach it to other people on the team.

After Ohno studied mass production at Ford Motor Company, he went back to Japan to begin a quest to eliminate waste. He added cross-functional teams and the idea of continuous improvement. By the early 1990s, Toyota consistently achieved four times the productivity, and 12 times the quality, of General Motors. The gist of the Lean philosophy is that anything that is not providing business value to the process flow is an impediment and should be removed, leaving all the remaining processes contributing in a positive way to the end result.[7]

But how did software development fit into this Lean process? While the first computer arrived on the scene in 1944, it wasn't until the mid-1960s when IBM released its System/360 that computers became an important part of the business world. Originally controlled by machine code unreadable to the human eye (assembly language, wired boards, or programmed through punchcards), by the mid-1980s the field had progressed to systems engineers writing in programming languages that were more decipherable to the people working with them.

On a timeline (Figure 3.1), we now have the project practices of the manufacturing, construction, defense, and other industries that were tested and proven to work. PMI promoted the idea that others could take the best practices of these industries and apply them in an intelligent way to other industries and projects. Organizations interested in running better projects used the *PMBOK® Guide* processes and found that they were more productive. Their projects were completed closer to the goals of on time, on budget, and with a higher degree of the positive quality metrics by which most project managers are taught to evaluate project success.

Subsequently, organizations reasoned, "Hmmm…. If this specific process we used worked once, let's make it a rigid methodology and force every project in the company to be done in exactly the same way." First, you *must* do this process, and then you *must* create a document from this template, and so on. This was never the intention of the volunteers from all over the world who participated in the creation of the first *PMBOK® Guide*. So, the problems in traditional project management came not from PMI, but from those who took the PMI best practices and misapplied them. People had found a good thing, but took it too far. They calcified a process structure they had developed in their own organization and, in far too many cases, almost made it into a religion.

The book *Canticle for Leibowitz*, by Walter Miller, is a science fiction tale set in a Roman Catholic monastery in the desert of the southwestern United States after a devastating nuclear war. The story spans the thousands of years that pass as civilization struggles to rebuild itself. The monks of the Abertian Order of Leibowitz take up the mission of preserving the surviving remnants of man's scientific knowledge until the day the rest of the world is ready to appreciate and benefit from it again. All that has survived, however, is one tiny fragment of paper with a few cryptic words written on it. The heroes, the monks, fiercely defend and protect the priceless relic with their lives, but at the end of the story, the artifact that they have fought to preserve and devoutly worshipped—on which they built an entire faith—is nothing more than a grocery list from an ordinary man named Leibowitz, who lived a mundane existence in the pre-war world.

The moral of the Leibowitz story for us as project managers is that no process should become rigid, solidified, and worshipped for its own sake. If each and every team member does not understand the value of a project artifact, perhaps it should be replaced with a more useful one embraced by everyone on the team and throughout the larger stakeholder community. Each project approach should remain adaptable to respond to the changing needs of the business as it navigates the swift, flowing waters of the economy.

In the real world, some companies have adopted PMI processes and still keep the assembly line mentality. Do the math: managers from 1930 to 1950 progressed into upper management between 1970 and 1990. They mostly kept the same mindset that had made them successful: the more they could document a set of procedures and force everyone to follow a list of requirements, the faster they could produce cars, refrigerators, or televisions. And, the more they could grade an individual's performance against a list of requirements, the more they could micromanage and squeeze the last drop of performance out of interchangeable and expendable people.

The asterisk within Figure 3.1 marks the spot where software development came into its own as a profession, around the early 1980s. To place the timeframe in context, this is only about 15 years after computers entered the business world. So, picture yourself as an early software developer and ask yourself the following questions: "What is a computer? What am I trying to make it do? What are my limits? How does this machine work? How long will this take? How much will it cost? What tools do I use to communicate what I want it to do?" Answers to those questions were, in the beginning, "I really do not know."

The computer field was so new that no real business theory had considered the difference between what employees working with computers were doing compared to the employees typically working in construction and manufacturing. With software development, men and women were creating totally new products and services, often on equipment that would evolve and be replaced in a year or two. There were few reliable metrics for estimates at the beginning, and the complexity involved was woefully underestimated by stakeholders who were unfamiliar with this emerging type of software project.

Due to the tremendous uncertainty and innovation necessary to complete software development projects, the heavyweight structure that worked for other industries was totally inappropriate and did not work, much to the frustration of the software engineers, as practitioners in this field came to be called. Scrum, as a development methodology for software, began to evolve from multiple, unconnected sources when developers read Takeuchi and Nonaka's article, *The New New Product Development Game*.

To Takeuchi and Nonaka (1986), *Scrum* meant cross-functional teams engaging in the dynamic conflict of ideas that generates *ba*, the energy flow that surfaces the knowledge that eventually forms new products. Takeuchi and Nonaka were not writing about software development, but rather product development in general. The essence of their article was that new product development had become fast-paced and competitive. Managers needed to realize that the traditional, sequential approach to developing new products would not work any longer. Instead, they must adopt a more flexible and holistic product development strategy where a development team would work as a unit to reach a common goal. Do you hear the Agile principles in that description, still as fresh and workable today as they were years ago?

By 2001, these same ideas had inspired software developers to adopt these suggestions and try out the resulting practices at work. At various companies around the United States, early innovators had already developed a number of fragmented approaches to address the challenges in software development. Finally, in February, 2001, seventeen people representing Extreme Programming (XP), Scrum, Dynamic Software Development Methodology (DSDM), Adaptive Software Development, Crystal, Feature-Driven Development (FDD), Pragmatic Programming, and other fledgling approaches met at The Lodge at Snowbird ski resort in the mountains of Utah to compare their ideas and experiences.

What emerged was their shared consensus that they could not be successful in their projects doing the formal, traditional project management processes popular at the time in their organizations, because they did not know the answers to the questions asked of them by that type of approach: How long will this project take? How much will this project cost? How will you go about creating this new product or service? What will your upfront plan be for the project, from beginning to end? These questions were unanswerable when software was involved.

The group said, "This isn't working for us! We need alternative **processes** (*a series of actions, bringing about a result*) for software development. Our actions at work, and the reasons that we are not using the usual, traditional approaches, are based on our personal beliefs about how we can best serve our companies. We don't believe that the philosophies of a Waterfall process work for software development. We think the basic core values in the belief structure of the company need to be adjusted, and this will free us to produce software quicker and to end up with software that will actually work."

The result of this meeting was the formation of the Agile Alliance, which you can access at www.agilealliance.com, and the creation of the now famous Agile Manifesto, containing the names of the 17 original signers (see Figure 3.3).

The ideas proposed in the Agile Manifesto have had a far sweeping effect, not only in the software industry, but in all business theories. Out of this meeting came the birth of the Agile philosophy. In the book, *Where Good Ideas Come From*,

---

Manifesto for Agile Software Development

We are uncovering better ways of developing software by doing it and helping others do it. Through this work we have come to value:

Individuals and interactions   *over*   processes and tools.

Working software   *over*   comprehensive documentation.

Customer collaboration   *over*   contract negotiation.

Responding to change   *over*   following a plan.

That is, while there is value in the items on the right, we value the items on the left more.

Kent Beck	James Grenning	Robert C. Martin
Mike Beedle	Jim Highsmith	Steve Mellor
Arie van Bennekum	Andrew Hunt	Ken Schwaber
Alistair Cockburn	Ron Jeffries	Jeff Sutherland
Ward Cunningham	Jon Kern	Dave Thomas
Martin Fowler	Brian Marick	

Figure 3.3 The Agile Manifesto

Stephen Johnson talks of the 10/10 rule for social innovation: "A decade to build the platform and a decade for it to find a mass audience."[8] Agile has had its 10 years to build a strong methodology, and we are well into the next 10 years when it will find its mass audience of practitioners. You need to be one of them.

References

[1]Taylor, F. 1911. *Principles of Scientific Management*. Frederick Winslow Taylor: Philadelphia.

[2]Lang, Walter (Dir.). 1950. *Cheaper by the Dozen*. [Motion picture]. Twentieth Century Fox.

[3]Fayol, H. 1930. *General and Industrial Management*. London: Sir Isaac Pitman & Sons.

[4]July 2008 lineup. Sept. 29, 2008. *CNET*. Retrieved from cnet.com.

[5]Royce, W. 1970. "Managing the Development of Large Software Systems." The Institute of Electrical and Electronics Engineers, Inc.

[6]Takeuchi, H., & Nonaka, I. January 1, 1986. "The New New Product Development Game." *Harvard Business Review*.

[7]Sutherland, J. Oct. 22, 2011. "Takeuchi and Nonaka: The Roots of Scrum." *scruminc*. Retrieved from http://www.scrum.jeffsutherland.com.

[8]Johnson, S. 2010. *Where Good Ideas Come From: The Natural History of Innovation*. New York, NY: Riverhead Books.

4

What Are Agile Practices and How Do They Work?

As described in the background of Agile principles in Chapter 3, ideas from several business theories of the 19th and 20th centuries merged to form the foundation of Agile principles. People are not interchangeable cogs in a machine, but rather, as Drucker expressed, they are knowledge workers who are needed in order to solve the massive, ongoing business problems that organizations face. Plus, organizations are nothing without customers, so we need to work toward providing customer value, not only toward making money. McGregor added the concept that people, when managed appropriately, are motivated and will do their best for the company.

Reddin's idea was that it is important to move from scrutinizing individuals and look instead at the collective success of the team. If the team delivers, the people and the managers are doing their jobs well. Additionally, Goldratt's Theory of Constraints and the Lean philosophy professed that the best way to create business value was to focus on moving customer value through the process flow of the project, as quickly as possible, by removing impediments or constraints.

Agile Principles

There are 12 principles that form the Big Agile philosophy. They are based in a respected and valued legacy of business theory that is a part of history, but which has not always been fully implemented in business practices. Although the same principles originally focused on software development, you can easily translate them to be appropriate for all types of projects. Some non-software ideas appear within the parentheses.

1. Our highest priority is to satisfy the customer through early and continuous delivery of valuable software (or products and services).
2. Welcome changing requirements, even late in development. Agile processes harness change for the customer's competitive advantage.
3. Deliver working software (or products or services) frequently, from a couple of weeks to a couple of months, with a preference to the shorter timescale.
4. Business people and developers must work together daily throughout the project.
5. Build projects around motivated individuals. Give them the environment and support they need, and trust them to get the job done.
6. The most efficient and effective method of conveying information to and within a development team (or a project team) is face-to-face conversation.
7. Working software (or a product, feature, or service) is the primary measure of progress.
8. Agile processes promote sustainable development. The sponsors, developers, (project teams) and users should be able to maintain a constant pace indefinitely.
9. Continuous attention to technical excellence and good design enhances agility.
10. Simplicity—the art of maximizing the amount of work not done—is essential.
11. The best architectures, requirements, and designs (creativity and innovation) emerge from self-organizing teams.
12. At regular intervals, the team reflects on how to become more effective, then tunes and adjusts its behavior accordingly.[1]

In addition to the 12 Agile Principles, another outcome of the meeting of software developers in 2001 was the **Agile Manifesto** (shown in Figure 3.3). Its authors said, "We feel that the software goals of our organizations are best served by a new philosophy called the Agile Manifesto". A manifesto is nothing more than a public declaration of intentions, and this one showed their philosophy and how they intended to approach projects.

In essence, the Agile Manifesto authors explained that the items shown on the right in Figure 3.3 were what they saw valued in the Waterfall, or traditional project management process:

- Highly defined processes and tools
- Comprehensive documentation
- Contract negotiation
- Following a plan

The signatories of the new manifesto agreed that they also valued those processes, but they valued these new principles even more:

- **Individuals and interactions** *over* processes and tools
- **Working software** *over* comprehensive documentation
- **Customer collaboration** *over* contract negotiation
- **Responding to change** *over* following a plan

The Agile Manifesto is the common rallying point for the current Agile movement. If you go to www.agilemanifesto.org you can view a copy of the *Manifesto for Agile Software Development*, along with the names of the original signers. Take note of their names, since this isn't a relic from a past century but a current and important addition to the project management landscape. These men are still actively speaking, writing, teaching, and practicing these principles on a daily basis. You may give a little more credence to an article, book, or speaker if you recognize that the person was a founder of the Agile movement.

The Agile Manifesto is available in multiple languages if you scroll down on the www.agilemanifesto.org web page. You might like to have a copy for your team workspace as you try to move into this methodology. If it isn't available in the language you prefer, there is a link where you can create a translation and submit it to the site to help others who speak that language. On the same page, you can download a copy of the *12 Principles of Agile Software*.

This statement of value coincides nicely with a major value shift that has taken place over the last few decades. Many of us may work in a top-down organization structured like the one shown on the left side of Figure 4.1. Our earlier management philosophy was reflected in the organizational hierarchy of companies. The prevailing assumption was that the hierarchy (meaning an organizational structure and its financial success) rested on the customers.

The bottom strata in a traditional hierarchy may be called the teams, the workers, or the employees. One level up are the project managers, department managers, and other individuals who work in a supervisory capacity. Listen to the words embedded into the language of business that define these relationships: Managers "oversee" the work of those "below" them. At the top of the pyramid are executives, who are "top management" or "upper management." We send decisions "upstairs" and talk of "climbing the ladder" as we garner promotions, and envision information flowing either "upstairs" or "down to the troops."

A more modern representation of the corporate structure based on Drucker's respect for the customer and the knowledge worker employees can be seen on the

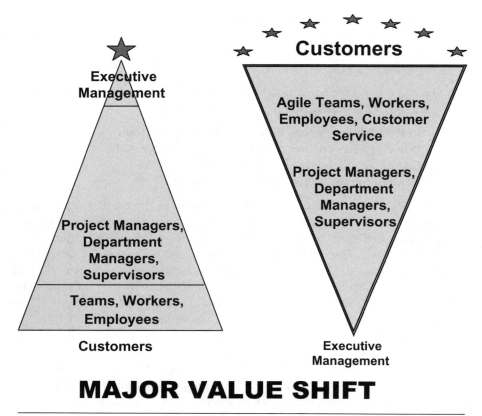

MAJOR VALUE SHIFT

Figure 4.1 Traditional and Modern Organizational Hierarchies

right side of Figure 4.1. Owners and executives now see themselves at the bottom of the pyramid and view their role as supporting and balancing the organization in the face of outside threat factors from the economy, competition, regulation, profitability, and shifting customer taste. They support the project managers and other managerial staff, who in turn are responsible to be a communication conduit in both directions. Centered in the organizational structure, the middle level now provides information and shares the vision with the employees, while working with executives to remove obstacles and impediments for workers and project teams.

The highest stature in the corporate heavens is reserved for the customers, because they are the most important people to the business. Being responsive and supportive of customers and their desires is the reason that the organization exists. In fact, we might prefer to remove that third, top side of the triangle, as increasingly customers are invited into the decision making process of new products and interface design as we add Agile to more traditional practices.

There is a similar flipping of traditional representations of project constraints occurring as more organizations move to Agile. We all have seen the time, cost, and scope parameters that define the ultimate quality of a typical project. With Waterfall technical and functional requirement practices, the idea was that an external, legal contract, or a position-power driven internal document, led the project team to try to manipulate time and cost to insure that the scope remained constant. Only as a last resort were we trained to consider adjusting the actual work that would be completed within the timeframe of the project. That worked well under the previous century's manufacturing and construction paradigms.

In a more Agile environment, the team and the stakeholders accept the fact that things will change during the course of the project, sometimes because of the speed with which the team is able to produce, sometimes due to extenuating circumstances around materials delivered, and so on. Project managers constantly have to balance time, cost, quality, and scope. However, if you are working with a dedicated team, you have fixed resources once you know how many people are on the team. With work periods timeboxed into iterations, your costs for resources and time are pretty much set. This gives you solid data on the two factors that cost the organization the most money.

That leaves scope as the only constraint that can change, while maintaining the project quality. Rather than consider changing scope as a negative, it is the flexibility to adjust the scope of the project for any internal or external reason that gives great value to the Agile approach. Since work is prioritized based on business value and the most important things will be done first, no matter where the project stops we will always have created value.

Find Errors Early

Both common sense and the *PMBOK® Guide* teach us that if change is going to occur in a project, the earlier the better. This also reverses another traditional idea. In Waterfall, we move heaven and earth to not fail, and to have every iota of what we produce be part of the final deliverable. In Agile, we've learned that every iota is impossible, or at the very least, unnecessary.

In fact, we may try out a couple of inexpensive prototypes first. Based on Lean principles, we are going to make our decisions just-in-time, often called the "**last responsible moment**" in Agile circles. This allows more leeway to do research and conduct small tests that might fail, but we are no longer afraid of failure. The mantra is, "Fail early, fail fast" because at the start of the project you are doing the least harm to the project.

Common cost of change charts illustrate that the earlier in the project you make changes, the lower the cost. Think about it. The further along you go in a project, the more you have invested in time and materials. Waterfall project structures can lead you through a one-pass process where you find problems too late to effectively adjust the work, resulting in huge losses from sunk costs.

One technique used in software development to find necessary changes early in the project is **pair programming**. The practice involves *two programmers working together, one at the keyboard and the other sitting next to him or watching over his/her shoulder*. Many programming errors result when the typist inadvertently leaves out a curly bracket or a colon. Plus, it is hard to be doing the actual typing while considering all of the complexity of the development architecture at the same time.

With one person doing the coding and the other watching for errors and having their mind free to consider whether or not this is the best approach, many time consuming bugs are avoided. Rather than costing double as you might assume, pair programming can actually save money, as it is less costly to fix problems as you go, rather than have to hunt them down in the complexity of thousands of lines of code at a later time. It is a low cost fix to remove a problem found by a pair of programmers, one at the keyboard and one looking on, correcting the code on the spot for only a few cents of time.

It is also a low cost fix if you find problems by *constantly fitting new pieces of the software, product, or service into place as you complete them* in a traditional project, rather than waiting until the end of the project to discover problems. That way you will not invest in volumes of items only to find out in the last phase of the project that things do not "fit" as you had anticipated. Assembling pieces as you go is called **continuous integration**.

Test Driven Development (TDD), covered in the later chapters on little agile, is *a way to write lines of code first to create a test to check other lines of code as they are written*. As more code is written, it has to run and pass all the earlier tests that have been created. TDD automates error spotting and finds problems at a time when you know it is in the lines of code you wrote today, not buried in the work from the last six weeks. Another low cost fix.

If the customer, or the project owner, is present at your end-of-iteration demo, you can find out what he or she does not like, forgot to tell you earlier, or did not realize until a portion of the project work was made tangible or observable. And, if you are mocking up or building small prototypes to test things, it is cheaper than investing in a wrong decision that you only discover much later.

Prototyping

It is not only the cost of change that leads Agile teams to use prototyping—it is also about flexibility. Many project managers new to Agile are uncomfortable with flexibility because it leaves loose ends. Most of us became project managers because we have a personality type that thrives on order. We like to see things decided up-front and then play out according to plan. If you have all of the information you need to make an informed decision, go right ahead. However, if you are forced to make decisions without all of the crucial information available to you at the moment, it may be a more viable option to delay the decision to the last responsible moment.

An excellent illustration of this way to deal with uncertainty comes from *Machine Design* magazine.[2] As an example, it describes a project to design and develop a new hub for a spoked bicycle wheel. If you are not a bicyclist, bike wheels can have narrow or wide flanges (the round part in the center where all the spokes come together). Most non-bicyclists assume that the wheel is one piece, since that is how we see wheels replaced at the gas station or sporting goods store.

Although it looks like one piece when all the parts are assembled, a bike wheel is actually the outer rim (to support the bike tire), spokes, and a center cylinder (which looks like a horizontal tube) called the wheel hub. Each wheel has a pair of flanges on either side of the hub, with holes to hold the spokes in place. Narrow flanges, closer to the same circumference as the hub at about 1.8 inches, are lighter weight, use less material to produce, and are cheaper to manufacture (see Figure 4.2, upper right corner). However, many bicycle enthusiasts believe the wider flange, measuring about 3 inches, allows for more stiffness and shorter spokes, and provides a wider spoke bracing angle from the flange to the rim, resulting in better power (see Figure 4.2, lower left corner).

The engineers on the hub design project were anxious to proceed, so they decided to build the narrow flange option, as they agreed that it was structurally adequate and also the cheapest. You can see the planned budget and schedule for this project in Plan A, Figure 4.2. It was budgeted to be a $100,000 project that lasted three months. Two months into the project, the marketing department was working with a group of bike shop distributers on the plans to launch this product, and found out by chance that they strongly preferred the wide flanges. They insisted that their customers, the end-user bike enthusiasts, would not purchase the narrow ones.

So, the project was forced to change to the wide flange option. See Plan B, Figure 4.2, for the impact that this change had on the project's cost and time. The project had already spent $70,000 of the $100,000 budget and eaten up two-thirds of the three-month project time. Now, they were forced to go back to the beginning and start over designing and testing the wide flange. These cost $10 each

A	Project Info	Planned Project Expense	Time	Cost Per Hub	
	Develop Narrow Flange	$100,000	3 months	$7	

	B	Project Info	Project Expense	Time	Cost Per Hub
		Sunk Project Costs	$70,000	2 months	$7
		Redesign Using Wide Flange	$100,000	3 months	$10
		Project Total	$170,000	5 months	$10
		Plan Variances	+ $70,000	+ 2 months	+ $3

C	Project Info	Project Expense	Time	Cost Per Hub
	Prototype Both Hubs	$5,000	none	0
	Develop Best Hub Choice	$100,000	3 months	$7 - $10
	Plan Variances	$5,000	0 months	$3 Max

Figure 4.2 Bicycle Wheel Flange Project

rather than $7, but that increase was through no fault of the project team. A wider flange requires more raw materials to manufacture it.

When you review the metrics of the project, there is the extra $70,000 of money spent on partially developing the narrow flange, and two months were wasted. So, the project cost was $170,000, or $70,000 over the initial cost estimates. The schedule took five months, between the aborted narrow flange work and the final production of the wide one, making the project run two months over schedule.

However, there was an alternative process that could have served this team well. At the beginning, the team could have realized the uncertainty surrounding which hub flange to produce and built prototypes of each one, or at least constructed a mock-up of the two options. These could have been shown to prospective distributors, and also to their customers, to see which flange they preferred and would be enticed to buy. It would have solved the problem of which item to manufacture before the company had invested large amounts of time and large numbers of dollars into either one.

The schedule and budget might have looked like Plan C, Figure 4.2, using the prototype approach. The cost for the hub flanges to be prototyped was $5,000. Since it was done before the project began, in an Iteration Zero scenario, it would not have added any time to the project schedule. Once the prototypes were shown to customers, the team would only work to produce the one that the distributors and their customers thought would be the best seller.

Granted, using this approach, the flange eventually brought to market would cost the organization $5,000 more than if the engineers had made their guess and it had turned out to be the right one. Consider that $5,000 an informal insurance policy categorized as risk management. The $5,000 investment would have saved the $70,000 of sunk costs which were wasted by making the wrong product when they guessed incorrectly, for an eventual savings of $65,000.

More importantly, the 2 months that were saved on the schedule might have made a huge difference, since it would have meant this manufacturer would be able to get the hub flange to market quicker and capture more market share before competitors sold to the limited pool of prospective buyers. The cost per hub could be $7 each (the narrow flange cost of production) or $10 each if the end-users chose the wide one. When project decisions are uncertain, Agile risk management suggests that you wait until the last responsible moment and get as much accurate data as you can before committing to a decision. And, you can always try the prototype route.

Early Customer Involvement

The next project example again shows the need to get the customer involved early. It is very costly on the cost of change curve to discover that the product owner doesn't like the results if you wait until the project is almost finished to show what you are doing. Most costly of all is when you finish the software, product, or service, but the marketplace rejects it. Remember, "fail early, fail fast." The faster you get feedback, the faster, easier, and cheaper it is to make corrections.

In *97 Things Every Project Manager Should Know*,[3] one tip involves an international training company franchise that provided classes on desktop software products like Microsoft Word, Excel, and PowerPoint. They marketed to companies who needed their employees trained to a higher level than what each person may have been able to learn on their own. Each software application had a Beginning, Intermediate, and Advanced class.

Originally, the ordering system worked great. The fastest way to pull up an item for reordering was by entering the item number.

- 4125 typed into the system, and you have ordered a Beginning Word student manual,
- 4225 was the accompanying student exercise disk,
- 4325 was the instructor's manual,
- 4425 was the course outline for marketing purposes, and so on.

If you went to the **5***x***25** series, where *x* is the variable number, you would be ordering the Beginning Excel manual, and so on. You could look the numbers up on a Master List the first time you ordered a new item, but administrative coordinators in 140 locations around the world ordered the same kinds of materials over and over again on a daily basis, and they soon memorized the item numbers.

The organization decided to redo their order processing system for training materials as part of a larger redesign of corporate management software. (Actually, the existing system worked beautifully, but the CEO's brother was an unemployed IT department manager in need of something to do.) During the redesign, the brother's team forgot to consider the way the ordering system was used by real people, so they changed all the item numbers and did away with any logical relationship between the items:

- Item 4125, formerly the Beginning Word student manual, was now 6358,
- The accompanying student exercise disk was 8872,
- The instructor manual was 3394, and
- The course outline was 1001.

With the "new and improved" system, not only did the data entry person have to look up each new item number and "forget" the old numbers and system, but now, each type of manual, disk, or sales sheet was part of an unrelated series of numbers. To make the situation even worse, each item had to be ordered by moving to a totally separate page, one for manuals, one for student exercise disks, one for instructor manuals, and still another for course outlines, rather than having everything on a one-screen list.

The administrative coordinators responsible for placing the orders for each franchise were furious when this new system was rolled out. Ordering slowed to a crawl. If you have ever had the misfortune to be a part of something that has made an administrative staff angry, then you already know that they had to redo this project. By the time it was redone, the redesign far exceeded its time and cost baselines, and it was never a good system or totally accepted by the users.

This idea of customer involvement is important in the emerging Agile methodology, which is no longer only for information technology (IT) departments but for all departments throughout the entire company. What do the chemists really want in their new lab? They do not really know every detail, but quickly lay out a lab design and show it to them and they will be able to immediately spot the missing emergency eyewash station in case caustic chemicals splash or explode. They will easily point out to you that the stations with Bunsen burners and the cabinets for compressed gas cylinder storage cannot be located next to one another, as you have shown in the your original floor plan.

Get the customer involved early and often

How much better it is to find out that there are problems with what we are developing early on, when change is cheap, rather than after the project is complete! Here are three other Agile ideas to consider for your team:

1. Deliver incremental change in order to maximize feedback.
2. Accept change continuously in order to minimize waste.
3. The cost savings that result from making changes early in the project will far outweigh and offset any costs associates with changes that are made early.

At this point you may have enough of an idea about Agile to ask yourself, "Should I be Agile?" Here is a quick way to see if you are a viable candidate. Make a list of numbers 1 through 9 on an answer sheet for yourself, with Yes and No columns to the right of each number. Or, use the form found in the Web Added Value section of the publisher's website (www.jrosspub.com) if you would like to try this with your team or customers. Check Yes or No to the following questions:

1. Do your projects need knowledge workers who are important to solving the difficult questions that your project faces?
2. Are your projects very, very complex?
3. Are you trying to do or create something new with this project, so there isn't much literature or any experienced people at your company to guide you?
4. Do you work on projects so complicated that no one person can have all the answers and plan out all of the solutions? In other words, do many specialists and many knowledge workers all need to contribute?
5. Is your team interested, or perhaps even pushing you to allow them to try out a new way to improve projects?
6. Would the management of your organization or the head of the project management office (PMO) be willing to have your teams try something slightly different? If not, could you convince them?
7. Would your customers be willing to try something new?
8. Do you have someone within your organization, or someone you could hire, to help your team get off to a good start in the Agile space?
9. Are your current projects not meeting time, cost, quality, and scope goals no matter now hard you try? Or, do you have other problems surrounding your current processes?

These are all issues that can be softened or made easier through a more flexible, more Agile process. Now look at your results. If you have four or more check marks in the Yes column, Agile could be in your future. You should definitely consider it. However, the No column is equally important. The check marks in the No column are a gap analysis of the organizational and customer issues that you will need to address, and problems you will need to solve, to be successful in moving to Agile processes.

Agile vs. Waterfall

Now that you may be serious about what Agile can offer your team, let's compare Agile and the more familiar Waterfall process. Often the easiest way to understand something new is to see what it looks like next to what we already know. The nickname "Waterfall" came from its resemblance to cascading levels of water pouring over the stair-stepping rock outcroppings on a mountainside. There is no need to go into it in detail, as most of us use it every day.

In Waterfall, we plan out a schedule and do *all* of the project Analysis before we flow down to the next level and start Design, as shown in the sample Waterfall phases in Figure 4.3. When the Analysis phase is finished, we do *all* of the Design.

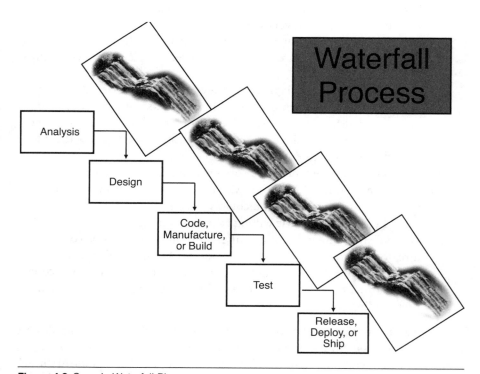

Figure 4.3 Sample Waterfall Phases

After that we do *all* of the Coding, Manufacturing, or Building. Next we Test, or do quality analysis, or get the trade inspectors on-site to approve the construction, and so on.

This is called a sequential approach. One phase must finish before the next one can start. However, this is not the only way to do a project. It is just the most controlling, based on manufacturing and construction history and an old picture of the role of the employees in our organizations. Remember, when Royce wrote his original white paper from which this idea was taken, he warned, "Be careful, you may have feedback loops that require change late in the process." But people read right over that warning and embraced Waterfall anyway. *One of the key oversights with this process is that it focuses on delivering product, but not necessarily on delivering the business value to the organization it expected to receive by investing in the project.*

Plan, Do, Check, Act

Most project managers are familiar with the **Shewhart Cycle**: Plan, Do, Check, Act (also called the PDCA cycle). It was created by Walter Shewhart and popularized by William Deming in their push for continuous improvement. In essence, this cycle *contains a continuous feedback loop in order to instigate continuous improvement in the processes.* So, let's use that as the basis for learning about the Agile process. We are still on Big Agile because, remember, the overriding belief structure is more important than the details of who does what on a daily basis.

Plan

In the Plan portion of the Agile project cycle, as shown in Figure 4.4, you have a dedicated team with only one project to focus on at a time. Researchers Joshua Rubinstein, David Meyer, and Jeffrey Evans suggest that productivity can be reduced by as much as 40% by the mental blocks created when people switch tasks.[4] There already are so many other interruptions during a workday that the mental leap from one project to the next really reduces the value an organization gets from its workers.

Hopefully, *the team is located and working together in one area*—that is, **collocated**. To help with creating a participative environment, Steelcase, the office furniture manufacturer, has taken a patent on new, more collaborative office space furniture. This includes desks on rollers, large moveable whiteboards that can be used for projection devices, a dry-erase board, a magnetic surface, and other types of adaptive furniture for a cube-free, open workspace. The company makes the point that with today's technology, why come into the office at all if you are not going to work together in a collaborative manner?

* Have a dedicated team. (Working on only one project at a time.) Cross-functional and collocated and self-directed.

* Meet as a group and have the customer pick the most important features from a pre-defined list *(Backlog)* to do first.

* Estimate how long each item will take; not in duration, but in difficulty.

* Commit to creating the number of features that will fit into the time period of your Iteration, usually 1-2 weeks. (During this time, there will be **no** customer changes).

* Display the stories or features you will create during an Iteration on sticky notes in a highly visible area.

Figure 4.4 Plan Cycle Process for Agile Teams

In the Plan phase, you meet with the customer and the customer chooses the most important features (the stories) to create during this 1 to 2 week iteration. Next, the team estimates how many hours it will take to complete each story or feature. The team chooses and commits to as many of the stories as it can do, considering the number of team members and the hours that they work. The work committed to by the team can be displayed on sticky notes in a highly visible area.

Do

The Do part of the cycle is where the daily stand-up meeting happens, with each person reporting on the work done the day before, the work to be done today, and the impediments or roadblocks that they need removed. Whether you are developing software or working with other kinds of products and services, the concept of Do and Test, Do and Test, Do and Test as you go is still important. When the item passes the test, the team member who completed it moves the sticky note to the place for completed tasks.

At this point, a team member can choose another task or help someone who is having problems. Rather than taking on additional tasks, many teams find there is

DO:

* Each day, have a stand-up meeting where each person says what they completed yesterday and what they will do today and what is in their way.

* As you complete each task, you immediately test it or check it for quality. Then you move the sticky note to a "completed area".

* If there is still time in the day or the Iteration, choose another task or offer to help someone who is behind.

CHECK:
* Do all quality checks and testing during this 2 to 4 week iteration. Usually it's more like this…you create something and you immediately test it…because if your work in incorrect it could cause a problem for someone else.

* At the end, demonstrate or show the customer the features, functions, or items you have completed and get their feedback.

Figure 4.5 Do and Check Processes for Agile Teams

more value in allowing the people to have a little time to catch up on other pressing business, or to have a moment to talk with other departments, customers, or vendors. Allowing time to mentally process information and think about better ways to do the work of the project is also of value (see Figure 4.5).

Check

Now it is time for the Check phase. We have created and tested during the Do phase, but if some activities cannot be done this way as they need to be checked after being assembled into a larger feature or product portion, at least be sure to do the initial check process of your assembled item during the same 1 to 2 week iteration in which the work was completed. At the end of the iteration, show the customer the features, functions, or items that you have done. After seeing them and trying them out, they can approve them or ask the team for a redo. Figure 4.5 shows the processes found in the Do and Check portions of the Agile cycle.

 At the end of each Iteration, place any unfinished items or work discovered into the Backlog (pool of features and stories yet to be done).

* Check your velocity (speed with which the team has completed features or stories), and adjust your work for the next Iteration. unfinished items or work discovered into the Backlog (pool of features and stories yet to be done).

* Do a Retrospective, a look back to see what worked and what needs to be changed for the next Iteration. (Why wait until the end of the project, when it's too late.)

Figure 4.6 Act Cycle Process for Agile Teams

Act

During the Act phase, place any unfinished work, or additional work you realized must be done after the initial planning, back into the backlog. Check the speed of your team. Did they accomplish the work in the time that they had estimated? If the individual story estimates were high (and they did not select enough work) take on more stories for the next iteration. If the estimates were too low (and they fell far short of completing the selected tasks), take on fewer stories next time. After each iteration, each 1 to 2 weeks period, do a retrospective to see what worked and what processes need to change for (see Figure 4.6). The Agile Plan, Do, Check, Act cycle is now complete for this iteration and ready to begin again for the next iteration.

References

[1]"The Twelve Principles of Agile Software." (2012). *Agile Alliance*. Retrieved from http://www.agilealliance.org/the-alliance/the-agile-manifesto/the-twelve-principles-of-agile-software.

[2]Mraz, S. "Dealing with Change in Design Projects." March 17, 2011. Machine Design, 83(5): 38-41.

[3]Davis, B. 2009. *97 Things Every Project Manager Should Know.* New York: O'Reilly Media.

[4]Rubinstein, J. S., Meyer, D. E., & Evans, J. E. 2001. "Executive Control of Cognitive Processes in Task Switching." *Journal of Experimental Psychology: Human Perception and Performance, 27*(4): 763-797.

5

What Are Some More Agile Concepts?

Favor the Simple Over the Complex

Some critics of the Agile process say, "Well, wait a minute. If we don't list *all* the features we want at the very beginning and get a commitment from the team to do them, some things may take longer to complete than expected and we'll run out of time and won't get as many features as we want for our money." However, do they really need all of those features?

Another tip in the book *97 Things Every Project Manager Should Know* is entitled "Favor the Simple Over the Complex" and is contributed by Scott Davis, who humorously, but thought-provokingly considers the same question of the necessity of extensive lists of features, stating:

> "As far as I'm concerned, my microwave oven only has one button: 'add a minute.' To boil a cup of water for my coffee, I press the button three times. To melt cheese on my crackers, one click. To warm up a flour tortilla I press 'add a minute' and then open the door after 15 seconds.
>
> Would a one button microwave oven even make it out of the planning committee on a traditional project? Probably not. I can tell by the never-used features on my microwave that the committee who designed it favored complexity over simplicity. Of course, they probably cloaked "complexity" in the euphemism "feature-rich." No one ever starts out with the goal of making a product that is unnecessarily complex. The complexity comes along accidentally.

Suppose I have a slice of cold pizza that I want to warm up. According to the manufacturer's directions, I should press the "menu" button. I am now faced with the options "speedcook" or "reheat." (Um, reheat I guess, although I'm kind of hungry. I wonder if speedcook is any faster than reheat?)

"Beverage," "pasta," "pizza," "plate of food," "sauce," or "soup"? (I choose pizza, although it does have sauce on it, and it is on a plate.)

"Deli-Fresh" or "Frozen"? (Neither, actually—it's leftover delivery pizza. I'll choose, Deli/Fresh, I guess.)

"1 slice," "2 slices," "3 slices," or" 4 slices"? I have no idea how much longer this interrogation will last, so I press "Cancel," and then the "add a minute" button.[1]

So, Scott's thinking is that although projects generally solve complex problems, they often erroneously do it by creating equally complex *products*. The question is, how much of that inherent complexity is really of value to the end user?

There is an interesting study done by the Standish Group, the research organization that is centered on collecting statistics of why projects succeed or fail. They found out that of all the successfully delivered features—all features that the customer put into long requirements documents of traditional Waterfall projects—45% of them were Never used by the end user anyway. An additional 19% of the features fell into the Rarely used category. Totaling those percentages, as shown in Figure 5.1, and you'll realize that 64% of the features could have been eliminated, and no one would have cared.[2]

The Always, Often, and Sometimes used features total 36%, just slightly over one third of the features created. So, if a customer has you produce features in the order of importance, they will get total usability at the end of the project with workable, well-tested software or products, even if you don't have time to deliver the 64% of the requested features no one will ever touch anyway. But, the ones you do deliver are the important ones, and they are ready-to-use to garner business value.

Scott also raises the question of whether your project deliverable is a complexity amplifier. He poses the idea that great software, products, or services are generally a complexity "sink." They bear the brunt of the problem on behalf of the user and provide a clean, streamlined, and simple solution rather than amplifying a problem. According to Davis, simplicity does not happen accidentally. Rather, it needs to be cultivated. Complexity is what happens when you are not paying attention.

As a project manager, you need to ask yourself, regardless of the type of project you work on, if you, personally, are a complexity sink or a complexity amplifier. The best project managers who work in an Agile manner assume a role whereby

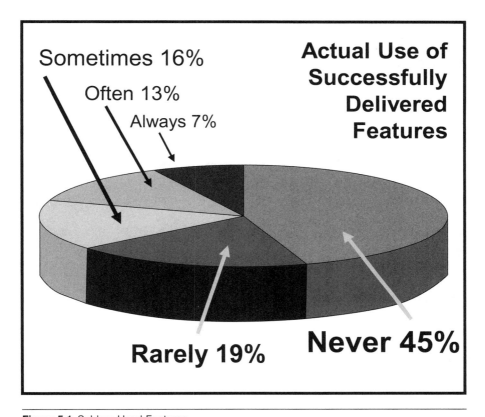

Sometimes 16%

Often 13%

Always 7%

Actual Use of Successfully Delivered Features

Rarely 19%

Never 45%

Figure 5.1 Seldom Used Features

they absorb complexity from all sides—from the project team, end users, product owners, customers, and the management of the organization. They take it upon themselves to remove the constraints and obstacles in the way of the team's performance and make the path smooth. They never amplify the problems facing them, even if it makes a great story over coffee.

The old traditional project management pattern is gathering requirements, designing the solution, developing or creating the solution, and then testing it, as shown in Figure 5.2. The newer Agile model suggests that you start with a list of features or user stories the customer has prioritized, let the team choose how far down the list they can commit to for each timebox, and move those items over to become iteration features. Once the team begins creating the actual project work, it is a cycle in which they plan and develop, evaluate their work, learn from their successes and errors, and keep the cycle going until at the end of the iteration they

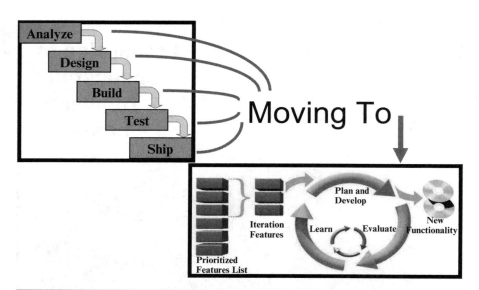

Figure 5.2 Traditional Processes Moving to Agile Processes

have a piece of product, service, or software that can be put to use for business value.

Another way to describe the cycle is to figure out the first thing the user wants, build a small portion of it, and make sure you are on the right track. Then, check with the user to see if he or she would like it altered or adjusted, and continue that process until the user is happy. Remember, it is not just doing actions or activities that "look" Agile; it is about embracing the philosophy behind Agile and using it in a way to achieve greater *business* value by creating greater *customer* value. It's about moving the software, product, or service, through the project team process flow with a minimum of impediments or constraints.

Phase-to-Phase Relationships

Many people continue to think Agile is new, rather than the more than 12 years old it really is. They may also think that these heretical processes are "against the rules" set out by PMI, despite the obvious misconception that PMI "sets out rules," rather than sharing effective practices found and contributed by their members. The acceptance of Agile project management has been in the *PMBOK® Guide* since the Third Edition was published in 2004. In the Fourth Edition, which came out in 2008, there were three basic types of phase-to-phase relationships:

- **Sequential**, where *one phase must finish before the next begins*. This is what we have come to know as Waterfall.
- **Overlapping**, in which *the next phase may start before the preceding one is completed*. If you speak project management, you will be familiar with this idea that we frequently use in attempts to bring projects back on track with the techniques of schedule compression or fast-tracking.
- **Iterative**, which sounds exactly like a description of Agile: "*... an iterative relationship, where only one phase is planned at any given time and the planning for the next is carried out as work progresses on the current phase (iteration) and deliverables*. The scope is then managed by continuously delivering increments (small parts) of the product and prioritizing requirements to minimize project risk and maximize product business value."[3]

At a high level, a Waterfall project might look like the top of Figure 5.3. In this example, the Design Phase is broken into several Sub-Phases. The length of time planned to complete the Design Phase is the total of the three Sub-Phases; however, the phases as the higher level such as Planning, Execution, and Test can vary in length from one to the next. One might be two weeks long and another three months. The Sub-Phases can also be quite different lengths in the time it takes to complete each one.

In the lower portion of Figure 5.3, you can see an Agile project sample. For purposes of comparison, you might like to think of a Release as being equated to a Phase in the Waterfall diagram. As you can see, the Release is also broken into smaller parts called Iterations. The difference is that the Iterations will all be equal in length. That length can be 1 week, 2 weeks, or up to 4 weeks, but if you choose 4 weeks for the iteration timebox, each and every Iteration must also be 4 weeks. So, in the example, if we plan a 4-week Iteration, the first Release will be 16 weeks (four months). The entire project would take a year, since there are three Releases.

The Non-Software Agile Process

There are many books on Agile for the software industry, but for those of us who are not software developers, they use many terms and processes that do not translate to the non- IT world. For our purposes, an overview of a non-software approach to Agile would be more useful. Almost all people retain information best through pictures, so in its most simple form, a non-software Agile process would look something like the bottom of Figure 5.3.

As with all good project initiations, a non-software Agile project starts with a company vision that can be achieved through the success of the project. *Someone who knows and understands that vision, and has some personal interest,*

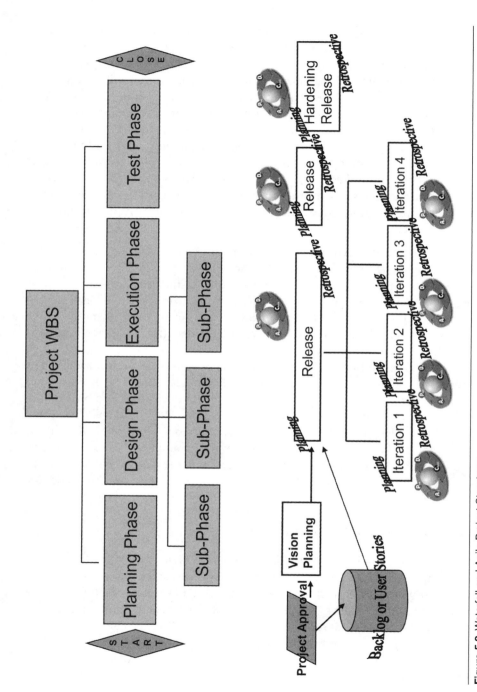

Figure 5.3 Waterfall and Agile Project Structures

involvement, or responsibility for the outcome, needs to commit to be the management link to the project team and the project manager. A common title to designate that role in the project is **product owner**. You may commonly see it written as Project Owner to show that this is a specific Agile role with distinct responsibilities.

In different organizations, the title of the person who will take on the role of the product owner will vary. For a small organization, it could be the owner. In a larger company, it might be a department manager, and in an even larger enterprise, it might be a program or portfolio manager. When the infrastructure has many levels, there may be an intermediate representative who reports to that person with the ultimate responsibility, who is chosen to be the project liaison. Perhaps it is a business analyst. If this project is for an external group, you may hear the person who performs the product owner responsibilities labeled the Customer, with a capital C.

Ideally, the product owner or customer must be prepared to be available to the team on a daily basis, and preferably they will be collocated with the team. The idea is that they are there to guide the team and answer questions that occur as the work of the project progresses. Having immediate feedback keeps the team from creating incorrect choices, which, as we saw in the bicycle hub flange example in Chapter 4, can add time and cost to the project.

At the start of the project, the product owner writes stories of what they want in this product or service, rather than create a long list of technical and functional requirements. This is typically done with the help of the project manager. Again, in its attempt to deal with the realities of the world, Agile approaches acknowledge that while the product owner knows best what he or she hopes to gain from creating this new deliverable, this may not be a person who also knows the details of *how* it can best be created. So, that is left to the project team.

When the scope of a project arrives on the desk of team members in the form of a 210 page, single-spaced technical and functional requirements document, it is hard for them to see the vision that was intended when the project was originally approved and funded. But if they attend a meeting where the product owner tells them in person what this product should do, why it is being proposed at this moment in the company's lifecycle, and how it needs to perform to make the work or life of the end user/final customer easier or better, the team member is better prepared to share this vision and bring it to life. A Vision Statement of what this project is intended to do should be posted on the wall of the team room to keep it constantly in focus.

User Stories

In the Agile world, technical and functional requirements are written in a way that is easy to understand. They are *descriptive, short explanations of a feature* called **user stories**. There is no one way to create user stories, but a successful sample is shown in Figure 5.4. It is written to give the team the knowledge of who the end user or beneficiary of the feature would be, and what need it would meet. A common way to write user stories is:

> As a <Insert the Role of the Ultimate Person Who Needs This Feature>, I want <Insert the Functionality/Feature/Service that the Ultimate User or Person Wants> to <Insert the Business Value or Benefit to the Customer/ Organization>.

This is usually shortened to:

> As a *<Role>*, I want *<Functionality>* to *<Business Value or Benefit>*.

User Stories – As a <Role>, I want <Functionality> to <Business Value or Benefit>

Story 43

As a Vice-President of Membership, I want to get a report of expiring members (within one month) to send them renewal incentives and prevent loss of their membership.

Priority: High
Story Points: 5

Figure 5.4 A Sample User Story

Imagine that you work for a professional organization that represents the security industry. Your funding is based on membership dues, and without a robust enrollment, you will not have enough money to provide the services that the security professionals have come to count on. As part of a project to fulfill the vision of the organization to support its members, you might fund a project to retain and increase memberships. One of many user stories you, as the product owner, might write to share with your project team, could read:

> As a <Vice President of Membership>, I want <to get a report of expiring members (within one month prior to expiration)> to <send them renewal incentives and prevent loss of their membership>.

If you were on this team, you would clearly understand what needed to be done. (You don't need to include < > marks. They just help to show where the template and the sample fit together.)

By the way, all joking aside, you might want to be sure that your team did not misunderstand the word "expiring" and think that you wanted a list of dead members. But that discussion might prompt the addition of another user story to read:

> As a <Vice President of Membership>, I want <to get a report of deceased members (within one month)> to <remove them from mailing lists or deduct that projected income from the balance sheet, or activate their insurance settlement paperwork>.

Each of those needs could also be a separate story. You can find a user story template on the Web Added Value section of the publisher's website (www.jrosspub.com).

Some teams prefer to get very specific with their descriptions of the end users, developing several pages for each **persona**, or *character they are going to use to represent the ultimate customers.* They tend to describe jobs, hobbies, families, interests, and other details for each person. Then, when discussing a feature, they have a communication shortcut to say, "How do you think Ethel would like this?" (a grandmother persona that has little experience with technology), or "Would these colors be an attraction for Jason?" (the sports minded professional persona with four children).

In order to know when each user story is done, it needs to have pre-planned approval or acceptance criteria. These will be written or stated by the product owner and captured by the project manager or the team. **Acceptance criteria** *allow the person working on the feature or service to know when this user story is finished, that is, when it meets the standards or requirements set out for its approval.* For example, acceptance criteria for a new printer being created might be that it prints two-sided documents at speeds of 7.4 pages per minute in black and 5.4 pages per minute in color, based on the International Organization for Standardization (ISO) standards for measuring print speeds.

Traditionally, these criteria come in the technical requirements document. Now, we are going to find them out from the product owner, or perhaps the team has the authority to suggest some themselves. Regardless of the lighter form of documentation preferred in Agile approaches, there is no dishonor to having product requirement specifications on a list. In an Agile project, it is incredibly important for the product owner to spell out what he or she expects, so the team is always clear as to what they need to accomplish.

The difference is in how requirements are kept in front of the team as they work. One workable method is to have the acceptance criteria written on the back of the same sticky note that contains the user story. At any time, any of the stakeholders on the team can flip over this project artifact and see the technical goal for the item. So, when the printer meets the ISO standards for speed set out in the acceptance criteria, we can move this sticky note to the "Done" pile. Because there are two color speeds to achieve, perhaps the speed requirement will be broken into two, separate user stories.

Each project will have a number of stories, and *all of those stories that describe product, service, or software features are placed into an imaginary bucket* called a **product backlog**. Now the customer or product owner prioritizes them by their importance, business value, and risk. Those at the top of the list will be completed first. In the earlier membership example, we might decide that the need to contact existing people whose memberships are due to expire is a story that belongs at the top of the list, since it will be easier to retain members than attract new ones. It also brings money into the coffers earlier if we notify them ahead of time, rather than waiting for the membership to expire (reach its renewal date) before reminding current associates to rejoin.

Let's switch examples, and look at how this approach might compare to a traditional project. In Figure 5.5, we see that this project has a Company Vision to "Be the online bank of choice to small business customers." The Specific Company Goal is to "Increase customer retention on our website." This Company Vision and the Specific Company Goal could work for either a Waterfall or an Agile approach. At the third level, where, in a traditional project, the team could expect to receive technical and functional requirements; instead the Agile team gets an **Epic** story, *a large umbrella collection or group of related user stories*. In our example, the Epic story is: "Add a self-service Customer Center for frequent customer needs."

Now, the *Epic story is broken down into* **Features**, telling what the customer will be able to do that provides value to the customer. Using an online bank, a customer might find value in the ability to access past statements, stop payment on a check, and find a branch location to provide the services that cannot be provided by the online functionality. The Features are now divided into Stories

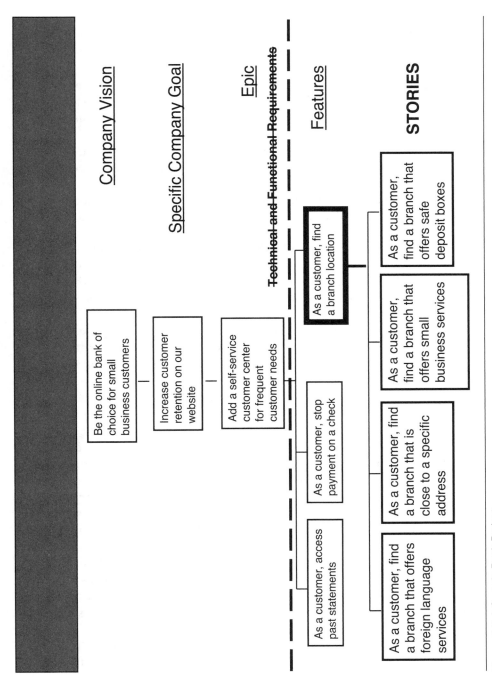

Figure 5.5 A Sample Bank Project

(user stories), showing that the customer may want to find a branch with foreign language services, close to their home or office, a location with small business services available (since all branches do not necessarily maintain identical offerings), and pinpoint which branches offer safe deposit boxes. If the Stories are too large to do in one iteration or as one unit, or some parts deliver more business value than others, or some parts have differing levels of importance, they can be further separated into **tasks**. At the task level, the work of the project is in *a small enough piece for the team members to assign story points, based on the difficulty and ability to complete in one iteration.*

Notice that we deliberately do not tell the team *how* they are to do what is asked of them. In an Agile approach, control of the stories of *what* is needed and *when* it will be done rests with the product owner or customer. *How* those needs are met is in the hands of the team (within reason). Obviously, if the need is for a faster route between Omaha and Sao Paulo, Brazil, an airline team will be expected to think in terms of airplanes, not dog sleds.

The subject matter experts and technical experts from the team can also add infrastructure stories that need to happen to support the other stories, or add any additional work they can see from their own detailed knowledge of what it will take to complete these stories. They work with the product owner to get the team stories integrated into the prioritized line of work in the backlog.

Here is an example that may help you visualize how an Agile project would work with user stories rather than the traditional WBS approach. The dotted line in Figure 5.6 shows the process flow, or the project value stream. It maps how the software, product, or service moves from Company Vision to completion, and out into the marketplace or into internal departments. Since we are looking for a value stream with the fewest possible constraints or impediments, the project manager is going to get those out of the way for the team, who is doing the work of the project.

Remember, ideally we have a team all working in one room and they have cross-functional (overlapping) skill sets. We do not want to have only one expert on anything because it would delay the process flow if that one team member was busy on another task. Also, this team is dedicated 100% to this one project. Ahead of time, the project manager has worked with the product owner or customer to figure out what features this project is to produce, broken them down into stories (Customer User Stories), and written the stories on "sticky notes". Usually, the notes are in a format like, "As a customer I want to be able to search for a product on the web." These stories make up the product Backlog, shown as the large bucket. It has been prioritized by the product owner/customer based on which items would provide the most business value, and any additional, necessary work has been added by the team and worked into the prioritization.

For the first **Planning meeting**, shown as a vertical pillar labeled Planning, the product owner or customer is right there with the team face-to-face to present

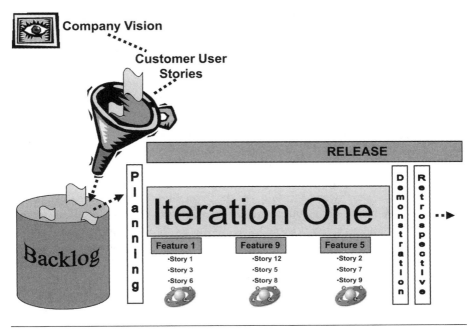

Figure 5.6 Sample Agile Process Flow

what he or she wants, tell the vision in person, and plan together roughly how long this project is going to take. This is without doing a WBS or getting into great detail. The group may say, it looks like we could get most of this done in about 9 weeks. So, we start out planning for 8 weeks and decide to work in 2 week increments.

Progressive Elaboration

Once there is a prioritized Backlog, we plan at a high level for a Release, the longest horizontal rectangle that you can note. There is a misconception regarding Agile that since it advocates lighter documentation, it is an *ad hoc* process that eliminates planning. Not true! It is just based on the reality that because of unknowns, or information that we do not know at this moment but may know more about later, it is best to *plan with broader strokes far out into the future and then add more detail just before doing the work.* This lowers the risk to the project and lowers the cost of change. This technique is called **progressive elaboration**.

A form of progressive elaboration, known as **rolling wave planning**, is also referenced in the *PMBOK® Guide* as, *"Planning where the work to be accomplished in the near term is planned in detail, and future work is planned at a higher level"* in the WBS.[4] Therefore, work can exist at various levels of detail, depending on where it is in the project life cycle. For example, during early strategic planning, when information is less defined, work packages may be decomposed to the milestone level. As more is known about the upcoming events in the near term it can be decompressed into activities. That exact philosophy is being followed in the Agile planning cycle. The Release shown in Figure 5.6, for example, might be eight weeks long. That is how long we anticipate the project will take, based on the high level look at the Customer User Stories in the Backlog. Now, we do some detailed planning for the next two weeks and decide how many features, divided into user stories we can create or produce during that timebox. In this iteration, we are going to do Feature 1, and Stories 1, 3, and 6, which will help complete that feature. We will also commit to complete Features 9 and 5, with the most important stories for each of them. Notice that we do this detailed planning for the iteration, which is set at two weeks just before we begin to do the work. You can see where this occurs by locating the vertical Planning pillar before Iteration One.

We then do as much of the work as we can during Iteration One, and put any leftover stories we have yet to complete back in the Backlog bucket. At the end of the timebox, we *demonstrate what we have created to the product owner/customer* (**Demonstration**), get his or her feedback, and hopefully get approval. This is sometimes referred to as, "Demo, not memo."

Now the product owner/customer chooses the next set of stories in importance or business value and the team gets to make a case to add any architectural or other supporting technical stories that need to be added to the backlog. We then begin the detailed planning for the next iteration, Iteration Two, which includes any changes we agreed upon during the Retrospective on Iteration One.

The final part of an iteration is to take time for the team to talk together about how the work went the last two weeks. This talk is called a **Retrospective**. Through this meeting, we get feedback from the team as to what we need to change for the next iteration. *Is there a better way for the team to do things in the way that we create this product or service? Also, teams talk about their processes.* Is there a better way to run the daily stand-ups, communicate, and make our progress visible? Do we need to change our team rules? This is continuous improvement in action, because we are going to improve both the product and the team's processes, or rules, at the end of each iteration. Retrospectives are far superior to capturing people's grumblings in a lessons learned meeting after 6 months or a year, and then filing them away, never again to see the light of day.

Be sure to review the project's vision statement and other organizational goals to check that what you are creating is aligned with what is needed. Think of the retrospective as if you are a powerful, up-and-coming sports team. Each Monday, whether you won or lost, you watch the game tapes from the weekend's game together as a team to enable you to clearly spot what you need to change in your own performance and what needs to be adjusted in the team's playbook to improve the chances of winning. The same self-awareness and openness to personal and group improvement will also work to hone a winning project team.

The issues that come out of the retrospective are added to the backlog and ranked. That way, they get addressed in the following two weeks. If there are impediments, the project manager puts his or her name on that sticky note and it is placed with the committed stories that will be done this week. However, the project manager tasks do not get counted for the team velocity figures. (You'll understand velocity later.)

If this is an IT team, or a team from any small department or small company, you may not have the luxury of being totally dedicated. Perhaps the team includes all the resources available to the company, and you must do both operational and project activities on a daily basis. In these situations, some teams have had success by placing the operational issues in the backlog as well, and have the product owner, usually a functional manager, rank them, too.

The product owner helps to decide what will be done in the next two weeks, and if he or she is not the functional manager of the people on the team, you can invite the functional manager into the meeting to help prioritize the backlog with the product owner. Let the two of them work out which tasks have priority, and after they have decided what to do, the team is left with a clear direction of the work they should complete, and left out of the middle of any conflicts. Both managing parties of this matrix organization, who have now been involved in the decision making process, also know about and have agreed to any delays in the work of the project or the operational work.

If we pull back for a higher, birds-eye view in Figure 5.7, we can see the whole project. This view of an Agile project is called a **Project Roadmap**. There are four Iterations in each Release. If we know that each Iteration is 2 weeks, in this example, the Release will be 8 weeks in length. There are three Releases, so the entire project should take 24 weeks (6 months) to complete. The other two Releases will eventually have their own 4 Iterations each, but they are not yet planned this early in the timeline, as there may be changes that would cause them to be reworked at an added cost to the project if they are planned in detail too early.

Hopefully, this brief overview gives you confidence that there is nothing in this approach to managing projects that could not be adapted for your own project environment, regardless of your product, service, or industry. Remember, the idea is *not* to slavishly follow every detail, but to use the spirit of it to find ways to ease project pain points and enhance customer satisfaction, speed to market, and profitability for your organization.

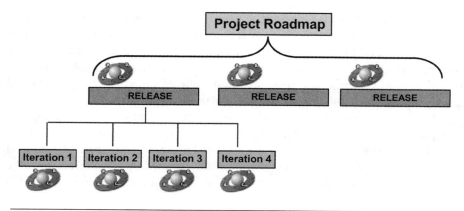

Figure 5.7 Sample Agile Roadmap

References

[1]Davis, B. 2009. *97 Things Every Project Manager Should Know*. New York: O'Reilly Media.

[2]The CHAOS Report. 2002. The Standish Group International, Inc..

[3]Project Management Institute. 2012. *Project Management Body of Knowledge (PMBOK® Guide)*. Fourth Edition. Newtown Square, PA.

[4]Project Management Institute. 2012. *Project Management Body of Knowledge (PMBOK® Guide)*. Fourth Edition. Newtown Square, PA.

Should My Projects Be Agile?

"I have been a project manager for a number of years and have been quite successful using my current PMI processes. Do I need to change all of my projects to a more Agile approach? If not, how do I decide which are to be Agile, and which should be Waterfall?"

–Confused Colleague

The question that puzzles most of us is similar to the one presented above. Do I need to change all of my projects, only some projects, or just change parts of some and leave other parts as I have done them in the past, and on and on? The answer is simple. As we evolve as project managers, we will all grow more Agile and flexible in the way we do projects. The reality is that some of us will do *all Agile, all of the time*, but *all* of us will do *some Agile, some of the time.*

The project managers who will do all Agile *all* of the time will most likely be those who lead software development teams, because Agile is most appropriate in those types of projects for the reasons that led to the Agile Manifesto (Chapter 4). When a project is very new, extremely innovative, or trying to solve a complex issue, it is hard to draw up detailed, comprehensive technical and functional requirements. Some undertakings are being started before market decisions or governmental regulations are finalized, for example, so there is a strong possibility of change. There may also be a strong potential for risks that would be very damaging to the project if they occurred, so it would be detrimental to make binding decisions too early.

Some organization have the need and/or the opportunity to release or sell products immediately, and then provide or market frequent upgrades or versions as a way to get their offering into the hands of the public in advance of the competition. Increasingly, organizations who create or consult for software and web development projects are reorganizing themselves to allow for the luxury of teams that are collocated (all team members under the same roof), cross-functional (team members with overlapping skill sets), and dedicated (teams work on one project at a time).

Places that find their projects have some or most of these characteristics requiring the ability to be flexible may benefit from moving to an Agile approach. But even in these environments, there will probably always be a few of the traditional methods surrounding the actual project, as program or portfolio management techniques will still be used to choose projects and authorize the funds. Realistically, you will also find that you may need to have some Waterfall/Traditional processes upfront to get the project authorized and do some high-level Vision Planning. In addition, there will still be a need for some version of a project charter up front, although it may have a different name.

In companies that have additional work at the end of the creation of the product or service, but not enough to take an entire additional release to implement, a type of iteration called a *hardening iteration* can be added. In this space,

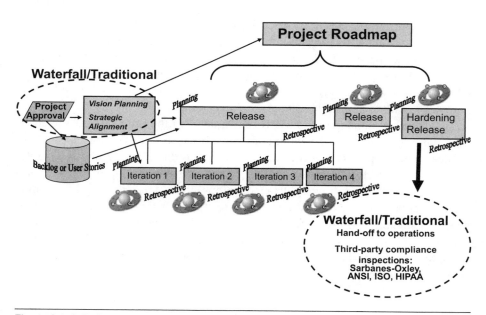

Figure 6.1 Agile Project with Traditional Bookends

traditional work to teach training classes, prepare compliance submissions, create archival documents, and other typical end-of-project work can be written into the overall schedule of one release of the Agile project.

At the end of the last release in the project, you may need *a wrap-up release to do training of operations personnel, train end-users, and do other little bits of wrap-up*. Then you may hand off the project to a more traditional operations team or a third party to do mandatory compliance inspections. This extra, clean-up release is often called a **Hardening Release**.

Perhaps some additional, traditional processes will also remain near the end of the project, especially if you work in an industry where you must meet government or industry standards, pass audits or inspections, or have other types of compliance requirements. The high level view of the project structure might look something like the one shown in Figure 6.1. You may hear this referred to as traditional bookends for an Agile team process core. Think of it as a "hard candy coating with a gooey Agile center."

Ideally, as many of those responsibilities as possible are moved up from the end of the project to instead be done in parallel with the work of the development team. So, for example, if there is to be training at the end of the project, an instructional design person will be working on creating the training materials at the end of each iteration (Figure 6.2). It is helpful if the person occupying this role

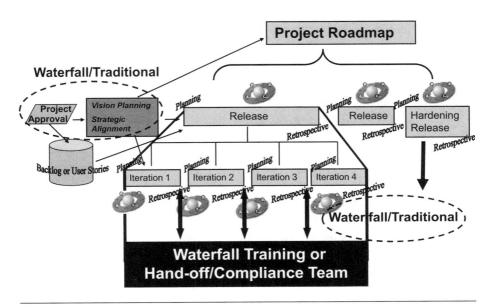

Figure 6.2 Agile Roadmap with Hardening Release

is also collocated with the rest of the Agile team so that questions can be answered on the spot, and feedback on smaller portions of the educational approach can be reviewed by the team. This training expert may also have a perspective that could influence the overall design of the deliverable.

Often there are hand-off documents to be given to the operations team that will be implementing, maintaining, servicing, or handling customer questions after the formal project ends. These materials can be prepared by a person occupying a non-developmental role on the team. Or, perhaps there are compliance tests, on-site evaluations, and formal paperwork to be created to meet third-party compliance standards or maintain third-party compliance certifications. It is ideal if those can also be done in iterative pieces in parallel with the internal product or service creation. Remember, to fully complete the Agile model, the PMO or other groups in the organization will need to track the success metrics the project was to provide. Time, cost, and quality are no longer enough. There must be quantifiable business value created if we are to put a check in the success column next to this project.

Waterfall Candidates

Some organizations will choose to stay with a traditional or Waterfall process. If everything is honestly working great, why change it? But you have to remain confident that it will keep you and your employer competitive in the future, too. Don't let anyone fool you. The traditional approach to projects is a proven commodity and is excellent for projects that have the characteristics shown in Figure 6.3.

- If you are in a well-established industry where:
- You are confident that you can prepare *highly defined and set requirements*.
- You have widely *distributed teams* across the city, the country, or the globe.
- You have a *rigid corporate culture*, and your management team or your project co-workers are very resistant to change, so it may be difficult to alter the way you do things.
- *New or less-experienced team members*, or people with single skill sets, are struggling to become adjusted to the organization and the existing ways things are done, and are not ideal candidates to learn something innovative right away.
- *High compliance regulations or government oversight* are often cited as a reason to choose another project technique rather than an Agile approach. This is certainly a valid consideration. However, many international regulatory organizations and governmental agencies are not

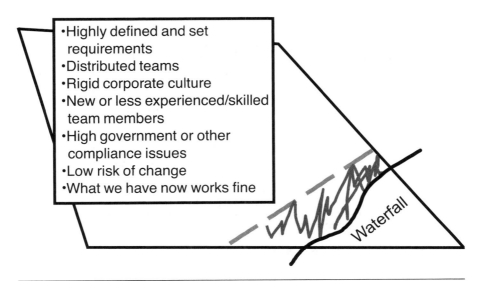

•Highly defined and set
 requirements
•Distributed teams
•Rigid corporate culture
•New or less experienced/skilled
 team members
•High government or other
 compliance issues
•Low risk of change
•What we have now works fine

Waterfall

Figure 6.3 Waterfall Process Selection Criteria

only allowing, but requiring, Agile approaches. So, you should check into the reality of your ability to change to Agile before you discount it based on compliance concerns.

• Projects with a *low risk of change* may not need the flexibility of moving to Agile.

• You currently use a process that is successful. As always, "If it ain't broke, don't fix it!" If *what you have now works fine* and the projects you do sing beautifully with the planning and execution you employ right now, you may be better off to find other, more volatile, projects on which to practice your musical flexibility skills.

Agile Candidates

Some organizations, on the other hand, have projects that are tailor-made for an Agile approach. As shown in Figure 6.4, they have:

• *Hard to define requirements* because the project results are so complex, innovative, or fluctuating that even if they were written down today, they would not be appropriate to direct the project path tomorrow.

• Extremely *strong possibilities of change*, because all of the decisions surrounding the project tasks rely on decisions beyond the team level

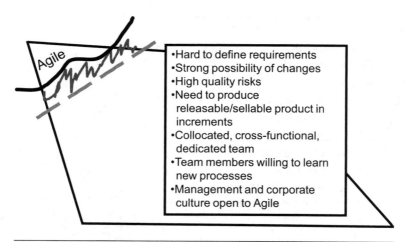

Figure 6.4 Agile Process Selection Criteria

that have not been solidified yet, or because the customer cannot yet articulate exactly what is needed.

- *High quality risks*, perhaps those related to physical safety, financial exposure, or product line remodeling.
- A business *need to produce a releasable/sellable product in increments*, either to fast-track time to market, to allow room for future customer value through updates and advanced uses, or to compress the company investment/return on investment timeline.
- A culture that is ready, or has already moved to, a *collocated, cross-functional, and dedicated team* structure.
- *Team members willing to learn new processes*, or are young and/or early adopters who have experienced more flexible methodologies in an educational or previous job setting.
- *Management and corporate culture open to Agile*, or even driving the shift due to business pressures.

If these attributes describe the atmosphere where you report to work every day, you are in the enviable position to start an immediate move to Agile.

As shown in Figure 6.5, the hybrid sweet spot is where the majority of us who will do some Agile, some of the time. There are some practices that Agile does well that can be blended into even the most rigid Waterfall practices, and will only make the project stronger. That is where we want to focus our project evolution skills. But the question remaining is, "Is *my* project the one that I should be making more Agile?"

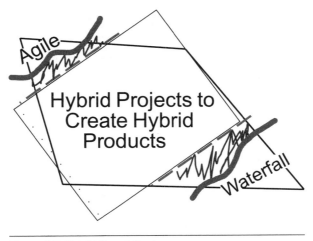

Figure 6.5 Hybrid Sweet Spot

The Agile Evaluator

To help you answer that question, Figure 6.6 shows an Agile Evaluator. Used in conjunction with the Agile Evaluator Checklist, shown in Figure 6.7, the Agile Evaluator helps you rank your project on a scale from 0 to 100, with 0 being the kind of project that requires the most traditional, Waterfall approach, and 100 being ripe for an extremely Agile process.

To use the Agile Evaluator, you read the question on both the left side and the right side of any horizontal line, then evaluate and estimate where you think your project, team, or organization, realistically would score on the scale. Decide which statement is more descriptive of your situation. For example, the question for line B asks you to decide between whether this project has a "Strong possibility of project changes" or a "Low risk of project changes." How true is this for your project? Is it 50/50? Is it lower risk, but not 0 risk? For example, if you decide that there is about a 70% chance that this project will have changes, mark the 70 on the left. Try it on Figure 6.6, or print off the Agile Evaluator from the publisher's Web Added Value site at www.jrosspub.com.

After evaluating this project on all the questions, Figure 6.8 gives you an idea of what a completed evaluation for a single project might look like. If most of your scores are points to the *left* of the center, or the 50% line, this project may be most appropriate for an Agile approach. If most of your scores are to the *right* of the center line, perhaps a Waterfall/hybrid approach will serve you best.

If you see that this project is mostly an Agile one, the few scores on the right side of the Agile Evaluator will help you to pinpoint issues you will want to address

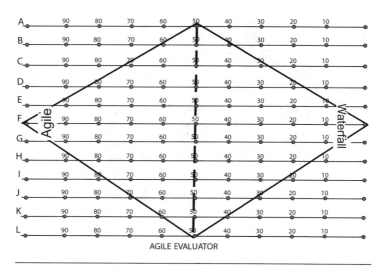

Figure 6.6 The Agile Evaluator © 2011 Davis Consulting.

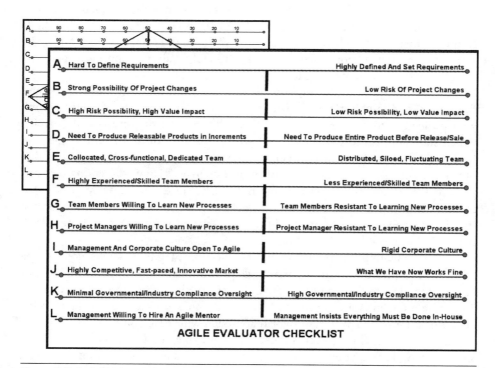

Figure 6.7 Agile Evaluator Checklist

in your team or organization to make your environment even *more* receptive and supportive to Agile. Conversely, if you have only a few scores on the left, you now have a list of issues shown on the right to change to get your team and your corporate culture started on a move to a more flexible approach. The Agile Evaluator Packet is available for download in the WAV™ section of the publisher's website (www.jrosspub.com). There are 12 questions shown, but you should feel free to change or add questions in order to customize this evaluation tool for your specific situation, organization, or industry.

If you are a Scrum supporter, be assured that this is not to suggest that anything be changed in a legitimate Scrum process that is being used for software or web development. You are golden. This also holds true for the other specific methodologies such as XP, DSDM, Crystal, and others. However, even the most successful Agile team, regardless of the success they have in the software milieu, may have to evolve a little. The real project culture change that will lead us to shift our project management practices resides in the middle of Figure 6.5 where we will need to create hybrid project management methods because we are creating hybrid products or services.

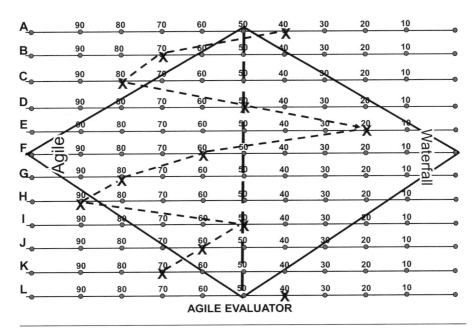

Figure 6.8 Agile Evaluator Sample Results

Hybrid Products

What's a *hybrid* product? Think of an iPhone® or smartphone. It is a hardware base, but the real value for the customer is the software that runs it (the operating system) and the apps (applications) for almost any conceivable customer need. As Peter Drucker visualized years ago, customers create their own value for products, and they decide what they are willing to pay for them according to the availability of software applications that they can download for entertainment, productivity, information, or convenience. Some user experiences are resident and unique to the phone via the brand and operating system purchased, but the driver that leads a potential buyer to choose one product over another is most likely the ability to access the largest-volume and most-appealing apps, in the most cost-effective and convenient manner.

Today's phone experience has become very complex. You may have seen this quote, "There's an old story about the person who wished his computer were as easy to use as his telephone. That wish has come true, since I no longer know how to use my telephone." The funny part is that this quote came from Bjarne Stroustrup, the person who wrote the programming language C++ which revolutionized the software industry.

Before C++, communication with computer hardware was more difficult than it is today when it is done in various programming languages. The first concept for a computer was imagined by Charles Babbage. His *Analytical Engine*, envisioned in 1837, was never actually built until the 1940s, when it was created for military use in World War II. The original concept of controlling mechanical devices by the use of punchcards originated in the early 1800s with Babbage. In his time, mathematical calculations were done by humans, and he saw the high error rate that was inherent with this process. He postulated that a mechanical approach could eliminate those mistakes and save time.

By the mid-1960s, businesses loved the speed and accuracy of electronic processing for payroll, inventory control, and other accounting functions. IBM was the leader in the field, but their machines were originally controlled by "wiring boards." IBM employees physically moved and relocated the wires on small, programmable boards for each customer and each application to communicate with the machine regarding the process that was to be performed. The board was then inserted by hand into the single-function IBM computer to say, for example, "This is a payroll function you are to perform." Next, the actual employee name, hours, and pay rate data was fed in through punchcards, and this combination of instructions allowed paychecks to be printed.

Assembler language was an innovation that allowed a live person to also code a small stack of punchcards to tell the mainframe the details of the application, removing the need for the physical step of wiring actual boards, but this language was not user-friendly. Assembler language was a computer code that was not easily readable by a person who did not originally create it, and it could not be read by the computer either.

This was the process. A programmer wrote "instructions" to the mainframe in assembler language and ran it through a piece of hardware called a complier. The job of the complier was to translate the assembler code into instructions that could be recognized by the computer (machine language). The computer then tried to execute the resulting "object" deck of cards that had been created by the complier. If it worked in tests, those instructional punchcards were fed into the machine to configure payroll, inventory, or other applications, before the cards with the data to be processed were run. Computers are a true hybrid product.

As the computer field progressed, more user-friendly programming languages were created. A programming language is basically a set of instructions to tell computers to perform certain operations. With inventions like COBOL, Fortran, RPG, C, C++, and today's Java, Ruby, C#, and Groovy, to name a few, programmers could write and read the code in a more decipherable set of rules that were easier to understand and proof with the human eye, which meant finding their own programming errors faster. Thus, Stroustrup made a significant contribution to the field by creating C++.

If your project experience is in a non-IT setting, it may be hard to internalize the problems faced by software developers in the 1980s who were trying to create original and unique software applications within a traditional project management framework. Remember, this was a new professional field. Hardware was being changed and improved frequently, so the learning curve was steep. Plus, the way in which instructions were written to the hardware was also constantly being altered.

As businesses found the power of data processing, they no longer wanted generic applications, but customized ones for the unique scenarios of their industries and organizations. As the computer field continued to grow, rather than one computer in a specially climate controlled room that produced the results, the model moved to cathode ray tube (CRT) screens with green or orange print, often called "dumb terminals," placed on remote desktops (not screens attached to a mainframe server). Now, a manager with a view-only screen could access processing results quickly and obtain financial and production metrics. That setup evolved into workstations with their own stand-alone computing capabilities to do word processing, Lotus 1-2-3, or Excel calculations, and continued to evolve until the workstations were then linked back through a central server creating a local area network (LAN).

The one main server with a network of workstations became many servers, each with specific functions such as e-mail, payroll, accounting functions, and customer relationship management (CRM) uses; housing websites, print servers, and backup or data storage systems. With the advent of mobile handheld devices such as smartphones, tablets, e-book readers, and gaming systems, software applications need to be tested so that they will function on a myriad of operating systems and devices.

End-user customers might have any number of brands and types of hardware, but they expect your organization's software, websites, and service interfaces to work with whatever they have. Each system runs on software written by people who may not have known what the future needs would be when the original operating systems and applications were developed, but new applications must "play nice" with those old, legacy systems. So, creating today's solution to a business problem may uncover a myriad of problems with existing software, both within the same company and in terms of compatibility with outside devices and servers.

Perhaps this can help you understand the frustration that the software developers who wrote the Agile Manifesto were feeling when they were asked to plan development projects using the same processes that would be excellent for building a road or manufacturing living room furniture. The uncertainty of what the features needed to be in the project software, coupled with the fact that they could not predict what incompatibilities they would encounter as they tried to test it with internal and external legacy interfaces, meant it was truly impossible to accurately estimate how long it would take to have fully tested software that included all of the features that a customer requested. Add to that the issue that the customer may not know or understand all of the underlying work associated with writing and testing the new application, then testing it against other software, hardware, and far-reaching connectivity over which they had no control, and you can begin to embrace their need for a more flexible way to approach their projects.

The New Marketing Strategy

Despite Stroustrup's frustration with his own phone, the latest smartphones are exploding a new type of marketing strategy. No longer is the product itself the sole profit maker for the organization. Under the old product-centric selling model, the only profit was from the single sale of the basic product. After that, you had to wait for it to break, wear out, or be dramatically changed to get additional revenue associated with that item.

As in the past, the automotive industry has been a leader privy to this after-sale revenue stream idea for many years. New car sales are important, but the money generated from aftermarket services such as oil changes, repairs, parts, and other routine servicing recommended by the manufacturer is an equally critical source of company income and profitability. That is why the first oil change may be free: To get you into the habit of coming back to the dealership's service center when you need to purchase additional products or maintenance components.

Based on that mindset, the modern paradigm is that the hardware item produced is only a vessel to ignite interest in the myriad of downloadable products that can be purchased in a seemingly endless stream. Meaning, the revenue continues to flow in long after the initial sale of the hardware product. In another seemingly counter-intuitive shift based on the speed and competitiveness of today's marketplace, manufacturers are now working in collaboration with other vendors to coordinate their mutual offerings. As recent as 10 years ago, products or services were stand-alone. The old business model was to segregate yourself as an organization and try to make all the profit you could by providing to your customers only things that you sold yourself. Everyone else was your competition for the buyer's dollars.

Now, you see automobiles created by Ford, Chevrolet, or Toyota that include built-in global positioning satellite (GPS) software that they have purchased externally. T3 Motion, Inc., a California based company, is producing the GT3 car, a zero gas emission, all-electric vehicle that includes a dock for an iPad, ready and waiting. Volkswagen is following suit, and the Consumer Electronics Show in 2011 displayed a car dashboard with an integrated iPad dock that controlled not only entertainment and navigations native to the Apple device, but seat positions, climate controls, and other automotive functions traditionally expected to be hardwired into the automobile itself by the manufacturer. An iPad can be removed for portability, replaced when a newer, more powerful version of the hardware is announced, or used to easily access later versions of the software to control automobile features. Thus, the customer is not forced to buy a new car to get enhanced usability.

So, we have to evolve as project managers because our projects and the marketing strategies of the economy are evolving. Think of an old Chrysler car from the mid-20th century. It came off the assembly line customized with a customer-ordered color, seat fabric, tire choice, and accessory package. It was a product that was self-contained within its manufactured package of nuts and bolts. Compare the project to create that automobile with the one needed to produce the new Google car.

The Google Car

The Google car, shown in Figure 6.9a, is a true **hybrid product**. And by hybrid, this does not mean a car that runs on electricity, or with an alternative or more energy efficient fuel source, although those features are no small part of its appeal. In this case, hybrid is used to mean that the car is *part hardware, part software.*

Amazingly, it can drive itself without a human being, without a live person at the wheel.[1]

Think about the provenance of this innovation. Google's expertise is in mapping systems, so the Google car has a GPS system, mapping software, a laser range-finder, video cameras, and radar sensors to detect other cars. One of the models being tested between San Francisco and Los Angeles is a Toyota Prius, converted to be controlled by artificial intelligence software. So far, it has driven over 1,000 miles without a traditional driver, and 300,000 total test miles out on actual roads and highways next to other normal cars with normal drivers, with only minimal human intervention.

Of course it is a test, so they do have a live driver ready to grab the wheel and take over in case anything goes wrong. But since it is a hybrid—hardware plus software—they also have a software engineer sitting right beside him. So far, the only accident that occurred when the car was self-managed was when it was correctly and safely stopped at a red light, and a human driver accidentally rear-ended it.

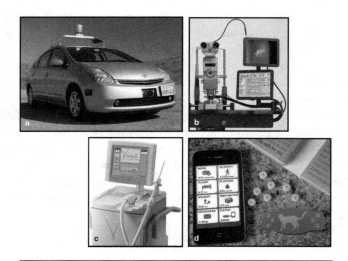

Figure 6.9 Hybrid Project Examples
a) Google car provided by Google.
b) PASCAL Streamline 577, courtesy of TOPCON Medical Laser Systems.
c) Visica 2™ Cryoblation Treatment System, courtesy of Sanarus Technologies.
d) Raisin System, a product of Proteus Biomedical.

What would be the advantage of a self-driven car, other than allowing you to drink coffee and complete the morning crossword puzzle in your newspaper on your trip to work? Think of the faster reaction of an automated system when compared to the reaction of a live person, and the value of that split-second response time when reacting to unexpected road behavior from other vehicles. Artificial systems do not drink and drive, get sleepy on long trips, get distracted by other passengers, or turn to admire the beautiful scenery out of the window.

Another positive of self-driven cars would be that the capacity of roads might double, as sensors to avoid other vehicles could allow cars to drive closer to each other while still being safer than those manned by humans. Since the car is less likely to crash, much of the construction of an automobile that is currently based on making the outer shell and inner passenger compartments more protective could be omitted or lightened, lowering the weight of the vehicle and thereby reducing fuel consumption and wear-and-tear on the roads. The Google car could be a win for consumers by being more green, less costly to operate, and less risky for highway travel.

This innovative, hybrid approach to solving business and consumer issues was developed by Sebastian Thrun, Director of the Stanford Artificial Intelligence Laboratory and co-inventor of the Street View mapping service. If you have ever used Google Maps to get directions to a customer site or a new restaurant, or to preview the looks of an unfamiliar location, you may be familiar with Street View. Google projects that they can cut the 1.2 million traffic deaths in the United States each year in half with self-driven cars.

Hybrid Medical Devices

When we create products that are part hardware and part software, we may need to use traditional project management techniques, but also use the Agile techniques that are increasingly successful for creating the software applications that run them. And, if it is rolled up into one project, both sides will need to work together with compatible approaches. However, remember that there are parts of the Agile practices that we can add to normal processes for manufacturing, construction, and other projects that would usually be traditionally run.

Cars and smartphones are not the only offerings that already take advantage of blended products. Figure 6.9b shows a hybrid medical device. People with diabetes can have problems with the blood vessels leading to the retina of their eyes and often go blind as a result. More than 50% of diabetics are at risk of developing diabetic retinopathy, which commonly leads to blindness. The treatment for this affliction is to use laser burns to prevent abnormal blood vessels from growing into the retina, which reduces the oxygen demand to the rest of the eye and retards, or even prevents, the blindness that at one time was inevitable.

While laser treatments for retinopathy have been around for over 35 years, the treatments have been long and tedious. Older equipment allowed only one 100 millisecond burn at a time, and successful treatments needed up to 2,000 burns. This might mean two to four session of 15 minutes each for the patient, and the success of the process relied heavily on the skill of the doctor. Not a risk you might want to take when the organs in question are your eyes and the risk is permanent damage to your eyesight, which also will be damaged if you *don't* have the procedure.

A newer technology, the PASCAL photocoagulator, a combination of TOPCON Medical Laser Systems of Santa Clara, CA hardware running on LabVIEW FPGA software, has changed the experience for both the ophthalmologist and the patient. This machine, created for eye doctors (hardware plus software, and notice the monitor on top for teaching institutions) allows the ophthalmologist to use a laser to treat retina and glaucoma disease in a series of shorter, 10 millisecond pulses up to 56 spots at a time.

Shorter pulse durations minimize the collateral damage to the sensory retina and also result in less patient pain. Plus, there are additional electronic/software safeguards to prevent damage to other areas of the eye. Shorter and fewer sessions translate to greater success, less risk, and better patient compliance.[2]

Tumor treatment is another use for hybrid machines. Figure 6.9c shows the Visica 2™ Cryoablation Treatment System. This is a device for tumor cryoablation surgery (a process that uses extreme cold to destroy tissue), created by Sanarus Technologies, that has revolutionized how doctors treat benign tumors. Again, note the software screen attached. Using this equipment, the doctor can locate, freeze, and destroy tumors in a nearly painless, outpatient process using local anesthetic, rather than the traditional hospital in-patient, invasive surgical procedures. Inserted through a tiny incision, this equipment freezes the targeted tumor and destroys it via the freezing and thawing process. The entrance opening is so tiny it does not need even one stitch to close it, meaning a quicker recovery and less painful experience for the patient, and a faster, less risky procedure for the physician.[3]

Another even more ingenious application of hybrid innovation is the raisin monitor shown in Figure 6.9d. This medical innovation is the size and shape of a raisin (a dried grape), and that is where the device gets its name. Visualize the typical band-aid you might stick on a child's knee if they fall off their bike. This product uses a very similar, although slightly larger, band-aid like device for the arm. The patient takes the prescribed medications and *swallows* the raisin monitor.

Once in the stomach, this indigestible sensor made of organic materials ordinarily found in foods is activated by stomach fluids and proceeds to record the date and time, the type of drug taken, dosage, medicine's place of manufacture, and the body chemistry's physical reactions to the drug. It can capture heart rate, respiration rate, sleep state, temperature, and other bodily responses to show both that the patient took the medication and also the patient's physiological reaction to it. All of this monitored biological data is transmitted through the wearable physiological monitor that looks like a band-aid stuck on your arm, to a cloud service where a medical analytics program integrates it with other previous recorded medical information about the patient, like blood pressure, weight, blood glucose, and any other additional feedback the patient has generated.

From there, using a smartphone, the patient can see their own results, in addition to it being immediately visible to the doctor back at the office or hospital. This allows the doctor to monitor each patient's condition, see if they are taking medications on schedule, see if the prescribed drugs are working correctly, and so on.

Not taking medications correctly can be a particular issue within an aging population, plus the surveillance necessary to prevent a negative or allergic reaction often leads to extra hospital time or expensive, at-home nursing supervision. The Raisin Personal Monitor system, created by the device manufacturer Proteus Biomedical, gives patients the peace of mind that they are being cared for, even in the privacy of their own homes.[4]

With the increasing focus on our global energy footprint, hybrid environmental devices are also in widespread usage. Many of us are familiar with gas meters on houses, complete with equipment to track and record the monthly usage. Technology has progressed from having a meter reader come into your backyard once a month to write down and take the gross usage back to their office, to more technologically savvy handheld devices that allow usage data to be entered into a phone, transmitted back to the power company, and automatically calculated, recorded, and billed. But none of that improved meter reading progress gave you any real knowledgeable control over your personal utility usage, except hearing your parents yell, "Turn off the lights!" in your mind whenever you left a room.

There are now devices to fit between the electrical wall outlet and a computer, coffee pot, TV, or gaming device to show the amount of electricity you are using. Some electronics use power even if they are not turned on, so knowledge of how many watts are being wasted may encourage people to unplug the device when it is not in use and save both energy and money on their power bills. There are versions that will record and print weekly or monthly usage, or transmit the information they collect wirelessly, so customers can view it on a cell phone, tablet, or computer from wherever they are. Many communities are checking out similar electrical monitoring items for free from public libraries, power companies, or other local utilities.

Creating hybrid projects will, of necessity, involve both traditional project teams and software development teams. In order to work together and coordinate the work of these products, which are unlike anything most of us have experienced producing in the past, the best process seems to be a product team that may leverage the more familiar Waterfall processes by adding some Big Agile philosophies of how to work with customers and teams. Those teams will need to coordinate their work with the software team that most likely will be involved in a full-blown, specific little agile methodology.

The New Product or Service Measurements of Quality

With hybrid products as the goal, it will be necessary to see if some of the software development qualities for desirability can be echoed in the traditional hardware portion of the deliverables. In *The Seven Qualities of Wildly Desirable Software*, Mike Gualtieri[5] talks about what to look for when creating software. This is applicable for the software portion of a hybrid product. However, these ideas can also transfer over to the hardware side of the project.

Think of the *user experience* as the most important focus of your software, product, or service. The users should find it useful, easy to use, intuitive to operate, and more desirable than past versions that they have owned or accessed. With internal customers, what you create should bring them more advantages and make them happier with the change than continuing to work with what they had before. For external customers, it should help them fill a gap in knowledge, information, or need, or it should have new features and functionality that will entice them to purchase from you rather than somewhere else. Users should be able to accomplish their goals easily. Creating something the team thinks is awesome matters little if the users don't gladly flock to adopt this as a solution.

Next, think of the *availability to the user* as a second evaluative quality. Is what you created ready to perform when the user needs it? If this is software, it might mean that other than scheduled downtimes for maintenance, installing new versions, and testing, the application is available for the "Five 9's." In other words, the service or product is online and accessible 99.999% of the time, meaning only about 5.26 minutes per year of downtime for unexpected problems. Or, in unique circumstances, there might be a sliding, downward scale that is acceptable.

For products, how reliable are they? How often do they break down, and how long does it take to get service for them? After each use, what is the cycle time for the device to be ready for a second use?

Performance metrics have to do with the speed with which your creation performs its intended function. Project owners will usually have some response time goals, or they may be added by the project team. How quickly will the web page appear, the smartphone connect a call, or the scanner capture an image? In addition to the response time of a single application or product, how quickly can you get the same results if you increase the number of users, or the amount of data that has to be loaded? If the marketing department requests automated estimating systems for customers who want to apply for a loan online, how timely does it work if 6,000 potential home buyers want to use it all at once?

Seldom do we go to the trouble of financing an entire project to create something for a single end-user or marketplace customer. So the concept of *scalability* is built into most projects. We build plumbing systems into homes, but what is the water pressure when there are two toilets flushed at the same time, the washing machine is running, the dishwasher is on its rinse cycle, and the automatic sprinkler system is watering the lawn?

It is common in software design, at least with the "rock star" level of designers, to code an application so that portions can be reused for other functionality, and also so that it can be changed quickly to a new version to address changing business needs and customer expectations. No one wants to start back at the beginning each time there is an alteration needed. This is called *adaptability*. By the same token, how well are manufactured products designed so that a faster motor, a better cooling solution, or a lighter battery can be integrated into a new version without major design rework, altering the case, or costly retooling of machinery on the assembly line? Creating interchangeable pieces allows for adaptability.

Security is a concern that is growing as more and more outside organizations or individuals try to access private information to use for their own purposes, to cause problems within your organization, or to show off their own hacking prowess. Creating software that allows data to be viewed only by the people for whom it was intended, that allows data to only be changed by authorized individuals, and that ensures that no viruses or malware will keep the applications from being ready for use when accessed, are three important security standards. Other standards, such as "authentication of a person's identity before access" must be added if anonymous people are not welcome, people should be allowed or denied access by a set formula such as their onsite location or role within the organization, and there must be tracking so that actions can be traced to the person who performed them.

For hardware products, security can take a slightly different form. Are harmful chemicals or dangerous wiring housed in a way that the consumer cannot access them? Is a moving mechanism equipped with a safety stop in case foreign objects, or user body parts, are accidentally introduced? Are there built-in locks opened through number codes, biometric eye scanners, or fingerprint recognition?

Gualtieri's final quality metric is *economy*. Every project decision has an associated cost. The time and organizational capital that must be invested should not exceed the value of the outcome produced. Risk is always a factor. Choosing the cheapest, fastest solution is not ideal if you do not also weigh the risk factors inherent in that decision. In the final analysis, after weighing time, cost, and risk, focusing on the full benefit of each choice to the organization may provide the best guidance regarding which path to take.

Finding the perfect approach to project requirements may involve finding the right balance between these seven qualities. In Agile planning meetings, whether it is the project manager who is participating at the portfolio level when original project funding selections are being made, or at the planning level for a project roadmap, release, or individual iteration meeting, it is your responsibility to bring up these qualities and ensure that they are all being considered in the overall project decisions.

References

[1]"Google tests driverless car." October 10, 2010. *The Telegraph.* Retrieved from www.telegraph.co.uk.

[2]PASCAL Streamline 577 with Video Teaching System, TOPCON Medical Laser Systems, Inc.

[3]Visica 2™ Cryoablation System, www.sanarus.com.

[4]Johnson, R. C. Nov. 16, 2011. "Smart Pills Transmit After Being Swallowed." Smarter Technology. Retrieved from www.smartertechnology.com.

[5]Gualtieri, M. January 24, 2011. *The Seven Qualities of Wildly Desirable Software.* Forrester Research, Inc.

How Does an Agile Team Get Started?

As you can probably already tell if you are a project manager leading Agile or hybrid projects, there will be more emphasis on communication and facilitation skills. No longer will you work alone to create a Microsoft Project file, assign tasks, and upload individual team progress reports on Friday. You will be heavily involved in the coordination between your team and other teams on the project, work to remove constraints and impediments, and find yourself tasked with the responsibility of supporting self-directed groups of highly-skilled people.

Let's first distinguish between a hybrid project and a hybrid team. The **hybrid project** *blends products (hardware or manufactured items) with software.* The **hybrid team** *blends Agile approaches to projects with more traditional or legacy ways you managed projects in the past.* So, how do you as the project manager—assuming you have little position power to change the whole organization via personal mandate—go about setting up this new genre, a hybrid project team? How do you fit Agile changes into the existing corporate culture?

Create Team Operating Rules

One often overlooked first step in setting up a project team with a hybrid methodology is the need to set up team operating rules. Since the team will be self-directed and not come to you to set up the working rules, you will need to facilitate a discussion right at the beginning for the team to set up its own rules.

Here are some items that should probably be covered. This list does not suggest all of the questions are viable possibilities or encompass all of the items you should have on the list, but it should help you think of business issues to discuss in advance of starting the actual project processes:

1. How often will the team meet? Once a month? Once a week? Every day? Every Thursday at 4:00 p.m.?
2. Where will the team meet? In a conference room? In the aisle next to their cubicles? In your office?
3. When a team member has an idea in a meeting, does he or she just speak out? Should a person raise their hand? Will they go around the group in turn?
4. What will happen if someone does not do his or her work as planned? Will the group do it for him or her? Will the team need to work overtime? Will the person whose work is incomplete be fired?
5. How will the team resolve conflicts? Will there be a mediator? Will you, as the project manager, get involved?
6. What will the team processes be? What are the reporting procedures? What are the available tools?
7. What is the rule for punctuality? What will happen if a person is late?
8. What is the team agreement regarding honesty? Is the main focus to protect ourselves, or is there trust within the team that allows open discussion regarding the work?
9. What are the attendance rules for meetings? What will happen if a person does not attend?
10. What are the ground rules for participation? How will the team ensure that everyone's ideas are heard and considered?
11. How are vacations, illness, and other absences coordinated within the team?
12. Who will document what happens in your meetings? What method of documentation is appropriate for which types of meetings?
13. If a team member finishes his work ahead of time and wants to do more work, can they take the next activity from the backlog list of prioritized tasks?
14. What will the team do about having phones, tablets, or laptops in use during the meetings?

You can add to the list from your own past experiences of working with previous teams. Add all of the other things you can think of that have caused problems on previous teams. Despite the Agile idea that a team is dedicated to one project at a time and will remain a cohesive working unit from project to project, in the reality of your corporate landscape, those ideal situations may not be possible at the moment. Leading a team over whom you have no functional authority is also always a challenge, but it seems to go better if the team has created their own guidelines and know the behaviors expected of them, what the conflict resolution procedures are, and what will happen if they do not follow the rules.

Capture the team rules on a sheet of flip chart paper or a white board that can remain in the team space throughout the project. Having the team-generated rules of operation visible at a glance rather than buried in a folder somewhere, or worst yet just lingering at the edge of memory, is the best idea. You may also want to visibly display on the wall the definitions of some common project management terms, using the Glossary of the *PMBOK® Guide* as your reference. Not everyone on the team may be certified, or their certifications may be older, so some of the vocabulary details may be foggy. Include new Agile terms that the team needs to use and understand, too.

Teams that are able to set up their own rules and be self-directed tend to have a higher level of motivation. This can lead to an increase in the productivity of the team as a whole. Decisions are made more quickly, as the team bonds and works through problems. As the project manager, a good concept to support with the project owner is that he or she creates the user stories (what the project will provide) and the team decides how that goal will be achieved. This empowers the team with the authority to make day-to-day technical decisions to get the job done.

Since there is better communication within a small team, there is less opportunity for misunderstanding and wasted time. Collocation also provides a way for people to increase their skills informally, as they work together and socialize at lunch and breaks. Also, since ideally this is a team consisting of 5 to 7 people, there are fewer hand-off issues than might occur with larger teams, whose members are loaned for a few hours a day, but remain in departmental silos.

Select Techniques to Reach Consensus

One of the most common problems with teams is that it is hard to reach agreement or consensus within the group. The most vocal members speak up often and, frankly, can monopolize the discussions, while the quieter members, who may have great ideas or knowledge, do not get a chance to be heard. As the project manager, you have a responsibility to create an atmosphere where all people feel comfortable to speak freely.

One technique popular in the Agile community to combat this problem, and allow us to fully utilize all of our knowledge workers to solve project problems and ensure that all team members are heard, is the **Fist of Five** (or, the more technically accurate Fist *to* Five). It is similar to the children's game Rock, Paper, Scissors where you close one fist and hit it three times into the other palm reciting, "One, two …". On three, you display either a closed fist (Rock), an open hand (Paper), or scissors (first and second fingers snipping to resemble a pair of scissors).

A question is posed to the group, perhaps the idea that you will meet informally each morning at 8:00 a.m. to quickly discuss the work of the project, for example. After a Rock, Paper, Scissor-ish, "One, Two…" count, on "three" each team member displays a visual vote ranging from a closed fist to an open hand showing all five fingers (Figure 7.1). Each response has a meaning:

- Five open fingers mean, "Yes, definitely. This is a *great* idea."
- Four fingers convey, "I think this is a good idea."
- Three fingers say, "OK, I'm not really excited about this, but I can live with it."
- Two fingers are a maybe, "This might be alright, but there are some things we need to discuss first."
- One finger (and notice that it is the first finger only) means, "I want to block this proposal until there is further discussion, and probably will insist on some alteration to it before we pass it."

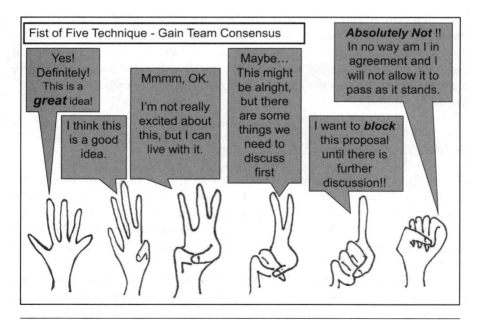

Figure 7.1 Fist of Five Technique

- A closed fist shows very strong opposition, "Absolutely in no way am I in agreement to this proposal and I will not allow this to pass as it stands."

Let the "one finger" and "fist" voters tell what is troubling them. They may have knowledge or experience about the issue that others on the team do not. Or, they may be thinking of concerns that have escaped the notice of the rest of the group. Also, allow the people who were strongly in favor of the proposal, the five finger voters, to tell their reasoning for having such strong positive feelings. They may want to voice continued support in the face of the new information, or acknowledge that they overlooked key elements that now make them want to alter their position.

If you, as the facilitator, sense that any of the comments have shifted the opinions of the team members, you can alter the proposal appropriately and the group can vote again. Continue this process until you have a proposition that the whole team can live with, and all of the risks or subject matter expert knowledge is out in the open. Or, if it seems more reasonable, you can just vote a second time on the original proposal. Perhaps getting their ideas out was all it took for the more opposing voters to reassess their own positions. When you see only three, four, and five finger responses, you can consider the topic "approved."

Confirm Initiating Processes

In a Waterfall organization, project initiation is traditionally the time when the project manager is asked to build time and cost estimates, and a projection of the physical and material resources needed, either alone or with the help of the project team (if it is already in place). In some organizations, a formal work breakdown structure (WBS) is even required to get the funding to support the project. The project manager may rely on pulling up similar projects, usually archived in his or her automated software, to provide data to management.

Since the Agile approach does not espouse long-term planning in such detail this early in the project, you are left with a decision. If you are trying to add a more adaptable process approach to the one team you lead without full organizational support for the change, you may need to pull back from your attempts to change processes for the moment and go ahead with the required, full estimates required to complete the project charter. Once you get the project approved and the charter is signed by management, you have written authorization to use the resources of the organization to complete the work if the project and can inject some more Agile practices into the team ethos.

Even if you are required to start with a more formal, traditional beginning, you can still use Agile principles and include many of the tools and techniques that make the team more flexible as you get into the core of the project work. It is common for project managers to learn about Agile ideas and become frustrated when they cannot implement all of them immediately with the full support of their organization. As you know, changing the processes and corporate culture of your workplace cannot happen overnight.

Do not be discouraged when easing into Agile practices. Instead of expecting perfection and a total "about face" in the way that you and your team work, add what you can as you go. Remember, it is the philosophy and attitudes toward customers, teams, your own behavior as project manager as you lead the team, and a focus on delivering business value that count. Once you and your team are alone and begin to work, ordinarily executive management does not micromanage the day-to-day activities and the techniques you use to complete deliverables. This is your opportunity to try new ideas and show improved results in order to convince management to give you more opportunities to keep moving in this new direction.

If you are fortunate enough to work in an organization that already is trying to make this culture shift to Agile, there may need to be a timeboxed work period added to the project ahead of the first iteration. Usually called **Iteration Zero**, *this is a time for the team to do some prototyping to facilitate better decisions around risk issues, and to find out how quickly the team can produce work.* Using actual data for how fast a group works allows better projections for time and cost than any of the traditional estimate approaches or calculations. Sometimes you can actually complete usable parts of the work of the project during this iteration, which is impressive to management. If calling this period Iteration Zero raises any eyebrows, just call it a feasibility study. Remember, do not focus on new Agile buzzwords, but rather the intent of why and how you now work differently.

Planning Agile Work

Once your project is formally approved, you will need to involve the extended team in understanding what Agile is all about. This is the point where you need to get the Customer (with a capital C) involved, so a good idea is to choose an internal project for a first Agile venture, where you have a positive track record and a good personal relationship with the Product Owner (your internal Customer), who perhaps is a department manager. Rather than saying, "I am now going to have an Agile team, and you are required to do user stories and come to all of our meetings," a successful entrée into a new customer/team relationship might unfold like the following scenario.

Set up a meeting with the project owner and say, "You know, Bill, the last time we worked together, we had some challenges in making sure the team delivered exactly what you wanted," citing specifics of timing failures, cost overruns, or other problems that occurred on a recent project to get his attention. "I've got some ideas about how we could avoid those frustrations this time around, if you'd be willing to work with me." You have three goals in this conversation. To get the project owner to work with you on creating user stories, to get him or her to be available to the team for questions, and to get him to look at what you've created at a set time every two weeks (or the length of the iteration).

Try to keep the conversation informal. Since you are making a change without a corporate mandate that requires all project teams to switch immediately to Agile, the project owner may already have created technical and/or functional requirements for you, or is having them prepared as you speak. Tell the project owner that despite the information that comes from those documents, you think you could avoid some of the problems of the past if he would allow you to supplement those documents with some more informal information for the team to be sure that they are on track with what he really wants and needs.

Have the project owner tell you the vision he sees for this project, and how he sees it as important to his department and to the organization as a whole. Now you can explain user stories, work with him to create them, ask him to prioritize them, and ask him to be involved in the meeting to present the stories to the team. Explain that the team will add their own work that needs to happen to support the creation of what he has placed in the user stories, and you will need him to reprioritize the backlog at that point.

Iterative Development and Risk

The best results from iterative development come when you are working to create value as early as possible in the project, but you are also trying to complete the stories with a high risk at the same time. Remember, the cost of rework and the impact to the project as a result of risk events is lowest at the beginning of the project. Ideally, over the course of the project lifecycle, as shown in Figure 7.2, the value of the output of the team continues to grow, while the risk continues to plummet. So, as you work with the product owner/customer to prioritize the user stories for this project, look for those that have the largest business and technical risk, but at the same time are part of the series to bring about the biggest return in business value. Risk and value are not an intuitive pairing, so this is a new mindset to learn, along with other Agile principles.

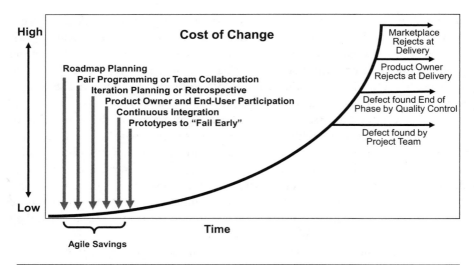

Figure 7.2 Cost of Change Over Time

The Agile-ish WBS

Some organizations that are highly invested in Waterfall may not be ready to give up the WBS, and require that you do it. Here is how you can create a WBS and still move into a more Agile, or hybrid, process during the execution of the project. As described above, get the project owner, Bill, down to work with the project team and have him work alongside the other members of the team to think of the major parts of the project, the deliverables, that need to be created. For example, let's say the project you are doing for Bill involves a philanthropic outreach program that he has committed to helm, to work with small coffee growers in Uganda, each of whom is trying to support a family on a plot of farm land only 30 feet by 30 feet. They grow an excellent product and charge less than current U.S. market value, but in Africa, they have no market. So, the idea is to import and sell the coffee in the United States, and reinvest the profits back into things to help the coffee growers.

You have a long-term, third-party vendor who has a great relationship with your company. He has agreed to donate downloadable games to the project in return for free advertising, which the public will see as they come to your not-for-profit website to buy or rent the games. People can also use this site to donate money to the program and eventually the site will sell the Ugandan coffee. Bill and his bosses think this will grow goodwill for your own organization, which can also advertise on the site. The philanthropic mission statement for the project

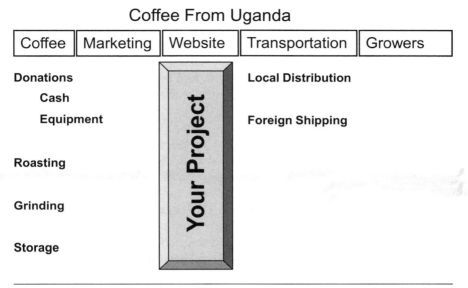

Figure 7.3 Uganda Coffee Project WBS

is, "Serving people by increasing their markets through quality marketing and support."

Let's try an exercise around this project to show how you can blend a traditional WBS into a more Agile approach if your organization is adamant that you must do one. Your project might look something like the one shown in Figure 7.3. You will have some items to consider in the categories of **Coffee**, **Marketing**, **Website**, and **Transportation** for the coffee, and some dealings with the **Growers** in Uganda. When we complete our work, we will have the tangible deliverables to show for it, but there are also some subtopics to consider.

For example, under **Coffee**, we might have subheadings like *Donations, Roasting, Grinding,* and *Storage.* **Transportation** could have subheadings such as *Local Pick-ups* and *Foreign Shipping.* Breaking this hierarchy down further, *Donations* might have still smaller categories of "Cash" that is donated from various cost centers in your organization to fund the project, or opportunities might be opened up to include employee or public donations as well. Under "Equipment", it will be important to consider items that could be donated like roasters, grinders, or bags. You do WBSs for a living if you are in project management, so there is no need to complete it here in full. But you get the idea.

Remember in pure Agile, Bill, your product owner, would be writing user stories with your help as the project manager. But this is a hybrid process where your organization is married to your being able to show a WBS. So, once a skeletal WBS is designed at this high level, place each of these headings at the top of a flip chart page and tape them to the wall. Have the entire team, including Bill, as the executive sponsor of the project, or in Agile terms, the product owner, write on sticky notes the activities or tasks that would need to be done to allow the coffee to be collected, the publicity to go out, the website to be created and function, and so on. But, be sure to keep Bill there during this process, so the team gets his first hand participation on what he envisions is to be done for this charity right upfront.

Instead of writing these as traditional activities, for example "build website," "contact growers," "ship coffee," and so on, write each sticky note as a user story: "As a <insert the role>, I want <add the functionality> in order to <add the business value or benefit>." After the extended team captures the activities or actual work that needs to be done in each category, the sticky notes can be removed from the WBS headings and placed on one sheet of flip chart paper. This will be the product backlog, and its items can now be arranged by the product owner, Bill, in order of their importance or value. We want to spend the team's time and energy doing the most important and valuable activities first, plus those with high risk.

Getting money to fund the project (Cash) and acquiring roasting machines and bags (Equipment) are very important. Finding how to contact the Growers to get the coffee into the United States is also very important. Those things should be done first, because they bring the most value to the project. Also, those same things bring the most risk. If we cannot get, or raise, money to fund the project, or cannot get coffee into the United States, the project will fail. Worrying about getting grinding equipment has less value, because prospective customers may have coffee grinders at home, and we could always sell the beans whole as a last ditch option if grinders become the project constraint.

So, the things that are the most important, the ones that bring the most value, should be done first. One of the ugly issues with Waterfall projects is **scope creep**. As team members notice additional activities that need to be done that may not have been added when the WBS work packages were first broken down, and the customer needs change, *the work of the project tends to expand.* Aggressive change control policies present in most workplaces are an attempt to keep the lid on these expansions.

However, there is no scope creep when stories are ranked on value. The customer and the team may add as many items as they like at the end of each iteration. Then, the backlog is re-prioritized and the next group of stories is selected for completion. At the end of the project, the low value items, or those that will cost more to produce than the value they will add to the final product or service, are dropped.

Imagine you are moving to a new town where you are unfamiliar with housing and prices. You hire a realtor who asks you what you want in a house, and he or she keeps prompting you for more specifics: How many bedrooms? Should each bedroom have an ensuite bathroom? Before you are done, you may say you want a swimming pool in every room, beer on tap in multiple locations throughout the property, a 15-car garage, and so on. But, when the realtor then asks for your budget for the house, you quickly begin to look down the list and pick out what you really need and know you can actually afford. You do not regret scaling back to one pool and a three-car garage, because you went through the process to arrive at those compromises on your own.

For this reason, the usual attempt by the project manager to get the customer to list and sign-off on the details of the project early on is exactly the wrong approach. The main reason scope creep occurs is because the customer did not get all his wants and needs out in the open from the first. Project managers were trained at one point in time to use this technique of asking for more and more specifics from the customer. We were taught to capture everything the customer could possibly envision from the beginning, rather than interrupting along the way with, "Oh, that will take too long," or "How could we realistically maintain that?" Then, when all of the wishes and expectations were out on the table, like in the imaginary house search, we began to talk time and budget. The customer could then go back down their list and choose what they really wanted, needed, were willing to pay for, and were willing to wait to get.

Agile is using this same old, traditional technique with a new name, *prioritizing a backlog*. We say, "Put in anything you want in your list of requirements, Mr. Product Owner. Then choose what you consider to be the most important to you (what creates the most business value) and what worries you the most (highest risk), and we will do those things first." As time and money are used up, "fluffy" items may need to be dropped, but of course, we never call them fluffy in front of the customer. The euphemism is "low value items."

Moving User Stories Into Iterations

Let's put some user stories that we created for the Uganda coffee project into iterations, as shown in Figure 7.4. If you prefer, print them out from the publisher's Web Added Value site (www.jrosspub.com), cut between the stories, and actually arrange them on a flat surface. This is a good activity for you to repeat with your team as you are trying to lead them into more Agile ways of working together.

For this exercise, your iteration, or work time between meetings, is 2 weeks. You have four people on your team who can work 2 weeks, or 10 days, each. Ten days times 4 people means that you have 40 days of work available in each iteration. After four iterations, the team will open the project's website to the public. *Take the stories and arrange them into the order in which you think they should be done, based on business value and risk, and then break that list into iterations.* Take a break and do this yourself before you read further.

Uganda Coffee Website Exercise
You will fund your project to market coffee from Uganda by creating a website to sell and rent games.

2 Week Iterations (10 day Work Periods)

4 team members per team = 40 days of work each Iteration

Arrange The User Stories Into Four Iterations of 40 Hours Each
A sponsor will provide free games in return for web ads. After 4 Iterations we will open our website to the public.

---

7 Name:
As a subscriber, I want "Purchase Games" functionality so that I can download games to my personal devices.

Actual Hrs/Days:

Business Value	Project Risk	Estimate or Difficulty Points
High (Worth $2,500 per month)	High (After 6 Done) Needs 1, 2, 3, 4, 5	15 Days/Points

---

17 Name:
As a subscriber, I want a "Rent Games" functionality so that I can play games on my personal devices.

Actual Hrs/Days:

Business Value	Project Risk	Estimate or Difficulty Points
High (Worth $4,500 per month)	High (After 6 done) Needs 1, 2, 3, 4, 5	15 Days/Points

---

1 Name:
As a product owner, I want to "Build A Games Database" functionality so that I can store and deliver games to purchase/rent online.

Actual Hrs/Days:

Business Value	Project Risk	Estimate or Difficulty Points
Low	High	5 Days/Points

---

4 Name:
As a project team member, I want "Build A Website" so we can sell/rent games online and accept donations.

Actual Hrs/Days:

Business Value	Project Risk	Estimate or Difficulty Points
Low	High	5 Days

---

15 Name:
As a subscriber, I want a "Games List" functionality so that I can see what I have previously purchased or played.

Actual Hrs/Days:

Business Value	Project Risk	Estimate or Difficulty Points
High	High Needs 5	10 Days/Points

---

8 Name:
As a subscriber, I want a "Free Test" functionality so that I can try games before purchase.

Actual Hrs/Days:

Business Value	Project Risk	Estimate or Difficulty Points
Low	Low	10 Days/Points

---

18 Name:
As a product owner, I want "Subscription Renewal" functionality so that we can bill renewal fees and capture new customer info.

Actual Hrs/Days:

Business Value	Project Risk	Estimate or Difficulty Points
High	Low Needs 5	5 Days/Points

Figure 7.4 Uganda Coffee Website Exercise

13	Name:
As a subscriber, I want "You Might Like Hints", based on previous browsing so that I might find new games I might like.	
Actual Hrs/Days:	

Business Value	Project Risk	Estimate or Difficulty Points
Medium	High	
		15 Days

14	Name:
As a subscriber, I want a "Write Review" functionality so that I can share my personal experiences with others.	
Actual Hrs/Days:	

Business Value	Project Risk	Estimate or Difficulty Points
Medium	Low	
		10 Days/Points

10	Name:
As a product owner, I want "Click Through Advertising" functionality so that I earn additional revenue.	
Actual Hrs/Days:	

Business Value	Project Risk	Estimate or Difficulty Points
Medium	Medium	
		15 Days/Points

12	Name:
As a subscriber, I want "Tell a Buddy" functionality so that I can earn free games through referrals.	
Actual Hrs/Days:	

Business Value	Project Risk	Estimate or Difficulty Points
High	Medium	
		15 Days/Points

3	Name:
As a potential subscriber, I want "Add New Customer" functionality so that I am registered to start purchasing/renting games.	
Actual Hrs/Days:	

Business Value	Project Risk	Estimate or Difficulty Points
Medium	Medium	
		10 Days/Points

9	Name:
As a product owner, I want a "New Subscribers Play Free In May" functionality so that new customers are attracted rapidly.	
Actual Hrs/Days:	

Business Value	Project Risk	Estimate or Difficulty Points
Medium	Low	
		10 Days/Points

11	Name:
As a product owner, I want "Sell Customer Information Opt-in" functionality so that I might earn additional revenue.	
Actual Hrs/Days:	

Business Value	Project Risk	Estimate or Difficulty Points
Medium	Low	
		5 Days/Points
	Needs 5	

16	Name:
As a potential subscriber, I want a "View Reviews" functionality so that I can evaluate games I would like to purchase/rent.	
Actual Hrs/Days:	

Business Value	Project Risk	Estimate or Difficulty Points
Medium	Low	
		5 Days/Points
	Needs 5	

Figure 7.4 Uganda Coffee Website Exercise (*Continued*)

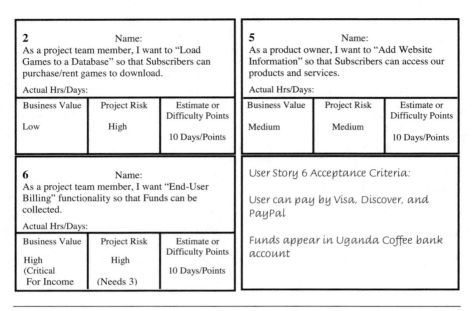

Figure 7.4 Uganda Coffee Website Exercise (*Continued*)

So, do you have the user stories for each iteration chosen and prioritized? If so, here is a way to look at your choices. There is no "right" order for the user stories, as each backlog list will vary according to the perception of the importance of each of the items in the eyes of the product owner. Here is a logic you could follow to stimulate your own thinking. Iteration One might include stories 4, 1, 5, 2, and 3. Item 4 is to create the website so that we can raise money, show the sponsor's ads, show our own company's ads, and get online coffee sales. Not much else can happen until we have a website.

Item 1 is to add the games database where we can house the games once we get them donated from the third-party vendor. The website shell is not of much use unless there is a place to store games to rent or buy, so that we can raise money for our cause. Both Item 4 and Item 1, you will note at the bottom, have low business value. Neither of them will bring in any money just by creating them, but nothing else can happen until they are created. Also, they have high risk. If they are not done so that they work properly, the whole project is at risk.

Story 5 might be next. Again, the website is not much use without content, so we create content such as information about the project, copy describing our cause and the reason for supporting the Ugandan growers, how to donate money, coffee ads, the vendor's ads, and our own organization's advertising. Then, in Item 2, we load the database with actual games. With Item 3, we need to have people sign up as members, so that they are eligible to begin renting and buying games. Those stories total 40 days of work for our first iteration, or Iteration One.

During the second two weeks of the project, Iteration Two, we might do activities 6, 17, and 7. Seventeen is rent games functionality, including the ability to download games from the website. It is worth $4,500 per month toward our Uganda project, but you will notice that it is dependent on Items 4, 1, 5, 2, and 3 being completed—that is why we did those in the first iteration. It also depends on Item 6 being done, the ability to bill customers and collect funds.

Item 7 adds the ability for a customer to rent a game, but it also depends on Item 6 being completed first, which in turn was dependent on 4, 1, 5, 2, and 3. This item is worth $2,500 per month. So, doing Item 6 first in Iteration Two makes sense. We want to be able to bill the customers for the games they can now download and buy or rent, because that is how we get the funds for our project. And that totals another 40 days, or 2 weeks, of work on the project.

The rest of the activities probably plan out like this:

- Iteration Three: Items 12, 11, 13, 18. These add up to 40 days of work.
- Iteration Four: Items 15, 10, 16, and 8, again total 40 days.

You may have these in a different order, which is OK. Remember, each team with the participation of the product owner decides how they think the work should be prioritized, with the product owner having the deciding vote. But the team can only commit to 40 days for each iteration.

After Iteration Four, it is time to open our website to the public. But, we still have Items 9 and 14 that haven't been done, "Create a place for customers to write reviews" and the "New subscribers play free" in May promotion. What will we do? This illustrates why it is so important for the product owner to share his or her vision for the project and why it should have a mission statement. The mission statement allows us to be sure that there are not activities being done that do not really work to promote the goals of the project. Again, this is the art of maximizing the amount of work not done by eliminating work that is unnecessary.

Our mission statement was, "Serving people by increasing their markets through quality marketing and support." When you compare the two orphan items remaining to it, you can see that it obviously says nothing about providing a way for customers to write game reviews and nothing about a goal of providing customers free games to play in May. It is not that these are bad ideas, just that they are not crucially important to the mission of the project, making them the least valuable items in the backlog. We can probably just cut these low value items off the list at this point without any harm to the project.

Many teams find a two week iteration is about right. It is short enough to give you quick feedback, but long enough that you can do enough work to demo that the customer has something to see, evaluate, and approve. At two weeks, the overhead of Agile meetings for planning, demonstrations, and retrospectives is not so proportionally substantial, compared to the time spent on actual project work, that it isn't balanced out by the real value the team can create in that time.

However, keep in mind that Big Agile is a philosophy, not a set of specific rules, so there is nothing to limit you to a two week iteration, if three or four weeks makes more sense for your project. A good rule of thumb is to strive for the shortest possible timebox, because if you are going to postpone scope changes until the end of the iteration, your stakeholder may become anxious to see project results. He or she may also know there are upcoming changes, and you do not want to complete work that will be discarded or become obsolete at the end of a longer timebox.

Each iteration should also back right up to the next one with no lags. In other words, perhaps your demonstrations and retrospectives are always on Wednesday, so that on Thursday you can begin planning the next iteration. The regularity of the cycle—from planning to executing to demoing to retrospectives—allows the project team to adapt to a productive pattern.

Here is an example to further support choosing shorter iterations. If the project length is estimated at roughly three months and you have four week iterations, this allows only two opportunities, at the end of Iterations One and Two, for the product owner to make scope adjustments. If the retrospectives elicit product or team process adjustments that would help the success of the endeavor, again, only two chances to use the flexibility Agile provides. Software changes tend to arise more frequently than hardware changes, so if you can, you may prefer shorter intervals with the programming team.

If you and/or your team are new to Agile, particularly if you are doing this without the oversight and support of an experienced outside mentor or consultant, shorter iterations give you more practice in your team processes of working with the backlog, planning, demoing, and retrospectives. With a two-week window to work, you can also adjust the team course more quickly if the iteration meetings are closer to one another.

There is some project overhead that must be acknowledged for the team to do the Agile meetings required, but on a software team it is an acceptable number of process hours, which are offset by working hours on project products and services. Hardware project teams may have a proportionately larger number of hours to plan, prototype, and test before they can complete the work of a single iteration. Therefore, you may prefer slightly longer iterations to allow sufficient time between them for the team to do work that creates completed and testable business value.

How Do Agile Teams Estimate?

Once you have a list of the user stories you will do prioritized in the order in which you will do them, you need to decide how much you can do in the first iteration. In construction projects where brick walls are built every day, we have metrics based on actual experience to know how many bricks it will take to build a wall that is 1,000 feet long by 3 feet high. Standard bricks are 2" x 3" x 6". You can choose a pattern that places the bricks so that the long side (the 2" x 6" face) is exposed, called the *stretcher,* or so that the 2" x 3" end, called the *header,* makes up the portion of the wall we see.

Various common patterns show how the bricks are potentially positioned, either directly aligned over each other or offset. Perhaps stretchers and headers are alternated or varied in a set motif. There are charts to show how much mortar is needed based on the number of bricks, the number of hours or days it will take, and the design pattern chosen to create the wall. You can even differentiate by the time it will take an apprentice as compared to a journeyman union bricklayer.

Team Estimates

Anyone who has estimated a project by traditional means tries, when possible, to rely on specific metrics available to the industry. But, no matter how experienced or mathematically skilled you are as a project manager, while you can calculate how the project *should* run, there are always unexpected variables of people, weather, and other factors that rely on the foundation team or the framing team, which mean you cannot guarantee that your team will meet the numbers on your estimate.

Although the traditional project management processes consistently employ the word estimate, which clearly states this is a "best guess" based on as much empirical data as can be obtained at the moment, management habitually reads it as a guarantee that we will finish the project in the time stated. Between 75 to 110 days in "management speak" equals, "They can do this in the low 70s, but if I push them harder they could actually do it in 60." So, project managers build in more and more contingency space, which leads to additional mistrust from management, and more arbitrary slashes in budgets and time. Agile can help our teams move beyond this cyclical stalemate of distrust and misrepresentation.

For the Uganda coffee exercise in Chapter 7, we worked with the traditional estimate of days for each activity. However, the preferred way in the Agile community is to estimate a user story is by its **degree of difficulty**, rather than by trying to guess how long it will take and delivering an estimate of duration or work hours. Traditionally run projects are estimated in time. The project manager, working with his or her own experience, archived past projects, industry metrics, and team input, estimates how long they think each task should take, and then assigns the work to individuals based on their availability.

Agile teams look at project work as an assignment to the collective team. Rather than working in the units of time it will take to finish each piece of work, they think about *the amount of effort that will be required to complete the work, and the complexity and amount of sustained concentration it will take to produce it in a finished, tested, and workable form.* For example, it may take an hour to change a tire and also an hour to rewire the fuse box in your basement, but there is a pronounced difference in the complexity and knowledge the person will need to embrace in order to finish each task to a workable, usable, stopping place. The sustained concentration and testing is much more difficult on rewiring the fuse box than merely changing a tire.

Since the team will be committing to complete this work as a single entity, it makes sense that they should also be in charge of looking at the details of what will be produced and figuring out a way to show *a relationship between tasks in terms of their difficulty.* Then, a relative number, usually called **story points**, can be assigned each task (a smaller portion of a user story) to allow the group to intelligently assess how much they can do in the upcoming iteration.

The Fibonacci Sequence

One effective way to rank user stories by degree of difficulty is based on the Fibonacci sequence. Leonardo de Pisa, also known as Fibonacci, was an Italian mathematician in the early 13th century who found unexplained, yet repeating patterns in nature. One of the interesting problems that Fibonacci investigated in 1202, was how fast rabbits could breed in ideal circumstances. Remember, this was an attempt to find mathematical patterns in breeding, not an attempt to start a rabbit farm to supply the historic equivalent of a Pisa branch of a Kentucky Fried Rabbit franchise.

Fibonacci posed the question like this: suppose a newly born pair of rabbits, one male and one female, are put in a field. Rabbits are able to mate at the age of one month, followed by a one month pregnancy. By the beginning of third month the female of the first pair produces a second pair of rabbits. Also assume, for the purposes of our experiment, that our rabbits never die, and that the female always produces one new pair (one male, one female) every month from the second month of her life forward. The question posed by Fibonacci was, how many pairs of rabbits will there be at the end of one year?

According to Fibonacci, at the end of the first month the newly born pair of rabbits mate, but there is still only that original pair because there is a one month gestation period to wait out before the birth of the second pair, as shown in Figure 8.1. At the end of the second month, the original female produces her new pair of offspring. So, by the beginning of Month 3, there are two pairs of

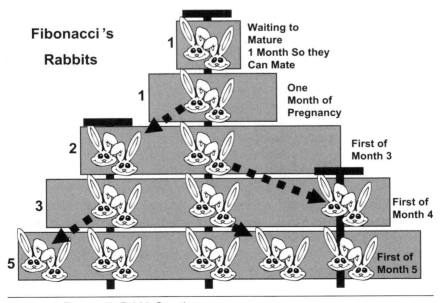

Figure 8.1 Fibonacci's Rabbit Question

rabbits in the field. At the end of the third month, the original female produces yet another pair, making three pairs in the field at the beginning of Month 4. The newborn female offspring has used Month 3 to mature from birth to a place where she can now mate and begin to produce her own baby rabbits. She is pregnant during month 4, as is her mother, the original female.

At the end of the fourth month, the original female has produced yet another new pair of rabbits, and the female born at the end of Month 3 has matured, mated, and now delivers her own first pair of bunnies. So, by the first of Month 5 there are five pairs of rabbits in the field. If we continued the chart, the number of pairs in the field each month forms a mathematical sequence of 0, 1, 1, 2, 3, 5, 8, 13, 21, 34, 55, 89, 144 and 233. At the end of one year, there are 233 rabbits.

People who are set on criticizing Fibonacci's findings say that his logic seems to imply that brothers and sisters mate, which would lead to genetic problems, and not all of the offspring are guaranteed to survive. It you want to get this technical, you can remove these concerns by adding the assumption at the start that the female of each pair mates with any male (not just the male she was born with) to produce another pair. Another stone that naysayers throw at these hapless bunnies is that each pregnancy would have to produce exactly two rabbits, one male and one female. The answer to these skeptics is that, as stated at the start, *this is a mathematical formula, not a breeder's guide.* Fibonacci's purpose was to see if there were mathematical relationships present in nature, and he found them. This same series of numbers occurs not only with rabbits, but with the proportions in the spirals of sea shells, in the growing points (or shoots) from plants, in the spirals of pine cones…well, you get the idea.

Fibonacci even found his numbers in the proportion of the human body. Look at the top surface of your index finger (your first finger). If your fingernail is 1 unit in length, each section from the tip of that finger to the base of your wrist is larger than the preceding one by the Fibonacci number series, 2, 3, 5, and 8. He also saw this relationship in flowers, where he observed that we seldom see a flower with four petals. We all know the four-leaf clover is very rare.

But we do see flowers with petal numbers that form a sequence. The Calla Lily has 1 petal, the Euphorbia has 2, the Trillium 3, the Columbine 5, the Bloodroot 8, and the Black-eyed Susan 13. This is the familiar sequence of 1, 2, 3, 5, 8, and 13. If this mathematical sequence of relationships is found everywhere in nature, it is not much of a leap to think it might also be found in the relationship between the degrees of difficulty in various Agile tasks.

There is a further interesting thing about the Fibonacci sequence. They are formed by a mathematical formula. If you add each of the numbers 1, 2, 3, 5, 8, 13, etc., together with its immediate predecessor, you get the next number in the sequence:

$$1 + 2 = \mathbf{3}$$
$$2 + 3 = \mathbf{5}$$
$$3 + 5 = \mathbf{8}$$
$$5 + 8 = \mathbf{13}$$

You can begin to see the Fibonacci sequence form vertically in the sums of each of the two preceding, horizontally consecutive numbers in the series.

Planning Poker

For Agile purposes, there is a user story sizing technique, created by Mike Cohn of Mountain Goat Software, called Planning Poker. It is a form of the estimation technique known as Wideband Delphi. As a project manager, you may already know the Delphi technique in which experts fill out forms to estimate a specification, the coordinator collects the estimates, and then the experts discuss the points where the estimates vary widely. But Barry Boehm and John Farquhar originated the "wideband" version that involves greater communication by using more interaction and communication between the participants.

Planning Poker uses a modified set of Fibonacci numbers in conjunction with the experience or ideas of the team members to *estimate how hard it will be to do a task, rather than how long it will take to do it.* For Planning Poker, we have actual playing cards with numbers limited to the numbers of the sequence 0, 1, 2, 3, 5, 8, and 13. We have arbitrarily added the non-Fibonacci numbers of 20, 40, and 100.

We do not want to waste precious work time in debating whether a story is 6½ degrees of hard or 7 degrees of hard. The idea is to get a relative idea of how stories rank in relationship to each other, so the team can figure out roughly how many they can get done in an iteration (Figure 8.2). When you use this with your Agile team, each estimator (each member of the team) needs a set of cards. You can make cards with paper and a marker, print them from the publisher's Web Added Value download resource center (www.jrosspub.com), or there are companies like Mountain Goat, Version One, Incrementor, and others that sell the decks. If a team is distributed in different physical locations, there is a free online site at www.PlanningPoker.com that protects private information, but allows you to use this technique with a non-collocated team.

The process for this technique is every person on the team holds his or her own set of cards with all of the choices. Each person considers the user story, (or subdivision of it, which is a task) in terms of difficulty, and pulls the card from his hand that represents his or her choice, keeping it turned face down so no one can see it. On the count of three, everyone shows his or her card. Most people will have similar numbers, and the longer the team works together, the more skilled they

Figure 8.2 Planning Poker Cards

will become in having closer evaluation scores. But what is key in this game, is to look at the outliers, the scores that are very high or very low and out of keeping with the majority of the team choices. In traditional project management "quality speak," we are considering the special, or assignable, causes of variation.

If most people have 5s and 8s, for example, but one person has a 2, that is the individual who needs to explain the choice. This is not, "Explain yourself! Why don't you have the correct answer!" It is a way to get all of the team to a common understanding of the work of the project. He or she may not fully understand the task, or conversely, may have a clever way to make the task easier.

If most people have 5s and 8s, but one person has a 40, he or she may have some experience or technical knowledge about this activity and can predict difficulties that others do not see. So, you play your card, or "vote", and hear from those people whose scores are outside the norm. Other team members can ask clarifying questions and get additional information, if needed. Then you re-vote.

When you have most of the team estimating at about the same number, that is the number you go with. For example, if you get to the place where the votes are all 5s or 8s, then that task is an 8. Remember, this is just a best guess, so do not waste time on minutia. After completing this Agile step with the team, you have a backlog list of activities ranked in the order of their value and risk, and you can now add the degree of difficulty from the team estimates in lieu of creating estimates by hours.

If your workplace insists that estimates be done in hours, you know how to do that from the Uganda exercise in Chapter 7. You move to the top of the list any activities that have other activities that depend on them. Note that this process replaces the traditional sequencing process, but again if you are forced to do it by the organization, this information could still be sequenced and entered into an automatic software program.

At this point, you, as the project manager, can begin to figure out budgets, quality metrics, costs, and answer most of the other knowledge area questions on risk, communications, and so on. If you are exceptionally skilled in traditional project estimating and you hit your baseline goals pretty regularly, or if your organization is adamant about that as the way you must estimate, you can certainly continue to do that part of the process. Being more flexible yourself, particularly when you are attempting to make this change on your own at the project team level, may mean continuing to do some traditional activities that you know could be handled better with another, more Agile technique. But continue to add what you can as you build your case for a more widespread movement toward Agile.

Planning Poker gives you an option that involves more of a team approach and is a way to begin to alter your facilitation style to get more involvement from the people who ultimately will complete the work of the project. The idea is to get everyone engaged, thinking and sharing their experiences. It is much better than saying, "Brad, tell me how long you think it will take you to do these six tasks I am assigning you, and either get back to me via e-mail or put your estimate into Microsoft Project by Friday."

Team Estimation Game

While Planning Poker works great for a team that has some experience, many brand new teams are at a loss as to how to get started. They know that one task is larger than another, but is it a 2 or a 20? In this team estimation game, Steve Bockman has a good technique for helping your group begin to find relative relationships between user stories or tasks before they assign story points. This activity happens after the user stories are created and prioritized by the product owner. Now the team takes over:

> **Step 1**. A team has a stack of the user stories in prioritized order. The first person picks up the first story and places it in the middle of the table.
> **Step 2**. The next person on the team, Player 2, now has a turn. He or she picks up the second story from the backlog stack. This person cannot express a personal opinion and can only ask clarifying questions about

the task from the team and the product owner. Then, he or she compares the story to the first story on the table. If Player 2 thinks it will be harder, it is placed to the right of the first story; if easier, it goes to the left.

Step 3. The next person, Player 3, picks up the top story from the backlog stack and places it where he or she thinks it belongs relative to the first two stories. Or, if Player 3 disagrees with any earlier story placements, he or she can move any one previously placed story to another location instead. Again, the player is entitled to ask questions from the rest of the group during a turn.

Step 4. One person at a time, the team goes through the rest of the stories on the stack and places them in probably 6 to 10 stacks, relative to the other stories. Stories that seem to take the same amount of time are placed in a vertical line below the "stack" of earlier placed stories (see Figure 8.3).

Step 5. Once the stories are sorted into groups by degree of difficulty, the team can pick a story point amount for the middle stack. For example, say that they chose 8. Now, stacks to the right, the more difficult ones, can be assigned numbers higher than 8, using the Fibonacci sequence. Those to the left, the smaller ones, can be assigned numbers lower than 8. Not all

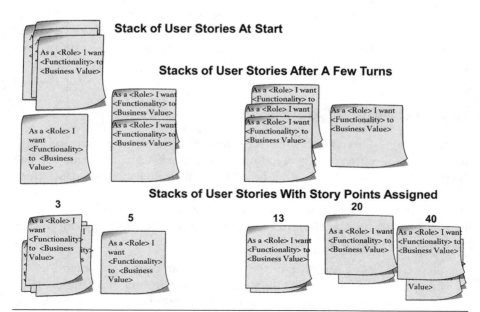

Figure 8.3 Team Estimation Game

of the numbers must be used; in other words, it is fine to have gaps in the numerical Fibonacci sequence of points.

Advocates of this technique say that a fairly large product backlog can be estimated in about one hour by using this technique. Even if you are staying quite close to your traditional roots and need to estimate in hours, a variation of this idea that involves the team could help close the gap between reality and the usual assessments of task durations.

Dog Estimates

Yet another form of relative story point estimates from Mike Cohn centers around the relative size of dogs. Imagine a Chihuahua as 2 story points, and a Great Dane as 13. A Beagle is roughly twice as large as a Chihuahua, so it might be a 5. A Labrador is bigger than a Beagle, but smaller than a Great Dane, so it is maybe an 8. Once you have the relative size headings, you can then place the user stories or tasks in their relative spots on the "dog scale."

T-shirt Sizes

Perhaps your team would prefer to work with yet another type of affinity estimating, the relative sizes of T-shirts. A story could be a XS, S, M, L, XL, or XXL. The idea is to give the team *a way to relate story size to something with which they are familiar,* like T-shirts, and to have a common method to exchange ideas. "Man, that looks like an XXXXL!" is a cue that the story is too big to be completed in one iteration, and it needs to be broken down further into smaller tasks.

Which method or clever convention you choose for your team isn't important. What matters is that the team shares a common understanding of the scale it uses, so that every individual on the team is comfortable with the meaning of the scales' values.

Selecting Tasks

The next step in imagining how Agile might look in your team setting is selecting tasks. From your prioritized backlog, the team chooses how much they think they can do in Iteration One. If you did an Iteration Zero, you have some actual data to use. If not, based on the degree of difficulty and the priority value of items, the *team* picks the number of stories that they think they can get done in the first iteration. This is emphatically *not* the project manager or the product owner/customer making the decision, but the people who will actually do the work.

If this is your first stab at an Agile approach, one way to get started is to draw an arbitrary line on the backlog list as a starting point. Then allow each team member to pick the stories (or tasks, if the stories have been broken into smaller parts) that he or she will commit to completing during the next two weeks. If there are items left unchosen that are higher in priority, or need to be done first because they have other tasks that are dependent on them, you can negotiate with the team members to switch out their chosen tasks to do these higher level ones instead. If you need more items, move the line on the backlog list further down.

Actually, even when your team becomes more experienced, the idea of letting the team members select their own work rather than having it assigned by the project manager works well for a number of reasons. It is human nature that people are more willing and likely to work harder on tasks they have chosen themselves and committed to do within the two-week iteration timebox. Plus, they have probably selected things that they feel they have the skills to do well, or tasks that seem interesting and challenging to them.

If they have been the person to add certain infrastructure tasks because they saw their importance, they are more likely to choose those to do themselves, feeling a special, protective emotion and interest that they be done correctly. Self-selecting tasks fits into the Agile philosophy of respecting our knowledge workers and trusting them to bring their best to the work of the project. Feeling part of the solution, rather than just an interchangeable cog in a random process, is a powerful motivator.

Tracking Agile Progress

Tracking Agile progress differs from the traditional project management reliance on automated software or Excel reports. It tends to rely more on whiteboards or flip chart paper with sticky notes that can be readily moved. This *ad hoc*, light form of documentation makes change easier to consider. The project has not been planned in detail beyond this iteration and there are no cumbersome Microsoft Project or Excel reports to manipulate and update when the anticipated and acceptable frequent changes occur. The other advantage to posting things on the wall of the team room is their constant visibility, or **transparency**, as *the team operates in such a way that it is easy for others to see what actions are performed.*

This method of displaying progress is often called an **information radiator**, a name coined by Alistair Cockburn, a signer of the Agile Manifesto, whose work grew into the Crystal methodology. He defines it as, *"... a display posted in a place where people can see it as they work or walk by*. It shows readers information they care about without anyone having to ask anyone a questions. This means more communication with fewer interruptions."[1] Steelcase Furniture has already created a collaboration tool in its interactive board that allows impromptu projections in the team space, and houses both a dry erase surface and a magnetic surface, giving the team options in terms of how they share information.

A typical chart for your project to post on the wall to share the team's progress might include columns for the *items the team has committed to do this iteration* along the left in a *To Do* column (Figure 8.4). These tasks are also known as the **Iteration Backlog**, to separate them from the **Product Backlog**, *the larger container holding all of the potential tasks of the project.* While the whole purpose of a small area on which to write the information is to get each part of the feature decomposed into a single, doable idea, if you need a slightly bigger surface for greater viewability from a distance, there are 4 × 6 sticky notes available.

As people self-select a task, they put their initials on it. Once they begin to actually work on that user story, they move it into the *In Progress* column. Some individuals may have chosen the task as a way to expand their skills, and as described earlier, with pair programming or pair collaboration, this is not a problem. Sometimes people work together from the beginning, as one person

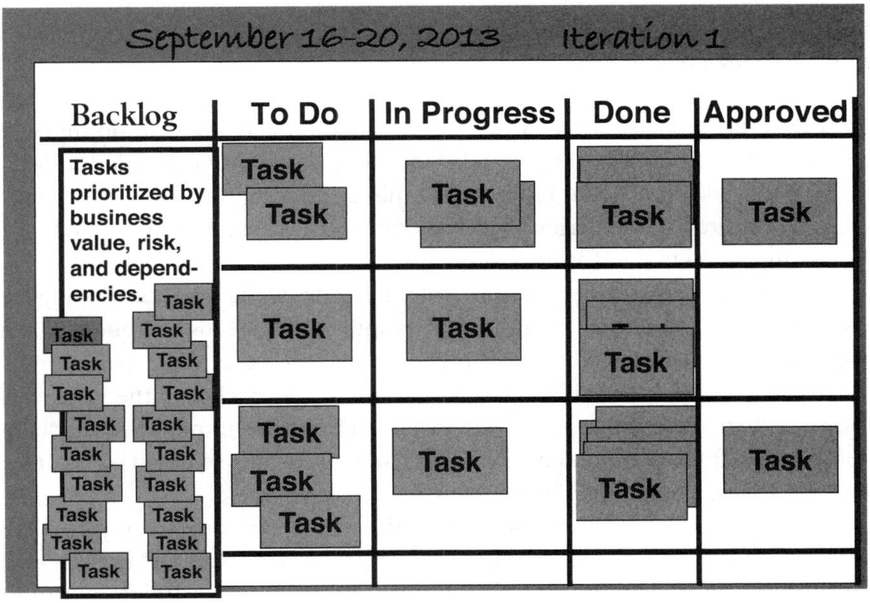

Figure 8.4 Agile To Do Chart

codes and the other watches over his shoulder for errors and helps brainstorm the approach.

In a non-programming environment, two people could collaborate on creating an Excel report, a marketing brochure, or a high level roll-out plan for a new pharmaceutical. You may not think of everything when you are heads-down in the typing and your own thoughts. Sometimes a team member works alone, but in this collaborative environment where everyone is in the same vicinity, it is easy to call a colleague over for help if the tasks prove too challenging or if you just want a second opinion without too much fuss. Or, it could be as simple as asking a colleague to look over your work before it is submitted.

When the task is finished, the doer (person who has chosen and initialed it) moves it to the *Done* column to show it is completed, or leaves it in the *In Progress* column if it does not get finished by the end of the Iteration. You may also need an *Approved* column and an *Outside Approval* column. **Approved** means *the customer has seen it and agrees it is done to his or her satisfaction.* The **Outside Approval** column is for *sign-offs that come from outside the team,* such as government inspections, quality team inspections, or regulatory inspections. A task is never truly done until it is approved.

Even though user stories were self-selected and initialed, if one person finishes her own tasks early, she can certainly ask to work on tasks left in the iteration backlog. That is the reason for having cross-functional teams; most people are capable of doing any of the user stories on the project. At least, this is true on beginning, small teams.

Earlier, in the team rules that were set, the group decided whether or not a person who has finished all his work for the iteration and wants to do more, can take the next activity from the iteration backlog. Many Agile teams decide that they will not take additional tasks unless this is an early iteration, like Iteration Zero, or they are an inexperienced team that is just learning how to judge their capacity to complete the stories.

One thought about Agile is that in order to facilitate the team developing truly cross-functional skills, they need time to shadow, or at least discuss questions that arise, with other workers. So much of the Agile space involves projects where there is great value to innovative ideas and new, creative approaches to the work of the project. If the team members are never given a moment to think, do research, talk to other departments or companies, or exchange ideas informally with their own teammates, their merit as a knowledge worker is diminished.

Defining how Agile teams spend their time also brings up the topic of overtime. Traditional Waterfall teams know all too well how projects work in practice. If the estimates were faulty, or any unexpected problems or constraints appear and the project metrics fall behind, suddenly everyone is working evenings, weekends, holidays, and is expected to skip lunch in order to meet baseline metrics. But if you work in an organization where that is the norm, you know the catch. Once the team exerts superhuman effort to complete the project on time, regardless of any adverse situations, they are expected to continue to work large numbers of hours, often without overtime pay, to make sure *all* projects come in as originally "guesstimated."

Research done with Agile teams highlights some interesting statistics. When Agile teams are asked to work over the normal number of working hours, their velocity, the amount of work they can produce in an iteration, goes up. But only for that one iteration. After that it goes lower and less work gets accomplished than usual, and the velocity *never goes back up*! One attribute of the Millennium and Generation Y workers' value systems is a focus on friends and family, and a desire to have a positive work-life balance. Having that balance disrupted seems to have a lasting effect on worker morale.

The takeaway is that Agile teams who are working on new, complex, and innovative projects should not be asked to work overtime. They need the downtime for their brains to process solutions. You can remind companies that try to drive speed as an end they think justifies the means, that what they really want is *speed that delivers usable outcomes*, which they won't get by overworking teams. As an aside, whether organizations know it or not, increasingly they will realize they also want project managers who can keep one eye on the portfolio and the other eye on the delivery process.

Daily Agile Stand-up Meetings

From the first day the work of a project begins, a good practice in the Agile world is to have a **daily stand-up meeting**. Just as it sounds, the team members literally stand. The thought is that once people get settled in with their morning cup of coffee and a comfortable chair, meetings drag on too long and can be an excuse for avoiding the real work of the project. If you stand, there is more impetus to keep a meeting short. The format of this meeting is that each person has about 1 minute, at the maximum, to say:

1. What they completed yesterday,
2. What they intend to complete today, and
3. Any constraints or obstacles that are in their way.

This is a great way for the entire team to see where the project stands and what prerequisites have been completed that may affect their own tasks. They may be waiting for you to finish your task before they can move on. Problems are noted, but they are *not* discussed during the daily stand-up. After the meeting, small groups with *only the team members involved* can form to find solutions to the problems raised.

The project manager, product owner/customer, or other team members can also meet to discuss what can be done to remove obstacles. But problems and ideas are discussed *after* the stand-up meeting. The rest of the team goes back to work on the project deliverables and it is the responsibility of the project manager to remove the roadblocks (constraints) presented in the stand-up meeting, so that the team is free to spend their time on creating the software, product, or service features for this iteration.

Other stakeholders such as the product owner/customer, other project managers whose teams' work will be coordinated, and outside vendors, are also welcome and encouraged to attend. However, *only team members are allowed to speak during the stand-up meeting* itself. Afterward, it is important to remember that the team needs to immediately return to their work. This leaves the project manager to answer questions or help moderate short, after-stand-up conversations.

Only allowing the team participants a voice during the daily meetings is based somewhat on the old "chicken and pig" joke. Mike Vizdos of Vizdos Enterprises, a Scrum training organization, is infamous in the Agile community for his cartoon version of this joke (see Figure 8.5). The Agile software community likes to think of the core Agile team of developers as the pig, fully committed and with "their bacon on the line." While the product owner or customer, and perhaps other project stakeholders, tend to be characterized as the chickens—interested and involved, but it is not a life and death scenario for them. They have something to gain by the work of the pigs, but they are not involved in the day-to-day process of actually completing the work.

As clever as the analogy is, there may be a case to be made that actually the product owner is the pig. He or she may be funding the project out of a departmental budget, and may have corporate responsibilities to deliver a certain percentage

By Clark & Vizdos
© 2006 implementingscrum.com

Figure 8.5 The Chicken and the Pig. Cartoon courtesy of Mike Vizdos.

increase in sales, or decrease in expenses, or whatever, to upper management. The product owner may certainly have his neck on the line. And you could make the case that project team personnel seem to go on and collect a paycheck, regardless of the project's success in meeting its metrics, and regardless of whether or not the deliverable is useful, successful, profitable, valuable, or competitive for the organization. But if you open your mouth in the "little agile" world, or sit for a certification, remember *team = pigs*, and *product owner/customer = chickens*.

The daily stand-up meeting is an Agile practice that was recently added to the staff procedures of an Arts Council in the Midwest. It is an interesting example because they are a not-for-profit state agency, and do not produce an actual, tangible product. However, they are expected to provide value to the state, as a robust arts community attracts relocating corporations, pulls visitors into the state, and arts events add tax dollars to public coffers.

Previously, once a week, this state agency would shut off all of their phones, remove the receptionist from her post, and basically close the office. They were unreachable, to the great annoyance of their constituents, while they met every Thursday afternoon as a staff from 1:00 to 5:00 p.m. Twenty people times four hours each equals 80 hours of staff time per week. (Your tax dollars at work!)

Now, as a more Agile team, they all stand in the kitchen area with a cup of coffee each morning (which they were going to do anyway), and do a 15 minute daily stand-up meeting. Twenty people times 15 minutes equals five hours of staff time per day, or 25 hours for the week, compared to 80 hours. That is a savings of 55 hours each week, more than the salary and productivity of one entire full-time employee. Regardless of the hourly wage of the people participating, a savings of this magnitude is worth considering for your team. That does not even monetize the increase in value provided by the problem solving and communication exchanges that happen during that time.

Another hidden value of Agile may be the accountability. If you know that tomorrow morning you will stand up and share what you have done today with a team of your peers, you had better accomplish something. Now, the Arts Council finds that they are much better organized and more effective as a team. Oral sharing is much more motivating than handing in a written report.

Remember the Parkinson's Law principle, "Work expands to fit the time allocated." When we timebox the work into iterations, this principle is less likely to be a factor. In a traditional Waterfall process for projects, if you say, "Hey, Joe, how are you coming on your activities?"

Joe will always say, "Fine."

If you say, "Are you going to be done by Friday?"

Joe will say, "I sure am."

But when Friday comes and Joe's activity reports are submitted electronically through Microsoft Project via Project Server, his activities might be only 10% to 50% done. He was working on a number of other projects, and just did not get to yours. And, that percentage complete that he submitted is only an estimate.

However, if you say, "Joe, Mr. Product Owner is going to drop by the office on Friday morning at 10:00 a.m., and I would like to bring him by to see the checkout function for our online product sales. Can I count on you to be ready to show him by 10:00?" Now, Joe is going to put other projects on hold and make sure he gets *your* work done because he does not want to be embarrassed in front of the product owner by having nothing to show. It is the same psychology that was at work with the stand-up meeting. Knowing that you will stand up and share what you have completed with a live person, at a certain time, is much more motivating that handing in a written report.

References

[1]Cockburn, Alistair. Crystal methodologies. Retrieved from www.alistair.cockburn.us.

What Agile Tools Are Important?

End-of-Iteration Practices

At the end of each iteration, before the tangible demonstration of the work completed is held, it is time for you as the project manager to take a closer look at progress of your team. This is the time for each team member to make sure they have repositioned all of their sticky notes correctly to show what they have completed during the iteration, before an end-of-iteration meeting begins. Once the wall charts or whiteboards are updated, you can capture this information by taking a picture of it with a smartphone and attaching it in the Notes section of Microsoft Project, Primavera, or your proprietary project management software tool. Take a photo of your product backlog, too, so you have a record of how it changes from week to week. Be sure the photos are dated in order to keep a progressive record of the information.

As you can see, Agile philosophies move the stakeholder from being a remote person appointing an underling to write requirements, to an engaged participant in the team activities. Hopefully, teams are involved earlier in the project initiation process and can come to understand how projects are funded, the impact this one will have to the organization's strategic goals, and the expected business value it should return. The product owner will need to embrace his active participation during development, but in return will have the chance to hear options before needing to commit to a murky path forward. He or she will also have early access to see when the project may need to exceed its original limits to get the business return anticipated, or when the value of future work on the project will exceed the business value it would provide. The stop/go sign is always securely in the hands of the product owner.

Velocity

Velocity is the measured capacity of the team to deliver value. Once all of the progress for the iteration has been captured, add up the difficulty points (story points) of the work done by the team in Iteration One. For example, you had 5 people who completed a total of 50 difficulty points. Remember, this does *not* mean each person completed 10 points. We are not tracking individual performance, but **team velocity**. The number of points you completed in Iteration One tells you how many difficulty points you can take on as a team in Iteration Two. In this case, unless there were extenuating circumstances, such as team members out with the flu, or there was a national holiday, or a devastating storm and work time was lost, you should plan for your team to commit to 50 points for Iteration Two.

The rule of thumb is that you can never commit to more points for the next iteration than you completed in the last iteration. Estimates are OK, but we have already talked about their fallibility. The proof of how quickly the team can work is best measured by real data showing *how fast they really did work* in the preceding iteration. That is the only thing that matters as you move forward. However, if the whole team agrees that you all could handle more, for example, if you weren't busy enough the first iteration, or you underestimated the difficulty of the work and couldn't finish it all, you can have the team as a group agree to do more or less in Iteration Two, since it is so early in the project.

At the end of Iteration One, the product owner/customer joins you for the customer demo, formally called a **demonstration**. It is not a verbal presentation by the team and it does not include a "death by PowerPoint" presentation. This is *an informal time for the product owner or customer to try out what you have completed* during the last two weeks. If it is software, he or she sits at a computer and tests things out as an end-user might. If it is a portion of a product, have something for him or her to hold, inspect, and touch.

A demonstration is the bridge between the time when the customer described what was wanted in words and the moment he or she gets to see if the team understood. Based on what the customer experiences, you may have new sticky notes to move into the Approved column or additional items to add to the product backlog. Remember, this is OK. You do not mind changes because you have not yet planned for the next iteration anyway. The purpose of this time together is to elicit early feedback at a time when it can guide future team performance, allow the incorporation of changes or adjustments to the completed work, and to get sign-offs on the portions of the product or service already created.

Once the product owner/customer adds any new items to the backlog, the team makes their case for any additional back office items they may have discovered or thought of during their experience in completing the first iteration, and adds those to the backlog, too. They may also add items needed to structurally support the new things added by the product owner.

If there was any work that was committed to by the team for Iteration One that did not get completed, it is placed back into the backlog, rather than automatically moved to Iteration Two.

The backlog is now reprioritized by the product owner/customer. Also, the assembled group revisits items that were ranked further down the list last time, because after this first iteration on the project, you all know more. You may want to suggest a new order, or the product owner/customer may want to change the order of importance and value of items listed last time, before you choose what to do next week for Iteration Two. The team may also want to revise the degree of difficulty on some items since you now know more about them, especially if they move up the list and become a part of the user stories that the team will be working on in Iteration Two.

At this point, the product owner re-prioritizes the backlog yet again, and the team estimates the difficulty points for the next group of tasks down the line if they have not been handled already. Since this is progressive elaboration, the entire backlog isn't estimated—just far enough down the list to cover roughly enough tasks to allow you to get 50 story points for the next iteration in the project we are using in our sample explanation.

Depending on the project or the industry, for a short project, some teams prefer to use the T-shirt technique rather than Planning Poker, or another technique. As described in Chapter 8, the T-shirt technique asks the team to merely look at the relative size of the tasks in relationship to each other and judge them to be extra-small, small, medium, large, extra-large, or extra-extra-large. Often, the project manager will put six squares, or little T-shirt shapes, on the board showing a range from extra-small to extra-extra-large to help the team visually judge the relationship between the tasks. In some cases, that can be enough detail to allow the team to estimate the degree of difficulty for the items in the upcoming iteration. Regardless of the estimating technique used, at this point people choose their tasks for the second iteration from the prioritized list, initial them, and the Iteration Two of the project commences.

After the first couple of iterations, the number of difficulty points the team completes each week should be fairly stable. This becomes the team **velocity**, or *the measured capacity of the team to deliver value*. The team's velocity may grow larger over time if you have chosen team rules that allow people to take on new tasks during the iteration, or it may grow smaller if people consistently do not or cannot finish what they have committed to do. Over time, the velocity of the team will level out. Now that you know how much your team can do each iteration, you can use velocity to estimate how many weeks it will take to complete the rest of the work on the product backlog list. And estimating using team velocity is a more realistic projection than we usually have by using Waterfall techniques.

In Figure 9.1 you can see a team that had planned a backlog of activities that totaled 700 **difficulty points**, or story points. If the velocity was 100 points a week, they will complete the project in 7 weeks. But, if they have a lower velocity of only 70 points a week, it will take them 10 weeks to finish. If, after a week or two, you see that you have planned more work in your backlog than the team can possibly do in the time you have, you are early in the project. Remember, the team will not be required to work overtime; rather, scope or project features will be reduced and added back into the iteration backlog at the end of the timebox.

The intent is that the team develops a rhythm that is sustainable over the long term of the project. Short bursts may produce slightly more work for the moment, but have a long term negative affect on the morale of the team. A gain from any additional work in the short term will be negatively counterbalanced by an overall decline in the team velocity over the long term.

Another important truth about team velocity is that you cannot compare the velocity of one team to another in a judgmental way. Team Red may have a

Planning Project Length Using Velocity

Total Backlog of Story Points	700
High Velocity	100
Low Velocity	70

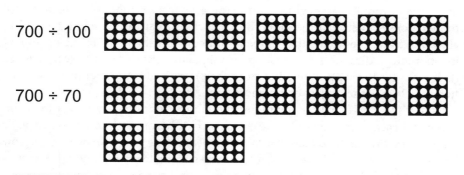

Figure 9.1 Planning Project Length Using Velocity

velocity of 70 story points per iteration and Team Blue may work at a rate so that they complete 50 story points per iteration. This does *not* mean that Team Red is a better team, or that Team Blue should work harder to match the performance of their competitor.

In fact, teams are not in competition, as speed is not a factor that can be transferred directly into business value or customer value. The complexity, innovation, and differences that we have toward estimating the size of user stories in great detail means that teams will always vary. The purpose of velocity is merely to allow the team to get a reasonable idea of how much to bite off for the next iteration, and to allow the project manager to approximate the overall timeline of the project.

In fact, you cannot even take the team velocity of 70 story points for Team A and assume they will perform at this rate, or a higher one, on the next project that they undertake. The next project by this same team will be so different that they will not move through stories at the same rate. A team that has a 1200 story point velocity on the Harper Project cannot be projected to have a 1200 story point velocity on their next undertaking, the Malloy Project. Velocity must be re-established on a project-by-project basis, as the variables of each project shift. Choosing which project team to assign to a critical project because they appeared to work "faster" on the last project is folly.

What you can do is establish a team velocity within normal parameters of being a little over or a little under the number of story points to which they commit each iteration, and use that to estimate how many story points can realistically be completed during the time allocated to the project. However, *there is absolutely no correlation between a story point and a guaranteed business value to the work that story point describes.*

Sometimes, a project manager finds the need to map out eventual team velocity before there is the actual data collected by letting the team complete an iteration or two. The idea of an Iteration Zero to compete just enough information to allow the project to be authorized can also be useful to get a preliminary idea of team velocity. But the team velocity cannot be known with certainty until the team gets into the actual activities of the project. A technique to use early on might be to informally notice the velocity of individual team members. A collective sum of the individual scores of the people on the team could be a very, very general starting point. When planning future iterations around a known absence by one team member, or when a person leaves the team or the company, you might choose to subtract that person's velocity from the team's story point commitment for those iteration weeks. However, this is only a stop-gap measure until you can once again use real data from the team as a whole.

While it is possible to collect individual velocity scores for the unusual situations just mentioned, keeping them private is of crucial importance. It takes a process of unlearning standing assumptions for the other teammates to not equate a high number of velocity points with getting the "best grade," a thought process left over from our collective school experiences. And comparative personal velocity scores should never be used to typify the worth that a person contributes to the team. In fact, Jerry, who produces only a few story points, may be extremely crucial to the success of the project. He may have been pair programming or co-partnering with others, helping with structural design issues, fixing quality issues, or spending the time thinking of creative ways to approach and solve thorny problems. The impact of how this person spent his time does not show on a scorecard, but the project would be much worse off if Jerry fell back into doing an isolated Waterfall activities list, even if by doing so he bumped up the number of story points he could claim for the iteration.

And never try to compare team members by some contrived metric you may see touted on the Internet, or by a prominent guest speaker, like taking the story points completed by our team player, Jerry, and dividing them by the number of story points in the team's velocity to give Jerry a recordable metric. You can get a number for an answer with that formula, but it has no merit as any sort of useful metric. It is like dividing Jerry's shoe size by the miles per gallon he get in his car. Iteration by iteration, the story points Jerry has chosen will vary in complexity and difficulty. He won't know what he faces until he is in the middle of the work to complete them.

Jerry may also be spending time learning new skills, which will be of value to the team by bringing in increased knowledge, reducing risk, lowering errors when working together with another team member, or as he mentors another colleague. If you make the rookie mistake of evaluating Jerry on the number of story points he completes, you will damage the team performance and negate the collaborative value an Agile team brings. Jerry may begin to focus on grinding out story points rather than completing things with an eye for quality, a nose for innovation, and an ear for customer satisfaction.

Other short-sighted attempts to apply meaningless metrics to Agile team members include tracking things that are not relevant to the goal. For software development, lines of code written per day are used as a common measurement of programming prowess. But clear thinking will lead you to realize that the shorter and simpler the code, the easier it is to test, integrate, and maintain. So, encouraging and rewarding the programmer who writes the most lines of code is at odds with our project goals. Following the same logic, if you track and reward the number of hours worked per week, you will undoubtedly get more people working overtime. That adds to the project cost, plus, studies show that people who work excessive overtime get tired and resentful, and do not necessarily produce more valuable results over time. That which gets measured, gets repeated. Be sure you are measuring the right things.

Both individual and group story points completed in an iteration are easy to calculate: Just add the number of story points that were moved from the To Do section of the progress chart to the Approved column. (In Agile, nothing can be considered "done" unless it has also been approved.) Individual velocity should never be used as a part of the employee evaluation process, and certainly should never be tied to raises or pay grades. Rather, the more both evaluations and pay issues are related to the team as a whole, the stronger you will support the Agile principles and mold your successful team.

You may not be in a position to change the way your organization words evaluations or uses the results, but you are the person who can calculate a collective score for the team for evaluations and then add the same score for each person into his or her personnel paperwork. Think back to Henri Fayol (Chapter 3). If the team produces a good result, then all members of the team and the manager were collectively successful. And if the team is truly self-directed, democratic, and cooperative in their approach with regard to team responsibilities, i.e., they are empowered, rather than monitored and controlled, you may not be able to differentiate between levels of contribution made by individual employees.

Social Loafing

The power of a group can be positive, but project managers considering moving to Agile often secretly fear **social loafing**; *the idea that people have the tendency to slack off or not work as hard either mentally or physically within a group* as they would alone? After all, a team gives you the opportunity to hide in a situation where your lack of effort may not be noticed in the overall output from the group. The tendency for employers to ask employees to adhere to rigorous methods and techniques, and monitor the metrics of their output, is based on the theory that it protects the firm from loss, since if not watched carefully, people will shirk their duties, right? Does this sound like Theory X?

The Agile approach, more akin to McGregor's Theory Y, stresses empowerment and trust in the team to the extent they can monitor themselves. They are responsible for the creation of the work to which they commit, and in the best of scenarios the group is evaluated as a whole, as opposed to as individuals. Research by Williams, Karau, and Bourgeois looked at the problem of social loafing. They described three factors that contribute to social loafing:

1. It increases when the work is based on group performance,
2. It is less likely to occur if the work is interesting, and
3. Working in a cohesive group can reduce it.[1]

At first glance, based on the group performance factor increasing the possibility of social loafing, their study could appear to support some minor concerns about the formation and operation of an Agile team and rating them as a group rather than as individual workers. An interesting study done by John McAvoy and Tom Butler in Cork, Ireland, proved that Agile proponents have no cause to worry, as their study found the opposite to be true. The first group studied was a team of seven people, plus their project manager, who worked on a project for a European government organization. They employed the Agile philosophy in a major way and were judged on their performance as a group and the results of their project.

The second team in McAvoy and Butler's research was made up of eight members, and a team leader, who were working on a project for a U.S.-based multinational telecommunications company. This organization needed to comply with TL9000, a standard for developing communications software, and also were regularly audited for their compliance to the Capability Maturity Model (CMM) for projects. They were evaluated as individuals in terms of their performance. However, they were still considered an Agile team.

You might predict, based on the earlier research on social loafing, that the first European team would be the most likely to shirk. Their work was based on group performance, they were self-directed, and they were allowed to be responsible for what they did and how they did it. For the second group, needing to adhere to the government standards and being regularly audited for CMM purposes, would make one think that they would be under enough scrutiny to never shirk.

The opposite proved to be true. The more Agile, European team developed a cohesive group that bonded at work, and then continued that close relationship outside of the workplace. They saw the work as "our" work, no matter who actually produced it, and they vigorously defended their decisions and supported each other. There was no social loafing perceived to be present.

However, the telecommunications team, the one you would imagine would be constrained by the presence of a high degree of monitoring and the necessity to adhere closely to company processes, exhibited more social loafing. In fact, there was little bonding and collaborative support for one another, except for "show" when they were meeting in a review process, or were trying to look busy and important when they were being evaluated by the team lead. The team members appeared at meetings without the proper preparation, and even the team lead would come to the meetings and try to quickly do his work on the spot.

McAvoy and Butler concluded, "The existence of a highly cohesive software development team, with ownership of, and control over, their work is, all things being equal, less likely to lead to the existence of social loafing among team members. It is also evident that Agile methodologies promote these high levels of social cohesion and a sense of ownership among team members." [2] In the end, Williams, Karau and Bourgeois were proven correct, too. While there is potential for loafing when the group's performance is evaluated as a whole, working in a cohesive Agile group can counteract that risk.

Individual monitoring and evaluation of teams who religiously apply formal processes can have the opposite effect to that predicted by existing research on social loafing. What was actually found was that individual evaluation allowed those that were not the focus of the evaluation to engage in social loafing. If a team fully adopts an Agile philosophy, team members tend to work better as a group by supporting each other, rather than hiding within the group to disguise problems with the quality of their work.

Project managers always have to balance three constraints: time, cost, and scope. Together, these constraints box in the amount of time and money available to create the quality of the project. Since Agile projects are typically laid out at a high level with a fixed time and a fixed cost, and inherent in the methodology is a burning commitment quality, when you can determine actual team velocity early in the project, rather than be obligated do all of the activities you originally planned, the product owner has time to reassess. He or she can choose what portions of the project you will continue and what parts you need to cut off. There is also the option to choose to invest more time and money in the project to lengthen the number of iterations and get a fuller rendition of the entire product backlog. The good thing with this approach is since you have put all the things of low value to the bottom of the list, the important things will still get done, regardless of whether or not the product owner extends the project.

Remember, you never require people to work overtime, come in on weekends, or even pressure them to speed up. The truth is, when the team members are engaged and feeling excited about their work, they are naturally going to stay a little later on occasion to finish up a task before they leave for the evening, or spend some time thinking about ways to improve the final product on their personal time. Allowing those additional contributions to be voluntary, at the discretion of the employee, brings great value to the team.

In our Agile team example, at this point in the process, people choose their tasks for the second iteration from the prioritized list, and the project continues. If you are managing a hybrid team and must have hours worked for an automated software report, have team members write the actual number of hours they worked on a task on its sticky note, whether you work in difficulty points, hours, or days. This will help if you are in an organization that requires traditional reports. You as the project manager can translate the data into the proper software to generate reports, while the Agile team moves along swiftly, focusing on the tasks of the project.

Interacting with Traditional Teams

Keep focused on the idea that the technical terms, and the tools and techniques of an Agile team, are not the important part of being Agile. If Agile means more flexible, then you need to exhibit that flexibility around working with other types of teams, too. For example, Brendon was a software developer/consultant who was working with a major television brand name to develop a TV that had the equivalent of a digital video recorder (DVR) in the clouds. In other words, you could record on any TV in your house and with no extra equipment, like a TiVo or your cable company's proprietary DVR box, view those recordings on any other TV or electronic device you owned, such as an iPad or smartphone. Find a program in the online program guide, but you are currently watching another channel? It will record the program simultaneously with the one you are viewing and store it on remote servers for you to recall at any time. Concerned about storage space? It is virtually unlimited. See something on the program guide but the broadcast started 20 minutes ago? No problem, the entire episode will be recorded for you from the beginning.

The project management challenge was that the hardware team was Waterfall and Brendon was running the software team as Agile. With this opposite mindset towards running projects, the simplest things became problems. In Brendon's team, they freely spoke of iterations and releases. That really threw the traditional project manager, Jake, who kept misinterpreting the term "release" and saying, "But we can't sell this TV until it is completely finished and tested." Since Jake was thinking as a hardware project manager, we cannot fault him; but he was missing the idea that some of the software features could be released with the basic TV set in order to get this product into the market before a competitor announced it first, and stole the market share and reputation for being the creator of this new feature. The rest of the software features could be added later.

Another miscommunication arose when Brendon who, from his software viewpoint, was trying to coordinate the iterations and releases that he had broken into consistent short timeboxes, so that as much functionality as possible could go with the first shipments. The traditional project manager, Jake, shared that the company did not use consistent phases. They ran all their projects by setting major checkpoints to correspond to major holidays. So, deadlines or milestones would be tied to New Year's Eve, St. Patrick's Day, Mother's Day, Fourth of July, Labor Day, and Election Day. He said that the teams had found they had a better internal sense of when those days were, as opposed to just a random date on the calendar picked by the project manager.

Brendon was stumped! Usually, in the Agile world, iterations were consistent periods of time. But he was an outside consultant and could not afford to fight with the higher ranking internal employee. So, Brendon looked at a calendar and determined the time between each of the holidays was roughly about 2 months. Typically, each iteration is the same length as every other iteration, and each release has the same number of iterations, but he fudged it. He counted the number of two week iterations that would fit between the holidays, and ran his Agile team on that cycle. The last iteration in each release might be a little long or short, but the slight variation in that one timebox was not a deal breaker. When the holidays came, that's when he coordinated his team to meet, collaborate, and sync up progress with the TV hardware team at the end of their own phases.

He also addressed the problem of the word "release," which concerned the other project manager greatly, by calling it a "phase." Within his team, they had release targets. When he went to meet with the TV team, it was easy enough to switch to the terms that made him more understandable and acceptable to the other team. The point of this example, is that there while software development teams have specific processes they follow with excellent results, based in this case on the little agile product, Scrum...the most crucial skill regardless of which side of the aisle you are on regarding the project processes, is to concentrate on what gets the product out the door and brings return on investment value for the organization.

Getting Started with Agile

If we want to move from a Waterfall process to a more Agile process, what should we do first? If you are a project manager with authority only at the project team level, where should you start? How can you make changes and still have it all fit into an existing corporate culture that has yet to make an extensive organizational change in this direction? An Ambysoft Agile Practices survey[3] (see Figure 9.2) shows that the first most effective practice is the *daily stand-up meeting*. Project teams universally hate a 6-hour team meeting once a week in a conference room. You'll recall that, in Agile, the entire team meets every morning and, literally, stands for the entire time while each person quickly says, "This is what I did yesterday", "This is what I am going to do today", and "These are the roadblocks that I see." The project manager's job is then to remove those roadblocks, so that the team can focus and spend their time on creating the software, product, or service.

A second effective practice is *continuous integration,* which is building in small parts, and making sure each new thing works with the others, before moving on. Also in the top three effective Agile processes we can implement for non-IT teams is the *retrospective*. At the end of each two week iteration, for example, the team meets to consider what went well and what needs to change before they start the next iteration.

First Agile practices to introduce

 • Daily stand-up meetings

 • Continuous integration

★ • Retrospectives

• Short iterations

• Work prioritized by the customer/product owner

• Customer demos at the end of each iteration

• Collocated, cross-functional, dedicated teams

Figure 9.2 The First Agile Practices to Introduce

In a well-done retrospective, two sides of the team experience are evaluated. First, how well is the team doing to create the product or service and what should be changed. Second, how are the team's processes working and what should be altered? The mantra for the open discussion is "No naming, no blaming."

We all know at the end of a traditional project there should be a lessons learned session that is documented and accessed for guidance when beginning future projects. If you are honest, you know these sessions may turn into gripe sessions with finger-pointing and assigning blame for problems, rather than an attitude of capturing what went well and what needs to change. Worse yet, the session results tend to be archived to never again see the light of day. After all, if this is a temporary, traditional team, the members may be anxious to get back to their regular work and forget about this experience.

With the Agile retrospective, rather than a year or so of data to review, your team only needs to consider what has happened in the previous two weeks, or whatever short period you have sent for the timebox. Rather than documenting ideas that may never be needed again, or never actually be used, changes the team sees that need to be made will be implemented on the next day the team meets to work.

In addition, the retrospective is a time to also see if any team issues have arisen that would lead to an addition or change to the team rules. Maybe the team did not think to consider what would happen if someone was unexpectedly taken ill. Or, the team may have learned they should add a rule where at least one other person on the team needs to have a colleague's password for access into each other's computer in case of an unforeseen event. Perhaps they did not create a rule about how absences or tardiness to the daily stand-up meeting would be resolved. It saves a lot of resentment by addressing these practices as a group as they occur, rather than letting them fester throughout the project or leaving it to the project manager to be the attendance police.

The changes of the team may be added to the backlog, posted to the team rules, or simply agreed upon by the group and posted as a reminder, but the value of considering them while they are fresh in people's minds and correcting or improving things quickly as you go is the essence of the Agile attitude. Change as you go—the retrospective leads to continuous improvement in action.

A fourth effective practice to use in traditional projects is *iteration planning*. The user stories are prioritized and chosen, and the team plans in detail what they will do during this next few weeks. If, as an Agile/Waterfall hybrid team, you work with a parallel traditional team, it is easy enough to translate this term to rolling wave or sub-phase planning, if necessary.

How hard is this to do? The same Ambysoft survey found that the same practices that were the most effective were also the easiest to add. Here is a review of the things you might be able to introduce without a major culture shift or too much upper management concern:

1. Daily stand-up meetings.
2. Continuous integration.
3. Retrospectives.
4. Short iterations.
5. Work prioritized by customer.
6. Customer demos at the end of each iteration.
7. Collocated, cross-functional, and dedicated teams, if possible.

The only item that requires you to have some outside organizational cooperation is getting the customer involved, but you can be smooth about it. You do not have to say to the product owner/customer, "I am now doing an Agile process and you are required to come to my customer demo every two weeks." Try starting with an internal project where you already know the product owner and have worked together before. Instead, say, "We've got some (creative, innovative, valuable) stuff done on your project already. The team and I are excited about it, as I know you will be, and I know that you're going to want to see this. Could you stop by on Friday morning at 10 a.m.? The team will be there so that we can show you what we've done. We'd sure like to get your feedback to be sure we are going in the right direction and that this is what you had in mind."

However, always keep in mind that doing the list of activities above is not being Agile. There is no magic in doing these tools and techniques by themselves in lieu of your current organization's traditional or Waterfall project management processes. The trick is to think about how you and your team can be lean, and focus on getting your team working together on a process flow to drive value through the project with no impediments. Keep rereading the principles of the Agile Manifesto and the philosophies behind them. It will lead you to change your relationships with the team, functional managers, internal and external customers, and vendors. Change your thinking to change your results.

Iteration Time Breakdown

How should the two weeks of an iteration be spent? Obviously, if there are planning sessions, stand-up meetings, demos, and retrospectives, how much time remains for actually completing the features and functions of the item you are to create? Figure 9.3 illustrates the way that a two week or 10 day iteration might lay out. For a first iteration, there will need to be some big picture, long-term planning called Roadmap Planning. Then there is the smaller division, the release, to be planned.

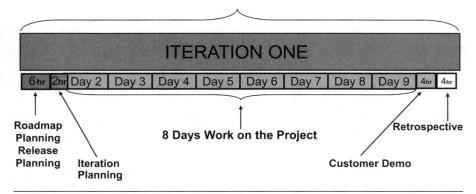

Flow of the Iteration

2 Week or 10 Day Iteration

Figure 9.3 A Two-Week Iteration Time Breakdown

This is done in a meeting with the project manager, team, product owner/ customer, vendors, and any other collaborating teams and their corresponding stakeholders. Each person attending may have information that is crucial to share, will need a common vision of how the project will proceed, and will have to agree on a realistic timeline. This meeting, like other Agile processes, should be time-boxed (limited) to about 6 hours.

Once the high-level Roadmap Planning and the more detailed Release Planning for the first release is done, the group can disperse. Now, your core team of you as project manager, the team members, and the product owner/customer (or a representative) can meet for an additional 2 hours to have the product owner prioritize the backlog of user stories, break larger user stories down into more workable pieces, have the team estimate the story points for each one, and let the team select the ones they will commit to complete during Iteration One. The team now has 8 days to work on the project, protected from change.

As show in Figure 9.3, the last day of the Iteration One is the Customer Demo. This is set for 4 hours, allowing plenty of time to show the completed work of the iteration, get customer feedback, and begin to capture any new user stories for changes or additions that originate with either the customer or the team. After the Customer Demo, the product owner/customer is free to leave.

For the afternoon, the project manager and core team meet for their Retrospective. They can refine how they might address some of the changes that came up in the Customer Demo meeting, and take a look at how well the team worked together during the last two weeks. If there is time, it might be appropriate to look at the team velocity for this first iteration, and consider whether or not it appears to be a realistic and appropriate pace for the next iteration as well.

At the end of each iteration, the cycle repeats itself. Roadmap and Release Planning may go a little faster, but there will be changes and work to be done to accommodate alterations that result from what was discovered in Iteration One's Customer Demo and Retrospective. Remember, any unfinished work from Iteration One does *not* automatically get moved into Iteration Two, as it would in a traditional project. Incomplete or never started activities go back into the product backlog. Keep in mind that once you adopt the Agile mindset, every feature and function initially conceived may not appear in the final result, but rather the process is intended to sift down to the key and crucial things that will be "barely sufficient" to create the business value or fulfill the precipitating business objective for which this project was funded.

Lest you think this idea is an anomaly within the current project management field, in both the 1996 and 2000 editions of the *PMBOK® Guide*, the Knowledge Area of Project Integration Management is defined as including, "the processes required to ensure that the various elements of the project are properly coordinated. It involves making tradeoffs among competing objectives and alternatives to meet or exceed stakeholder needs and expectations."[4] In later editions, the idea of exceeding stakeholder expectations was removed, as the cost and speed of doing business made it a poor choice for project managers to attempt to do more than the exact details of what the customer wanted, needed, and requested. In fact, they were cautioned that it was an unethical use of company funds to expand the scope of projects to "exceed expectations" in a business world where projects were having difficulty even meeting minimum requirements.

So, the shift in business philosophy was already underway before it was codified and named Agile, but the trend continues at a faster pace today as teams now try to find the simplest method to obtain the most streamlined project results that will bring the maximum value for their customers. Remember, success is not having the highest number of microwave buttons and functions, but zeroing in on which buttons the customers want and which will lead them to purchase your product in a sea of similar items.

After time for the iteration meetings is taken out, plus 12 to 15 minutes per morning for the daily stand-up meeting, there are approximately 8 days of work time remaining for team productivity. The project manager, or ScrumMaster for an IT Scrum team, will work to resolve issues with management, get decisions made to move the project forward, coordinate with other teams who may be working in parallel, resolve internal team conflicts, and do the paperwork necessary to generate the minimal reports the organization will accept from the team.

When you do not see it drawn out as in Figure 9.3, it may sound to management, the PMO, human resources, or your customer, as if Agile requires an excessive amount of "wasted time in meetings." The facts are that traditional projects also take planning, its just that the weeks of planning may all occur upfront, rather than being interspersed in a more useful way across the entire time span of the project. Often, that traditional planning time is not captured as a part of the project time and cost, since the WBS is not built until many of these meeting have already been held. And the traditional lessons learned sessions, if they are done at all, may be held after the project budget has already been closed. Using 20% of the Agile integration project time for planning is usually less than the time actually spent for planning with a Waterfall project, but the difference is that this evolved approach offers a better return on investment.

References

[1]Williams, K., Karau, S. & Bourgeois, M. (1993). *Working on collective tasks: Social loafing and social compensation.*

[2]McAvoy, J. & Butler, T. (2006). *Looking for a Place to Hide: A Study of Social Loafing in Agile Teams.* ECIS 2006 Proceedings.

[3]Ambler, S. W. (2009), *Ambysoft Agile Practices Survey.*

[4]Project Management Institute. 2000. *A Guide to the Project Management Body of Knowledge.* 2000 edition. Project Management Institute, Inc. 20–22.

How Does Agile Scale to the Enterprise Level?

Most Agile methodologies and training focus on the single project team. The optimal size is said to be 7 people, plus or minus 2. Think of the massive amounts of face-to-face communication necessary on an Agile team, so the idea is to keep the team small. However, the reality is that most of us work in companies that are large enough to need project managers. We do not have the luxury of having only one team of 6 or 7 people doing a project. So, how do we scale Agile up to an enterprise level?

One Backlog—One Team

When you scale up through the enterprise, every project becomes a hybrid even though you may yourself work with one small, Agile team. This is because of the bookend, traditional processes discussed in Chapter 6. Even if you are part of the world's most dedicated, disciplined, and successful Scrum team, if you are in the middle of a large organization that is not 100% Agile at every level, you will have some Waterfall type requirements at the beginning and end of the project. Think of the mandatory initiation, quality, and compliance requirements at the start and finish of each project. So, let's start from the single team structure and work up.

Remember, Peter Drucker said that "the customer is king." This role may be either a traditional customer from outside your organization or an internal product owner. He or she might be the department head paying for your project, the higher-up manager in the area of the enterprise responsible for your project, or an intermediary such as a business analyst who is appointed by upper management to serve as the project liaison. In the example shown in Figure 10.1, you may have a Customer or Product Owner who holds a list of work or user stories, the product backlog, that make up the project. You, as the project manager, are part of the Project Team shown at the right.

People often are great in their roles on a team, and from that success they are elevated to a project management position. Most of us who come from a production background on the team find it hard to get free of continuing to perform at least a portion of the work of the project. Theoretically, it is easy to see that once the project manager has project activities assigned to himself or herself through virtue of personal expertise, or because they enjoy doing a particular sort of work and choose to keep it for themselves, there is a potential for disaster. Should the project fall behind in any of its metrics, or should unusual problems arise, the project manager is the one pulled off tasks to put out fires. The activities the project manager kept go undone, and the project slips further and further behind schedule.

One Backlog – One Team

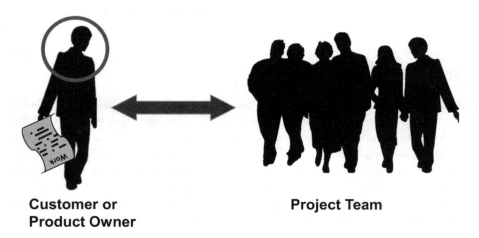

Customer or **Project Team**
Product Owner

Figure 10.1 One Backlog—One Team

Perhaps this is one of the reasons that, although the project manager, or in a specific methodology like Scrum, a ScrumMaster, is a part of the team, he or she does not occupy a role that is involved in completing the work of the team. The **project manager/ScrumMaster** role *works only to facilitate meetings and remove obstacles for the team and to coordinate with other teams throughout the enterprise,* so the teams are free to complete their user story responsibilities.

One Backlog—Mixed Teams

As we begin to talk of adding another team to the structure and mixing approaches to arrive at a hybrid approach to projects, it is common for people to visualize an arrangement where the Agile software development team and the non-IT team are mixed together into one big, happy family. A hybrid team is *not* where some people on the team use a Waterfall method and others on the same team use an Agile approach (see Figure 10.2). You do not *ever* want to structure a small project team like this. In fact, actively avoid this situation at all costs! Mixing people who are doing all Agile, or perhaps the precise methodology called Scrum, into the same team with those using a traditional Waterfall approach is a recipe for disaster.

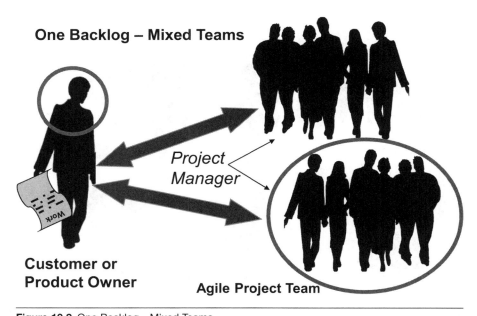

Figure 10.2 One Backlog—Mixed Teams

Here's the trick. You can mix Agile and Waterfall actions together to make a hybrid process that pleases you and keeps the organization satisfied, too, but *the whole team must be on the same hybrid process*. That hybrid team can then coordinate their work with a pure Agile Scrum, XP, DSDM, Crystal, or other type of stand-alone software development team to create the larger hybrid project.

Or, on a team so small that it makes no sense to divide it, software-centric team members can use a more precise set of practices for their code development, testing, and integration testing, while others on the team responsible for other non-software items can work in the way that makes the most sense for them. However, the length of iterations and releases are standard for all, they share product and iteration backlogs and visual team progress charts, and everyone participates in the daily stand-ups and other Agile meeting frameworks.

In fact, once you make sure that all members of your group are on the same hybrid methodology, teams do function better when they are composed of 5-7 people. You may choose to divide a larger team into two or more sub-teams, and then manage the coordination of those teams for greater flexibility and productivity. However, you can only do this if you become skilled in managing the communication and lining up the interlocking results from all of the teams in each iteration. Then, there could be one backlog worked on by two teams using different methodologies, managed by one project manager.

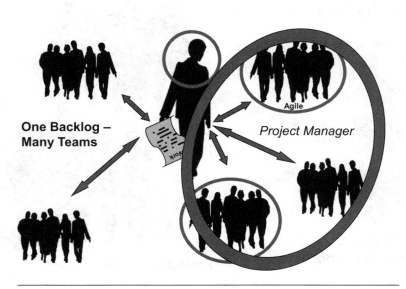

Figure 10.3 One Backlog—Many Teams

One Backlog—Many Teams

One product owner may have such a large project that multiple teams are working on the same product backlog (Figure 10.3). Since you, as the Project Manager, have worked to perfect your managerial skills, you may find yourself managing several self-directed teams and coordinating their work to complete a large portion of the overall project. In this example, you are managing the two Agile teams on the right (circled in gray), as well as the traditional team. Your total team responsibilities are shown encompassed by the wider gray circle, but you will also need to coordinate your three teams with the two traditional teams (on the left), probably managed by other project managers.

Multiple, Independent Product Backlogs

If we scale up to larger projects, you might find multiple Product Owners, each with his or her product backlog that multiple teams are working to fulfill. Each of those Product Owners would then report up to a Product Manager (Figure 10.4). The project for each Product Owner can be totally independent of those managed

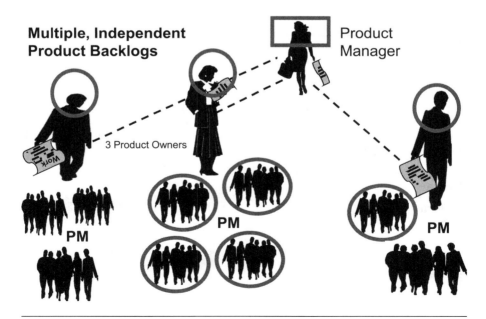

Figure 10.4 Multiple, Independent Product Backlogs

by his or her colleagues, or all of them might be coordinated at the program level for a companywide initiative. You can see that the Project Manager (PM) will manage multiple teams that could be all Waterfall, all Agile, or a mixture of both types, each in their separate team groups. If this is a large company initiative, your responsibilities may include coordination with the other project managers to keep all of the teams in sync.

Separate, But Cooperating Teams

Teams can be from different organizations and still work together. For example, a project management consulting company that has an Agile approach may supply the oversight to a construction and remodeling project that is done using a more Waterfall approach. This situation is not a mixed team, but rather a project manager who is skilled in both Agile and Waterfall, acting as linguistic and process interpreter between the teams.

For example, you might be the Project Manager at a management consulting firm in Dallas, TX, and your team is sold on and skilled in using Agile to manage projects in numerous different industries. However, your latest client, located in Rio de Janeiro, Brazil, is a local college looking to remodel their library and add a

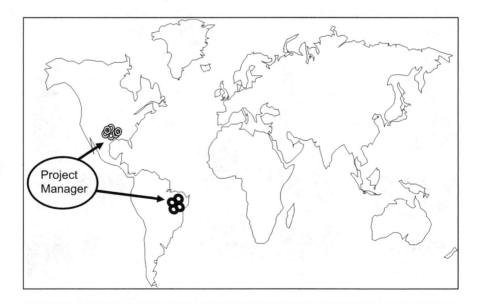

Figure 10.5 Separate, But Cooperating Teams

student dormitory to the campus. This is the first project that they have done, and they don't have any processes, only the approval, financing, and the vendors they have already hired. The subcontractor they have chosen to do the construction is a very established, traditional group, and they will use a rigid Waterfall approach that has proven extremely successful for them. You, as the Project Manager, should be able to successfully coordinate between all of these groups (Figure 10.5).

Collocated Teams

An important feature of Agile is collocated teams. All of the members are hopefully working in the same room at the same time, if at all possible. That allows the best chance for the team to put together the pieces of the project puzzle. We also want them all to be dedicated, to work exclusively on this one project 100% of the time.

Think of your favorite sports team, and you will know in your heart that collocation, cross-functional skills, and dedication are keys to winning. Imagine how ridiculous a game would be if part of the team was on the field, but the rest were teleconferencing from home, at a soft-drink endorsement shoot, or on vacation. Or, visualize a team where each player could *only* perform a narrowly assigned role and not have any meaningful interchanges with fellow teammates. The ball is coming toward the player near the end zone, but he is not the receiver whose role it is to catch it and score, and no one has signaled him to go ahead, so he lets the ball hit the ground, bounce, and roll out of bounds for an incomplete pass (a wasted opportunity). Or, even more ludicrous, your key players are participating in four games at the same time. After every play, each teammate gets on public transportation and they all rush in different directions to another game, and another, and another, keeping the circle going until the time on the clock runs out for each game.

The reason for keeping the team dedicated 100% to this one project is that studies show that a huge amount of productivity is lost if people are moving from task to task on different things. The idea of multitasking as a way to stretch resources and save money is a myth. You have your best performance when you can focus on one thing at a time. Each additional task from a different project, or operational responsibility, lowers your ability to concentrate and deliver your best work on this project.

You may think, "OK, my workplace needs to become more Agile, but we have too many non-project tasks each day to work in dedicated teams. So, if 100% of the team's time focused on one project is not possible right now, try to gain as much of the dedicated, collocated advantage in any way you can. (Scrum teams, rather than continuing with the next few paragraphs, please skip over them and use the time to get a cup of coffee to prevent your having an untimely seizure by reading them.)

Involve your own team in brainstorming ways that you could get at least a portion of their time where they can focus on this one project. Ask, "What could we do if we cannot have a dedicated team that works 100% on one project?" Here are some ideas to get you started.

Interest Teams

Project managers who become believers in Agile often are disappointed to realize that the other members of the team have not gone through the same discovery process and may not be excited about changing their practices. Remember, many people are not immediately open to changing the way that they work. They are heavily invested in sustaining a homeostatic balance.

Choose people in your workgroup who have the necessary skill sets, and are the most interested in exploring Agile, to work on an initial Agile team. Often, the competing projects are not technically "projects," but merely the day-to-day operations of the department that must be handled along with project work. Perhaps you could allow people to volunteer to be on the new, Agile team. The other members of the department can handle the day-to-day work for the length of the project.

It is not uncommon to find that there are people who would prefer to work on the operational work of the department exclusively, and not be submitted to the pressure and constantly changing job responsibilities that go along with projects. Since the project manager seldom has the functional authority to change job titles and pay scales, as long as those remain in place and promotional opportunities are not affected, you may find the best of both worlds and have happier people surrounding you by letting each person decide which work is the best fit for them.

Reserve Mornings

If organizational issues, or the reality of your workflow, do not allow you to have both an Agile team and an operations team, try to have each team member devote mornings, or as much of the day as possible, to the project. Facilitate stand-up meetings to present what was accomplished yesterday, what each person will do today, and what is standing in their way. Then, there should be several hours to focus on accomplishing project work, undistracted by other obligations. Routine, non-project work can be done at the end of this reserve period.

This is a good option if you work in a functional organization where your team is assembled out of individuals "on loan" to the project, or who may expect to perform assigned tasks from the project WBS in isolation at their own desk in remote, siloed departments. Finding a space, such as a conference room or break room, where people can group together for the daily stand-up, work on laptops, and at least develop a team identity together, will be very advantageous. In the worst case scenario, at least they are at their desks and have their hearts and minds on your project each morning when you contact them by phone during this reserved time block.

Add a Special Skill

While there is real value in having an intact team work together over the entire project, there are times when a special skill is needed for only a few days, or the skill is in such short supply in the organization that this in-demand person must be available to multiple teams. To make the best use of a short-term subject matter expert or consultant, see if he or she can attend the early product owner/customer meetings to gain a full grasp of the purpose of the project. If this is impossible, make sure this person understands the project vision and the specific reason this feature or function is important to the customer or product owner. That way you get the best and most useful work out of the short time that this expert can work with your team. Having the expert attend iteration planning meetings, daily stand-ups, customer demos, and retrospectives is also ideal.

These next two ideas *are not good ones*, but they may work as stop-gap measures until you can prove the usefulness of Agile and get managerial support for dedicated teams.

Team Switch

A team switch is far from a desirable solution. A large amount of the worth in an Agile team evolves over time. As the unit learns skills due to the close proximity and collaborative nature of Agile, plus the honing of the way the team works together at each retrospective point, keeping the same team intact makes sense. Otherwise, a lot of the value of the team learning is lost. However, if you have substantial work to do that is not related to this Agile project, try forming two teams that are equal in skills.

One team completes this project and experiences and learns the new Agile processes. Meanwhile, the second team will have a chance to work in this way on the next project. Those on the "off" team complete the department's routine operational work and other project work managed in a traditional way to allow the Agile team to be dedicated to the primary project. Again, this is *not* a good solution, but could be a temporary approach to get success metrics during the time that you are testing Agile processes and trying to make your case to management.

Iteration Switch

Remember, these workaround options are *listed in order of desirability and an iteration switch is the last one on the list*. When planning the project, you can try to anticipate which skill sets will be needed during the upcoming one to two week time period (iteration). All team members and stakeholders should attend the stand-up meetings to keep in touch with the project. Then, those whose skills can be covered by someone else in this iteration can take care of the operational and other project work, while the Agile project team moves forward to create project features and functions. Switch team members by iteration, so that no one group gets designated the "Agile experts" by virtue of working on the first project. Your positive outcomes may be slower with this approach, but at least you are gaining a small amount of experience for your team. This will *not* work with software or web development teams, and do not use it if it does not make sense in your situation.

Ideally, your Agile team is dedicated to only one project at a time. If that is unrealistic, find creative ways to get the most focused work periods possible to complete the work of the project. Then, work within your corporate environment to get management to rethink the way they assign teams.

How Do I Work With Distributed Teams?

Distributed Teams

The reality of the modern corporate environment is that there will be many occasions when not only is collocation within your office impossible, you may be required to manage geographically distributed teams across the globe. The distance for a distributed team may include groups from different floors of the same building, various locations around the country, or opposite corners of the world. Frequently, the term *distributed teams* describes teams separated not only by distance, but perhaps by language and culture as well.

If each distributed team has all of the needed skills in one location, and they are truly cross-functional, then each group can work in a different location on parts of the same stories or features from the same product owner backlog. You might think that the logical next step would be to divide the work so that Team A Dallas is doing its own, self-contained features and Team A Paris is doing separate software features, which can then be integrated at the end of the iteration. However, experienced veterans of the Agile system suggest that it is a better practice to have the split Agile team continue to work and function as one unit on the same shared backlog, and to have team members on both sides of the ocean involved in tasks to produce the same features.

If you fragment a team along the lines of the work, you will end up with experts on one thing in the U.S. and experts on a different area in France. When not managed thoughtfully, dividing work in geographically split teams can lead to specialization, and that hurts the team in the long term because they lose their cross-functional nature and sense of team oneness. If a "plus" of the Agile team is their cross-functional skills and the abilities of team members to learn and grow from working with more experienced or innovative co-workers, you need to let them bridge the communication gap and continue to share ideas and expertise around the same user stories.

However, Team A, US/Europe, might do the software and Team B, South America/Australia, could do the product. But the work needs to be coordinated under the guidance of one project manager. In the example shown in Figure 11.1, the Agile team is split between Dallas, TX, and Paris, France, and the traditional team is split between Lima, Peru, and Sidney, Australia. Yet, the same Project Manager is managing both teams in all four locations.

You can split the project into multiple teams working between different offices or different cities, if necessary. But the teams who work together as one unit must *match* on their project methodology. Another structure is to split the Agile team and have them work together, and split the Waterfall team, but allow all teams to still share work from the *same* iteration backlog. The project manager now coordinates the two parts of the Agile team, and two parts of the Waterfall team, and then blends the work of those two mixed teams together to coordinate the single project goals they are fulfilling.

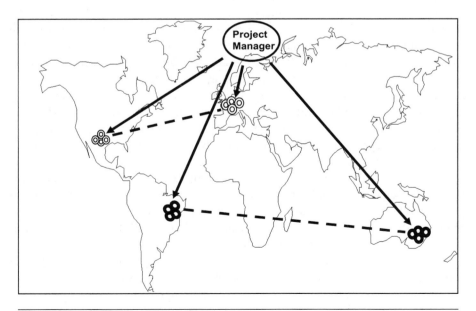

Figure 11.1 Divided, Distributed Teams

Again, the key to success is a skilled project manager. You are managing an Agile team and a Waterfall team, but in four locations. Although you will see even more fragmented teams commonly structured in organizations, usually it is best not to divide a single team between more than two locations. A better structure is to have three, four, or five intact teams that are in widespread locations, coordinated through one project manager and one product owner, or possibly multiple project managers reporting to one person at the program level. As project manager, you have to work within your organization's structure regarding the distribution of teams, but know and spread the word throughout your organization that each level of separation from collocation reduces the power of the Agile process.

In a recent survey of Agile projects, success rates for teams located in the same room were over 20% higher than those for geographically distributed teams. But despite those statistics, in the 2012 State of Agile Development survey conducted by VersionOne,[1] 57% of the respondents stated that their teams were distributed. Furthermore, 41% of the participants said that they were currently using, or planned to combine, Agile with outsourced development. When faced with these large numbers, it seems that the Agile practice of placing the entire team in a single room is at odds with what is actually going on within a large part of the business world. While collocating your team is clearly the recommended approach, many teams are unable to do this and are faced with trying to stick to Agile principles and also apply Agile practices to distributed development.

As project managers, we certainly do not have control over the decisions of our organizational leaders, and we do not have magical solutions for what upper management faces in today's world. With economic crises and the ease of international contact, as businesses seek to expand into new, global markets they need to gain expertise and a physical presence in those locations. Perhaps foreign locations are acquired through mergers and acquisitions, or perhaps it is prudent to set up subsidiaries located overseas to tap into emerging markets.

With news of high unemployment rates all over the world, finding workers seems like an easy problem to solve. Yet, increasingly, companies are casting nets wider when looking to hire quality employees with specific skills that are in short supply in the local workforce. Work visa availability, relocation costs, and the willingness and practicality of having new hires move are factors that tend to increase team distribution.

Companies also have their eyes on the bottom line and may seek to reduce costs through outsourcing to regions with less pricy resource pools and cheaper overhead. This can be an excellent solution, as there are skilled and motivated workers available all over the globe. An offshore provider may represent an apparent cost savings as high as 25%, although estimating actual savings is not always that clear. There are challenges in the management and communication of a distributed team structure that may add undetected overhead to the cost of a project, and there is more to the success of a geographically split team than just hiring workers with cheaper salary and benefits packages.

The hourly cost of individual team members may be lower, but reduced productivity and additional travel costs to manage, train, and coordinate the teams can negate a portion of these savings. It may become your job as project manager to track and compare costs to see if the savings are real, compared to the loss of flow to the value stream when a distributed team, by its very nature, adds an impediment to the communication flow of the project.

To see if distributed teams are a wise option, you may ask your boss if you can do a feasibility study to determine the actual savings compared to the outlay of cash needed to set up successful divided team work, communication, and reporting channels. It is important to realize that there is a tradeoff being made when a team is distributed. The benefits of team distribution, if not managed well, come at the cost of reduced performance and potentially, team dysfunction. Understanding the likely impact of distribution on your team, avoiding distribution when possible, and mitigating its impact when it is a necessity are key to success.

While there may be business reasons for distributing a team, distribution can also contribute to team dysfunction by inhibiting communication. Agile teams rely on intensive person-to-person communication, both within the team and with the customer. This allows them to forego some of the additional processes— like writing detailed specifications—that are usually associated with a more Waterfall approach.

Most of the practices discussed here can also be applied to teams who are in separate offices or floors of the same building. In all cases, teams need to be sure they have pinpointed ways to increase their communication and productivity when they move away from a "reach out and touch someone" team experience. Here are some issues that can cause team dissention and some suggestions for how to avoid it.

Casual Conversations

Casual conversations within the team room, in hallways, and other shared spaces make a significant contribution to the team's collective understanding of the project, the problems it faces as they evolve, the group's decisions to solve challenges that contribute to the feeling of "oneness" and team consensus, and the ongoing exchange of ideas and information that allows each person to grow and develop. This closeness also feeds into the personal needs of the individual to feel a part of things, to feel they are making a contribution, and to want to work to the best of their ability for the sake of the group.

So, when the communication bandwidth is narrowed by time and space, and garbled with language and cultural roadblocks, there must be new techniques deliberately introduced and mastered. Otherwise, poor communications can seriously reduce the most enthusiastic and talented team's agility.

Story Cards

In Chapter 2, we talked about user stories placed on story cards as a primarily tool to display and convey project direction and progress. In reality, a story card is a reminder that when the time comes to work on it, you may need to have a conversation with other teammates and the product owner to coordinate and double check your solution intent. Everything about that need cannot be contained in a few words on this small sticky note. It is a conversation placeholder until you arrive at the time in the project to collect the latest, freshest information, and get to the "last responsible minute" before you proceed to flesh out the specifics of a particular piece of functionality.

These two things, the story cards and the conversations, replace a more formal specification writing process for technical and functional requirements with something that will give the customer a more desirable and acceptable product. When teams are remote, the information contained on the story cards is insufficient to communicate what needs to be done, so they need to be supplemented with more detail. Plan for this to add more time and more cost to the project, but if the new goal is not just "done" but providing greater customer value, artificial means to simulate face-to-face exchanges will be a necessity.

One tip that enables sticky note user stories to be sent to remote teams is to use printable sticky notes. The originating team would use their usual "marker plus sticky-note" technique to hand write the story cards, capitalizing on the quickness and flexibility it allows for rapid change and easy prioritization. Then, the project manager or an administrative aid converts them into the printable Post-it note software application supplied free from 3M Corporation. The configured file can then be sent to the remote team. By printing the notes out on their end and posting them on a wall chart at their remote location, each team can see the same information in their own team room. Be sure to use an enormous font. Remember, the point is to be able to read these items from across the room. There will be a little more coordination required to keep the charts identical, but it is an option for you to consider.

Time Zones

How far apart are the time zones of the two parts of the team? Teams that span time zones have further challenges when it comes to communication. There are times during each person's working day when other members of the team are not available to them. If it is only about four hours, the morning of one team and the afternoon of another will overlap, allowing them to be in touch and receive quick feedback during at least part of the day. But there are negative impacts to team cohesiveness and the project timeline when, for half of each day, the other half of the team is not reachable.

This time zone gap can be mitigated somewhat by shifting core working hours on both teams to better align the teams. Inevitably, work will be delayed because clarification is needed from the unavailable team, or rework will need to be done when one person's best guess did not pan out when reviewed by the other half of the team. Regular reworking for this reason can also impact the team's progress, and morale suffers when people are repeatedly asked to rework yesterday's tasks.

If the time zone gap is 12 hours or more, the teams will never actually work at the same time, and the critical path, or the priority items from the backlog, can suffer while one team waits for a response, or a piece of the product, from the other team. Extra time equals extra money, and the lower salary savings of offshore teams can disappear in the cost of longer hours worked to coordinate activities.

One technique to keep opposite sides of the clock teams in sync is to have a team representative work late to contact the other team and share the progress and problems of the day. The remote team will also need their corresponding, local team representative to perform the same outreach and update function at the end of their day to close the two-team feedback loop. In addition to the regularly scheduled data and reports, be sure that these after-hours liaisons also capture water cooler and hallway conversations that open up team issues, potential project risks, or upcoming bottlenecks. Do not forget to capture overtime and phone call expenses for these solutions to evaluate for impact to the project cost.

Language

Do the teams speak the same language? If not, will there by an extra expense to have a translator in each location or to purchase translation software? Will there be a risk of errors from misinterpreted requirements or customer requests due to language and/or cultural differences? What will the time zone delays do to the ability to complete work within the iteration timebox when each team member adds on the extra burden of translation time? The informal team bonding and innovative solutions that may result from chatting over coffee in a collocated experience can be lost for both sides in a remote team structure.

When working with team members from another culture, especially over the phone when each side is removed from the non-verbal face and body language, try to be very clear. Have you heard the story about the project manager whose wife left him a voicemail that said, "After work, could you please go to the store for me and buy one carton of milk...and if they have eggs, get six." When the husband arrived home, he had six cartons of milk. His wife asked, "Why in the world did you buy six cartons of milk?" He replied, "They had eggs." The same type of language miscommunication can occur between distributed teams, leading to different results than intended in the work of the project.

Avoid informal jargon and cultural idioms that are conversational shortcuts for one team, but meaningless and indecipherable to the other. For example, sports metaphors and references to movies, TV shows, and popular song lyrics are often lost on people from a different culture, which has its own popular idioms and catchphrases.

For example, in North America, we might talk of an overkill of extra features as "Carrying coals to Newcastle," "Gilding the lily," or "Selling ice to the Eskimos." The Chinese might characterize "overkill" as "Drawing a snake and adding feet to it." This saying is based on the story of a man who gave a jug of wine to his servants. They did not know how to divide the wine, so they decided that each person would draw a snake on the ground and the person who finished first would drink the wine. One man finished drawing, but the others were still busy, so he decided to add feet to his snake. Before he completed the feet, someone else finished and grabbed the wine, saying, "Who has ever seen a snake with feet?" The saying would mean nothing to North Americans without an explanation.

Reduced communication has even more impact when coaching new team members and integrating them into the team. Many of the practices used by Agile software teams, like pair programming and test-driven development, are learned and grasped most rapidly by demonstrating them in a one-on-one coaching session. Again, not an insurmountable obstacle in the face of the reality of a distributed team, but one you must plan for and implement the solutions with additional care.

Since distributed teams are a growing part of the project management team environment and often make excellent business sense, a part of your evolution as a project manager is to become skilled in new techniques. To keep communications flowing, teams need access to international phone calls, automated project software linked to a server, and opportunities for webcam, video conferencing, and other electronic links for team meetings to capture and exchange information. You can price these services and collect other hidden costs for teams that are non-collocated, subtracting the costs from resource payroll savings, to show your organization the true cost of distributed teams and to push for realistic project budgets.

Communications Tools

There are some simple practices and easy-to-use tools you can implement to improve communications between teams.

Video Teleconferencing and Web Conferencing

One way to minimize the overhead of setting up meetings across locations is to have a conference phone and projector easily accessible—ideally in the team room of both teams—for impromptu meetings. There are many third-party vendors to facilitate teleconferencing calls. Allowing the team to get together regularly, as well as spontaneously, when a small group of two or three members need to brainstorm, check data, or show results, is crucial.

Teams can use Web conferencing software in conjunction with a projector to either show on a screen in one location, or have all team members see the slides on their own laptops or other electronic devices. Video conferencing, if available, is even better than just a voice presentation with slides, as participants are less likely to disengage or to do other work at the same time. If meeting rooms are hard to find on short notice in your building, can each project team "own" a dedicated conference room with a phone and a projector? Third-party conference services are low cost, and allow groups with access to a computer the opportunity to set up and hold conferences with audio and video features without the need to purchase, install, and house the software locally.

Collaboration Technology

One Agile practice is that two people might work together to create, innovate, and proof documents on the go, rather than one person writing it alone and then sending it to someone else for proofing. In software development, it is called pair programming, but the technique is equally workable for other types of projects. For example, think of two marketing people working on ad copy for a product release, or two trainers collaborating on the user training for your product's customers.

Hands-free headsets for a long-distance phone connection and collaborative software that allows two people to share their computer screens over the Internet can help disparate locations bridge the distance gap. Check out free phone services like Skype and other software solutions for screen sharing that allow free tests to explore the possibilities.

Instant Messaging (IM)

Although many corporations frown on the use of individuals communicating during work hours via a smartphone, instant messaging by phone or Windows

Live Messenger can give the teams almost synchronous peer connections. Again, an immediate interface with your corresponding member of the remote team can be key to overcoming the negatives introduced by distance. Questions can be answered quickly through IM even when the colleague is out of the office.

Web Cams

Some organizations are experimenting with live Web cams that are turned on all the time to connect two geographically separated team rooms, replicating the advantage that a collocated team has of seeing who is at their desk and available to talk at any given point in the day. An always-on Web cam is often coupled with a conference line that is constantly open; no dialing, just pick up the phone and ask for the person you need to talk to on the other end. You may want to see if there are problems with speed or bandwidth limitations, depending on the location of your sister team, but those challenges should disappear with time. You can expect to see more sophisticated devices that are designed for routine business exchanges in the near future.

3D Telecommunications

Web cams allow you to see a person's face, but the two-dimensional limits of a screen do not convey the same sense of reality as having the person in-the room. Queen's University in Ontario, Canada, has developed a new product called the *TeleHuman*. If you saw the *Star Wars* movies, you may recall the Sith Lords looking at tiny representations of humans, with whom they could carry on conversations. Similarly, TeleHuman is a life-sized cylindrical pod that allows a telepresence of the person on the other end of the conversation. You can walk 360 degrees around the projected 3D presence of a remote colleague, who appears inside the physical pod that sits in the conference room. Sensors on your end capture your placement, and allow the 3D person to turn and follow your movements, too.[2]

Cisco Corporation, in cooperation with Musion Systems, has had their own product, TelePresence, at work in 28 countries since November of 2007. TelePresence allows speakers on a stage (or in two mutually equipped conference rooms) to see and hear people as far apart as the United Kingdom and India. The 3D holographic display technology allows people on both sides of the interaction to appear, hear, and speak as though they were standing right next to you in the presentation venue. In addition, multiple people can appear at the same time, and be further rebroadcast out to any type of broadband device. Other team members, or stakeholders, could participate from their respective workspaces, or even from home. Think of adding in product owners to meetings, even if their executive travel plans have them away from your home office.[3]

You may be envisioning the positive effects this type of communications tool could have for remote collaboration between distributed teams. The missing body language cues inherent in remote team interchanges are crucial. Even in communication between people who speak the same language, 93% of understanding is often ascribed to the non-verbal signals. That percentage goes up when working in a cross-cultural, cross-language team.

Another capability for group collaboration over long distances is the HoloDesk, by Microsoft Research, an invention that allows for virtual, rapid prototyping between distributed team members. It might also be used as a solution for remote product owner demonstrations by the "away team." This will be of special interest to the product development community. HoloDesk allows you to reach into a physical box at your location with your bare hand, and pick up and manipulate virtual 3D objects. Bounce them, roll them, stack them, or re-arrange them—it is up to you to envision the value of this technology for distributed project teams.[4]

Work Tracking Tools

Despite the popularity of the sticky note information radiator to show work and track progress, in a divided team it can be less effective. Instead, there are several brands of virtual whiteboards, where what you write is duplicated via a wi-fi connected second board in the remote site. What is drawn on one appears on the other, and a camera and audio connection may also be bundled into the product. After the data is handwritten, the board can print out hard copies on both sides of the globe. Software exists that can allow you to use the concept of sticky notes to arrange and rearrange user story type documents electronically, viewed by all team members who have computer or Internet device access.

Even familiar solutions such as e-mail or automated software tools are also becoming increasingly customized for Agile teams. Often, they allow you to visually format things as though they were written on sticky notes, so the remote team can project the image on a wall or screen, and share the advantage of having an easy-to-see tracking tool that is shared by both teams on a constant basis. The market has lagged in software that uses this approach for more hybrid teams, so if this is your area of expertise, here is an idea to make your first million.

Remote Daily Stand-ups

Remote teams, denied the privilege of talking to other colleagues throughout the day, may need to extend their virtual communications into slightly longer daily stand-up meetings. One prototype procedure could be the regular "what I did, what I will do, what I need" report from each team member. Then, although the main team meeting ends, the remote team can ask (or be asked) to remain "on the line" for additional questions, comments, or issues to be discussed in smaller groups of team members directly involved in the issue. Your teams may find that the additional time for these daily meetings reduces their velocity, but it is part of the reality of distributed teams.

Travel

In most organizations, cross-country or international travel is usually limited to individuals at the management level. However, companies are finding that extra dollars spent to allow teams to meet and spend a few days working together, perhaps for the first few iterations at the beginning of a project, can recoup that cost in the speed and smoothness of the project's productivity. Travel would make good business sense in the case of a standing, dedicated, but distributed team that will work together on many projects. This allows the team members to get to know one another, and to build rapport and trust.

The more the entire team can assemble and be a part of hearing the project owner describe the vision and the reasons that the project is of importance, the more fully the people will commit to the goal. Being involved with the initial decisions about the project is extremely motivating. Do not make the mistake of thinking that the team members are not equally skilled knowledge workers in every location around the world.

During shared visits, it is effective to arrange social events, so that people can get to know each other on a personal level. Plan for team members in the host location to join the visitors for lunch and coffee, talk informally, and build a bond during the day. Arrange evening events such as dinners or opportunities to meet the host team's family members. If travel is not in the cards, be aware that there will be a longer ramp-up time for the team to gel, and begin to work in a cooperative and cohesive manner.

The Lone Expert

One of the hardest situations to facilitate is when you have the bulk of your team together, but one lone consultant or remote expert is located off-site. This person does not constitute a critical mass to justify round-the-clock Web cams or fancy projection equipment. Usually, this person is joining by phone, while the rest of the team benefits from the whiteboard drawings, silent gestures, facial expressions, and side conversations. Fortunately for the lone person's feelings, they often do not realize what is happening that they cannot see. But unfortunately for the team, here is an important member that is missing out on the full experience of the team discussions.

Daily Agile stand-up meetings are self-directed by the team, rather than facilitated with the project manager as the leader. So, remind the team at the start to be mindful of the "lone" expert on the other end of the phone, and remember his or her point of view so you can describe visuals that cannot be seen. Another option is to ask one of the team to be the expert's "buddy," making sure that what is said is understandable to the person only connected by phone.

Some project managers attempt to solve this issue by saying that if one person has to be on the phone, they will level the playing field by having *everyone* go back to their desks and the whole team will be on the phone for the conference call. This is a poor solution. It punishes the entire team and inhibits their ability to participate in one of the most valuable parts of the Agile experience—face-to-face communication. It also adds resentment toward the off-site participant, which is the opposite of your intended agenda. Instead, have team members take turns being the person who accesses the meeting by telephone. To experience what it is like to be that person may make them sensitive to the feelings and needs of the lone, remote caller.

References

[1]State of Agile Development survey conducted by VersionOne, 2012, Retrieved from http://versionone.com.

[2]Wagstaff, K. May 4, 2012. "Videoconference like a Sith Lord with 3D Hologram Telepods." *TIME Techland*. Retrieved from http://techland.time.com.

[3]"3D Hologram: Best Video Conference Ever." November 15, 2007. *Singularity Hub*. Retrieved from http://singularityhub.com.

[4]"HoloDesk—Direct 3D Interactions with a Situated See-Through Display." September 23, 2011. *Microsoft Research*. Retrieved from http://research.microsoft.com

What Do I Use for Agile Documentation?

Agile means lighter documentation, so often things are done on sticky notes. Visibility of team progress is better since it is in full view at all times. Management, customers, and other interested department personnel can also see how the team is doing as they walk by on the way to the lunchroom, or the bathroom.

To save less rigid information, you can roll up paper charts and save them, take a picture of a whiteboard to archive, or attach a photo to a Microsoft Project, Primavera, or other software file in the Notes field. Notes could also be photographed and forwarded directly to other interested stakeholders right from your smartphone.

Perhaps you can create other minimal ways to record a project. Remember, we are using Agile because we are working on innovative projects with highly changing requirements, so what we did on the last project may not be that important to spend days documenting. Next time, we will likely be doing something totally different.

Earned Value Method

Software developers and other departments dealing with uncertainty are increasingly convinced that a more flexible, Agile approach to creating project deliverables is the best way to produce high-quality, working features that solve customer problems and provide business value. However, project management offices (PMOs) are continuing to develop procedures and train project managers in traditional approaches that have worked successfully in the past in most other parts of the corporation. Is there a way to blend the reporting between the two factions, so that upper management can have matching metrics such as earned value variances from both areas? Yes, sort of.

If you are new to the **Earned Value Management** (EVM) method, it is *a numeric tracking of progress and the business value of that progress* on a weekly, monthly, or quarterly basis. The *PMBOK® Guide* defines it as, "A management methodology for integrating scope, schedule, and resources, and for objectively measuring project performance and progress."[1] Performance is measured by determining the Budgeted Cost of Work Performed (Earned Value) and comparing it to the Budgeted Cost of Work Scheduled (Planned Value). It is intended to fill in the gap to show team progress in lengthy projects where little or no tangible evidence is available for the stakeholders see to assess movement toward the project goals. In an over-simplistic explanation, ignoring the cost factors, the project manager (and other stakeholders) define requirements and estimate the amount of time it will take to do the work of the project. These estimates are converted into a schedule.

Let's say the reporting time period was one week and the traditional project team was assigned 40 pre-defined tasks to complete in that week, a certain number to each team member. On Friday afternoons, each team member reports their actual progress. If everyone got all of their tasks finished in those 40 hours, they "earned" 40 hours of value (Earned Value or EV). They had originally estimated, or planned, 40 hours (Planned Value or PV) worth of value would be done during the week. The formula to use to see if the project is on schedule is:

$$\text{Earned Value (EV)} - \text{Planned Value (PV)} = \text{Schedule Variance (SV)}$$
$$40 \text{ hours EV} - 40 \text{ hours PV} = 0 \text{ SV}$$

A clearer way to state it is, "What I got minus what I planned to get," shows me if I am on track with the original plan. In this case, they had zero Schedule Variance. The work had been done exactly as planned.

However, if the team got behind and finished only 36 hours of work, the schedule would be behind and other workers down the line need to be alerted. If the team finished early, the original time estimates might have been excessive, and incoming materials vendors or other project participants will need to be alerted that their tasks may start earlier than anticipated. Remember, the scope (work) of the project has already been set in a traditional project.

For the Agile team, velocity is the method used to measure the productivity of a team. It is used to allow the team to undertake a specific amount of work for an upcoming timeboxed period, not to exceed the amount of work the team completed during the last iteration. However, since this team is being compared to themselves and their last iteration user story choices, rather than to a long-term schedule plan pre-created for the entire project, there is no need to reschedule the work of others if the total number of story points created varies. Others will note the progress line on the wall charts, or hear about it in the daily stand-up meeting.

Further, the tasks for this week may be easier, have fewer bugs, or be more familiar to the group. In the Agile project, the total number of features of the end product has not been set in stone. So if the velocity is not as fast as originally estimated, the scope (amount of features delivered) can be adjusted.

The project manager who is rolling together reports from the software development project, or other Agile projects, in with marketing, manufacturing, training, etc., needs a common reporting metric. The simplest approach is to give information technology (IT) or the non-IT Agile team a block of time (and a corresponding payroll amount) to work on the features and functions of the project. On the reports, show two weeks of time, for example. When you submit Agile team reports, also submit the features/stories completed for the project manager to convert to task names and fill in after the fact. This allows traditional reports to show Agile progress alongside more traditional team numbers.

Agile Earned Value

Some organizations are big on Earned Value. If you manage both an Agile team and a Waterfall team, here is a way to calculate **Agile Earned Value**. Figure 12.1 shows a **Daily Burndown Chart**. Although traditional project management approaches for tracking a project that may extend months or years typically capture progress on a weekly basis, since the iterations in an Agile process are so short, teams may prefer to track their work and see their accomplishments on a daily basis. If your company insists that you calculate Earned Value, you can do it from the information shown. The grey dotted line in Figure 12.1 is the plan. That is the amount of work scheduled… the number of difficulty points, story points, or estimated hours that your team committed to perform for the iteration based on their velocity in the preceding iteration. It has been arbitrarily divided by the number of days in the iteration, less the time set aside for Agile team meetings.

The grey dotted line on the chart, your plan, is also called the BCWS (Budgeted Cost of Work Scheduled) for software tools, or PV (Planned Value) for Waterfall people. Start at the left of the chart and you can see that your team committed to do 63, then 56, then 49 points, and so on. On a Waterfall team, since the activities of the WBS were estimated in time, it is easy to convert the total time for all tasks assigned to one person to a dollar amount, by multiplying the total hours times the person's hourly wage.

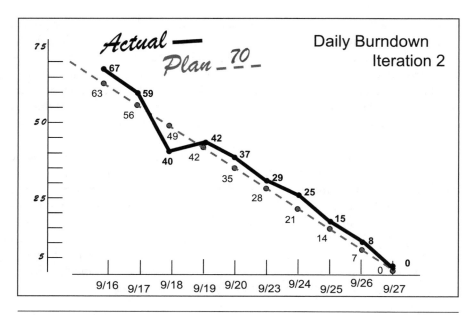

Figure 12.1 Daily Burndown Chart

The black line on the chart is the actual amount of work performed (EV), the number of difficulty points or story points your team completed. Perhaps someone was ill or on vacation, so the amount of the team work accomplished was lower for Day 3. In most project management software applications, this is called BCWP (Budgeted Cost of Work Performed), but it was renamed EV (Earned Value) at the same time BCWS was renamed PV (Planned Value) in recent versions of the *PMBOK® Guide*.[2] Both BCWP and EV mean exactly the same thing, just as BCWS and PV are identical.

For Agile-ites, PV is your velocity, the number of difficulty or story points the team has committed to complete this iteration. If the black line is above the grey dotted one on your Daily Burndown Chart, as shown in Figure 12.1, you did more work than you planned. If the black line is under the gray dotted line, you completed less work than planned. Remember, with an Agile team, or a team to which you are adding more Agile behavior, unless we are forced to do so by organizational rules, we are trying to get away from wasting time doing lots of metrics looking backwards. What we chart on a daily basis is immaterial compared to the quality and releasability of what we create by the end of the iteration.

Earned Value is a backwards look at what numbers show was accomplished during the previous measurement period. It is used when there is no tangible result to show to the customer or product owner at the end of the work period. That is why you will hear people in the Agile world say, "There is a reason a car has a bigger windshield than rearview mirror." The team tends to look forward to the work of the next iteration, rather than backwards to the metrics of the past, which cannot be changed.

Plus, the goal of an Agile team is not to just finish story points to rack up scores that equal velocity projections. They are committed to providing business value and return on investment in complex project settings, so quality issues override meeting abstract number quotas. Showing the customer actual progress in tangible form at the demonstration after each iteration eventually negates the need to figure Earned Value as a way to show mathematical progress, as compared to that need in a long, Waterfall project where nothing was assembled until the last few weeks of the schedule. And, if you can include levels of management above the product owner in demonstrations, you can eventually lighten the need for formal documents.

For the traditional team, there is another part of Earned Value that measures the *cost* of completing the work done within the measurement period. It is called ACWP (Actual Cost of Work Performed) or AC. This is the metric involved in tracking the budget of a project. If you budgeted that in this measurement period, you would spend $40,000 in payroll and material costs. That amount could vary if you lost an employee, or received materials either ahead time or later than scheduled. BCWP (Budgeted Cost of Work Performed) compared to ACWP (Actual Cost of Work Performed) gives you the Cost Variance (CV), showing how far you are from the budget you planned for the time period in question:

$$\text{BCWP (or EV)} - \text{ACWP (or AC)} = \text{Cost Variance (CV)}$$

Particularly in software and web development, Agile teams have little cost to the project other than payroll amounts. If new equipment is needed, it may be figured as a total amount charged against the project rather than tracked iteration by iteration. But, if it is necessary for the happiness of your corporate home for the Agile team to track costs, you can take the hourly salary of each team member and multiply it by the number of working hours your company considers a standard work week, to come up with a weekly total for the team. In organizations where individual salaries are proprietary information, a standardized or median hourly salary figure can be substituted. That is your Actual Cost per week. Multiply it times the number of weeks in the iteration if you are tracking by that timebox, rather than week by week. It is a pointless metric if you are working with a dedicated team, as each person will be estimated at a 40 hour work week and complete a 40 hour work week. Vacation time and sick leave are still charged against the project.

If this is an Agile project where you track your own materials costs, add them as they are received. Since the story points axis of your Burndown Chart,

Figure 12.1, is not in dollars, you can track this cost metric on a second chart where the vertical axis *is* in dollars. Agile teams, particularly those that are dedicated, seldom see a fluxuation in salary costs during the short time of the project (as opposed to longer Waterfall projects where overtime and raises may occur), so they soon abandon this extra work unless it is mandatory in your business setting.

If the PMO, or the organization's management team, insists on seeing Earned Value Management (EVM) numbers, Agile EVM can be figured by using story points completed or finished for the iteration. Finished Story Points (FSP) are the equivalent of Earned Value (EV) or Budgeted Cost of Work Performed (BCWP). Committed Story Points (CSP) are the difficulty points, or story points, the team has opted to complete during the current iteration. CSP is the equivalent of Planned Value (PV) or Budgeted Cost of Work Scheduled (BCWS). The Finished Story Points (FSP) less the Committed Story Points (CSP) for the iteration gives you Agile Schedule Variance:

FSP (or EV) – CSP (or PV) = ASV (Agile Schedule Variance)

Although you can figure Earned Value metrics for both traditional and Agile teams, it is relatively useless to try to use them to compare the progress or success of the team by using these values. In order for this to work, on a traditional team, each member must supply the project manager with his or her individual number of hours worked on each activity during the reporting period. That in itself is hard enough to track, so there is a lot of acknowledged "estimating" when people report status. And, what percent complete are they? How does someone estimate if they are 22.75% complete or 62.75%? Even the most skilled team members have to just make a best guess. Agile teams track work that is *done* and *approved*.

To add to this challenge, there are various methods by which the company may ask you to determine when to credit the progress on an activity. In some organizations, merely starting a task may give it a value of 20% complete by using the 20/80 technique, and 50% if you choose to assign half of the value of the activity when it is begun and the other 50% at completion. When comparing statistics between teams, the project manager must be sure that the same **start-finish rule** is in use in each instance.

To ease this confusion, Agile teams do not assign any value (completed story point credit) to the work of their task until it is 100% done. In traditional project lingo, they use the 0-100% method, i.e., the task has no value when it is started, or at any point along the way. Only when it is completely finished can the team member move it to the "Done" or "Approved" column, and take 100% credit for the story points. In fact, Agile teams even question the term "Done", asking each other, "Is it "Done", "Done Done", or "Done Done Done"?" referring to various acceptance standards. Only the last answer garners permission to add the 100% value to the project schedule.

There are different metrics and standards to use with your non-IT team to define "Done." Be sure to talk about them in the early session when you define team rules. You might consider something like a user story is "Done" when the team member finishes his or her work and tests on it. "Done Done," may mean it passes internal quality inspections, integrates with other necessary parts of the product or service, and works when checked out with a larger group of users than just the team member. "Done Done Done," might be reserved for when it passes outside compliance inspections. There are no specific rules as to when you take the 100% "Done" credit for finishing a user story, but be sure to have all your team in agreement on how you will judge it. Setting out these completion metrics upfront is your best bet.

Since the team's velocity, or ability to complete the story points to which they have committed, tends to remain fairly stable over the course of the project after the first week or two, as project manager, you can figure Earned Value for use by the people upstairs, but it may provide little value to managing your team and completing the work of your project. If you only take on story points based on what you actually accomplished last week, your schedule variation will be very small from iteration to iteration, and not a useful metric for management to use to judge the effectiveness of the team. However, if you are forced to figure EV, have this be your own task as the project manager, considering it your contribution to removing constraints from the value stream of the project. Free your team to work on the actual production of business value by completing the project work.

While no one disputes the value of well-done metrics, unfortunately too many organizations measure what is easy, instead of what is valuable and relevant. Note that the value of any metric diminishes over time, but completed project deliverables do not. It has been said that too many unnecessary metrics can be like a vampire, draining the life-giving blood of time from the project team.

Software Documents

If you have a project with many teams scaled up through the enterprise, or geographically dispersed around the world, realistically you may have to revert back to automated software for record keeping. There are many vendor solutions. A Microsoft Project example is shown in Figure 12.2, which is a continuation of the sample project from Figure 5.5. If this was an Agile team's information included in a larger, enterprise Waterfall project, notice that you could create a summary task of "Online Bank for Small Customers." (This means low dollar business, not tiny people.)

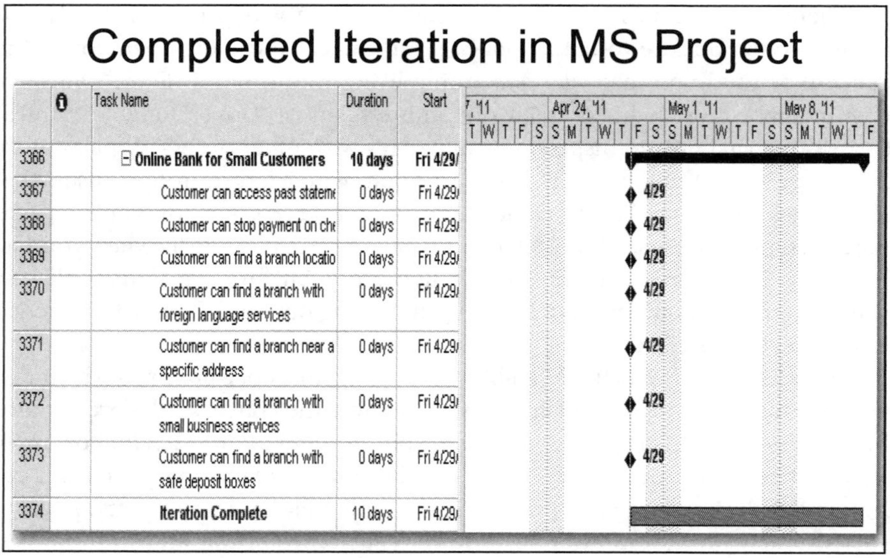

Completed Iteration in MS Project

🛈	Task Name	Duration	Start	...11	Apr 24, '11	May 1, '11	May 8, '11
				T W T F S S	M T W T F S S	M T W T F S S	M T W T F
3366	⊟ **Online Bank for Small Customers**	**10 days**	**Fri 4/29/**		▽		▼
3367	Customer can access past stateme	0 days	Fri 4/29/		◆ 4/29		
3368	Customer can stop payment on che	0 days	Fri 4/29/		◆ 4/29		
3369	Customer can find a branch locatio	0 days	Fri 4/29/		◆ 4/29		
3370	Customer can find a branch with foreign language services	0 days	Fri 4/29/		◆ 4/29		
3371	Customer can find a branch near a specific address	0 days	Fri 4/29/		◆ 4/29		
3372	Customer can find a branch with small business services	0 days	Fri 4/29/		◆ 4/29		
3373	Customer can find a branch with safe deposit boxes	0 days	Fri 4/29/		◆ 4/29		
3374	**Iteration Complete**	**10 days**	**Fri 4/29/**				

Figure 12.2 Completed Iteration in Microsoft Project

The two-week iteration for the Agile team means that they will have 10 working days, so enter 10 days for the Duration. Heresy, you say! We *never* assign a Duration to the Summary Task in an automated software tool! Just go along with this for a moment—we're evolving!

Next, assign the *entire* Agile team to this summary task. No, you say! We *never* assign Resources to the Summary Task. But watch how this works out. The next step is to indent and put in the stories from the backlog the customer has said are of highest value and that the team thinks they can complete this iteration. As a customer, I can access past statements, as a customer I can stop payment on a check, as a customer I can find a branch location, and so on.

Notice that there are no Durations for these sub-task items. We do not usually estimate in hours or days for Agile; we look at degree of difficulty and story points, so leave the hours blank. Plus, we do not really care which day these things got done or who did them—we only care that, as a team, we completed a finished portion of a workable product or service that provides value to the customer by the end of the iteration, and that when we show it to him, the customer is happy.

At the end of the iteration indent, type *Iteration Complete*, and add 10 days as the Duration. All of the team's Resource Hours calculate at the pay rates that they have been assigned in the hidden Resource Sheet. All of the stories show as completed tasks on the Gantt Chart along the right side of the screen and calculate to show your Project Statistics, including number of work hours, behind the scenes in the Microsoft Project database.

This is very minimal, "barely sufficient" documentation, but it will work if your organization insists that you must put Agile team progress into Microsoft Project, or similar software. Really, we are still running the work of the Agile or hybrid team from the wall charts in our team area, our constantly visible information radiator. This automated software work is just to humor the organization and submit the required reports in the approved format.

If you are using the proprietary methodology, Scrum, for a software or web development team, there is a free add-on to Microsoft Project 2010 called the *Microsoft Project 2010 Scrum Solution*. The link for a free download and license is on the Web Added Value page of the publisher's site (www.jrosspub.com). This add-on forces you to estimate by hours, rather than degree of difficulty, which is not really a true Agile practice, but for more traditional teams working in organizations with a heavy commitment to Microsoft Project, it may be a solution worth exploring. As this and other products are improved, you can expect to have more functional software to blend both Agile and more traditional team documents. There are also many programs specifically intended for Agile software development teams, but you will need to evaluate how well they track and show the data that your management needs you to capture in the non-IT world.

So far, we know why we are changing to Agile, some specific changes that we can make to our project practices, and some ways to revise documentation. Keep following the "barely sufficient" theory. Ask management what numbers or reports they absolutely must have and explain why heavy documentation and reporting can drain team productivity. But, be a realist. Changing project culture is not fast or easy. Sometimes when you start to move to a more Agile process, it is necessary to work with the tools that your organization already has and requires.

Burndown Chart with Scope Changes

A traditional team focuses much of its energy on upfront planning, with the specific goal of minimizing change during the course of the project. But, if the whole point of Agile is to be more responsive to changes in the business and economic development, we have to have an easy way to show scope changes, and using traditional methods may prove challenging.

It is simple to start with a fixed amount of scope per iteration and show normal team progress. But when scope changes adjust the original amount of story points in the product backlog, being able to still adequately show the team progress is challenging, but not impossible. Simple math on a spreadsheet will never tell the story as clearly as a visual will. For example, if the product backlog for the entire project is 600 story points and the team velocity is 60 story points per iteration, after Iteration 1 you might expect the backlog to be reduced from 600 to 540 points. Makes sense, right?

But if the product owner has discovered the competition has recently added new functionality to its product, he may have added 50 new story points at the end of Iteration 1, as he is welcome to do. This brings the backlog back up to 580 points. Looking at the numbers alone, it is hard to see the truth of what has happened during this iteration. Did the team complete only 33 1/3% of the story points it committed to? Was their velocity only 20 points instead of 60? The Backlog only shows a reduction of 20 points. We know the truth; the challenge is how do we show it?

Here's one successful technique. You can see in Figure 12.3 that this new project originally had 150 story points as its scope, as each box along the left is 10 story points. Assume this team had a velocity of 40 story points an iteration, so at the end of Iteration 1 this chart shows that they have burned down (completed) 40 story points and ended up at the 110 point mark. A dotted line projection

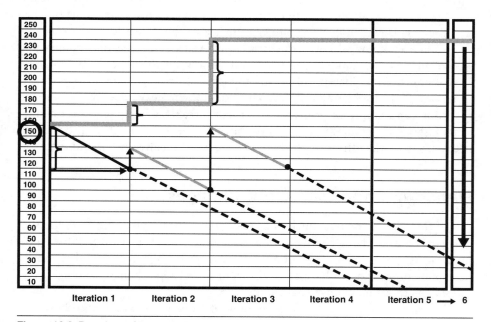

Figure 12.3 Burndown Chart with Scope Changes

shows that we are set to complete the work of the project at the end of the fourth iteration, as planned.

But after the demonstration at the end of Iteration 1, the customer added an additional 20 story points of scope to the project. That's OK. That's why we are Agile. We are here to create what the customer wants and needs, to drive business value, not to protect our pretty documentation. So, we go to the original scope line of the project, 150 story points, and move the scope line up 20 points on that same vertical line that shows the end of Iteration 1, and begins Iteration 2. Our total scope for the project is now 170 story points.

At the end of Iteration 2, once again our Agile team met their velocity goal of 40 points, so we show that with a line from the 130 point mark (110 points where we ended Iteration 1 plus the 20 story points added by the customer). Subtract the 40 points for this iteration and we end at the 90 point mark.

As we project out towards the finish line with the dotted line, we see that the team will not finish everything by the original finish date. But that's OK, because the customer who added the extra 20 points also re-prioritized the backlog of stories and knows the team won't get them all completed. But she also knows that they are working on the ones she has told them are the most important ones. The decision to add scope was a customer one, not a team one.

At the end of Iteration 2, after the demo the customer has found serious gaps between our product and that of a competitor; plus, she even has some user surveys that ask for additional features. In response, she ups the scope by 60 story points. So, we up the scope baseline from 170 to 230 story points. We also move our team starting point up 60 points, from 90 up to 150, to account for this second scope increase. We have the customer re-prioritize the backlog again, and we begin Iteration 3.

At the end of Iteration 3, the team has still met its planned velocity of 40 story points, so we mark the progress line from our new 150 point starting place down to the 110 point mark. At this point, we can see that it will take well into a sixth iteration to finish all that is in the backlog. The customer can decide if she wants to pay for the additional iterations, or if at the planned end of the project, Iteration 4, the work that will be completed is enough for the project to deliver the value she needs.

The documentation clearly shows that the team did their part properly, hitting their planned velocity each iteration. It is also clear that voluntary scope changes by the customer added more than the capability of the team to complete within the original estimated project roadmap, but she knows that it was her choice to expand the features and functions of the project, so it does not reflect poorly on the team. Also, by moving the high value items to the front of the queue each time, the customer has us focused on returning value on her investment in each iteration.

Burnup Chart

Another version of an information radiator by which Agile teams can track progress is by using a **Burnup Chart**. Think of a Burnup Chart in terms of the earlier example of building a brick wall, discussed in Chapter 8. Sure, there are industry metrics that give time and scope, but what really shows progress to the client is seeing the actual wall grow in height, day by day. That is the premise behind the Burnup Chart. Each day of the iteration, or each iteration of the release, the team, project manager, and the product owner can watch the completed work grow toward the "finish line" at the top.

In Figure 12.4, you can see the volume of project work measured along the vertical axis, and the completed work by the team is tracked on the horizontal axis. The top gray line represents the scope, and you can observe that it increased at the end of Iteration 4. You can also see the gray line for the planned delivery assumes that the team will achieve a consistent velocity, and then the black line shows the actual delivery rate.

Cumulative Flow Diagram

Another popular visual look at the work and progress of an Agile team can be found in a Cumulative Flow Diagram, ordinarily created in Excel or other software

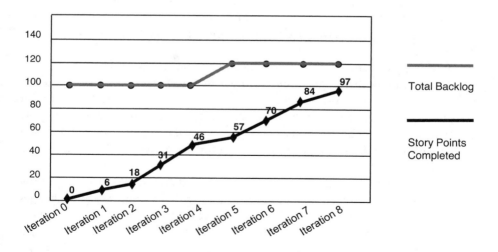

Figure 12.4 Burnup Chart

applications. As shown in Figure 12.5, this example allows you to view the Total Backlog of the project, plus, shows how much work was In Progress each month compared to how much of the work has been Done at any given point.

While this chart is prepared using months, you can adjust that metric to show whatever timeline you want. This is an excellent diagnostic tool for process flow. You will note that in July, there was not a large amount of work completed, but this could be due to the fact that this was Iteration Zero, a time when design and prototyping issues were being resolved. Once those decisions were made, August shows great inroads toward completing work.

At the end of September or beginning of October, you can see that less work was In Progress, but the amount of work Done grew nicely. Perhaps some of the user stories proved to be more complex than anticipated, so fewer were worked on. Or perhaps, this is reflective of a team member missing from the team for any number of reasons. Do not get the number of story points for the iteration confused with the number of story points that have been moved to the In Progress column of the To Do list.

You can see that at the beginning of November, the amount of work In Progress grew. The missing team member may have returned, and some snags on user stories may have led to a larger than normal amount of stories awaiting final approval authorizations. These suggestions regarding how you might interpret this chart are not necessarily accurate. The point of a Cumulative Flow Diagram is that you, as the project manager, can clearly observe fluxuations in the process flow

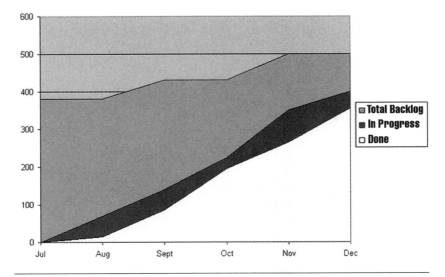

Figure 12.5 Cumulative Flow Diagram

and look at your own teams to see how and why they occurred. Are there changes you could make in the organization processes to smooth them out? Are there still constraints blocking the work of your team that need to be removed? This is your diagnostic tool to look at the overall flow of business value.

You can also look at project statistics other than just the three in this sample. Where is your project team feeling the pain? How can you diagnose the cause and remove it? It is not necessary to choose only one chart, or one way to represent team progress on the walls of the team room. Use them all, or whatever best fits the team situation you have and the requirements of your organization.

References

[1]Project Management Institute. 2008. *A Guide to the Project Management Body of Knowledge (PMBOK®)*. 4th ed. Project Management Institute, Inc.
[2]*ibid.*

What Needs to Change in My Own Skill Set?

So far, we know why we are changing to Agile *now*, and some specific changes we can make to projects and project documents to blend Agile attributes into Waterfall teams. However, we still need to talk about some additional things that we need to do *personally*, as project managers, to evolve. Obviously, you need to know both Agile and Waterfall processes for managing projects. Reading this book means that you are off to a promising start. Remember, the good news is that there is a huge demand, and corresponding financial rewards, for project managers who have a firm foundation in traditional Waterfall processes, but also know Agile and how to blend it into an organization's existing corporate culture.

Self-managed Teams

It is important to know how to lead self-managed teams. There is often some confusion over terms here. The technical term for how Agile teams work is that they are *self-directed*. If you are communicating with people on the "little agile" side, go ahead and use that term. But it has a connotation for most of us that means the team generates their own path. This is far from true. The project manager still works with the organization to coordinate the direction of the team, and make sure it is working to fulfill the organizational vision and goals, regardless of the methodology, or mix of methodologies, that they employ to do it.

The real idea is that the Agile or hybrid team members are now managing themselves. They don't have an overseer that tells them every small detail of day-to-day work. The knowledge workers set up their own team rules, communicate daily with each other and with project stakeholders, work together to solve problems, and rely on the project manager to remove the organizational roadblocks that keep them from driving product value through the value stream.

If your background is heavy with experience that is more autocratic, you may need to take a course, read books, or work with a coach to learn a new style of management. We all think that we know how to manage. However, most of us do not have those skills innately embedded, and in particular we do not know how to manage in a way that we have never experienced in our days as a "worker bee." In our role as a project manager, we may not have stopped to realize that we are called project *managers*. Now, we are being asked to shift to become project *leaders*.

There is an old saying that "a good manager does things right, while a leader does the right things." Managers are focused on the details of the project: paperwork, reports, and metrics. Leaders inspire people, convey to them the vision that drives their work, and motivate people. Many Waterfall teams are over-managed, but under-led. A common joke that rings all too true is, "A good project manager is never around when I don't need him." An important transition for project managers will be to summon up their inner leader when moving to work with Agile teams.

Collocated and Dedicated Teams

One way to get started is to focus on becoming an advocate for collocated and dedicated teams within your organization. Begin to reach out to departments and upper management on a formal or informal basis to help them understand the corporate value of this shift to a more Agile team structure.

In the book *Where Good Ideas Come From*, Stephen Johnson talks about the phenomena of the greatest concentration of innovation coming from cities. There is a special type of incubation and hatching of new ideas that is protected and nurtured in places where diverse populations are pressed together into common, close spaces. The cross-pollination of ideas from dissimilar cultures, languages, professions, religions, and other background uniqueness provides a rich source of opportunity for one person to hear practices of another segment that can inspire people to rethink their own emerging creations. Ideas flourish when they are allowed to be connected, rather than protected.[1] the scientist Stuart Kauffman calls this tapping in to the "adjacent possible."[2]

Facilitation Skills

You will want and need to brush up, hone, or learn skills in *facilitation*. Again, most every project manager considers himself or herself excellent in soft skills. After all, it is merely being nice to people, right? No! Facilitation is a legitimate profession. Find a source of support to become proficient at it, because your main role is morphing into facilitating meetings for hybrid projects, between multiple projects, and with upper management. You will be involved in roadmap planning, release planning, iteration planning, demonstrations, and retrospective meetings. You will be more visible to the customer and interact more with higher management people in your organization as an advocate for your team. If you coordinate the work of your team with other Agile or traditional teams, you will lead meetings with peer-level project managers and with product owners, program managers, and portfolio managers.

When working with one team, the daily stand-up meeting team members report, "What I did yesterday," "What I'm going to do today," and "Roadblocks or impediments in my way." But when you, as the project manager, move up to the level where you are having meetings with other project managers to try to coordinate multiple projects into a program level entity, these same questions are only slightly adjusted.

At the group meeting, you must share, "This is what my team has done since our last meeting that will affect other teams," "This is what my team plans to do before we meet again that might affect other teams," and "These are the problems my team is having that we could use help on from other teams." As with the team's daily stand-up, the problems are not discussed at this point. After the short, 15-minutes or so sharing window, you can meet in a smaller group with the other project managers who might need help, or who can offer assistance to you. Again, paralleling the way your agile team might add issues to the backlog, this group of project managers would be wise to keep their own issues backlog to be sure that problems that arise are addressed, not just brought up and then forgotten.

When you realize that you will be working in a collaborative way with other teams, stakeholders, suppliers, and management, you will have plenty of opportunities to practice facilitation skills. Add to this participation in vision, iteration, release, retrospective, and team meetings to introduce group decision-making techniques, and you will see that this is *not* an ability that you can afford to overlook.

Here are some simple ideas to get you started:

1. Facilitation skills are process skills. The project manager becomes the person to lead people through a process together, *not a person who shares his or her own ideas*. Your role is to draw out the ideas of the group and get opinions from the rest of the team about them.

2. Facilitation is not focusing on the *what* of the meeting, but on the process. You guide and monitor the *how*. The content, the *what*, comes from the team or the group.

3. After years of being the final word on project issues, you now need to step back and be neutral. No one is criticized, and everyone's idea is supported. You do not take sides, and you are no longer the deciding vote.

4. One of your roles is to make sure that everyone on the team feels comfortable participating and feels good about what they contribute, regardless of whether or not it is the final choice of the team.

5. It is your job to develop a structure so that each team member is heard, not only the most outgoing or experienced people.

Sales Skills

Often, those in internal organizational roles consider the term *salesperson* a slightly dirty word. However, a project manager who possesses exemplary sales skills will shine. It is not that you will go door-to-door to sell the product that your team creates, but as you transition your teams to become a more Agile/Waterfall mix, you will need to sell the ideas of adding Agile practices. The grand concept of a more flexible approach is great, but you will need to present and engage management, vendors, government regulators, other project managers, and probably your own team, to truly embed this new idea of shifting to more flexible ways to approach projects.

The wise project manager is realistic enough to assess what he or she can "sell" to the organization right now in terms of change, and consider that a small step on the path to having an Agile team. If your organization relies on distributed teams for cost and market presence consideration, you will fail if you insist that the teams must all be immediately brought to your geographic location. Instead, opt to lobby for some low-cost technology that would help the teams be more closely linked for communication purposes, as shown in Chapter 12. Or, choose another Agile practice entirely to implement as a starting point.

For example, focus your efforts on encouraging a customer or a department manager to get involved in prioritizing the requirements or technical features for the team. Rather than insist that your quality team no longer perform tests far along in the project schedule as they do now, but instead be immediately integrated into the team to test as you go, work with the quality people and your team to find the largest number of problems and see if there are ways to avoid those issues earlier in the project flow so that fewer defects are created.

Implementing Agile practices on a piece-by-piece basis is not ideal. It can cause its own set of conflicts and concerns. However, it is better than not moving in this direction at all. In a non-software development project, adding a few concepts of Agile should begin to give you some improvement in the value that your projects deliver. Be sure to capture those increases in a tangible way when they can be linked to a process change. Then, you will have specifics to use to show management why Agile practices should be spread to other teams, and why there might be corporate benefits to supporting your drive for additional Agile processes with your own team.

A skill set to add to your backpack of tools is definitely the ability to act as an advocate or a salesperson for more flexibility in projects. You may not be in a formal presentation asking listeners to make a decision on the spot, but you can bring up the topic in a non-threatening and informative way with management, vendors, and outside compliance inspectors. This insures, to be sure you are spreading the seed of Agile gently and allowing it to grow in their minds so they are sensitized to listen more intently as they encounter it from other outside sources, too.

Coordination Skills

Yet another skill that you will need is to be an effective *coordinator* with groups outside of your own teams. In an environment where a hybrid method is activated, every day you will find yourself managing the communication between your own teams. There will also be other project managers who will need to coordinate their projects with your project. At the end of each iteration, you will be the representative who coordinates with the project managers of the other teams. You will step up to the primary communication role between the team, the product owner, and all of the other stakeholders to be sure that everyone supports a smooth, lean process to produce the product, service, or software. Anything in the process that is not providing direct customer value is wasteful and should be removed (such as heavy documentation and unnecessary managerial approvals, hint, hint.)

Collaboration Skills

As an Agile project manager, you will need to have the ability to foster *collaboration* between team members. Provide a workspace and generate an attitude that allows the team to build trust among its members. Then, they will be more willing to share ideas and ask for help in areas where they do not know how to proceed. The collaboration that becomes dependent on you is not only at the team level. Your team must work with other project teams, with internal and external stakeholders, suppliers, and management who become product owners or internal customers.

Remember, collaboration is a sharing between equals. It is *not* that each side takes turns giving in so that no one makes waves. *Conflict* in a team merely means that more than one idea is being discussed. If there is no discussion, there may be no thinking and no innovative ideas working to benefit the team or the project. Disengaged workers have no conflict. Engaged workers each have a multitude of opinions, solutions, and paths that they think the project should follow. It is up to you to navigate, to guide the team through all of those thoughts, to make sure that everyone is heard, and that the best ideas are nurtured.

Team Building Skills

The term *team building* got a bad reputation during the 1980s due to training classes where the irritating mantra was, "There is no 'I' in team." Quick-witted people might have been heard responding under their breath, "But there sure is an 'I' in win!" In its positive form, team building is an important skill for the evolving project manager. It is part of the change from the organizational philosophy of viewing workers as independent, interchangeable parts, and instead seeing workers as members of cohesive groups of knowledge workers who are tasked to solve problems together that are too complex to solve alone.

The project manager, as a team builder, is responsible for providing a range of activities to improve team performance, ensure the development of team members, enhance communication, and create an environment in which the team can work together in harmony to create project value. Nurturing team building includes the courage to address conflicts head-on, and provide learning opportunities—not just classroom training, but opportunities for pair-programming or pair-work with a mentor to create "learn-on-the-job" options.

Conflict Resolution Skills

Call it what you will, the Agile project manager needs to acquire, practice, and become skilled in *resolving conflicts* within the team, or the trust and collaboration needed for Agile success will be elusive. There is often a misunderstanding that good leadership results in no conflict within the team. This could not be further from the truth. *Conflict*, if defined as people having different ideas on an issue, makes for a healthy team. Innovation, alternative ways to handle changing requirements, and collaboration between team members, requires encouraging individuals to bring their ideas and knowledge out into the open at every turn.

The conflict that needs to be discouraged is that which becomes abusive, argumentative, or angry, or results in two or more people refusing to work together and avoiding each other. Although this is an uncomfortable situation, you as the project manager need to pull those participants aside and find a way to re-establish a smooth working relationship.

The human reaction is to just pretend that the conflict will somehow magically go away, but it never does. Like a nasty infection, it may appear to dissipate, but more likely it goes underground in the team, leaving each party wasting work time to explain their side of the conflict in hopes of gaining support for their "rightness." This adds stress to the team space. As the project manager, you need to pull the involved parties aside—together—rather than you and one person at a time. In other words, you are better off to have a meeting with the three of you. It is harder for each person to adjust or slant the story slightly to make his or her own position justifiable if all parties are present.

If the conflict involves differing ideas about how to do the work of the project, you might allow the first person to present his or her idea. Ask the second person (with the conflicting idea) to paraphrase the first idea fairly, and state it clearly. Once the first person is sure that the idea is understood, the second person now presents his own conflicting idea. At this point in the process, the first person paraphrases and states his opponent's thoughts. Once the two ideas are out in the open, and each participant is sure the other has understood his or her position, see if the first person has anything to change, or if he or she sees a solution. Allow the second person the same opportunity. Often, just being able to sit quietly and be sure an adversary understands one's point is a "magical" starting place to work out a third answer that is best for the project.

Since we are fostering Agile, self-managed teams, it is inappropriate for the project manager to step in and make a decision or choose sides. These are adults, and your job is to facilitate discussion, letting the participants come to their own resolve. It is, however, appropriate to talk in a frank way about the disharmony that conflicts bring to the team, and how it slows the progress of the work on the project.

Make it clear that you think it is important for each person to bring forward their own ideas, even if they are opposing the ideas of another team member. The last thing that you want is people holding back and letting the team drift into apathy. However, since this is, hopefully, going to be a long-standing, dedicated team, say you hope that each person will listen carefully and clarify any murky comments before reacting in haste. Ask each team member to find a way to be respectful in their presentation of an opposing idea, challenging the content of the first idea rather than the person who is presenting it.

Training Skills

Mentioning a project manager's role in also providing training may lead you to push back, "My organization has cut way back on training to save money. We're all on our own." But the training needed by an Agile team can be done without expensive outside classes. Understanding and encouraging paired work on activities, informal mentoring, or quick, informal knowledge sharing presentations over a brown bag lunch can fill that gap to keep the entire team cross-skilled. You can fill in the information about how Agile teams run for your group, and then also establish an environment where they are free to try it out.

Actually, if your company will allow it, the best success in shifting a team to Agile seems to come when a well-vetted outside consultant comes in to lead the team for the first project or two. This eliminates a lot of the touchy spots, as the guru can share his or her experience with other Agile team participants to guide yours in the right direction from the beginning. There is no need for your team to recreate the same mistakes already made by others. If your company will not provide a consultant for you, for whatever reason, the mantle falls on you to be this leader.

Group Decision Making Skills

You will need to gain experience in *group decision making* skills, such as Planning Poker, Fist to Five, and other Agile techniques. Learn on your feet by trying them with your own team. After the first few exposures, let the team lead these consensus-building activities on their own. Allow them to be self-directed (self-managed), while you become an observer.

Agile leadership suggests that the project manager treat the employees like volunteers. It is an interesting concept, because volunteers are looking for things other than a paycheck for the work they contribute. It is a meaningful analogy to remember, because today's team members are also looking beyond a paycheck for their satisfaction, too. If you happen to work in an organization that is a non-profit, engages volunteers to complete project tasks, or is aggressive in making sure end-users give their input before product decisions are solidified, your Agile mindset will work for you here, too.

If you have already worked with volunteers, you can understand the challenges of leading a group where you have no formal authority. At any moment, a volunteer can walk away from the task and leave you to complete the work on your own. A volunteer may have more knowledge or better social/political connections than you do, and you must be ever mindful that the impact of treating him or her poorly may extend far beyond not getting a few tasks finished.

Be aware at all times that leading an Agile team is all about the "volunteer" team mentality. People are far more important to the success of the project than the process you choose. Good people with no process have still been known to produce great product results. If you do not allow good people to work in an Agile or hybrid environment when the project calls for it, the best process in the world will not make much difference. Post this on your Team Room wall, write it on your personal planner, and make it the screen saver on all of your electronic devices: "People are 10 times more important than tools and processes!"

Social Styles Skills

Every list of ways to improve your managerial skills is sure to include the word *communication*. Unfortunately, the list may not include detailed, useful ways to accomplish this personal improvement. One technique that has a proven success rate is the Social Style Model™ from Wilson Learning Worldwide. (Note: other similar models from the TRACOM Group or the Trigon Systems color-coded approach also work well.) Wilson Learning's logical approach to altering your behavior as you interface with other people was based on research done in 1964

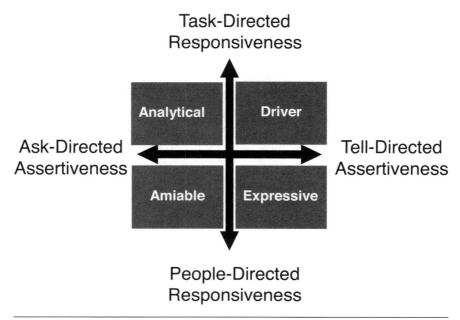

Figure 13.1 The Social Styles Model. Copyright © Wilson Learning Worldwide. All rights reserved. Used with permission.

by David W. Merrill. His concepts were based on the earlier, original work of James W. Taylor.

As an industrial psychologist and university professor, Merrill hoped to create a model that could predict success for people who wanted to have a clear direction to follow in bettering their chances in management and sales careers. Through his research, he found that people have consistent, observable behaviors as they engage with others. These actions, sometimes called *communications styles,* are fairly well set by the time a person is 3 years old, and seldom change over time. While this personality trait is constant, you can learn to deliberately adjust your behaviors temporarily in order to build a better bond between yourself and a person with a different communication style. Statistically, people tend to divide fairly evenly between the four communication styles, regardless of their location in the world, culture, age, or education.

Rather than being a deceptive or dishonest way to act, it can be a very honorable and respectful way to reach out to others if you consciously speak and act in the style they can most easily relate to, much as we may try to speak French to those we come in contact with in France. This ability to work productively with others is called *Versatility*, and it was found to be a reliable predictor of managerial success.

Wilson Learning says, "Versatility is the ability and willingness to adapt one's own behaviors to meet the concerns and expectations of others. It is not changing who you are, but making the effort to adapt your behavior. Greater versatility minimizes relationship tension and maximizes your effectiveness on the job."

Companion work that influenced Merrill, and his co-researcher Roger H. Reid's model, was done by Robert Blake and Jane Mouton. At the University of Texas, Blake and Mouton developed a behavioral leadership model called the Managerial Grid.[3] The most desirable style of managers in this model was based on Douglas McGregor's Theory Y. The vertical axis is Concern for People, while the horizontal axis allows for evaluation of a manager's Concern for Production. The managers who are found to be in the upper right quadrant, the Team style, with a high interest in people and equally high interest in production, most closely mirror the desirable qualities that McGregor labeled Theory Y.

By contrast, the lower right quadrant is where "Produce or perish" style managers score. With a primary focus on production to the exclusion of interest in people, this dictatorial or "command and control" style is more closely aligned to the older, industrial model of the Theory X manager. These contrasting types of managerial approaches became the foundation for an axis in the Merrill and Reid Social Styles Model™.

Adapted for Wilson Learning's model of Social Styles, the axis and their meanings no longer map to the Blake model, so there is no correlation between people within quadrants. In the Social Styles model, Figure 13.1, the vertical evaluation scale revolves around one's *Responsiveness*. Responsiveness is the way in which a person prefers to place their initial focus when communicating with others. Some of us like to target the tasks first (Task-Directed), while others prefer to deal with the people working on the task first (People-Directed).

When trying to decide by observation on which part of this vertical scale your colleagues would fit, Responsiveness may also include the way in which a person is perceived as expressing feelings when communicating with others. You may observe them either being very controlled in their emotions, or being more emotive. Controlled would be at the top of the model as an observable trait, and typically found in the two communication styles at the top. People who are more open with their emotions would be at the bottom of the model, and typically seen in the two communication styles found across the two lower quadrants.

On the horizontal scale, individuals are evaluated in terms of *Assertiveness*. Assertiveness is the way in which a person is perceived as attempting to influence the thoughts and actions of others. The Social Styles model ranks individuals between Ask-Assertive and Tell-Assertive. This means that the people on the left side of the model are more likely to phrase their verbal interactions in the form of a question to engage the other people, while those on the right choose to make comments in the form of a statement.

Both, "Can you help me with this user story?" and "I need your help with this user story!" convey the same thought. However, by noticing the way in which a team member, product owner, customer, or other stakeholder formats or articulates an idea (as a question or a statement), you can find a better way to exchange project information and solidify a cooperative relationship on a personal level.

These two evaluative scales cross to divide the model into four quadrants. The upper right is the *Driver* style. This person is Task-Directed/Controlled (focused on the task first, emotionally controlled) and Tell-Assertive (speaks in statements). Not to suggest these styles are stereotypical, but merely to help you form a mental image, this might be what we typically picture as a person in upper management. In a meeting, they will move directly to the work of the project, and they may exhibit a more reserved demeanor with few physical gestures. These are people who like to get right to the point. You will probably see a clean desk with a sparseness of decorative items on it, or around the office in general.

The primary focus on the tasks does not mean that the Driver is not interested in people. It only means that their approach to an interaction will be to get the work issues discussed first. Then once that is completed, they can move on to the more personal portion of a conversation asking about you, your family, your golf score, a televised sports event, or other more non-work related topics. A typical opening statement might be, "I need this done by Friday."

In the lower right of Figure 13.1 is the *Expressive* style. Here you see the People-Directed/Emotive colleague (focus on people first, effusive or animated in conversation—perhaps displaying more gestures) who is Tell-Assertive (speaks in statements). To help you form a picture of this style, think of someone in sales or marketing. In a meeting with you, they are interested in you and want to do a little personal networking and discussion before seguewaying into the content of the experience.

This person in interested in big, over-arching ideas and concepts, and may illustrate them enthusiastically with large, sweeping gestures. Their desk may be slightly messy, with lots of awards, stacks of ideas, and brightly colored folders. A typical statement might be, "How exciting it is that we are going to create this new product!" Do not misread this to mean that an Expressive cannot be detail oriented, concerned for people, or a person who cannot drive work to completion. We are just talking about a preference for the order and way in which they address things.

Amiable style individuals are in the quadrant formed by People-Directed/ Emotive (consider people first, conversationally open, perhaps more "touchy-feely") and Ask-Assertive (forms communication into questions). People with such a primary concern for other people are often found in the human resources department. A quick look at the desk of an Amiable and you might see family photos, photos of team outings, or photos or memorabilia associated with their pets. The Amiable will remember in detail the information about your family, friends, team, your pet cat, and any issues or concerns you have previously shared… and will want to ask about those things upfront before you move on to the reason for your visit. They may enjoy hugging you when you arrive and when you leave. The opening statement often is, "How are you doing, and how is (your family member mentioned by name)?"

This leaves the upper left quadrant, home of the *Analytical* style. Here, we find those who are Task-Directed/Controlled (focus on the task first, emotionally controlled) and Ask-Assertive (forms communication into questions). The analytical worker will commonly be found in the accounting department or on an IT team, whether in operations or software development. The desk of this person will be stacked with well-organized files containing statistics and proof for any questions they intend to pose to the team. They may appear to be more reserved, and gestures are usually small and contained, if they are used at all. The opening statement might be, "Have you seen the metrics on the Wilson project? What can be done to bring them back within the allowable 5% variance?"

Despite the attempt to allow you to visualize a style by painting the broadest possible image, there is no good or bad, right or wrong, no more or less successful style. Style just "*is*", and, in fact, each style has its own strength and perspective it brings to a team setting. The Expressive can get the group excited about new and changing possibilities, while the Amiable makes sure that the changes do not have negative ramifications for the people on the team. The Analytical can ask important questions to get the group considering fact-based data or financial realities when making decisions, and the Driver can do just that—drive the team to move forward and make decisions in a timely fashion. If fact, should you have a choice of team personnel, having a good representation of each communication style on a team will increase the chances of a successful project.[4]

Here's an example of the four styles, trying to go to lunch together. See if you can identify which is which:

- "Let's go to lunch at McDonald's! It's close and fast." _____

- "Did you see that McDonald's has a 45% coupon that could save $3.65 cents per meal? Would that be a good lunch spot today?"_____ _____

- "How many of you think that McDonald's would be a good place to eat today? Can we all be free around 11:30, or is there anyone that could not come at that time—or wouldn't be hungry that early?"_____ _____

- "I'm dying for a McRib today. I'm so excited that they are back! You know, they only offer them for a few weeks each year. I heard that it was developed as part of a major initiative to find better ways to utilize all the parts of the pig, and that the University of Nebraska was the place that invented it. My cousin, Sam, played football for Nebraska in the late 90s." _____

- (*Answers:* Driver, Analytical, Amiable, Expressive)

All joking aside, the reason for learning more about your own style and those of the people you deal with is not to label or pigeonhole them. The key is to learn Versatility in communicating with every style. Here is an actual experience to show how powerful simple observation can be in activating Versatility:

"I was a new Social Styles instructor for Wilson Learning and had the opportunity to fly to the corporate headquarters in Minneapolis for a training class. Since the organization offered many other courses, all of which I would eventually need to be certified to deliver, I thought it would be the perfect opportunity to gather all of the sales information brochures.

From the Social Styles profile tool that I filled out ahead of time, and from the similar evaluation tool others who worked with me had confidentially filled out before I came, I knew that I was an Expressive. It made sense to me. I had a background in the theatre and was aware that I enjoyed telling people about what I knew via a traditional teaching role, sharing my personal excitement about the new material with the class.

When the class took a break, I called the Sales Department and in my typically Expressive way, and said, "I'm Janine, a new instructor here for training (Tell-Assertive) and I'm here for my Social Styles certification class. I am really excited about teaching for you. I'm new to the company and Mrs. Hooper said that you were the person who I should contact to get all of the other sales materials." (Can you hear all of my Expressive/People-Directed focus as I talk about myself, my excitement, using the name of the person who referred me, and asking for the materials from this man on a personal level?)

Here is how the rest of the conversation went:

Man on the phone: "What exact materials do you want?"

Me: "Everything you have!"

Man on the phone: "Do you know how much material we have in this department?"

Me: "I want all the sales information for all of the courses in the company."

Man on the phone: "Do you have the names of any of the specific courses?"

Me: "No, I just want everything there is."

Man on the phone: "Can you understand that we have 26 individual courses, and each of them has multiple brochures, marketing sheets, and advertising copy samples?"

Me: "I'm sure it will *all* be useful to me to help me understand the courses."

Man on the phone: (Resignedly) "When do you want it?"

Me: "I want to pick it up at 4:00 today when I get out of class."

Man on the phone: "Can you come to the 4th floor at 4:00? Do you have the time to look through some things to see what you want?"

Class was about to begin, so I said, "See you at 4:00! Thanks so much for helping me out on this! I look forward to meeting you!"

As I went back to class, I thought about what a difficult person that man was. I was really annoyed that he was refusing to be more helpful. After all, I worked for this company now, just like he did, and it was important that I have the material about the classes to take home with me on the plane. I thought he should have welcomed me to the organization, asked where I was from and how I was enjoying the class, and been much more interested in helping. How dare he dampen my enthusiasm!

As I was mentally enumerating the injustices being done to me by this rude, indifferent individual, it dawned on me. I'm an Expressive! Here is a mini-test to see if you've been paying attention. What Social Style was the man on the phone? If you said Analytical, you are right.

The content of the training that afternoon, to my good fortune, was about which styles work best together. You can look at the Social Styles quadrant model in Figure 13.1 and see that Drivers and Expressive share their Tell-Assertiveness, and only need to adjust their Versatility by choosing to become either more or less Task vs. People focused. Each pair of touching styles only needs to adjust one behavior, but styles that rest diagonally across the model have the least in common and require the most Versatility if they are going to communicate successfully. Note where my Expressive style lies in relationship to the Analytical man on the phone. Direct opposites!

So, as the class ended and I headed down the elevator, I decided to put what I had learned into practice. I found the room and consciously changed to be more Ask-Assertive and Task-Focused. I said, "Is this the right place to pick up my sales materials?" (Rather than, "I'm Janine who talked to you on the phone earlier and you said I could come down here to pick up my sales materials," which would have been my normal Tell-Assertive approach). Here is the rest of our conversation, with me deliberately attempting to try out my newfound Versatility:

Man in the office: "Are you Janine?"

Me: (With one small shake of my head to nod yes, rather than throwing my arms wide with a big smile and announcing, "Ta-da," as I might have done if I were not consciously thinking about adjusting my style.) "What would you suggest I do to become more familiar with the courses we offer?"

Man in the office: "Have you seen any of the Versatile Sales Performance literature?"

Me: "Is that one of the more popular series?"

Man in the office: "Do you want to see the sales numbers broken down by courses?"

This conversation went on, and included more of the same types of exchanges, so you do not need to hear about all of it. But rather than a disinterested ogre, Max, proved to be a delightful, helpful, and knowledgeable asset. By approaching him in the way he found most comfortable, i.e., being Versatile, I got what I needed, and then some. After I had viewed and selected the appropriate things to take home, we had a nice conversation about how each of us had gotten interested in working for the company, where we originally grew up, our favorite football teams, and other more personal things. From that day, I have been sold on the power of Social Styles to transform communication.

Many team conflicts might be avoided by awareness of Social Styles. The Expressive's excitement and global statements for solutions are the antithesis of where the Analytical's thinking lies. It's a time-waster to them. The Driver, wanting to get a solid plan going forward in the shortest amount of time, is annoyed by the Amiable's concern for interruptions to the work schedule of future users during a product change. But with the presence of representatives from all four approaches on your team, softened by each person having an awareness of his or her own behavior patterns, each style can add crucial ideas to the team discussions and bring up risks, concerns, and innovative ideas that might otherwise be suppressed.

This is a much more complex topic than can be presented in this small space, but if you see merit in it you might do some further research online. In order to speak to IT teams you might manage, or work with in a joint hybrid venture, you will need to know something about the little agile processes they will follow. You will need to understand the vocabulary and be able to translate back and forth from Agile to Waterfall verbiage. A grasp of Social Styles, plus the ability to "speak their language" and use terms that are meaningful to each group, will become mandatory.

Servant-Leader Skills

As you move into the Agile space in your further reading, or even just your personal awareness of the field, you are sure to come across the idea that the project manager should transform his or her prevalent leadership style from "command and control" to the "*servant leadership*" model. But what is servant leadership? The phrase was coined by Robert K. Greenleaf in a 1970 essay, "The Servant as Leader."[5] His important concept was that in the hyphenated term servant-leader, the person (project manager) is focused on the servant part first, "to make sure that other people's highest priority needs are being served."

This concept reminds us to think of Maslow's hierarchy of needs and remember that our knowledge worker team members are looking to reach their highest level of self-awareness. Greenleaf also says, the test for whether or not you are successful as a servant-leader, is to ask, "Do those served (your team) grow as persons? Do they, while being served, become healthier, wiser, freer, more autonomous, more likely themselves to become servants?" (in the sense that they choose a servant-leader managerial style for themselves rather than "command and control.")

Servant-leadership is a concept that has become a buzzword, although few people really understand how to implement the concept in their own teams. It might be worth taking the time to read what a few contemporary leaders say with regard to explaining this term, driving home the importance that it brings to the workplace. Business theory guru, Stephen Covey, wrote the Foreword to a collection of essays, *Insights on Leadership*,[6] eloquently describing the crucial role that the shift to a servant-leader management style has on success:

> A great movement is taking place throughout the world today. Its roots, I believe, are to be found in two powerful forces. One is the dramatic globalization of markets and technology. And in a very pragmatic way, this tidal wave of change is fueling the impact of the second force: time-less, universal principles that have governed, and always will govern all enduring success, especially those principles that give "air" and "life" and creative power to the human spirit that produces *value* in markets, orga-nizations, families, and, most significantly, individual's lives.
>
> One of these fundamental, timeless principles is the idea of Servant Leadership, and it will continue to dramatically increase in its relevance. You've got to produce more for less, and with greater speed than you've even done before….. The only way you can do that in a sustained way is through the empowerment of people. And the only way you get empow-erment is through high-trust cultures and through the empowerment philosophy that turns bosses into servants and coaches. Leaders are learn-ing that this kind of empowerment, which is what servant-leadership represents, is one of the key principles that, based on practice, not talk, will be the deciding point between an organization's enduring success or its eventual extinction.

Ann McGee-Cooper is a consultant for Anne McGee-Cooper Associates (AMCA), and her team created the first Servant Leadership Learning Community in 2000. She is skilled at defining servant leadership. As you read further, notice how closely her comments align with the descriptions of Agile philosophies, and the idea of a self-managed team with the project manager's role to support the team and remove obstacles from the project value stream. McGee-Cooper says that servant leadership is not about a personal quest for power, prestige, or material rewards. Instead, leadership begins with a true motivation to serve others. Based on earned trust, people choose to follow you. The old methods of management tended to focus on people as "things we use to do other things," almost as if they were objects rather than people. We talk about controlling and motivating people as though they had switches the project manager could learn to flip to get the desired behavior. Rather than controlling or wielding power, the servant-leader works to build a solid foundation or shared goals by:

1. Listening and asking insightful questions, which encourages the team to bring more to the shared vision of the project.

2. Working thoughtfully and humbly to help build a creative consensus, stepping out of the way to let the team create its own solutions.
3. Honoring the various ideas of the group members and guiding them to find the "third right answers" that are more than reluctant compromises. This is how people are led to step in and take ownership of the work of the project.[7]

The focus of servant leadership is on sharing information, building a common vision, self-management, high levels of interdependence, learning from mistakes, encouraging creative input from every team member, and questioning present assumptions and mental models. In order to capture the power of the knowledge worker, we must change the ways that we manage the organization's human capital, and change how it is used. These are all Agile principles, too.

Millennium Management Skills

While all of the individuals we manage are unique, there are characteristics that may be found in groups of employees based on age and the historical time period in which they lived. Growing up in a different era can cause people to see things differently. The term *Baby Boomers* refers to the group of babies born to the returning veterans of World War II. Born between 1946 and 1964, today, those Baby Boomers are reaching retirement age, or at least will anticipate leaving the workforce over the next few years. Since they have provided a huge portion of the workforce over the past few decades, it is important to look at the next generation of workers (potential team members) and see how we might need to adjust our managerial style to interest them, keep them, and make them productive.

The new group flowing into the workforce is called the *Millennials*, or *Echo Boomers* (children of Baby Boomers), or *Generation Y*. Isn't it ironic that we need to move to Theory Y to manage the Generation Y employees? Birth dates range from the late 1970s to early 2000s. Estimated to number around 4 million, larger than the Baby Boomer generation and the *Generation X* group that preceded them, Millennials are the fastest growing segment in today's workforce. The prediction is that they will be 75% of the workforce by 2025, so as a project manager, you will need to adjust your managerial philosophies if you are going to be able to attract and retain them on your project teams. They have different priorities for job satisfaction, so even if your previous teams have always liked you and worked well for you, you may need some new skills for this age group. Common traits assigned to Generation Y/Millennials include:

1. **Tech-savvy**. This generation has had technology at their fingertips from day 1, and they not only use it on a daily basis to complete

job tasks, they are plugged-in 24 hours a day, 7 days a week. Their preferred method of communication is text messaging, Twitter, and e-mail. They are probably at the power-user level of any technology they own.

2. **Tech-trained**. This is a group that does not find value solely in instructor-led, classroom instruction. They prefer webinars and online classes. You could see how the collocated team with the opportunity for practical, informal, real-world, relevant, hands-on pair programming, or working side-by-side and learning through communication with a colleague, would appeal to them.

3. **Family-oriented**. This group is known to prefer family time over more hours at work, even if the additional hours garner a higher paycheck. They are looking for a better work/life balance than they saw in the lives of their parents, and perhaps the financial success and ongoing support of their parents has made them less driven by money. They value being a good parent and might be raising a child alone.

4. **Achievement-driven**. While not motivated by money, Millennials will work hard if they believe in what they are doing, but, they want to be self-directed. They typically want to work on things they care about, on their own schedule.

5. **Feedback-driven**. Perhaps as a result of attentive and supportive parents praising their efforts throughout life, Gen Y workers have an interesting approach to work. They want a challenge and they want to figure things out on their own rather than being told what to do. But at the same time, they want continuous feedback during the process.

6. **Team-oriented**. Baby Boomer parents enrolled their children in team sports, arranged play dates, and found other group activities for their Generation Y children. As a result, they now seek a creative group environment in the workplace. However, they usually value collaboration over a competitive atmosphere.

7. **Confident**. Millennials want to know why they are doing what they are doing, and are independent minded, optimistic, and confident. They expect to be given responsibility and be involved in the decision making surrounding their work.

Recent statistics show that only 7% of this generation work for Fortune 500 companies. The others probably do not, because they do not share the Fortune 500 values of how workers should be organized and managed. This is an unusual group. Rather than take a job for money and stick with it just for the paycheck, they are not afraid to take a big risk to get a big reward. So, more and more of them try start-up organizations where they feel empowered. They want to work on what they believe in.

Not long ago, a 10-year-old boy attending a "Bring Your Child to Work Day" at a Fortune 500 company was asked what he wanted in a job when he grew up. His answer was remarkably clear cut and mature for his age:

- I want a good boss who is not too strict or too easy.
- I want to work where they *need* what I know how to do, and they trust me.
- I want to work with people who want to do a good job, not people who are just there to get money.
- I want to do work that allows me to invent things and makes me learn.
- I like to work on computers.
- I want to earn enough to support my family and have health insurance.[8]

These thoughts line up with what older Millennials have polled as important in their own value structures.

- They want to be *self-directed*, but have someone or some process from which they can *have feedback*.
- Having been involved in group sports or other after-school activities from an early age, they *prefer a collaborative environment* rather than a competitive one.
- Having come from a background of plenty (Millennials will see the largest transfer of wealth ever from parent to child), they are more focused on *being creative and working to their fullest*, rather than viewing "good" employment as the highest paying position.
- Millennials are looking for *work that is challenging and fulfilling*. The preferred way of *learning* is *on a "pull" basis*. If a question arises, they want to have the answer now, not two weeks from now when the organization has scheduled a classroom experience for the whole team.
- Organizations that equate seeing a person online as someone "goofing off" or "surfing the web" will need to open their thinking to see that a quick webinar, Google search, instructional YouTube video, signing in to a communities of practice group, or e-mailing a colleague in the same industry anyplace in the world, is a plus for the speed with which business value can flow through the project process. Think *instant, self-directed learning*.
- Millennials *expect to have the latest technology available, and to be allowed use it to its fullest extent*. This is an extremely tech-savvy generation. A workplace that does not allow texting between team members two desks away, two floors away, or six time zones away, is short-sighted. Not having a constantly open web-interface, or at least

"always on" phone connections between geographically distributed teams, will be seen as unacceptable.

- *Balancing family life and work life* has taken on new value for Millennials, and flexibility with schedule and a stable work week commitment with few non-self-selected overtime hours is critical.[9]

Attracting and retaining team members from the Millennial generation will become a key project management skill set if we are to capture these high performers for project teams. You can already begin to align their preferences to those of the Agile philosophies and see how they would enjoy working on a dedicated, collaborative, and self-directed team where they are privy to the corporate strategy and vision, working daily with the upper level product owners, creating new and innovative products and services, having a set schedule where overtime is frowned upon, and perhaps working flexible hours. They would enjoy peer-to-peer informal learning and daily feedback from the other team members. And, they would be comfortable with any technology necessary to create a hybrid product or work with a distributed team.

The 2010 U.S. Census showed that, while Baby Boomers (ages 50 to 65) average 9.23 years on the same job, and Generation X (ages 29 to 45) stay for 4.1 years, Generation Y/Millennials are only investing a median 1.86 years before moving on to a new job.[10] Organizations with an older model of employee engagement will have difficulty competing for these talents and retaining them against a company with an Agile approach to projects. Some changes to envision would be movement away from the perception that someone on their smartphone, or on the Internet, is wasting time on personal matters. Team members might use push technology to text each other to confirm meetings, check on details before moving forward on the project, or ask for someone to come from across the room to validate a piece of work before they consider it complete. Interoffice texts allow the continuous flow of value without waiting for more formal, "pull" communications methods to be used, like e-mail applications that must be opened to be of value.

This section of the population is used to instant resolution of any question, or instant access to whatever they want at the moment that they want it. They do not wait to drive to their local movie theatre for the 7:15 movie on Saturday night, if they are awake at 4:00 a.m. on Saturday morning. Netflix, HBO To Go, Hulu, or their own TiVo/DVR movies are available on demand, so why wait?

By the same token, they prefer using a "pull" technology approach to training. A question comes up at work, so just Google or Bing the topic and a list of potential answers appear. Why wait for the corporate training for the entire team on a new software tool to be held next Tuesday and Wednesday, if you can answer the question you have about how to change to international fonts in 30 seconds on the Internet, allowing you to complete a marketing translation before lunch.

Webinars by vendors, research organizations, your customers, and even your competitors, can give you a 15 to 60 minute window into innovations and new business models while you sit at your desk with a sandwich over lunch. Consistently reading work-related blogs, or joining groups sponsored by professional associations such as the PMI Communities of Practice, allows the employee to tap into an enormous pool of free knowledge from people also wanting to share and trade ideas and technical knowledge without exposing company secrets. What you find on the web that relates to relevant project topics can instantly be forwarded to others in your project circle.

Allowing a team culture in which people are trusted to gather what they need from electronic sources only strengthens the knowledge base of the entire team. And, if you allow producers to extend the reach of their collaboration beyond the confines of the core team, you extend the value of their being self-directed.

Minecraft is a popular online game with people of all ages and sexes that is in essence, "virtual legos with zombies." It is free, and available to play as a single user. You can connect on your private web server site with a small group of selected friends, or play online with an unknown group of people from all over the world. It is not the complexity of the game that is fun; it is the challenge to discover on your own what this game is, and what it can do.

Minecraft comes without instructions, but when you have mastered all you can by your own initiative, you can go online. There you will find forums, Wikipedia entries, Minecraft wikis, the Minecraft corporate site with downloads, and even instructional YouTube videos of people showing how to do clever and creative moves you did not know the game allowed players to execute. There are Facebook links for fans and multiple other opportunities where you can post your own helpful hints for others.

As opposed to the idea of sitting down and learning all there is to know about the game, consulting a list of the manufacturer's printed rules, or scanning an instruction book before beginning to play; finding the answers to questions you really want to know and need to know through your own resourcefulness *right now* is the joy for the Millennials. To shut them off from their quest to discover similar tips, tricks, and ideas for the work of the project during the business day, is to deprive the organization of the true value of hiring these top-of-the-line knowledge workers. You are not paying them for what they *currently* know, because the knowledge base today is so large and so swiftly changing that no one person can know it. You are hiring them for their ability to locate what they need, at exactly the time they need it, so that there is no slowing of the process flow for the project work.

Today's workers are being sought for their ability to locate knowledge, not their brute strength. It is up to us as project managers to help our organizations attract and keep the best and brightest. By creating work environments that allow the Millennium generation to find their core values on our project teams through our project management styles, we secure our own place of value to the organization and help it complete in the ever increasingly warp speed marketplace of the 21st century.

Process Tailoring Skills

The byword in all Agile approaches is *flexibility*. This holds true for not only dealing with the features and services delivered by the project, but flexibility in adjusting the process by which the team functions on a project-by-project basis. As teams become more self-directed, project managers may break larger teams into smaller ones, take on multiple teams working on various portions of a larger project, and be responsible for integrating the output of the team with other teams on a hybrid product. So, even if you get the whole organization to "be Agile," there will never be a checklist of behaviors and tools that are used uniformly on every project outing.

One of the most important skill sets you can develop to ensure your long-term employability is the ability to guide teams through the process of choosing what processes are necessary and appropriate for each unique project, while being mindful of the documents, artifacts, vocabulary, metrics, and outputs that will be necessary to successfully merge information and integration production chunks in a meaningful way with the output of other teams.

Each product owner will have different levels of comfort with risk, different amounts of reporting overhead that they will need to pass up to their superiors, and different compliance issues to address. Each peer project manager will have his or her own additional set of personal preferences and team needs that must be considered and coordinated for the best business value to flow smoothly together from the various teams into a corporate value stream.

Each team will have specific tools and techniques that they will prefer based on their experience, what the company has available to them, the reality of the team distribution scenario, the content of what their output will be (i.e., software vs. traditional products), the originality or complexity of the project, industry standards, the level of comfort and familiarity the team has with each other, and their Agile aptitude and experience.

Do not underestimate the skills necessary to adjust team processes on a case-by-case basis (with the help and input of the team in a collective way). You must always be vigilant about acquiring new tools and keeping apprised of what others in your own industry are using. Take a look at the "adjacent possible" and remain informed regarding what other industries have found worthwhile that could be reconfigured for your own situation. You are in a unique position to be able to leverage the discipline of traditional project management processes when needed, and at the same time you will have the knowledge and understanding to integrate the flexibility and collaborative practices of Agile. However, keep in the forefront of your mind that the reason Agile is successful is that it is a mindset that frees the team members to perform in more successful ways than the old, lockstep approach to work allowed.

References

[1]Johnson, S. 2010. *Where Good Ideas Come From: The Natural History of Innovation.* New York, NY: Riverhead Books.

[2]Kauffman, S. February 27, 2011. *The Adjacent Possible and Unpredictable Future.* NECSI 2011 Winter School presentation, *Which Light Blog.* http://whichlight.com

[3]Managerial Grid Model. *Wikipedia.* Retrieved from http://en.wikipedia.org

[4]"Social Styles from Wilson-Learning—Leading provider of Social Style Training & Development." Wilson Learning Worldwide, June, 2012. Received through direct correspondence.

[5]Greenleaf, R. June, 1982. *The Servant As Leader.* Robert K. Greenleaf Center.

[6]Spear, L. 1997. *Insights on Leadership.* Hoboken, NJ: John Wiley & Sons, Inc.

[7]"Ann McGee Cooper – Define SL-1." Gonzaga Mentor Gallery Clip, 2003. Retrieved from www.youtube.com.

[8]"*What I Want in a Job.*" Interview with Chris Davis, April 28, 2012, conducted by Barbee Davis.

[9]Moore, J. T. & Mantica, D. "Millennials Rising." February 23, 2012. Webinar.

[10]"*Words for the Ys, How to Leverage a Generation's Strengths and Improve Its Staying Power in the Contact Center.*" [White paper]. Calabrio ONE, May 8, 2012.

Web Added Value™

What Needs to Change in My Business Skill Sets?

Six Changes to Embrace

The reality is that we have all come to be project managers by following different paths. Many project managers started into the workforce before the field of project management reached the significance that it has today. Others came into business with other types of degrees, and somehow were "anointed" with the title due to their excellent communication and organizational skills, or being good at managing a team. Still others studied to perfect their knowledge of this profession, and graduated with an official degree announcing a proficiency in creating, monitoring, and completing projects to pre-planned metrics.

For as long as you have been involved with projects, like the rest of the project management profession, you have been focused on a project-centric view of what is important. Are projects on time and on budget? Do they have the requisite quality? Can you turn in the proper documentation on time? Can you easily track earned value (EV) and project out budget at completion (BAC)?

With a shift to the Agile philosophy, projects have new goals that go beyond the traditional triple constraints of time, cost and scope. There is an evolution occurring in our profession's philosophy about projects, and project managers are focused on these six changes to the project milieu:

1. **More customer involvement and respect.** The product owner or customer is a familiar face around the project team, often located near enough to the team that there can be daily contact and a way to have questions answered almost on the spot.

2. **Smarter utilization of knowledge workers to provide solutions.** We are creating self-managed teams, giving the team the authority to make decisions in areas where they have the expertise needed to make wise ones. We are collocating them and providing a practical, collaborative team setting. Hopefully, we are able to keep dedicated teams intact from project to project, so that the learning curve gains are retained and used in future projects.

3. **More facilitating, less controlling project managers.** We have willingly given ourselves a promotion from endless paperwork and responsibility to deliver a portion of the work of the project and now are "fixers." We trust our teams and spend our own work day coordinating with other teams and stakeholders. In addition, we use Social Style abilities to function as a coach. The coach can only sit on the sidelines and help the players from that perspective. He cannot take over and walk onto the field to play a position.

4. **Accept project changes easily.** We have a more flexible approach to the project processes, which protects the team from changes during the current iteration, but freely allows product owners or customers, vendors, or team members with infrastructure issues or other unexplored user stories, to add scope (re-prioritized by the product owner) before the user stories are committed to for the following iteration.

5. **Greater focus on the value stream, less emphasis on individual or excessive metrics.** We protect the team from constraints and annoying paperwork, allowing them to focus on the work of the project. As the project manager, we see our role as removing as much stress and concern as possible from the team, and take it upon ourselves to negotiate with other parts of the organization to smooth the way for the Agile team. We have lobbied to have our team evaluated as a unit, and protect them from wasting working time creating obsolete metrics that serve no purpose.

6. **Better alignment to business strategy.** This is where there is often a huge gap in the ability of the project manager to fulfill all of the transitional needs of the project, because they have never been trained to understand and consider how to align a project to organizational strategy. The truth is, often project managers are not allowed to know the details of a vision or the corporate plans, outside of the information contained in the Project Charter. This becomes a Catch-22, as in many

corporations the project manager is asked to write their own charter and then submit it for approval. By writing his or her own charter, the project manager never has the chance to participate in the conversations that discuss the need for the project, so he or she is blocked from seeing how the team can truly contribute to the larger organizational goals.

As we switch from a project manager hat to an Agile hero and business guru hat, we have to remind ourselves to consciously make a mental shift and begin to view projects as investments, not team challenges. If we are not routinely given the organizational vision and goals, both in concept and in the dollar amount of return that upper management is counting on from our projects, we will have to learn to ask.

Rather than merely meeting traditional metrics, our job shifts to the main goal of adding business value to our organization by providing an organizational framework for successful projects. As the business environment changes and evolves, we have to evolve project support structures as well, so that they are flexible enough to anticipate and embrace those changes. The organization that does this best, wins.

As the project manager, you take on the added responsibility to optimize the employee skills and core business processes to be sure that each dollar the organization invests in a project brings an optimum return in business value. We need to be involved to be sure that each project selected is establishing a clear path, from organizational strategy to the project team, and aligning delivery to strategy.

Cost of Failure

Let's remove our project manager hat for a moment and look at project performance from another angle. Projects are organizational investments that are intended to create a positive return on investment (ROI). ROI is a performance measure used to evaluate the efficiency of an investment, or to compare the efficiency of a number of different investments. If an investment does not have a positive ROI predicted, or if there are other opportunities that have a higher ROI, then the investment—possibly a project—should not be done. Portfolio management teams calculate estimated ROI for projects long before they are authorized.

Every year, the Gartner Group has new statistics about the state of project management. In 2011, they showed that only about 40% of funded projects that are actually done are a Success. Thirty-six % of projects are Challenged, meaning that there is doubt that they can meet their original time, cost, scope, and quality metrics. The remaining 24% of projects are reported by their sponsoring organizations as Failures.[1] The statistics in the upper left of Figure 14.1 show that for 60% of

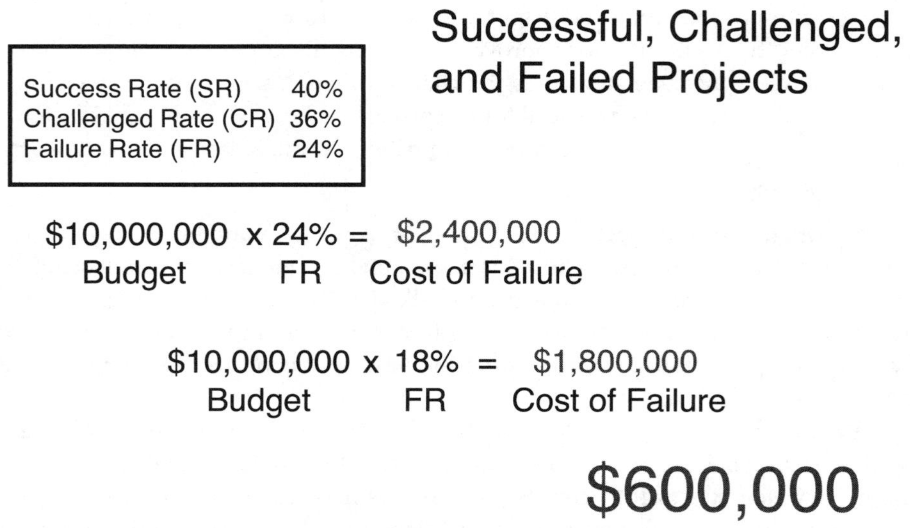

Successful, Challenged, and Failed Projects

Success Rate (SR)	40%
Challenged Rate (CR)	36%
Failure Rate (FR)	24%

$10,000,000 x 24% = $2,400,000
Budget   FR   Cost of Failure

$10,000,000 x 18% = $1,800,000
Budget   FR   Cost of Failure

$600,000

Figure 14.1 Successful, Challenged, and Failed Projects

our projects, the total of the 36% that are Challenged and the 24% that are Failures, the entire business value (ROI) we anticipated when this project was given the green light in the project portfolio is not realized. When a project is a failure or is cancelled, if we are comfortable in our familiar project manager hat, we can say, "Whew, at least I'm off that dog! Now I can move on and start again with a fresh project. My paycheck still comes in." But once we change to our Agile hero and business guru hat, we have to acknowledge some ugly truths.

Let's say that our organization's annual project budget is $10 million. Even if we ignore the losses from the 36% of the projects that are Challenged, believing that somehow the Project Fairy in the sky will bless them and move them into the Success column, we can monetize the failures: $10 million times a 24% failure rate.

$$\frac{\$10,000,000}{\text{Budget}} \times \frac{24\%}{\text{FR}} = \frac{\$2,400,000}{\text{Cost of Failure}}$$

Our cost of failure is $2,400,000. This is $2,400,000 of real money invested in projects that cannot be offset by any return on investment from those same projects. However, that money has to be recouped in some other way to keep the business viable. That is a lot of products or services to have to sell, savings to find on internal improvements, profit to be made on other projects, or income siphoned from other profitability streams, just to cover this year's project failure category on the balance sheet. This loss lowers the entire organization's profit, and perhaps negatively impacts the stock value. If these projects are not profitable, the question becomes where do we get the cash to replenish the funds we want to use to finance future projects for next year?

If we rethink the project philosophy and consider the benefits of an Agile approach, which allows us to do projects faster, cheaper, and get a quicker ROI, we might lower both the failure rate and the cost of failure. Let's say that we were able to lower the failure rate slightly, from 24% to 18%. Our cost of failure is now only $1,800,000 based on that same $10 million budget.

$$\frac{\$10,000,000}{\text{Budget}} \times \frac{18\%}{\text{FR}} = \frac{\$1,800,000}{\text{Cost of Failure}}$$

It is unrealistic to think we can wipe out all project failure right away, but as an example, if we can lower the rate by just 6% by adding a few Agile practices to our Waterfall projects, we are saving the company $600,000. The specific numbers in this example do not matter, but they illustrate the point that what we really want to do by adding Agile to our project philosophy is to move many more projects into the Success category.

Aligning Projects to Strategic Objectives

Next, let's grab a new managerial straw hat off the corporate shelf and see how we specifically work to align our Agile-ish projects to support the business strategy. We can start by looking at the corporation's Strategic Objectives. Strategic Objectives are statements of specific outcomes to be achieved, used to turn the mission and vision of the organization into reality within a well-defined timeframe. They could, for example, relate to greater profits, a higher rate of growth, innovative and new products, increased market share, higher productivity, or an increase in social responsibility. Let's say that in a simplified budget for the organization in the next year, based on achieving our Strategic Objectives, we have four main categories to cover: Overhead, Infrastructure, Growth, and Innovation (see Figure 14.2).

The first organizational budget category, Overhead, is the "keep the lights on" money. The metrics we have show that although our goal is that this cost should be 25% to 30% of the total budget, it is currently costing us 50% to 60% of that budget to keep the lights on. We cannot solve that problem all at once, but let's set a Strategic Objective, through projects, to *Reduce Overhead 10%* by the end of the first quarter.

Our Infrastructure goal, the budget we have allowed for computers, maintenance, and so on, is 20% to 25%, but actual numbers show that it is presently

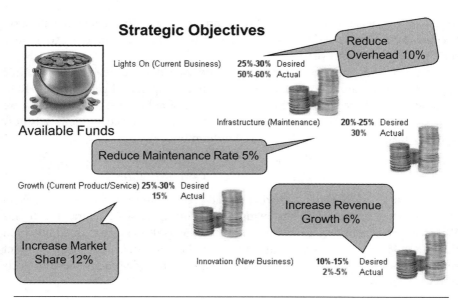

Figure 14.2 Strategic Objectives

costing us 30%. So, management sets a Strategic Objective that we will increase *Reduce Maintenance Rate 5%* by the end of the first quarter.

For the Growth of our Current Products and Services, we want 25% to 30% of the organization's budget to be met by the increase in income from sales of our current products and services over what we sold last year. However, we are really only covering about 15% of the annual budget from that source at this point. So, again, we cannot always solve this problem in one quarter, but hope to do projects that will *Increase Market Share* for current offerings and grow their corresponding income streams by *12%* as of the end of the first quarter.

For the Innovation category, which is new business, new products, or new services, we want the income to total 10% to 15% of the total corporate budget. Right now, that category accounts for bringing in revenue to cover only 2% to 5% of the budget. So, by the end of the first quarter, we want to *Increase Revenue Growth* (from new products or services) by *6%*.

Here is how we plan and track those Strategic Objectives to our projects. (Figure 14.3). Each project is directly linked to one of the objectives, and it may take more than one project to meet the percentage goals we have set. Ideally, one project manager would manage all of the projects that flow into the same Strategic Objective. If that is not possible, a program manager may be assigned to be responsible for being sure these projects bring in the requisite profitability

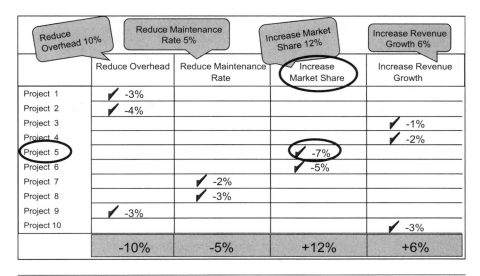

Figure 14.3 Projects Aligned to Strategic Objectives

the organization is counting on them to return, and to coordinate the work of the project teams so that they work in harmony toward a common goal. Take a closer look at Figure 14.3, and keep Project 5 in mind.

We are now going to align the Strategic Objective, "Increase Market Share 12%", with the Agile Project 5. In Figure 14.4, the objective has been brought over to become part of the Project Roadmap. Remember the misconception that there is no planning in Agile and that it is all sort of spontaneous and *ad hoc*? Nothing could be further from the truth. We see clearly here that the overall goal is to "Increase Market Share 12%", and the Project 5 team can see that they are being counted on to produce profit equaling at least 7% of that goal. (Multiplying the percentage numbers by the current corporate budget will give the dollar amounts, but here we are only working with the concepts.)

Once the Strategic Objective is tied directly to the Project Roadmap (or big picture) for Project 5, further planning can continue. The roadmap will then be divided into Releases, and at the end of each one we can release a major chunk of project or service into the company or marketplace, or not, depending on the project. Call these "phases" or "milestones" if you are working with primarily traditional teams. Remember, vocabulary is not the important thing. Thought processes and making sure that we understand the reasons for our actions are what make us Agile.

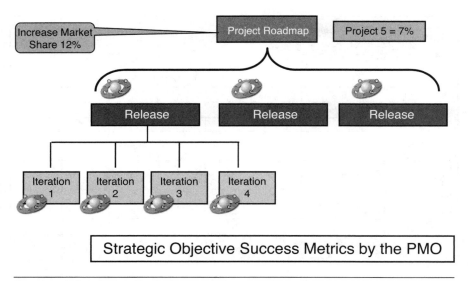

Strategic Objective Success Metrics by the PMO

Figure 14.4 One Project Tracked on a Roadmap

Be sure to post the Strategic Objective goal for the project on the wall of the team room to keep it front and center as the project team creates the features and services of the project.

Maximizing Revenue Streams and Flexibility

In this example, Figure 14.4, each Release is broken into four Iterations and the length of the Iterations and the length of the Releases will all be the same throughout the project. In this example, let's say the Iterations are two weeks each, so each Release is eight weeks. The roadmap is loosely planned, and Release 1 is planned a little more specifically than the others, but only Iteration One is planned in detail. Why get too specific too far into the future when things will change?

If we are truly going to link the project to its Strategic Objective, it is important, after the project team finishes its work, that a designated group tracks the metrics of the project impact to see if it fulfilled its goals. Did Project 5 actually contribute a 7% increase in market share? The fact that the project finished on time, or that it produced an agreeable number of user stories for the product owner, is not "success." The project success can only be evaluated if someone, possibly the project management office (PMO), actually tracks to see if the organization's market share does increase and if so, by how much. Can that gain be tied directly back to the work done by this project team?

As with any good measurement system, the parameters of how the business value gained from Project 5 will be measured, should be set out before the work of the project begins. If there is no clear way to track whether or not the project work had any impact, why spend the money to do the work in the first place? So, the way in which the 7% increase in market share will be tracked should be planned and shared with the team before the project begins.

Knowing how the measurement will be done may dictate the way the team chooses to produce its work. And, once result metrics are obtained after the end of the project, be sure they are funneled back to the project team. If we have teams driven by self-actualization, who are wanting feedback on their work, these are exactly the types of organization information that should be shared. Again, dedicated teams that remain intact from project to project can benefit most from this information.

While it is a good thing to have the Agile project team know the project's relationship to the strategic objective that is behind its authorization, which would be a good thing to know regardless of the project's chosen approach. Now, we are at a point where we can show the real reason for the emphasis on dedicated teams and their organizational value. Every project impacts the revenue stream of the organization. Its initial cost and the ongoing costs to keep the project running come out of the budget, so the faster the **minimum marketable feature** (MMF), *the smallest possible set of functionality that, by itself, has value in the marketplace or organization* can be created, the sooner the project ends and the less it costs.

A project impacts the revenue stream by whether or not it returns money or business value in the amount originally planned. We need to maximize that revenue stream and also start it flowing as soon as possible. At the top of Figure 14.5, you have a release that is 3 iterations long. Each iteration is 10 days, or 2 weeks in length. In each iteration, you are going to do the things with the most business value, and most risk, first. Remember, risk is cheapest and easiest to fix at the beginning of the project.

At the end of Iteration One, we have a portion of the product or service that is complete and ready to use or sell, if we choose to do so. For example, we could release it internally to one department and begin to get the return on investment (ROI) after 10 days. Iteration Two is done at Day 20, and Iteration Three is done at the end of Day 30. Make sense?

In a traditional project, usually we are *not* pulling business value and risk to the front, and since we are probably not a dedicated team, we may try to please multiple stakeholders by getting a little done on each part of several projects as we go. We do not see that it matters if we get any one part of this project complete *before* the end date, as long as we finish on Day 30.

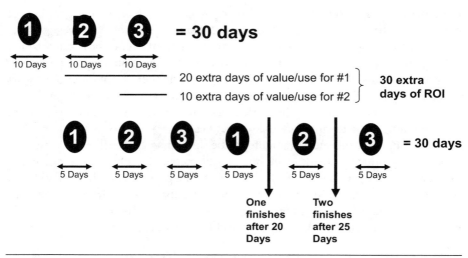

Figure 14.5 Why Agile Has Quicker Return on Investment

So, as a contrast, let's divide the work of the project into 5-day pieces and sequence them like they would be if we only targeted the end date at Day 30 and we try to work on the activities of the entire project at the same time. As shown in the bottom half of Figure 14.5, the pieces are sequenced like a traditional, Waterfall approach. We still finish on Day 30, so what's the big deal?

Well, in this Waterfall model, the work of #1 does not really finish until Day 20, instead of Day 10. And, since we have sequenced the entire project, rather than a two week increment of it that will provide a self-contained piece of the project functionality, we may not have a finished piece to deploy to begin to earn a return on our project investment dollars, even when #1 is finished. Remember, we also did not move the risk or the high value items upfront, so there may not be time to complete everything that is of importance to this feature of the product or service to make it useable.

The work of #2 finishes after 25 days, instead of 20, and the total work finishes after 30 days. But there is more to consider. In our three-iteration Agile project at the top, we deployed or released a portion of the project after Iteration One, so we earn 20 extra days of value (or use) for #1 while the rest of the project is being completed. And, we earn 10 extra days of value (or use) for #2. That totals an extra 30 days of ROI by structuring the project in three Agile iterations rather than in the typical Waterfall way.

Usually, the project manager is not responsible for reporting the project value and ROI to the organization; the PMO should be doing this. Someone needs to track to see if the organization got what they paid for. When a project is over, it is not enough to have an Excel pie chart showing whether the project met, or at least fell within, overage allocation metrics. The question is, did the project deliver the value to the organization that led them to invest in it in the first place?

If we create value in small increments, to be released internally as the project unfolds, we can shorten the time it takes to begin to have a return on how quickly we answer customer calls (new, automated call queue project), how fast we can bill customers which means a faster income stream of payments (new, improved billing process project), or whatever it was we were trying to achieve. The earlier we can use or release fully formed features and begin to recoup our investment, the faster those dollars can flow back into the organization and help fund this and other projects.

The reason that projects are funded in the first place is to receive a return on investment. The earlier the flow of return, and the earlier the flow of business value, the better. If a useable part of the product can be sold to the public, and then features added or upgrades made available later, we begin to generate revenue earlier. Many of us studied the present and future value of money for the PMP exam. Money we get now is worth more than money we get in the future.

You will never get backing to fund a change to Agile practices for your team by presenting it as a necessary infrastructure change, or by saying, "Everybody's doing it." If you want to be the project manager who becomes a catalyst for the Agile migration in your workplace, being able to show actual dollars flow more quickly from an Agile project is the path to management support. Couple that with Agile innovation as a way to differentiate the company, and as a way to fund projects that get things to market faster.

Handling Cancelled or Deferred Projects

As project managers, it is normal to become very attached to our projects and want to protect and defend them. We do not want our projects cancelled, or our resources pulled to be used on a project that we view as a "competitor," even if it is staffed by our friends on the other team. It is easy to feel it is a personal slap in the face and allow it to be a discouraging moment for the team if our projects, no matter how challenged they become, are not allowed to slowly and painfully limp over the finish line.

However, as we elevate ourselves and our points-of-view as project managers to the business strategy level, we accept that the organization needs to be able to constantly re-evaluate projects and stop them, if necessary, to reallocate resources and fund other more robust revenue or value-producing projects. At the organizational level, our marketplace competitor may announce a new product, stock prices shift, the company's ability to borrow money changes, or sales vary—either positively or negatively—and things need to be constantly adjusted in the business in order to cope. With an Agile approach, a project can be truncated early and still deliver the maximum business value from the work already done, since we are producing small, complete, and useable pieces with each iteration. We are virtually eliminating the financial drain of sunk costs when projects are stopped midstream.

Your mother may have already told you, "It is not always about you, you, you." As a project manager with a wider understanding of what makes organizations profitable and the need for flexibility in today's marketplace, try not to take a cancelled or temporarily deferred project you manage as a personal blow to your ego. Help your team understand that it is not a mark against their performance success, either. On an Agile team, once the group truly achieves a comfort level with changing scope and not always ticking the box "Done" next to every user story in the backlog, the self-worth that everyone feels from completing things incrementally will greatly overshadow other emotions.

Agile Budgeting and Forecasting

Moving to an Agile project management approach that timeboxes value in a one to four week period also allows the business to have an Agile budget and forecasting process. This frees the organization to adjust, postpone, or cancel projects in response to non-project related events that occur. Since that is a flexibility that is not found in a traditional/Waterfall project, the best practice seems to be to keep a separate portfolios for Agile projects and another one for more traditional projects.

A study in 2011, by the Aberdeen Group, found that organizations that were limited to changing their budgets and forecasts on a yearly budget cycle were only able to report where the organization stood financially at any given point in the year with about 70% accuracy. Those with a more Agile, monthly basis to reassess their budgets and forecasts, had an internal financial accuracy at any point in the year of 93%. This Agile reporting structure translated directly to an increased market share and higher profitability.[2]

Although budgeting, forecasting, and financial accountability for the company as a whole seldom falls under the purview of the project manager, it is good information to have when you are presenting yourself as a credible person to speak about the value of changes in the Agile direction. Don't forget to stress Agile's relationship with fostering innovation, since increased focus on innovation is essential for companies trying to stay afloat in today's markets.

Geoffrey Moore, the author of *Crossing the Chasm*, provided a seminal look at how technological advances move across the chasm between Early Adopters and the Early Majority. Moore's recent book, *Escape Velocity,* talks about the innovation that an organization can drive through Agile philosophies, commenting that the project manager can no longer afford to sit back and assume a passive role. The project manager needs to step up and drive business value.[3] However, Moore states that there is a major stumbling block standing in the way. CEOs, and high level management officials, are measured as successful in terms of the company's stock price. Their management compensation is tied to what their quarterly results were in the most recent three-month period. So, it makes sense for them to steer the time and resources of the company toward the short-term objective of looking good *now*, thus trapping the company in their legacy business.

If an organization is to flourish long term, it is important for the business objectives and the corporate budget to free human capital and allocate dollars to the innovation category of the budget to create future products and services, not just to optimize the business in which you are already engaged. But it is hard to free up resources for the future when they could be used to generate higher performance for the current quarter.

Moore continues that there is a misconception that large companies have an inability to create innovation and that creativity is relegated only to smaller, start-up shops. In his book, *Dealing with Darwin,* Moore says that in reality there is a large reserve of innovative products already in queue for release in major organizations, but the issue for the currently successful organization is getting the marketing dollars to bring them to the public. The larger and more successful a company becomes, risk to gain becomes asymmetrical: the less you have to gain from taking a risk and the more you have to lose. In project management terms, we describe that as management that is *risk adverse.*

But if marketing dollars are hoarded to drive current profits that make this quarter look good at the expense of supporting the release of new and innovative products in the future, eventually your corporation's core products no longer meet the needs of the marketplace and your company fades from view.

A good example of this might be Kodak. A January 19, 2012 headline from Bloomberg.com told it all: "Kodak Files for Bankruptcy as Digital Era Spells End to Film." The sad part of the story is that Kodak actually invented digital camera technology. But with their success through the years providing film to a marketplace stuffed with film-using personal cameras, as well as voracious customers in the movie industry, they failed to commercialize their own digital innovation. Robert Burley, an associate professor at Toronto's Ryerson University said, "They were a company stuck in time. Their history was so important to them, this rich century-old history when they made a lot of amazing things and a lot of money along the way. Now their history has become a liability." CEO Antonio Perez, after taking over Kodak in 2005 and understanding the need for change, tried to save the organization by cutting costs and finding a marketing opening for Kodak ink-jet printers at Wal-Mart and Staples stores. But the company was not able to sell enough printers to generate sufficient continuing revenue through replacement supplies and ink, the real source of a printer product's profitability.[4]

Proving the point that Moore made about there being plenty of bottled-up innovation in companies who were relying on old market prowess, rather than risking marketing dollars to introduce new products, Kodak deliberately shelved the digital camera it invented in 1975 so that it would not threaten its own lucrative film business. Organizations need to be adaptive and find a balance between supporting current products and developing new ones before their core businesses get too long-in-the-tooth and begin to dim in customer desirability and relevance.

Actively Seeking New Technology

The role of the project manager has traditionally been to direct his or her activities to finishing an assigned project within given parameters. With the speed of business firing up to light speed, you can gain stature and become a person whose voice is sought if you proactively look for new technology in the market that would advance the prowess of your project team and your organization.

Voice Biometrics

For example, one bottleneck or constraint for the team frequently cited by frustrated project managers, is waiting for sign-offs. In Microsoft Project training classes, the "go to" example to learn to set a Constraint is "Wait for Management Sign-off." It could be that the sales team has secured a new client and the internal administrative functions of the organization have alerted you to form a team and gear up for this new business. However, no one can pull the "Go" switch on the project until the formal contract has been signed by the customer and it is securely in the hands of the procurement division, the sales manager, or the corresponding administrative niche in the company.

One interesting new technology removes the delay between when the customer would traditionally place ink to paper and when the physical documents can be mailed, picked up, or otherwise transported to your offices. In addition, Angel, a provider of enterprise-focused technology, reports research that shows, "No matter what the industry, there is a 30% to 55% falloff rate when a paper process is involved in getting a signature from parties who are not face-to-face."[5] In other words, the deal is verbally closed, but up to half of them are never completely solidified because the paperwork is never submitted. This is a huge waste of time and resources throughout your organization as sales people and other administrative interfaces, down to and including your project team, may plan for this work in an already squeezed portfolio of projects.

Angel's innovation is that they eliminate the lengthy process after the contract is agreed to in substance by both parties, including signatures, copies, faxes, mail, or other forms of paper distribution used in contract processes. Plus, there are the same sorts of paper handling processes (read delays) within the hierarchy of the buyer. Their solution? Voice biometrics used to create technology to allow a voice signature solution. In addition to a faster return of contracts or other important documents, there are higher levels of data security since the virtual papers do not pass through multiple intermediaries, which could be a security hazard if corporate secrets leaking to competitors, or the press, is a risk. There are tighter audit trails with electronic solutions and a higher conversion rate from the spoken agreement to the signed contract. Increasing revenue as you raise the closure rate on negotiated contracts and an easier, faster customer experience as buyers deal with your firm are additional benefits.

We have become comfortable with biometrics for identification based on facial recognition, fingerprints, and iris and retina scanning. One small bank in Nebraska used a thumbprint for customer ID and touted the slogan, "At our bank, Thumbody loves you." Despite this groanable catchphrase, the bank gained acceptance because they removed the need for passwords, pin numbers, and challenging identifier questions.

Biometrics ensure that the person "signing" a document is, indeed, the person who has the authority to do so. The natural progression is to a voice print that digitally represents the algorithmically derived model of 100 points of physical and behavioral characteristics of a speaker's voice. Then the voiceprint can be compared to the stored one to authenticate the speaker.

Voice biometrics use existing phone systems, so no special hardware or software is needed. However, special, sophisticated techniques are employed to be sure that a recording of a speaker's voice does not match and "clear or pass" in the same way a live, spoken utterance would. Rather than a futuristic, science fiction dream, voice biometrics are already recognized by the FDA as legally binding, E-Sign Act compliant, e-signatures. Depending on the compliance hurdles you face, know that voice signatures satisfy FFIEC and FCC CPNI compliance requirements, as well as HIPPA/CMS guidelines if you work in or for the medical profession. Angel expands the value of return rates to say, "Businesses find that when using paper-based processes, 45% to 70% of contracts typically do not come back. That dropout rate goes to almost zero when a voice signature is obtained the moment someone says, "Yes".

Let's view this idea through our "What's In It for Me?" (WIIFM) glasses. Perhaps your main concern is not the closure rate of sales contracts for the business. Your personal pain may come from the delays in getting managerial and customer approval for project decisions and sign-offs before you can move on. If this could be given verbally, or captured in a phone call, think of the savings in time. Visualize this in an Agile environment where the project owner views the team's output at the end of the iteration and you can capture his or her spoken, formal approval into your cell phone. The idea is, "If you agree, speak on the dotted line."

In an organization wholly committed to Agile, lighter documentation and face-to-face, verbal OKs may suffice. However, if you are in a more structured organization that is in transition to being more Agile, or working with external customers on a contractual basis, the ability to capture spoken approval may have tremendous value to your team.

Moving beyond possible applications of voice recognition within your organization for the use of the sales and project teams, consider whether you might incorporate something from this technology into the projects themselves. Corporate servers today have various methods to check that users are who they say they are when accessing protected company information as employees. Some websites also require voice validation to access bank balances or the status of orders.

Perhaps you will be trying to attract more customers, or provide a higher rate of customers served with existing equipment, by shortening each interaction. Allowing the customer to speak, rather than type, to gain access to customer support lines or to register warranties might be a differentiator for you. In a study commissioned by Nuance Communications and carried out by Harris Interactive in 2003, 9 out of 10 participants said they preferred using a speech system versus traditional touchtone ("If you'd like to check the status of your order, press 1"). In the same study, 70% of the participants said their customer experience would be improved if speech were used instead of touchtone-only systems.[6]

In a Waterfall project life cycle, the end of producing the deliverables ordinarily also ends the concern of the team for the project. But within the new, Agile, order of things project managers are going to need to remind teams to think through the cost of maintenance and warranty issues when making their *how* decisions during project construction. As we all adopt the attitude that each of us has a responsibility to be concerned for the financial stability of the organization (and the ability to continue to have our paychecks not bounce), we will need to expand the range of considerations that go into making the best decisions for the project.

The point is not that in order to be Agile you need to have your company move to implement voice signatures immediately. As business moves forward at lightning speed, you need to not only be receptive, but actively seek out new technologies that you, as the project manager, could suggest that will solve common project problems. Who knows what will be available to you that seems unheard of today, but might be used by your competitors within the next few months to surpass you in the marketplace.

3D Printers

Fashioning prototypes of physical objects from 3D printers has been used in auto-motive industry prototypes of car parts for about 25 years. Today, Mercedes-Benz, Honda, Boeing, and Lockheed Martin, are only a few of the companies that use 3D printers to not only craft prototypes, but to actually make parts that are shipped in the final automobile or airplane.

Custom-made medical devices measured to scale for a particular client, architectural models of planned projects, and demonstration shapes for electronic devices to allow testing for internal space for parts, are a few of the practical applications of this printer. Want a Godiva chocolate with a 3D image of your face? It is in the works. Invisalign, the company which makes clear, custom braces that appear to disappear in your mouth finds 3D printing is a perfect production methodology for a one-of-a-kind product.

3D printing technology is so far advanced, even though it may be new to consumers, that there are "build-it yourself" kits for hobbyists, along with free software applications that can be downloaded from the Internet, to allow you to customize an "object", press print, and in a few minutes remove a fully formed three-dimensional creation from your home 3D printer.

Larger machines can create shopping carts, car dashboards, and other sizeable parts. This is another example of the type of hybrid projects you may be asked to lead. Rather than the project combining manufactured products that are coupled with software to produce their value, this manufactured product is actually *pro-duced* by the software, which can easily be customer designed. Again, project managers will need to be familiar with the needs and processes of both types of development teams

Will your future projects need to include an online application through which customers can create the small parts of your product that may break over time? If they need a special hex screwdriver to assemble the product, it might be cheaper to provide software online to allow the customer to "print" it at home, rather than include it in every box. But 3D is not the only changing concept for printers:

- The Environmental Pencil Printer uses black pencil lead instead of toner, so that mistakes to a printed copy can be quickly corrected with a common pencil eraser, and a small error filled in by hand with any regular lead pencil.
- The RITI Coffee Printer turns old coffee grounds into printer ink.
- If you'd like to appear at a customer's office "in person" (or delight the recipients of your cards), an Augmented Reality Printer prints your face on a postcard. When this card is held in front of a webcam, your likeness is transmitted to the computer monitor and becomes active.

So far this is more of a novelty, but the technology may have interesting business uses.

- Busy at work and no time to fix dinner? The Cornucopia Food Printer stores and mixes edible materials, then heats and serves them[7]

Food for thought as you plan for the flexibility that you may need to continue your project management success in the next few years.

Documenting Team Authority

In a Waterfall project, the decision-making authority is clear to the team. It *does not* rest with them. In fact, you as project manager probably do not have much authority either. When a decision needs to be made that is not found in the pages of documents e-mailed to you at the start of the project, you need to try to find out who does have the ability to sign-off on changes, and then get them to do so.

If agility is important because speed to market may make or break the company, you cannot have the value flow constrained while you chase down a functional manager. So, good Agile software practices start with a clear delineation that the product owner chooses the features that are the most important in terms of business value and risk, and the Agile team has the right to add support or substructure architecture to the backlog as well. The product owner prioritizes and the team assigns degree of difficulty points to the user stories. Very clear cut. Since the product owner, or his or her surrogate with decision making power, is available and closely housed with the project team, the constraint of needing a quick decision and having to wait for it is minimized.

However, once you move outside of the software team and into organizational projects that might be adding in Agile, there are also larger decisions that need to be divided between the various roles of the project upfront to minimize delays. These authorizations to make decisions may be non-traditional if you are used to performing in highly structured and controlling organizations. As the philosophies of Agile begin to infiltrate the halls of management, there may be additional authority entrusted at the team level, especially concerning *how* involved the team is in creating the work of the project.

Here is a partial list to help get you started thinking about decision points in your project.

Even if the person to make them in the past has been the functional manager, the procurement department, or you as the project manager, there might be value in moving authority to the self-directed team to decide answers to questions such as:

- **Who authorizes travel?** Is there value in allowing money in the project budget for the team to bring in representatives from distributed teams for coordination meetings? Could the team decide if and when that expense should be incurred? Could an allocation be made for travel between distributed teams, with who travels and when left to the team to decide?

- **Who selects the team members?** If this becomes a standing team built on trust and skilled at working together, should team members be allowed to interview and any choose additional members needed, deciding who has skills the team lacks and would fit into the team culture? Could the team, or a few representative members, be more valuable to sit in on initial interviews to assess technical skills and "fit" for Agile awareness and also experience, personal characteristics, and attitudes, rather than a random HR generalist?

- **Who should remove a team member?** Each team member should work within the Agile philosophies and practices of the team. If they cannot or won't, is their removal a decision that could be made within a self-directed team? Do they have the most accurate awareness of the hit the project work would take without this person's skill sets?

- **Who chooses training?** Does HR, the functional manager, or you as the project manager decide whether or not the team gets training, when it will happen, and how the training will be delivered? Do the team members have an allocation as part of the project budget for training, if needed? Do they have the time to do online training at work, or the ability to access it at home through corporate servers if they want to use their own time?

- **Who evaluates team member performance, compensation, and bonuses?** Is this done by the functional manager, the project manager, or other team associates? Is the team evaluated as a unit, rather than as individuals?

- **Who is responsible for team recognition?** Is it the product owner, functional manager, project manager, or Vice-President of the department? Does the team have a budget to use for expressions of internal team recognition and team celebrations for completing a project? Some people find public attention more of a punishment than a reward. Would the close-knit group be the best source of knowing what kind of gesture would be appreciated and motivating for a teammate? Would the team prefer to eschew individual recognition altogether for the more Agile practice of wanting to share all the spoils of success along with all of the pressures of performance?

Additional questions about team authority that may need to be addressed might be: Who will select and manage key business partners? Who will select and manage technology partners? Who selects and manages outside contractors? Who selects and manages outside vendors and suppliers? Who picks the team location? Who plans the layout of the team work area? Who selects the process methods used for the project? Who selects the test procedures and determines test criteria? Who sets the standards for documentation? Who sets the quality standards?

These questions are not to suggest that the team should be the responsible party in every instance, but that these are decisions that should be made, written out, and posted in a prominent site in the team workspace. The goal is to have decisions made at the lowest possible point in the organizational structure, so that teams are empowered to have both the responsibility and the authority to get the job done. If they require sign-off, they at least deserve to be able to quickly and easily see who it is, and perhaps have contact information available at a glance, too.

One way to see where these decisions should rest is to draw a visual model of the flow of the work of the project. Any point at which you are placing a constraint to wait for a decision by a customer, or an internal executive, might be a spot to consider if this could possibly be authority assigned to the team. The value of Agile will be negated if the work of the project must grind to a halt every time a decision is to be made. Again, once listed, authority decision points should be clearly posted on the wall of the team room.

References

[1]Gartner Group Study. 2011. Retrieved from http://gartner.com.
[2]Aberdeen Group. March, 2011. Retrieved from https://aberdeen.com.
[3]"Geoffrey Moore speaking on his book, *Escape Velocity: Free Your Company's Future from the Pull of the Past. BNet.*
[4]McCarty, D. & Jinks, B. "Kodak Files for Bankruptcy as Digital Era Spells End to Film." *Bloomberg,* January 19, 2012.
[5]"Speak on the Dotted Line." Angel White paper. 2012.
[6]Harris Interactive. "Speech Satisfaction Study," March 2003.
[7]Ionescu, D. "15 Amazing Concept Printers." *PC World,* March 26, 2010.

15

What Shifts in Business Will Affect Me?

One key way projects are shifting is in the business focus of what the project is intended to achieve. For example, traditionally, software was imagined as a support for the internal structure of the organization. It facilitated the transfer and storage of information, allowed people to pull together data for making better decisions, and performed a common, operational function such as payroll, inventory control, personnel records, or maintaining customer databases. But newer roles for software are emerging that show the need to oversee both software development and its increasing role in traditional product production. Managing these dual capabilities will become increasingly vital to the project manager who wants to move forward in the field.

A recent *Small Business Success* story about Shawnimals on CNN's Morning Express focused on a start up operation which illustrates software/product integration aligned with corporate intent.[1] The owner, Shawn Smith, talked of his passion for toy making and love of creating unique characters. We are familiar with the model of *Star Wars* movies, Disney or Pixar movie cartoons, TV series for children, and popular books or comics, evolving in their outreach for new income sources. Their creators find additional corporate revenue by adding merchandise sold online, in toy stores, or offered as extras in fast food bundles for children.

Smith knew he could not start as a new small business and hope to compete in these overcrowded arenas already filled with large scale competitors. As he searched for a way to use his own vivid creativity in a business through which he could differentiate himself in the marketplace, he realized that it was the engagement and interest in the story line that led kids to clamor for the accompanying figures. So, his innovative market plan was to design an online game with the specific, premeditated intent from the outset to create an imaginary world that included up to 23 mythical countries. Each unique land was populated with characters that could be leveraged into handmade, stuffed toys. A related Nintendo application also helped to widen the potential market and ingratiate these characters into the mindset of children, who would be the target market for his handmade toys representing each of these fantasy characters.

As project managers, we need to be aware that the road from creating merchandise as the end-goal, to seeing merchandise as a fortuitous by-product of an original sellable item like a movie, to creating online games with the specific idea and construct to maximize sales of tangible, related characters, is indicative of the path to new business models that we will be asked to serve in future projects. Again, both the ability to master and foster success in Agile software development, and the ability to coordinate with other, tangible products being produced by Agile/traditionally blended processes, will be important to our project management skill sets moving forward.

At the Shawnimals Company, they realized that creativity does not just magically appear in the quantity and frequency needed to keep expanding the product line and constantly coming up with new ideas to keep the fans interested. Every two weeks, the company has an Inspiration Day, where the entire team meets to listen to music, watch movies, and participate in other efforts that might stimulate their imagination. Can you see the common Agile workspace, the inclusion of the entire team as important knowledge workers, the servant-leadership attitude of the company owner/product owner, the focus on flexibility/creativity/innovation, the openness to change, and the regular, incremental, timeboxed periods set as boundaries to encourage the team to address issues sooner rather than later? All of these are Agile concepts, but appropriately configured for this unique project work.

Common Team Workspaces

Creating a common team space is an often overlooked, but critically important part of facilitating an Agile team. **Osmotic communication** occurs when *information flows in the background hearing of other team members as they pick up ideas and information by osmosis*, meaning the ideas are subtle or gradually absorbed. Close proximity, and the ability to roll a chair over to ask a question or to help a partner, is key. Having the whiteboard information, flip chart progress charts, burndown or burnup charts, and other forms of information radiators, as well as team rules and decision authority charts posted where they are impossible not to notice, is an advantage not to be underestimated. You might consider rearranging desks in a circle facing away from each other. This way, when walking to and from their own space, people can see what is on one another's screen. It makes it easier to stop by to make a comment, ask a question, or offer a suggestion on the fly. Chairs can easily be pulled together for a short meeting or for pair work. Other teams move away from desks entirely, preferring to work on an arrangement of common tables and a series of shared computer stations.

This shared team real estate is also the place to hold demonstrations at the end of each iteration. Assembling the shareholders here is a good way to make them feel a part of the team, know where to come to interact with the team, and has the added advantage of allowing them to review the team metrics on the walls in an informal way without the necessity of a mind-numbing PowerPoint presentation to tout progress.

Once stakeholders realize that they can answer their own concerns about forward movement of the work, you may find them coming to your shared space for a quick look on their own, rather than asking for a formal document about the progress. And, once they are voluntarily there, it is easy for team members to ask questions on the spot, rather than having to ask the project manager to get information for them, avoiding the lag time it takes to get answers that either delays the user story completion or forces the team to make decisions based on false assumptions.

Shared workspace also helps the team check their own progress and drives the forward movement of the team toward the iteration's goals. Other stakeholders coming into the area or moving through the area can also see the status. This motivational technique is akin to posting a picture of yourself on the refrigerator to support your diet attempts. Whether you post a current picture of yourself fat, or an old picture of yourself when you were thin, (i.e., burndown or burnup), the constant reminder of your goals is an incentive to not forget them. Although the common workspace works in practical ways, one of the new goals of many organizations is the need for innovative solutions to current problems. Collocation also has a positive effect on creativity.

In the book *Where Good Ideas Come From,* Stephen Johnson talks about how quickly technology is accelerating, producing wave after wave of new products. There is a change to our cultural acceptance of technology, too, as the marketplace is increasingly open to buying, learning, and using new items. In fact, as the lines outside the Apple store with each new version/product illustrate, we anxiously await the next, incremental advancement. We have moved from watching one of three network channels to watching content on the Internet, to embracing a participatory involvement as we upload video to YouTube and other Internet share sites. As we strive to become more creative, have better ideas, and become more innovative, Johnson's point is, "some environments squelch new ideas; some environments seem to breed them effortlessly."[2]

Johnson talks about the spaces that have historically led to unusual rates of creativity and innovation, and notes that we often have simplified myths such as Isaac Newton discovered gravity when he was hit on the head by an apple, or that one day it suddenly dawned on Charles Darwin that there was an evolutionary process at work that accounted for how life originated. The reality is that great ideas do not actually spring fully formed into our minds, but that there are many small, nagging hunches that over time collide and form a larger, more important idea. Often, the hunches that eventually erupt into an innovation may not all reside in the mind of one person. So the challenge becomes to provide an environment where those separate half-ideas can come together and be exposed to their other crucial half.

Many famous authors from Europe had the coffee house as their muse. Not only could they observe human behavior as an inspiration for their fictional literary characters, they had the chance to talk with people from all fields. The Elephant House, an Edinburgh, Scotland coffee shop posts a sign stating, "Harry Potter Born Here," next to a photo of J. K. Rowling writing on a pad. Around the mid-20th century, Ernest Hemingway, John-Paul Sartre, and Albert Camus wrote in the same French café, Les Deux Magots, which was also frequented by the painter Pablo Picasso. Writer Gertrude Stein hosted the painters Henri Matisse, Picasso, and Paul Cezanne at parties in her Paris apartment in the first half of the 1900s. Did you even stop to think why all of these successful, creative people are known for their social interactions in cafes or salons? Was it merely that it was warmer there? Or, perhaps you assumed it was that the strong coffee stimulated the imagination, or that the free party food attracted hungry artists. Johnson says that these coffee houses and private salons were crucial to fueling imagination and creativity because they "created a space where ideas could mingle and swap and create new forms." The increasing opportunities for connectivity through the Internet, international travel, and other technological advances allow us to reach out and make a connection with the ideas of others to borrow and combine with our own to thoughts to elicit a fuller, workable, and innovative idea in our own brain. So, naturally, we are recording an unparalleled age of technological advances. Johnson postulates that, "chance favors the connected mind."

This supports the idea that the shared workspace of the Agile team is more than a convenience or a signpost holder for passing stakeholders. If the collaborative work of the team is best served by innovation, innovation is best served by a common, relaxed place where people are encouraged to share ideas, present half-solved ideas to the group pool, and overhear conversations between people in related, but different, fields of focus than their own. The common team area is not only a convenience, it is a breeding ground for innovation. In the biological world, innovation is a mutation in a species that occurs when the species is under stress, and certainly our business world is currently under stress.

Design That Matters: Junkyard Incubators

Sometimes innovation is needed to find a way to produce and maintain an existing product to function in new circumstances, rather than create a new product. You are all familiar with the idea of an incubator used for a newborn baby. About four million babies die each year in developing countries due to low birth-weight, because they may not have access to an incubator to provide a clean environment and help them maintain their body warmth. Incubators may cost up to $30,000 each, but that is not the only stumbling block to their use in rural parts of India, Vietnam, Indonesia, and South Asia locations. There may be a lack of trained technical staff to operate them outside of major cities, local electricity may have incompatible connectors, power surges may damage what few incubators are available, filters that need to be changed every six months may be hard to find, and locating parts for repair when incubators break is a major issue.[3] Plus, who do you call as a trained incubator repairman when you work in a third-world clinic?

Timothy Prestero, CEO of *Design That Matters*, headed a project to investigate this problem. As researchers hoping to innovatively solve this problem, the team looked around one rural overseas area and found a big pile of discarded Toyota 4Runners. They took the SUVs apart and saw that they had discovered a group of things that were plentiful in rural, third-world areas: car parts. The team realized that automobiles are one of the few products that have a global supply and distribution chain, maintained by the automobile manufacturers, meaning that parts are available *and* there are people trained to fix cars all over the world.

The resulting "junkyard incubator" innovation uses two sealed-beam headlights (being careful that they are not brand specific) to warm a bassinette mattress from below, a dashboard fan for circulation to bring in filtered outside air for warming or cooling, and signal lights and a door chime to alert caregivers if the temperature of the baby, or of the NeoNurture unit, falls outside the desired parameters. It also uses a motorcycle battery plus a 12 volt car charger as a stand-alone power source for use during travel between the clinic and the infant's home. By constructing the incubator from auto parts, the team ensured that even something as simple as finding and replacing a 60 cent filter did not become a problem.[4]

You may not be creating incubators to tip the life/death balance for infants in poor, rural areas, but you might be involved in a crucial redesign of your organization's products where creativity may make the difference in competitive success. Johnson says, "The trick to having good ideas is not to sit around in glorious isolation and try to think big thoughts. The trick is to get more parts on the table." This is why cities tend to produce more innovation as people from various ethnicities, cultures, backgrounds, industries, and job related fields all come together and interface at work, at home, or in social settings from a Starbucks, to a golf course, to a PTA meeting. Translate this type of innovation process to bringing together the various teams working on a large project and allowing them to get to know each other on an individual basis.

Microsoft Research Division: Space Design

The research division of Microsoft in Redmond, WA, known as Building 99, opened in November, 2007. Building designer Martha Clarkson traveled to 26 Microsoft facilities around the globe and studied the way the teams worked. Some teams clearly preferred an open, collaborative work environment. To reflect this, the new office building has plenty of space for on-the-fly collaboration, with many small, meeting rooms where workers can relax and discuss ideas. Each day, the theory group from Microsoft Research, including physicists, economists, and mathematicians, meet for afternoon tea. It is a social get together, but they gravitate into conversations that end up relevant to their work. Many rooms have upholstered chairs around a coffee table to evoke a comfortable, living room setting. They also feature glass walls that can be used as white boards for drawing diagrams and capturing ideas on the fly.

Back in their own workspace, teams have options like offices with movable walls that can be converted into a larger, shared office space. What most offices have in terms of a kitchenette with a refrigerator is replaced by open "mixer stations," where employees gather to share ideas or gossip. The perfect location for the daily stand-up meeting.[5]

Steelcase, Inc.: Furnishings Design

Steelcase, once just a provider of office furniture, has become one of the leaders in new-age office space design. Based on their philosophy that business is increasingly a team sport, and that collaboration is trending up right now and unlikely to fade, they have used an Agile approach to design new building spaces and retool old ones. Capitalizing on the principle of involving the users early and often, the Steelcase Applied Research and Consulting (ARC) group set up user workshops to ask for their help in understanding how people work today, how they see themselves working in the future, and how satisfied they were with current workspaces. Steelcase looked at factors such as the need for collaboration, concentration, mobility, privacy, adjacency to other groups, storage, and technology to interface with other remote or distributed team members or vendors.

Steelcase also considered how the office design could support both local and distributed collaboration, and how to nurture communication and create a place to share and discuss ideas to incubate innovative products and services. Finding inspiration for spaces that allowed people to work easily together and were also flexible enough to provide quiet, private opportunities when necessary, seemed to spring forth best by involving the people most skilled in understanding the corporate culture and the work of the organization: the employees.

Using the same tools, methods, and processes employed when consulting with customers, Steelcase redesigned its own corporate headquarters in 2012. John Hughes, leader of the ARC team that redid the corporate space says, "You give people an environment that's open and inviting, where discussion is encouraged, where random encounters lead to more idea sharing, and spaces where people can easily work together."[6]

Skype: Virtual Space Design

Skype, the innovative communications leader that provides Internet connectivity through free text, audio, video, and desktop sharing connections, is another organization that has retooled its spaces to foster collaboration, in conjunction with Steelcase. Hughes succinctly comments in a way that shows office reorganization issues parallel other similar issues that are driving companies to move to Agile when he states, "There's no company that isn't struggling with this new business environment. Everywhere, resources are stretched thin from downsizing and a struggling economy. Business issues are more complex that just a few years ago, more organizations are working on a global platform, and every company needs its employees, along with every other corporate asset, to do more than ever."

Hughes' thought is also that the workplace itself can be a key factor in attracting and retaining the most talented knowledge workers. Skype knew that it was located just down the road from HP, Google, and Cisco, and competing with them to attract top talent. By offering a working environment that is both appealing and high-functioning, they hope to have that "extra something" that wins the top thinkers in the race to hire the best of the best. A recent Living Workplace Survey found that 37% of the respondents said that the quality of the work environment was one of the top three factors in determining their job satisfaction.[7]

Since good Agile teamwork relies on building trust, settings like Skype, where lunch each day takes place in an internal café with catered delicacies, foster a way for teams to get to know people from all over the company: engineers, marketing staff, IT professionals, and public relations staff. The conversation can move between family life, sports, entertainment, news, work, and into current challenges or exciting ideas that a person is thinking about on a project. This is the modern day version of the Edinburgh coffee house or Stein's Paris salons. It is a Petri dish for germinating innovative ideas.

Let's be honest. You may be slightly cynical and thinking, "Of course, Steelcase would support designing collaborative workspaces. It means a lot of revenue for them, consulting on what users want and then selling the organization remodeling contracts and new office furniture." But these ideas of what is important in creating a productive work environment did not originate with the furniture company.

Explicit and Tacit Knowledge

One of the original thinkers around how to foster the birth of new, breakthrough ideas was Michael Polanyi. The popular idea in 1958, when he wrote, *Personal Knowledge*, was that the best way to discover new things was by the scientific process. The scientific process was an impartial, unemotional exploration in a closed, laboratory setting to systematically move past the unsuccessful experimental results and eventually, by process of elimination, arrive at a new truth. In essence, science succeeded best when the scientists remained "value-free."[8]

By contrast, Polanyi felt that creative acts, especially acts of discovery, come when a person has strong personal feelings and a sense of commitment to discovering a new truth. He wrote that informed guesses, hunches, and the continuous processing of partial truths and half solutions motivated by what he called "passions," eventually could be coupled with those found in other places, or other people, to form a new model or theory.

Remember Nonaka and Takeuchi, the Japanese managers who were the first describers of Scrum and many other current Agile ideas? They were also interested in the process that led to new discoveries and talked about two types of knowledge, explicit and tacit.[9] **Explicit knowledge** is *the formal information you can write down and share in corporate documents.* The reliance of an organization on its training manuals, its PMO procedures, and the archived automated software reports of past projects, are examples of the use and transfer of explicit knowledge.

However, as we move into a new age of information transfer, companies are aware that they need to provide ways to capture and exchange **tacit knowledge**, *the knowledge embedded in a person's individual experience that is hard to articulate.* It contains insights, problem solving skills, intuitions, hunches, and other personal information. As teams become groups based on trust, this knowledge that is unwritten and cannot be formally captured is transmitted between people via stories, examples, and helpful suggestions informally exchanged in the group setting.

An organization cannot standardize the transfer of tacit knowledge, but can set up situations and work place environments that nurture it and enhance its exchange. The Gensler 2008 U.S. Workplace Survey identified four types of work modes that knowledge workers use: focusing, learning, socializing, and collaborating.[10]

Focusing

The first work mode is *focusing*, the time (often private time) that individuals spend "thinking, studying, contemplating, strategizing, processing, and other heads-down uninterrupted work." This is the way we picture a traditional project team member working at his or her list of Microsoft Project tasks in a private cubicle. Focusing also occurs at the point where an Agile team member takes the user stories to which he or she has committed for this iteration and begins working on the one with the top priority.

The workplace needs to provide space, whether it is a personal desk or communal private office, to which an individual can retire and escape noise if they need to work without disruptions. The trend in an Agile office space is that these are not permanently assigned, but there may be small conference rooms that are not continuously booked, leaving a spot to retreat for the person who needs some time to work alone.

Learning

The second work mode is *learning*. This is where a person builds on his or her own understanding and knowledge, which happens most readily when individuals share with each other. The learning is accelerated when thinking is made visible and exchanged with the team. Think of the consensus building practices of an Agile team like Fist of Five, T-Shirt sizing, or Planning Poker. Imagine pair programming, or pairs of people working on a non-software type project, but merging the development of the idea along with the secondary viewpoints added before any unchangeable commitment is made to any one path.

The collocated space with room for the numerous information radiators on the walls provide the visible part of the team thinking, while the other activities give members a chance to informally mention ideas that they have in process. Glass walls or low divider panels allow easier sightlines to the displays of team process. Easier access to the information encourages conversations. Or, perhaps there are a few computers stations dedicated to online training for employees to access as needed to enhance their own learning.

Socializing

Socializing is the third work mode. This is the best way for the knowledge that needs to be retained in the organization to be dispersed. Common lunchrooms, wide hallways that can be converted into temporary small group conference spaces, cappuccino makers, and makeshift libraries with research books and company information can provide places for teams to informally meet with each other and with other stakeholders in the business.

There has been specific concern that with a lot of the Baby Boomer generation reaching retirement age, much of the knowledge of the company they have acquired over their careers has not been adequately documented. When you now have the vocabulary to know that the loss will be in the tacit information they have swirling around, not the explicit information that can be recorded in a Word document or an Excel spreadsheet, you may have more ammunition to get a shared socialization space for your team before that knowledge worker carries the tacit information out along with a gold watch.

Collaborating

The fourth work mode is *collaborating*. It is the heart of the Agile process, where all ideas are respected and all knowledge is shared. In terms of work space, there should be areas for team meetings and stakeholder demonstrations, places for two or three team members to hold an impromptu conversation, areas where the tools are readily available to sketch out ideas, and technology to enable virtual collaboration with remote teams.

Because of the constant demand for informed workers and the inevitable, fast changes in skill sets they must possess, the idea of finding the person already trained and experienced in the talents you require is laughable. It would be better to spend your time considering the fastest way to integrate each person into the team. Lobbying for a collaborative workspace for your team, or cobbling together a makeshift one, may be one way to gain more job satisfaction for your project team, even if they are only at the beginning of a transition to Agile.

As proof that even the creators of Agile believe in a changing and evolving set of principles, on February 12, 2011, on the 10 year anniversary of the original signing of the Agile Manifesto, 16 of the original 17 signers met again for a retrospective to talk about what they had learned after 10 years of practice with their respective methodologies. They agreed that although they still supported their original statements—both their support for traditional values and the ones they created in 2001—they were once again ready to layer new understandings on top of their original thoughts (see Figure 15.1).

They said we now believe that team work and responsibility are more important than just the individual interactions, and that driving business value supersedes just completing working software, products, or services. Creating customer partnerships and elaborating on them takes precedence over just collaborating

Agile Manifesto   2001 - 2011

Team work and responsibility *over*
Individuals and interactions over
Processes and Tools

Products or Services

Business value *over*
Working software over
Comprehensive documentation

Partnership elaboration *over*
Customer collaboration over
Contract negotiation

Preparing for change *over*
Responding to change over
Following a plan

Figure 15.1 The Agile Manifesto, 2011

with customers, and preparing for change is more valuable that just being poised to respond to change. This is proof that Agile is alive and growing. It is an adaptive process, which is adjusting to the economic, social, and business environment in which it lives.

References

[1]CNN Morning Express, April 9, 2012 – Small Business Success.

[2]Johnson, S. 2010. *Where Good Ideas Come From*. New York: Riverhead Trade.

[3]Schultz, J. November 23, 2010. "A Baby Incubator Made from Car Parts." *The New York Times*.

[4]"NeoNurture: The 'Car Parts' Incubator." www.designthatmatters.org,

[5]Gohring, N. November 14, 2007. "Microsoft Goes Mod with Campus Expansion." *PC World*.

[6]360 Research. "Is Your Workplace Ready for the Interconnected World." Retrieved from http://360.steelcase.com/articles/is-your-workplace-ready-for-the-intercon-nected-world.

[7]*ibid*

[8]Polanyi, M. 1958. "Personal Knowledge: Towards a Post-Critical Philosophy." Routledge & Kegan Paul Ltd.

[9]Sutherland, J. October 22, 2011. "Takeuchi and Nonaka: The Roots of Scrum." Retrieved from scrum.jeffsutherland.com.

[10]Gensler 2008 U.S. Workplace Survey. Retrieved from http://www.gensler.com/uploads/documents/2008_Gensler_Workplace_Survey_US_09_30_2009.pdf.

16

What Changes Are Needed in My Organization?

So far we've been talking about changes that you might add to the project team. These are shifts that, with the support of the team, would fall into a grey area where your organization does not really care exactly how you do things, as long as the project results occur. In fact, minor shifts to a more flexible plan with more team empowerment will provide better outcomes. But if you want to move beyond the guerilla types of changes you can sneak in at the project management level, there will eventually have to be some organizational changes in awareness, acceptance, and desire, if Agile is truly going to make the dramatic impact that is possible.

The variations in detail of the changes needed by industry, individual organization, project team, and project are so widespread that there is no checklist and timeline to make this transition automatic or painless. Since Agile is based on a philosophy and requires a change in mindset, it is OK if end results vary from place to place. Thus, the road along the way to incorporating Agile practices has a different starting point in each instance. Despite the multitude of Agile success stories, the reality is that a mighty transformation will not come all at once, but change will evolve in fits and starts, victory by victory.

There are exceptions. Some companies that create and sell software, or those whose financial foundation is based on consulting around Agile processes, have an upper-management team that found this metamorphosis to be the life-blood of differentiation and profitability in today's markets. They have focused on transforming their cultures from top to bottom, and have backed their decisions with the formal authority and funding to make a radical change in a short period of time.

While you may not be that one person in the organization with the power to wave a magic wand and make the decision to head everyone toward a new way of doing projects, you are in a key spot to have the ear of the team, the customer, and the managers in a catalyst role. Here are some general areas in which you could work to evoke the corporate changes needed for an environment supportive to Agile. However, remember that implementing Agile as merely a new set of tools or practices will not give you the expected success.

Authorization

If you are in a large, traditional organization with heavy technical and functional requirements and a "say it all upfront or you'll never get it" philosophy, you probably also have a highly regulated process for project authorization. Typically, it involves estimating time and cost in some degree of detail before the project may even be officially sanctioned. If we are to shift to having product owners or customers create a backlog of user stories and a lighter form of information radiator documentation and tracking, your organization will need to rethink how projects are authorized, since it is not only difficult to estimate the total project upfront in Agile, it is the antithesis of the practices that make it worth using.

At a mid-level position in an organization, it is easy to erroneously assume that everyone who is higher than you on the organizational chart inherently knows more than you do—that's why they are there, right? But you can have an impact by sharing some of the Agile ideas as a vehicle to provide faster time to market, more portfolio flexibility, and the desirable ability to stop, pause, or discontinue projects without forfeiting the ability to have useable value from the portion that was already completed.

The mindset shift in the ranks of management needs to be that it is not the job of the project managers, or the project teams, to produce an unrealistic number of deliverables with a limited pool of time and resources. The organization must learn to do a better job of prioritizing the projects before approving them, and it may have to work from less detailed information for the initial authorization process. Then, the product owner must be realistic and involved in prioritizing the backlog to choose requirements by their critical importance to the organization, in terms of the amount of business value they will create.

Revisit the idea of an Iteration Zero, a short, pre-project period of time to collect high level stories, break down the most important ones into more fully-fleshed user stories, and then use this time period to prototype or model options for the project while discovering the team's velocity. This can provide management with a more realistic idea of the time and cost of the project to create the key features with the highest priorities. The results of an Iteration Zero are more meaningful, and more reliable for organizational planning than traditional estimates, because they are based on the most current decisions, actual work, and the true progress of the team as they create business value right now.

The pivotal factor is getting management to work from less detailed information when authorizing projects. There have been stories of victory based on the project manager and his or her team slowly and carefully learning to understand and embrace Agile principles. Projects that are done in "secret" and produce impressive results can move this issue of organizational support from something you are pushing, to something the organization realizes is better. You are in a stronger position to make your case if upper management is seeking you out to find the source of the sudden and mysterious higher productivity on your team.

Resource Management

Since the goal is to build dedicated, collocated, and cross-functional teams, you will need to find creative ways to alter the resource management practices and put together the best team structures you can manage. The complexity here is because you may have to convince the project management office (PMO) that standing teams are superior to those that are formed as fledglings at the start of each new project. In addition, you will have to work with human resources if it is appropriate for your team to have cross-functional, rather than siloed, skill sets.

Most organizations are currently hiring for a unique skill that is missing in a team, and plan to assemble teams in the same way one might collect colors for a box of crayons. Each crayon may have similar characteristics, but a single crayon may offer a unique and non-duplicated way to color the world, i.e., a single skill. Envisioning a box where the wax residents are used individually to create multiple-hued situations, or even utilized two at a time to create something better than a one-function stick, is a leap for most employers.

We often transfer the teacher/classroom motif to the manager/team member relationship. Human resources may be looking for characteristics like, "takes directions well" and "follows orders" rather than "colors outside the lines." Project managers hoping to move the organization toward an Agile destination will need to be able to identify and describe the types of people they want on their teams in great detail, and be prepared to explain why these newly requested characteristics are more desirable than the ones on the usual new-hire checklist.

Communications

If face-to-face communication is the Holy Grail that we seek, you will need to be creative in how you arrange space, secure dedicated team assignments, and provide technology bridges for those who are a virtual, rather than a physical presence on the team. Is there an unused conference room that could be hijacked for your team room? If you work in a "cube farm," can the cubical dividers be collectively reassembled to provide walls that slightly separate the team from the operational activities going on around them, rather than from one another? If desks cannot be reattached to the partitions since they no longer form multiple, tidy corners, can makeshift tables be constructed from leftover partitions using the old desks as bases, to provide a place where the team can work together?

If you are moving the team you manage toward Agile and have interface points with other teams, you are going to need to be skilled in translating the activities and progress of your group into language and artifacts/documents that are usable for the other teams. Part of your role as an Agile project manager is to do that sort of facilitation, leaving your team in a protective bubble to be able to focus on the work of the process flow.

Metrics

For a true Agile transformation, the corporation will need to sincerely move to the mentality that for a project to come out ahead of the game, you have to keep your eye on the ball, not on the players. In other words, you have to find a way to lead your organization to focus on how quickly project teams can push customer value through the system flow, not focus on micromanaging individual performances.

The metrics that the company uses to assess people need to be retooled so that the focus is on delivering small pieces of useable products or services that can begin to generate return on investment as quickly as possible. As an organization, do we really care how far we are ahead or behind our original guesstimate, or do we care that in this iteration we produced tangible things the customer loves, tests, and signs-off on so that we can move our attention forward to how we can do better in next week's iteration?

Years of research have left a common understanding in our minds as project managers that the act of measuring something alters the results, as "that which gets measured gets repeated." But obviously, numbers in and of themselves are of little use if they do not capture information that is truly relevant. If you want to improve quality, do not focus your attention on the statistics of how many issues were found, or how many were fixed. The relevant metrics are how many things *remain* to be fixed and how long will it take the team to do them?

Projects run by common sense, not with the goal of providing good looking numbers, will even evaluate the quality defects, bugs, or anomalies to see if they are even crucial to fix. If they are not crucial, is the cost to fix them more than the value that results? The goal of 100% perfection is unrealistic in our spouses or significant others, and also in project outputs.

When the underlying goal of the project work is not tangible, and therefore hard to measure, it is easy to substitute something that *is* easy to measure and convince yourself that it is worthwhile to track. For example, we all measure project costs, which do need to be tracked. But an embarrassing number of organizations do not use that data to figure an ROI percentage on the cost of the project, compared to the investment dollars spent to complete it.

Even more organizations do not track the business value of internal project outputs, for example, to see the long term return/savings that come from the project's completion. A larger number of organizations fail to track the detailed dollar amount of business return that can be traced back to a specific project to see if it met its goals. "Done is beautiful," indeed, but from a financial standpoint, "Done" is not enough of a goal if projects are to contribute effectively to survival in a competitive marketplace.

If the strategic objective connected to the project was to reduce the time to answer customer calls in the Call Center to less than a 2-minute wait, did anyone ever capture a response time before and after the project? Call Centers usually have automated ways to check these types of numbers, so maybe they are available. However, did anyone ever think to relay this information back to the project team, so that they could complete the circle and know whether or not their solutions worked? That feedback is crucial, especially for Millennials. If it didn't work, perhaps the team with so much tacit knowledge about the situation can come up with an additional way to cut waiting time. Closing that feedback loop with the team is a commonly overlooked failure in organizations, and an increasingly important one.

Contracts

Agile principles talk of respect and involvement of the customer, in essence, forming a *partnership* for mutual gain. This may mean that the way contracts are written must be altered. In most corporations, especially sizeable and geographically dispersed ones, procurement is done in a silo far removed from the day-to-day work you do to lead your project. Specialists in contracts produce the standard types of contracts, and legal experts scrutinize them before signatures are affixed. When a customer wants to purchase your services, the process is simple: you estimate how long this project will take, draw up a list of resources needed, check with your third-party suppliers for how much you will add for non-people costs, add in a profit percentage, the salesman quotes your potential customer a price, and everyone signs a legally binding agreement. The contract usually falls into one of three major types: fixed price or lump sum, cost-reimbursable, or time and materials.

Fixed Price or Lump Sum Contracts

With this type of contract, there is a *fixed total price for a well-defined product.* One set fee is agreed upon for all of the work. This type of contract has the least risk for the buyer (them). However, if the product or service is not well-defined, both buyer and seller are at risk. The buyer may not receive the desired product, and you, as the seller, may incur additional costs to provide it. Types of fixed price contracts are:

- **Firm fixed price (FFP)**–A type of contract where the buyer (them) pays the seller (you) a *set fee* regardless of the seller's costs. The pressure is on your team to deliver the project in less time and with less cost than estimated. Any savings increases the profit line of your organization.
- **Fixed price incentive fee (FPIF)**–A type of contract where the buyer (them) pays the seller (you) a *set fee*, but the seller also receives *an incentive fee if they finish their part of the project early.* If you are pressured to finish your traditional project early, this may be the motivator at work. If you finish early, the company in essence gets a "tip."
- **Fixed price economic price adjustment (FPEPA)**–A type of contract where the buyer (them) pays the seller (you) a *set fee*, but the contract allows for a *price increase if the contract is for several years.* Your organization receives a higher fee if the project takes longer than originally planned. It is fair if the project will span multiple years, as interest rates for cost of money, material prices, wages, and other financial portions of the project grow as time passes. There is considerable administrative overhead involved to track the growth factors, and there is not an effective way to anticipate them so that the cost increases will coincide exactly with the time when the contract allows a price increase. This is another benefit to shorter, Agile projects that can be completed in a reasonable timeframe.

Cost Reimbursable Contracts

In a cost reimbursable contract, there is a payment to the seller (you) for *actual costs, plus a* fee *representing the seller's profit.* In addition to the common thread that each of them starts, "the buyer (them) pays all costs…," there are additional incentives for meeting or exceeding selected project objectives such as schedule targets or total costs. The types of cost reimbursable contracts are:

- **Cost plus fixed fee (CPFF)**–The buyer (them) pays *all costs, but the fee or profit for the seller (you) is fixed ahead of time* to be a specific dollar amount. Excessive costs will not generate additional profit for the organization, so your project team is pressed to complete the project within the time and budget you originally estimated. Any metrics that go over the original baseline are a direct drain on the profitability of your company.

- **Cost plus incentive fee (CPIF)**–The buyer (them) pays *all costs, and pays the seller (you) a fixed fee determined ahead of time. Plus, the seller may receive a bonus for finishing sooner or coming in under budget* calculated at a predetermined amount for each day, week, or month they are early. Your team may be under pressure to finish extra early in order for your company to collect a larger bonus, but often management does not calculate the cost of finishing sooner than expected in terms bringing in materials early and the cost for overtime expenditures.

- **Cost plus award fee (CPAF)**–The buyer (them) pays *all costs and* also pays the seller (you) *a bonus, which varies based on performance standards* agreed upon earlier. Note that this type of contract does not have the fixed fee found in CPIF. Time may be a pressure point if it is a named standard, but quality criteria may also be the standard specified. Your team will need to know the details of the contract to know how to maximize the bonus.

- **Cost plus percentage of costs (CPPC)**–The buyer (them) pays *all costs, plus the seller* (you) *gets a percentage of the costs as a fee.* The higher the costs, the higher the fee or profit for your organization. The government will not allow this type of contract for their own purchases since it is to the seller's advantage (you) to run the costs up as high as possible.

There are also special contracts that include extra fees for your organization if the customer asks for scope changes, and increased prices per hour if additional team time is requested by the customer after the contract finish date passes. One can see that the careful use of resources cannot allow a lag between one customer contract and the next, as the people still draw their salaries whether working on revenue producing projects, or not. So, there is legitimate room to charge the customer extra for you to delay another project, or reschedule another customer, to allow the team additional time to finish unplanned work that comes from change requests. However, there is no honor in structuring contracts to make money only if the project is late and over budget due to change requests, or forcing customers to honor the original terms and to build functionality the end-users don't really want or need to finish out the duration of a contract.

Time and Materials

Time and materials (T&M) contracts are used for *small purchases that are priced on a per item or per use basis*. They are a hybrid of the other two types of contracts because they contain aspects of both fixed price and cost reimbursable contracts. The risk to the buyer (them) is minimal, since the dollar amounts are small and the period of time is short. They are like fixed price contracts in that the unit rates are preset at the beginning. Your buyer knows how much they will pay per item, just as they know the dollar amount for which they will be responsible in a fixed price contract.

Time and materials contracts are like cost reimbursable contracts in that they are open-ended. The full value of the arrangement is not defined at the time the contract is awarded. So, they can grow in value (cost) if the buyer purchases 10,000 items at $5 each, rather than the 20 items that they originally planned to buy.

Contracts used for traditional Waterfall projects place the buyer and seller in a win/lose situation. From PMP prep studies, we know that the parties on each side of the contract try to slide the scale in their favor, to elicit an agreement gaining them the highest profit with the lowest risk. It is a model of competition in which one side is trying to win at the expense of the other. As we move to projects developed in an Agile way, contracts must be adjusted to support the philosophy and changed collaborative partnership relationships between the parties involved in the extended team.

At the Agile Alliance 2011 conference, Angela Druckman talked about the practical considerations involved in adjusting contracts to Agile development practices, since allowing for change does not fit easily into the normal contract negotiation procedures. She feels that the product owner or customer, and the ScrumMaster (should the team be using Scrum) or project manager, should be involved in both the terms and the wording of the contract.[1]

Druckman's point is that Waterfall development often requires a business requirements document or another upfront capture of requirements for the entire undertaking before work on the project can begin. In contrast, a Scrum team would work with the product owner to develop the requirements into stories, which could be placed into the backlog iteratively throughout the entire project. So, contracts must now be worded to allow for that iterative development.

Contracts typically include a thick section on how change management will be handled and the specific scenarios in which the original requirements list can be altered. The flexibility to add new requirements (user stories) at the end of each iteration must be reflected in the wording of the document. Another issue could be who provides personnel for team roles. Up to this point we have assumed that the product owner, the ScrumMaster/project manager, or other appropriately titled corresponding person (depending on the little agile methodology), and the project team, are all from the same organization.

If we do not let the vocabulary get in the way, it is easy to see that a product owner could come from the customer side (the buyer) and be called the Customer. The project team would come from our organization (the seller) or from a third-party consulting firm, and the project manager or ScrumMaster, keeping in mind that they are *not* interchangeable roles, could be from either organization or from a third-party consulting firm. Since all of these possibilities exist, the contract may need to specify whether buyer or seller will "own" each role, and which role is the person authorized to prioritize and approve the work of the project.

Next, the contract should specify the methodology by which the team will make commitments (no doubt some form of maximum story points based on previous, proven velocity numbers after the team is a week or two into the contract) and place in writing that it will be the team that has the final word on how many story points they will commit to deliver in each iteration.

When both parties approach contract negotiations with mutual respect and a promise to work shoulder-by-shoulder in an environment of trust for mutual benefit, the Agile extended team is off to a good start. However, it is important to differentiate contracts between purchasers and software companies who are selling a finished, tested, and packaged off-the-shelf software application, and purchasers who are contracting with a firm to build customer software from scratch to fulfill a new or innovative business need, or customize existing software to fit the business needs of a unique environment.

With the off-the-shelf application, a standard and fixed T&M contract would be fine. You agree to purchase a guaranteed number of software licenses, and there may or may not be installation and maintenance agreements tacked on. The second situation, the creation of new software, or the alteration or customization of an existing package, is where Agile contracts come into play. The same ideas hold true for non-software contracts.

Allan Kelly, in his 2011 article "Agile Contracts," suggests these three ways, among others, you might consider the contracts dilemma: Hide it, roll it, or get money for nothing and your change for free.[2]

Option 1, Hide It

Hide the fact that you will be fulfilling this contract with an Agile team. This is a variation of the idea that as a project manager you might move your team to more Agile practices under the radar of your organization, or within a company that does not care too much about *how* the team accomplishes its results. It is also a viable option in a situation where you are newly merging some more flexible practices into your Waterfall team. It is possible to estimate and plan the work as you ordinarily would, and sign the usual type of contract. Then, you move to Agile techniques to improve your delivery. Test-driven development, continuous integration, and refactoring will help you improve your software delivery, and daily stand-ups, self-managed teams who are collocated, and other Agile practices will enhance the performance of a hybrid process team. If the customer contract lists delivery of detailed "progress against plan reports," you do not really want to go down the road of falsifying them and deceiving the customer. After all, honesty and respect for the customer are key principles on which the practices of your Agile team will rest. Hiding your processes may work in the short term to gain data to show the value of this approach, but always err on the side of honesty when dealing with customers.

Option 2, Rolling contracts

Rather than have the customer commit upfront to a large and lengthy contract, the customer and the supplier (you) can put together a series of short development mini-projects—think iterations. This type of relationship may be short on the up-front lists of final requirements. In fact, the work itself may be to explore options and evolve the final product as you go. Since something is delivered each iteration, each time the understanding of what else is needed increases. You discover the needs as you go.

At the end of each iteration, the customer pays for the work done in this wave and has the choice to stop the project here or to move forward to the next rolling wave (iteration). This alliance balances risk and reward for both sides. The seller (you) is motivated to produce something of business value that is useable, or releasable, and to show that there is more to be done that would increase the business value. This is often called producing a *vertical slice* of the product functionality. The vertical slice image comes from cutting a slice of birthday cake, for example. If you remove a small portion by cutting vertically, although you do not get the whole cake in this one slice, you do get an eatable cross-section of frosting, cake, filling, and bottom layer. If you need more after you finish this piece, you can negotiate another piece for next time. The nice part about a rolling contract, which is seldom acknowledged in contracts literature, is that sometimes customers are unrealistically demanding. You can see that they will never be satisfied, or they are uncooperative and generally difficult to deal with. This type of contract gives you a face-saving way to disengage from the relationship after an iteration or two, rather than facing the legal battle and expense of trying to back out of a long-term contract, or being forced to endure the disharmonious relationship for the original length of the engagement.

If the client thinks the cost of the work is greater than the value it will return to them, they can stop before they sink any more money into the project at the end of each iteration. The plus for the customer, even if they stop after an iteration or two, is that they walk away with tangible, useable project results rather than having to absorb sunk costs with nothing to show for them. Sometimes, both parties are in agreement that the product or service they explored at low risk, is not really appropriate to pursue.

Option 3, Money for Nothing and Your Change for Free

One of the Scrum creators, Jeff Sutherland, has written in detail about a type of Agile contract for big contracts that require large, upfront requirements analysis, called, "Money for Nothing and Your Change for Free." On the surface, it looks much like a traditional, standard FFP Waterfall contract and includes a T&M clause to be paid for work done as a result of changes. But, two additional clauses have been added.[3]

The first clause is the "Change For Free" option. To execute this option, the customer must show up and actively work with the Scrum/Agile team every sprint (iteration). Failure to do this will void this clause and the contract reverts back to time and materials. The value of this clause for the buyer (them) is obvious.

- First, changes in the scope priorities are free if the total contract work is not changed. In other words, if you start with 100 items, you can re-prioritize them in any way you like, as long as they are still the same 100 stories.
- Second, new features may be added for free at sprint/iteration boundaries (end of sprint or iteration) if low priority items of equal work are removed from the contract. For example, features 65, 66, and 67, which total 33 story points, can be added, as long as you swap them out for requirements that have not already been started that also total 33 story points.

Like a rolling contract, the customer pays in regular increments, probably monthly, in response to receiving working software. But this could work for other non-IT projects, too.

The "Money for Nothing" option sits on top of the "Changes for Free" option, starting with the same basic fixed-price contract with time and materials charges for changes. The team and the customer work together, to agree on estimates for all work items in the scrum (iteration) backlog. If they cannot mutually agree on the work item estimates, or the customer does not maintain participation with the team, the contract reverts back to time and materials for changes. The "money for nothing" clause allows the customer to determine the ROI cutoff where the implementation of the next feature would cost more than the value of the feature. So, at the end of any iteration, they can cancel the remaining work and keep whatever has already been created for them. For this privilege, they pay 20% of the outstanding cost of the work remaining in the contract. Since they get nothing for that 20% except an "early out" option, they in essence "pay money for nothing." If the customer cancels a 12-month, $10 million contract halfway through, they will pay an additional $1 million.

$$12 \text{ months} \div 2 = 6 \text{ months}$$
$$\$10 \text{ million} \div 2 = \$5 \text{ million for 6 months}$$
$$\$5 \text{ million remaining} \times 20\% = \$1 \text{ million}$$

Plus, they will have already paid the first $5 million dollars for the first six months and received the products it produced. But overall, they save $4 million dollars they would have spent on the total contract if they had continued to the end, long after the project stopped making business sense.

$$\$5 \text{ million for 6 months used} + \$1 \text{ million for early stop} = \$6 \text{ million cost}$$
$$\$10 \text{ million original contract} - \$6 \text{ million cost} = \$4 \text{ million savings}$$

As the supplier, your first thought might be that your organization is now losing $4 million dollars of potential profit. However, as you are paid $1 million dollars for the trouble of reassigning the project team, you are "getting money for nothing" and this can help bridge the profitability gap if it takes a short while to find other uses for these team members. If your organization has projects waiting in queue on which they can redeploy these people, the $1 million dollars is profit.

Right now the new types of Agile contracts are in the formative stages. Some people advocate offering the client a choice of contracts. If they know their requirements and want to freeze them upfront, they can sign a traditional "fixed-fee" option. If they are not sure of the specifics and need flexibility, they could try a rolling-Agile option. Agile principles talk of respect and involvement of the customer, in essence, forming a partnership for mutual gain. This may mean that the way contracts are written must be altered.

High-level Involvement

Most project sponsors think if they type up a large requirements document and hand it off to the project team, their job is done. Project sponsors, now perhaps re-titled project owners, either need to be available on a daily basis or appoint a surrogate as a full-time liaison to the Agile project. This stand-in must be available every day to answer questions about detailed feature stories, to set priorities at the appropriate points in the meetings, and to communicate risks and progress back to the project owner.

Not just any warm body or person who "won't be missed" in a department can be a successful liaison. This must be a person with subject matter knowledge regarding the work of the project, constant accessibility to the product owner, and the authority to make decisions on the behalf of the organization to guide the project's overall direction.

Cost Accounting and Other Reports

In high-ceremony situations, cost accounting can be intricately connected to multiple departments, and perhaps even tracked down to the feature level of a project team or to an individual WBS activity. Several departments may have gone together to fund a project that would be mutually beneficial, but the funding could be split equally or disproportionately, depending on the agreement made by the department heads.

If the tracking involves automated software traceability screens that link project work to details of a traditional technical or functional document, changing the way that the team slices and dices them into user stories may create a challenge. If this describes your traditional team situation, you won't be able to change your process by stealth. An alternate possibility is to pick a small project within your own department as a pilot and ask to be able to choose your own team.

With the go ahead to try this project using Agile principles and practices with full management approval, you have the advantage of being able to instigate a fuller transition all at once, and some position power to begin to work with the team to choose the appropriate tailored processes. Since this is now under the auspices of a single department cost center, it is easier to adjust the cost accounting codes, or create sub-codes to charge against the aggregate team payroll budget, and assign any hardware or materials charges to existing departmental accounts.

Some project managers may think that choosing a small, unimportant project whose outcomes will not matter if they are not realized is the best way to have a "practice round" with their first try as an Agile team. A counter thought is that if you finally have one shot to show the value of moving to this new philosophy, you need to have it be a project that matters and one on which you can show the positive impact of the new actions. After all, you want this to be the experience in your own organization that you can reference to support a move in a new direction.

A good choice is a small project of only a few months in length where it has importance to the company, but the doors won't shut if it does not go as planned. This project's success increases your chances of looking good and opening the door for additional Agile opportunities. Look carefully at the project team that you choose. If there is anyone who has had a positive team experience at another job with this methodology, grab them. Given the opportunity, the best and swiftest positive change for the team behaviors comes if you can get a seasoned Agile coach to guide you through the first project…or, at worst, through the first few crucial transformation iterations.

If you plan to be an instrument of change to roll this out to other teams and other portions of the company, remember that the human reactions and feelings about these new approaches are important to capture and document. Interview the future project owner. How have his or her projects gone in the past? What were the pain points? Did the project deliver the ROI, internal relief, or customer value planned? Did he or she feel in control, with a good finger on the pulse of the project as it unfolded? Or, was he or she comfortable that the team knew what was needed? Was the team receptive to changes that came during the various phases of the work? Were any resources of time or materials wasted through incorrect decisions made too early in the work? If you know of any irritations or dissatisfaction with previous projects, be especially sure that you get the specifics on any problems with the actual project time, cost, quality, and scope metrics. You will want to discover, did the project deliver enough value to make it worthwhile for the company to do it? Did the project get finished, or were important pieces left undone?

After the Agile project, be sure to re-interview this person, now known as the product owner. Ask the same questions you asked before. This time, listen for the differences in the project owner's feelings of understanding, being a part of the team processes, reactions to small, complete increments demonstrated every few weeks, as well as reactions to visual dashboards available at a glance on the walls of the collective team space. These interviews serve a multiple purpose. First, they help the product owner verbalize the differences in this experience from a traditional one. Second, they bring to his or her mind the increased sense of control he or she felt throughout the process. Third, this focuses attention to see if the approach produces results with more quickly realized recompense. Fourth, this is an opportunity to secure your second chance to practice Agile by asking the product owner if there might be value to doing his or her future projects in this way.

If the project shows gains over a Waterfall method, you now have a "believer" at a higher level in the organization than you occupy. It is fair to ask if this person would be willing to informally visit with some of the other managers in the organization who initiate projects for your team to share his or her positive experiences and encourage them to also try an Agile approach on their own projects. You might even ask him or her to give a short brown bag lunch session on this success story.

Team Member Reactions

In a hierarchical organization where personal status comes from tangible rewards such as private offices or a larger cubicle closer to the boss, moving the entire team to a collective area with floating workspaces can be a culture shock for certain team members. However, the satisfaction from self-actualization at the top of the pyramid's peak will triumph over time. Maslow was not ill-informed when he placed the need for self-worth near the top of the Hierarchy of Needs pyramid.

A smoothly functioning Agile team that is empowered, self-directed, and working in a collective environment is the preferred environment for most people who have a chance to see it function as intended. When a person with a private office is isolated and not in on the interactive, challenging nature of the work of the project, it is natural for that person to want to come out and be a part of things.

Clever project managers faced with asking a seasoned team member, who we will call Susie, to "give up" her office sometimes do not officially announce that she *must* move to the collective team space. They merely get her involved and out of her office by working in pairing situations. They may even provide her with a "temporary" workspace so she can be "closer to John while you are finishing these features." Then, when other team members need a quiet space to work, Susie can be asked if they could use "her" office. Over time, Susie is out working with the rest of the team and generously donating the use of her private office for situations requiring quiet and isolation. Asking her to make an official move becomes a moot point.

Radical Management Shifts

We talked earlier about how 20th century management theory influenced the way in which we produce goods and services, and the dramatic shifts in the corporate culture that came about when the business theory gurus found new principles for success. When a new body of ideas like the Agile Principles begins to gain acceptance in the business world, you will often see supporting corollary research and thinking appear. The following is one example of that new research.

The book *The Leader's Guide to Radical Management,* by Steve Denning, is a good example of this phenomenon. He says that management once again is being reinvented, and his principles are ones that we can apply to project management, too. His seven shift points for management seem to be a carefully constructed corollary for Agile philosophies. If an organization is going to embrace Agile as a project management approach, it will be important for upper management to make a parallel alteration in their own thinking patterns. This book might be a way to help them begin to think in new ways.[4] Denning's principles of Radical Management are:

Principle #1–Focus work on delighting the customer. This is a shift in goals from a singular focus on making money for the shareholders to delighting customers through continuous innovation. Does Drucker and the concept that the customer is king and creates product value, ring a bell?

Principle #2–Do work through self-organizing teams. Here is a shift in the role of managers from controlling individuals to actions enabling self-organizing teams. It also leads the way to move the communications channels from a top-down hierarchy to a horizontal communications flow. This sounds reminiscent of moving from a top down, industrial organizational structure to the flipped one shown in Figure 4.1.

Principle #3–Do work in client-driven iterations. Here is a shift in the way that work is coordinated in a bureaucracy to dynamically link the business needs of the client/customer/product owner with the work of the project team.

Principle #4–Deliver value to clients in each iteration. This idea parallels the Agile team practices of delivering demonstratable, minimal marketable features at the end of each consistent timebox. It also encompasses a shift in values from a preoccupation with efficiency, to a broader set of values that will foster continuous innovation.

Principle #5–Be totally open about impediments to improvement. This principle moves the corporate culture from a CYA (Cover Your A**) scenario to one in which the constraints and impediments to the process flow delivering value are freely communicated each day at the daily stand-up. They become the responsibility of the project manager (ScrumMaster, etc.) to track and remove with the help of upper management and/or the product owner, while the team focuses on productive work.

Principle #6–Create a context for continuous self-improvement by the team. The organization will need to move from the old thinking that people sitting together and talking are just "wasting time" to understanding that pair producing is not only more productive and reduces the risk of quality errors, it is a form of training and/or mentoring to increase the skill sets of the team as a whole.

Principle #7–Communicate these ideas interactively throughout the organization through stories, questions, and conversations. Only through the informal open, free-flowing, trust-based interactions between all parts of the organization can the larger group work together to build business value.

The result of implementing these principles is not reaching one final point where you can rest and say, "We did it!" It is the creation of a culture of continuous innovation that allows a consistently flexible and responsive organization; one that can compete and succeed within an ever-changing business environment.

The Growing Importance of Intangible Assets

In the Kotter and Heskett book, *Corporate Culture and Performance*, the authors found that 60% to 95% of the value of corporate stock is based on intangible assets. *Intangible assets* are things like corporate capital (how smoothly your organization can respond to change) and intellectual capital (the freedom of your knowledge workers to make a meaningful contribution).[5] Those two concepts are the very heart of all Agile approaches. Plants and equipment, *tangible assets,* are where most of the emphasis is currently placed, but that is only 5% of the corporate value. So, you can see that planning a management style to attract and keep Millennial workers, and providing a working environment and managerial support style to maximize personal engagement is key to long-term company stability.

A Need for PMO Refocusing

Some PMOs are quite forward thinking and are already working to move into the Agile space. In fact, a 2012 PM Solutions white paper said that 28% of PMOs today are already implementing Agile methods as part of their arsenal of project management tools.[6] Unfortunately, there are also a number of PMOs who are not truly performing the functions that can make them a vital partner in the business. They may be splintered to locations embedded within various organizational silos, with each addressing only the needs of their portion of the whole. Even if there is a coordinating PMO at the enterprise level, too many times it is relegated to the position of the "tools and techniques police" rather than being aware, aligned, and involved on a daily basis with working to fulfill the business needs of the company through the oversight of projects.

When resource capabilities are in short supply, the PMO may try to stretch the delivery output by doubling, tripling, or quadrupling the work assigned to each resource. It is a common misconception that this increases productivity for the organization. The misguided nature of these practices may have something to do with wanting to be sure all resources are "fully utilized," a manufacturing era thought that has been misapplied to a knowledge worker-based economy. Not all full utilization is positive. Think of a fully-utilized highway, or as we might also describe it, a slowly moving parking lot. Being "fully utilized" can result in mental gridlock.

The truth is that overscheduling actually hinders productivity, rather than help individuals do more than they think possible. Studies on human context switching show that multitasking is a myth, despite the fact we all believe that we can truly eat popcorn, play the trombone, and finish a project report in Excel at the same time. Gerald Weinberg, in his book, *Quality Software Management: Systems Thinking*, proposes a rule of thumb to calculate the waste caused by project switching: for every additional project added, you lose up to 20% of your productivity.[7]

At this rate, by the time you have moved from one project to five, you are losing 80% of your productive work time to the lag, as your brain stops one project, makes sure to save where you were, "opens" another project in your mind, and tries to mentally reload where you were the last time you looked at it, does some work, mentally saves that work, and on and on as you move back and forth during the day. Think of how many projects you may have in various stages of completion on any one day and you may be mentally picturing 5 to 7, an average found in an informal poll.

Recent focus on the dangers of texting and driving reinforce that the human brain is at its sharpest and most responsive when thinking of only one topic at a time. Instead of shoveling multiple tasks from multiple projects onto teams with a matrix reporting structure, the PMO needs to move to projectized teams that are dedicated to one project at a time, and who remain together from project to project, to leverage the cohesiveness and team bonding that builds as they move to new challenges.

Thus, the PMO cannot assume that all project request demands can and should be met. With a redirection of focus, they can help the organization prioritize projects and help educate the project owners regarding their blanket demands for lengthy lists of technical and functional requirements. They must learn to prioritize those to include only the ones they are sure are crucial and aligned with the organization's vision as to what provides business value. The question they should ask is, "How do we make the best use of limited resources and focus them on work that matters?"

The seminal thought is no longer to drive speed as an end unto itself, when what they really want is speed that delivers useable outcomes. The mantra on the wall gets repainted from, "*Are we doing projects right?*" to now read, "*Are we doing the right projects?*" PMOs must refocus their goals towards value creation, rather than managing and controlling rigid processes.

Scott Ambler, a thought leader in the Agile space, has a clear definition of the difference between governance and management.[8] He says, "*Governance* looks at an organization from the outside, treating it as a system that needs to have the appropriate structure and processes in place to provide a stream of value." Depending on the industry, there are outside, industry-wide organizations that develop and monitor this structure, so that it is uniform worldwide. However, the PMO can often perform a similar governance function for an individual organization, making sure that there is an objective structure and sets of process choices within its walls that are uniform and properly focused on organizational productivity.

In contrast, Ambler paints the picture of effective management, stating, "*Management* is inside the organization and ensures that the structure and processes (outlined in the governance standards) are implemented effectively." Too often, PMOs are tasked with enforcing an external set of governance standards so that the company can retain key certifications or endorsements that reassure potential customers that they meet consistent quality standards. The fallacy that they may embrace, however, is that a tightly controlled internal implementation policy is the most beneficial way to meet the governance checklist for the structures and processes.

A second, harmful assumption is that flexible processes will result in "sloppy" procedures that will be frowned on and rejected by external governance inspectors. Project managers are asked to manage in a "command and control" way within rigid, traditional processes that are detrimental to the core needs of the business. As Agile sweeps the world in all parts of the corporate spectrum, not just IT, most external governance bodies have gone on record stating that Agile processes are not only acceptable, but in many cases, preferable to more static ones. They provide dependable, quality end-results that customers and business partners can rely on when choosing to enter into a business relationship with your company.

PMOs will need to investigate their options for internal practices to meet external governance requirements. Once they are reassured, they can allow for various methodologies to be used on projects, each selected as the most beneficial and appropriate for the parameters of the project on a case-by-case basis. This will hopefully engender a relaxation of the pressure to force heavy documentation and micromanaging onto the project manager at the team level.

Successful PMOs of the future will also lobby to get themselves and the project manager involved in a project earlier in the timeline. At the point that the vision is being discussed and a project driven solution is being considered, the input from both the project manager and a lead technical expert from the team can help sculpt sleeker, more efficient projects from the start.

In the book *13 Fatal Errors Managers Make and How You Can Avoid Them*, W.S. Brown lists one error as "Managing By Group." The concept is that we are all individuals, and trying to avoid the hard parts of management by lumping everyone together with the misconception that treating them all the same, as the only "fair" way to manage, is erroneous.[9] The same can be said of a PMO that insists that every team's processes be identical, rather than tailored for the particulars of the situation.

Perhaps a side benefit of a dedicated, standing team would be that, over time, the team would prove itself to be trustworthy and reliable. Then, rather than insist that every team use a singular project management process and a set of uniform templates to manage each project, they would be allowed to choose among a sanctioned group of tools and processes to select only the most useful and productive ones for the project. All of the possibilities could be based on a compatible pool of core philosophies and principles that parallel the corporate vision. By eliminating the unnecessary waste of time and resources that would go into completing inappropriate work, reports, and templates, the project can be completed in a smoother and more efficient style.

Despite the constant push for standing teams, in some industries or project undertakings, the core of the team cannot truly have all of the cross-functional skills required. This opens the possibility to tailor the standing team concept to include an infrastructure of indispensible people to maintain the team foundation. Then, appropriate subject matter experts (SMEs) from both inside and outside the corporation can be added as needed. Over time, most companies find they do similar sorts of projects, so external SMEs in essence become an auxiliary, outer team layer that can easily and quickly blend into the standard processes and can be called upon when needed.

A Change in Human Resources Practices

Currently, human resources (HR) departments are the primary area involved in attracting, processing, interviewing, and hiring new employees for the organization. The administrative assistant, the maintenance engineer, call center worker, and project team member are each recruited, screened, and chosen, using the same set of checklist items. Technical skill sets, although important, are frequently the single, overarching deciders in terms of who is ultimately offered the job. While there are numerous positions that can be filled by running resume crawlers to pick key words out of a prospect's paperwork, there are different standards that may need to be introduced when it comes to hiring people who will work on Agile project teams. HR administrators are able to assess technical skills through certifications, verify past employment experiences, and purchase easily obtainable skills tests especially created for this type of HR sifting process.

What cannot be easily tested is the candidate's attitude and value set. Is this a person who is self-motivated when it comes to seeking out and learning new skills? Is he or she an innovative thinker? Is this person open and receptive to coaching or mentoring, and willing to do the same for others in return? Will this be an employee who thrives in an environment of collaboration? Can this applicant thrive in the uncertainty and challenge of a flexible environment to create innovative products and services? What kind of a fit is he or she with the company culture? Does he or she have a Social Skill type the team is missing?

These are personal attributes that will be crucial for people being hired for Agile teams. In order to attract the most desirable knowledge workers, particularly from the Millennium generation, HR interview processes will need to transition into a two-way conversation. One half will be the company checking for an attitude fit, along with technical skill sets. The other half will be presenting an honest portrait of the company as a place that allows a balance between work life and home life, houses a creative and flexible day-to-day work process, encourages those who are eager to learn, presents an achievable challenge, and offers a self-directed arena of trust in which self-motivated team members can excel.

The Society of Human Resources Management did a survey in 2011 regarding job satisfaction in a random selection of companies of all sizes and types. The idea was, first, to see what people thought about their jobs, and second, to give companies a benchmark to use to compare their own employee responses when they distributed the same survey internally. "Wow! We got a 37 on this," is hard to interpret unless you have a comparison with how other companies scored.

It takes about two years' salary to recruit, hire, and train a new employee. So, companies are still focused on keeping their people happy. If Agile or hybrid practices can address some of these issues and help retain employees, maybe that is even more reason to consider them. Here are some negative feelings that could be addressed by moving to an Agile philosophy.

Question	Indifferent or Unhappy
I have opportunities to use my skills and abilities at work.	53%
I have autonomy and independence to make decisions.	50%
My work contributes to the organization's business goals.	56%
I am passionate and excited about work.	44%
Employees take action when a problem or opportunity arises.	48%
Employees in the organization are flexible in unpredictable work situations.	58%[10]

Obviously, when looking at key engagement items, an organization in which about half of the employees are not engaged or aligned with the business goals of their employer highlights the need for a mandate to change practices. One evolving practice is the idea of setting a minimum number of work hours, but allowing employee driven self-scheduling as long as it is coordinated with the work of the team.

For example, each person must work 40 hours a week and attend the daily stand-up meeting, but time off for doctor and dentist appointments, children's school conferences and piano recitals, sharing child responsibilities with a spouse for a school vacation day or teacher in-service break, sick child care, or elderly parent care, can be possible as long as it is planned with the team. The time missed can be worked early in the day, or later in the evening, or by lengthening one day and shortening the next. However, this would need to be an experienced team that understands how to keep excessive colleague absences from disrupting the work of the team.

Depending on the project, unusual working hours can even be a plus if they mean a team representative is now available during the working hours of a remote team in a different time zone. Or, perhaps this is an odd time when two or more people can run tests that would be disruptive to the business and/or its customers if they were undertaken during the normal 8 a.m. to 5 p.m. day.

Some organizations are even open to vacations or personal family leave being split in half by the day. Time might be divided into a half-day of vacation and a half-day of work from a remote site, in special circumstances. During working periods, he or she can telecommute by using company servers to continue to upload work and confer with the project team on a regular basis. Say the flow of the project would be seriously marred by the absence of an important team member, despite the cross-functional skills of the rest of the team. Perhaps the seminal person can even work half-time at half salary for a week or two to accommodate personal responsibilities if they are short on vacation time.

Obviously, if this is totally inappropriate in your organization, don't do it. But, don't be afraid to think creatively about work time, if possible.

References

[1]Druckman, A. August 9, 2011. "Contract Negotiations Evolve with Agile Development." *Agile Alliance.* Retrieved from http://searchsoftwarequality.techtarget.com/news/2240039388/Contract-negotiations-evolve-with-Agile-development-QA-with-Angela-Druckman.

[2]Kelly, A. February 8, 2011. "Agile Contracts", Retrieved from http://www.infoq.com/articles/agile-contracts.

[3]Sutherland, J. July 12, 2010. *Agile Contracts, Money for Nothing and Your Change for Free.* Retrieved from http://scrum.jeffsutherland.com/2008/10/agile-contracts-money-for-nothing-and.html.

[4]Denning, S. 2010. *The Leader's Guide to Radical Management.* Hoboken, NJ: John Wiley & Sons, Inc.

[5]Kotter, J. P. & Heskett, J. L. 1992. *Corporate Culture and Performance, Corporate Culture and Performance.* New York: The Free Press.

[6]*"State of the PMO 2012."* PM Solutions Research. Retrieved from http://www.pmsolutions.com/collateral/research/State%20of%20the%20PMO%202012%20Research%20Report.pdf.

[7]Weinberg, G. 1991. *Quality Software Management: Systems Thinking.* London: Dorset House.

[8]Ambler, S. Governing Agile Project Teams White Paper. 2011.

[9]Brown, W. S. 1985. *13 Fatal Errors Managers Make And How You Can Avoid Them.* New York: Berkley Publishing Group.

[10]Society of Human Resources Management Employment Satisfaction Survey, 2011.

17

What Are Scrum, XP, and DSDM?

By reading previous chapters, you should now be very familiar with the mindset and principles of Big Agile, so let's move to little agile. Little agile is a set of approaches to software development and other types of projects that have developed specific, repeatable checklists to follow. In many cases, they have become productized with classes, posters, certifications, and a vocabulary built around their particular approach. However, they still are believers that agile is something you *are*, not just something you *do*. They ascribe to the same Agile philosophies and principles we have already learned.

You already know that when the signers of the Agile Manifesto met in 2001, each of them had already been experimenting with new methods of creating software. Remember, they never intended to blend them all into one big process that everyone had to follow. The premise of Agile is that methods should be tailored project by project, and industry by industry, but you will quickly note that each of the little agile methods shares much in common with its cousins. They were all based on common research papers available to the community, and accessed by free and open collaboration from person to person and company to company.

Software Development

The Scrum process is only one representative of the software development processes also know as *the software development life cycle (SDLC)*. Like other project beginnings, creating software requires getting the requirements from the customer. *Development* is the step where the programmers actually write the code for the project. Next, software *testing* is done to make sure the software meets the requirements set out, that it works as planned, and that it can be deployed to a wider set of users with the same quality that it had in the test environment.

In a more traditional setting, the software may be tested most vigorously after the code is completed. It may even be turned over to a quality assurance team to be tested by people outside the creative team. Test Driven Development (TDD), an agile method to be discussed later, differs from the normal process by placing more of the testing in the hands of the developers, rather than relying on a specialized tester from outside the development team.

There are multiple tests that code must pass. For example, user stories are most frequently written from the viewpoint of the end user, stating, "As a cell phone user, I want to pay my bill online." That is a *functional requirement* of the software and tests can be performed to make sure that action can be performed successfully. However, software performance depends on other, more hidden, performance standards that the non-IT person may not think to consider.

For example, *non-functional requirements* are things that the end user may never realize are necessary to test. *Scalability*, one such factor, means the ability of the software or hardware systems to work equally well when larger amounts of traffic or data must be handled. Perhaps the customer relationship management software works well with a customer list of 100 customers, but will it work the same way if you have 10,000 customers? A web hosting site may work fine with 1,000 hits a day, but if it houses *YouTube*, will it be able to handle 4 billion views per day?

Tests may need to check a product or service's *maintainability*. It works now, but if there is a problem in the future, how difficult will it be to repair or restore its function? Is there a simpler solution that would have a positive impact on the ease and cost of accessing and repairing the functionality?

What about *usability*? How easily can the end user learn to use this software? Is it intuitive, or will it take extensive training? Is there a simpler solution, using fewer lines of code and a more elegant solution, that will make it easier for programmers working with the next versions to understand how this was written, make it more compact to store with less server space, or more intuitive the first time an employee sits down to use it?

Still more tests might be necessary to check *technical performance metrics*. How many instructions per second can the computer hardware process, and what is the speed based on each watt of power? (Electricity to run systems always costs more than the system itself.) Does a piece of hardware with a smaller, physical footprint for tight spaces perform as well as a physically larger one? What is the impact on the environment from this solution?

Organizations want to be sure that their sensitive data is protected from hackers, from corruption that might make all of the saved data inaccessible, or from natural disasters such as fires, tornados, and floods. Therefore, testing for protection from unauthorized access and from unexpected, non-preventable damage means testing for computer security or *information security*. HIPAA and Sarbanes-Oxley are only two of the easily recognizable standards that must be met in this category.

While it is not creating code, *documenting* the internal design of the software is important for future maintenance and for enhancements that may be done in a future project. Newer programming languages allow the code to be written in clearer ways that require less in the way of secondary documentation to record what the lines of code are intended to do.[1]

Scrum

Perhaps the best place to start looking at little agile methodologies is with Scrum. Although it is only one of many approaches to agile, it is well-developed and has many training resources for you to use to educate yourself and your team, or coaches to guide you for the first project or two. Because it is easy to find resources when moving to this methodology, it is the fastest growing segment of the agile space. Gartner Group predicted in 2010 that by 2012, agile developments methods would be utilized in 80% of all software development projects.

Think of Scrum in contrast to Waterfall or traditional processes. *Predictability* is the cornerstone of Waterfall, so it works best when all of the details of the project can be known upfront. Since feedback is not usually available until late in the project, that means that change is expensive. On the other hand, Scrum is based on the premise of the value of *adaptability*. It addresses the reality that it is difficult to capture and freeze the project details at the beginning, so it is structured to support and implement change throughout the life cycle. Since there is constant feedback, change is cheap in terms of time, non-wasted materials and resources, and emotional responses from the team.

Developed by Ken Schwaber and Jeff Sutherland independently in the early 1990s, their jointly presented paper describing the Scrum methodology in 1995 was its first public unveiling. Scrum is a very specific process. However, it has a lot in common with the other Agile information you have already learned. Scrum also shares many similarities with other little agile approaches. To continue our comparison between Agile/Scrum and Waterfall/traditional practices, as project managers we all know the constant pull between the triple constraints, a framework for balancing competing demands. You may also hear it referred to as the "Iron Triangle." The idea is that in a perfect world, all three corners of the triangle (time, cost, and scope) balance and create a framework in which the project team can deliver quality (the center of the triangle). When all of the parameters of the triangle are in harmony, the shape remains consistent. However, if you adjust one side (for example, try to reduce cost), you will be forced to adjust the other sides, too, altering the time it takes to complete the work, and scope, which is the amount of work you do.

A familiar *plan-driven approach* to the work of projects (**Waterfall**) fixes the scope upfront and then adjusts the schedule (time) and the budget (cost) in order to achieve the scope promised. The thing to realize about traditional planning is that it is done early in the process and, over time, it becomes less and less accurate (see Figure 17.1).

Instead, the more **agile**, *value-driven approach* to completing projects fixes the schedule into set, timeboxed iterations that do not vary, and a fixed budget, usually the payroll costs of a dedicated team. The flex point then comes in the scope (the amount of features or services created), which is prioritized so that those features with the most business value are done first. Also, the items with the highest risk or uncertainty are addressed early in the project when change or failure is less costly. Value-driven approaches replace time estimates with the number of points the team thinks it will take to create a user story solution. They are also established early, but they become more, rather than less, accurate over time.

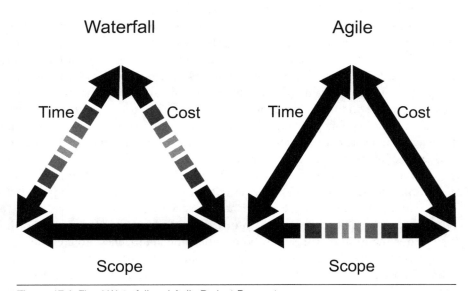

Figure 17.1 Fixed Waterfall and Agile Project Parameters.

The Scrum Alliance summarizes their specific process as follows:

1. A *product owner* creates a prioritized wish list called a *product backlog*.
2. During *sprint planning*, the team pulls a small chunk from the top of that wish list, a *sprint backlog*, and decides how to implement those pieces.
3. The team has a certain amount of time, a *sprint*, to complete its work—usually two to four weeks—but meets each day to assess its progress (*daily scrum*).
4. Along the way, the *ScrumMaster* keeps the team focused on its goal.
5. At the end of the sprint, the work should be *potentially shippable*, as in ready to hand to a customer, put on a store shelf, or show to a stakeholder.
6. The sprint ends with a *sprint review* and *sprint retrospective*.
7. As *the next sprint begins*, the team chooses another chunk of the product backlog and begins working again.

The cycle repeats until enough items in the produce backlog have been completed, the budget is depleted, or a deadline arrives. Regardless of which milestone signals the end of the work, valuable work has been completed when the project ends.

Scrum is unique because it uses the idea of **empirical process control**, which means it uses the real-world progress of a project to plan and schedule releases. Empirical means you are gaining your information through observation, experience, or experimentation. *Processes are controlled by inspecting for correct operation and results, and then adapting the process as needed.* **Transparency** means *the processes that affect the outcome must be visible to those controlling the processes.* Frequent inspection allows unacceptable variances to be spotted, and then the process or material being processed is adjusted if they are outside of acceptable limits and the resulting product will be unacceptable. The idea that the project can be adjusted after a few weeks based on a portion of the actual, completed work rather than metrics or speculation, has made it popular with upper management. The key idea here is the value of the feedback loops created by this agile methodology.

The Scrum Alliance offers training, which can lead to certification. Certification courses are taught by Scrum Alliance Registered Education Providers (REPs) and led by *Certified Scrum Trainers* (CSTs). One certification is the *Certified ScrumMaster* (CSM), which shows that the holder knows the terminology, practices, and principles to be a ScrumMaster or a Scrum team member. Participants are encouraged to work toward a *Certified Scrum Professional* (CSP) certification. In order to qualify for the CSP, you must already be a CSM, a *Certified Scrum Product Owner* (CSPO), or a *Certified Scrum Developer* (CSD); have a minimum of 2,000 hours of Scrum-related work in the past two years; and pass an online evaluation exam. Each CSM must re-certify every two years.

In terms of Scrum practices in the workplace, user stories create the **scrum product backlog** and the team takes a portion of that prioritized list to do for the upcoming iteration, but rather than be called the iteration backlog, it is called the **sprint backlog**, showing the work the team has committed to do within this iteration. Each user story, as prepared by the CSPO, focuses on *what* needs to be created, not the *how* of the method the team will choose to accomplish the goal.

The question always arises: Is ScrumMaster just a different name for the project manager? If you compare a ScrumMaster to a Waterfall project manager, the roles are very different. The ScrumMaster is the team coach and does not give day-to-day direction to the team. Instead, he or she protects the team, clearing the way for them to focus their time and energy on the work of the project. As you change from a Waterfall project manager to an Agile or hybrid project manager, you will assume those ScrumMaster-like responsibilities in addition to your other new skills.

The Scrum Alliance website at www.scrumalliance.com describes the role of the ScrumMaster very well when it says: "One convenient way to think of the interlocking nature of these three roles is as a race car. The Scrum Team is the car itself, ready to speed along in whatever direction it is pointed. The Product Owner is the driver, making sure the car is always going in the right direction. The ScrumMaster is the chief mechanic, keeping the car well-tuned and performing at its best."

It also suggests that some of the types of impediments that a ScrumMaster (or Agile project manager) might be asked to deal with could typically be:

- My _____ broke and I need a new one today.
- I still haven't got the _____ I ordered a month ago.
- I need help on a problem with _____.
- I am struggling to learn _____ and would like to pair with someone on it.
- I can't get the vendor's tech support group to call me back.
- Our new contractor cannot start because no one is here to sign her contract.
- I cannot get the _____ group to give me any time, and I need to meet with them.
- The department VP has asked me (a team member) to work on something else "for a day or two."

A software development product backlog differs from a non-software one in the types of things that you will find included. So far, we've limited the things on our iteration backlog to primarily product or service features. The programming team on a Scrum project can also include code bugs in the list. **Bugs** are *errors, flaws,* *or some other type of mistake that mean the software program does not give the expected results.*

Another addition to the backlog could be *technical work*, such as upgrading workstation software or installing a new communication tool. And, user stories around research or product selection which need to be done by the team in order to continue with the project, called *knowledge acquisition,* could be added to the list before it is prioritized by the project owner.

Numerous scrum teams can also be organized for enterprise projects that are too large for one team. When the ScrumMasters meet to coordinate multiple teams' information, it is called a **Scrum of Scrums.**

When the scrum team holds its **sprint planning meeting**, in addition to the sprint backlog, it may create a **sprint goal**. This is a *short statement that describes what the team plans to accomplish during this sprint.* The Scrum Alliance has introduced some new terms in describing the Scrum framework. They now say that Scrum is made up of three roles, four ceremonies, and three artifacts.

Three Core Roles in Scrum

These three roles make up the unit know as a Scrum team:

- **Product owner**: Represents the voice of the customer, whether internal or external, and is responsible for making sure that the team delivers business value from the project.
- **ScrumMaster**: Responsible for removing any impediments to the project that might keep the team from producing their sprint goal and their sprint deliverables. The ScrumMaster watches to be sure the team is following the Scrum process and enforces rules when the team cannot or does not.
- **Development team**: A small group with cross-functional skills who do the actual work of the project and are responsible for producing potentially shippable product increments at the end of each sprint. They are self-organizing.

Of course, there are other roles important to the project. These two additional roles are not technically Scrum team members, but they interface with the team frequently and their input is critical:

- **Stakeholders:** The end-users, the customers, and the vendors whose ideas and wishes are also important to the project.
- **Managers:** The internal organization people who might control the work space, personnel of the teams, and the surrounding environment of the Scrum team.

Four Core Ceremonies in Scrum

- **Sprint planning:** The team meets with the product owner to choose a set of work to deliver during a sprint.
- **Daily scrum:** The team meets each day to share struggles and progress.
- **Sprint reviews:** The team demonstrates to the product owner what it has completed during the sprint.
- **Sprint retrospectives:** The team looks for ways to improve the product and the process.

Three Core Artifacts in Scrum

- **Product backlog:** A prioritized list of desired project outcomes/ features.
- **Sprint backlog:** A group of user stories from the product backlog that the team agrees to complete in a sprint, broken into tasks which have been prioritized by the product owner.
- **Burndown chart:** An at-a-glance look at the work remaining that shows team progress during this sprint. You can have two burndown charts: one for the sprint and one for the overall project. [2]

To introduce Scrum into your organization, you need to understand the key drivers behind why it has achieved such a large base of acceptance. With a dedicated Scrum team, the work of the project flows directly into the team, eliminating misunderstandings and misinformation transfers. The focus moves to managing the work, rather than managing the people of the project. Dedicated teams quickly congeal to provide a sustainable velocity (capacity to complete work).

Extreme Programming

Kent Beck, one of the original 17 signers of the Agile Manifesto, is the creator of **Extreme Programming (XP)** and the key person in the rediscovery of TDD. Working in close collaboration with another signer, Ward Cunningham, in the late 1980s, they both refined their practices on numerous projects through the early 1990s. Beck had a chance to work out his ideas in practice on the Chrysler C3 project by creating cars, and the term "extreme programming" came into use around 1997.

Beck differentiates between values and practices. **Values** are *the knowledge and understanding that underlie the chosen approach to the project*, while **practices** are *the concrete, day-to-day things the team can do*. If you do not have a strong set of values, practices are just rote activities without a purpose. The *bridge between values and practices* are **principles**. So, the belief structure (values) can be listed as principles to be followed, and, based on those principles, the daily practices are chosen to correspond with the mindset driving the methodology.[3]

Beck describes XP as: "A lightweight methodology for small to medium-sized teams developing software in the face of vague or rapidly changing requirements." The gist of the XP process is constant integration and automated testing by a small, empowered team working in small, frequent releases that incorporate regular customer feedback to create an effective and flexible methodology for quick software development.

The name of the XP methodology comes from the idea that in this approach the beneficial elements of traditional software engineering are taken to "extreme" levels. While those who are not familiar with agile may assume that it is less rigorous than traditional techniques, that is far from the truth. In fact, XP got its name when its founders asked the question, "What would happen if we took each technique/practice and performed it to the extreme?" If code reviews are good, what would happen if you ran them constantly? That would be extreme, but would it be better? How would that affect the software process?

If a little is good, more is better. But don't misread this to mean that the emphasis is on process. XP is the antithesis of process-driven, and is preferably described as a "system of practices." You will find XP a close cousin of Scrum and many other agile methodologies. XP's unique feature is that the steps of the project are completed in extremely small chunks, e.g., within a day or week, rather than like Waterfall processes where a phase may take months or even years.

Rather than write code and then test it, this approach works in reverse. The developers write *automated tests* that must be passed to provide the functionality of a small portion of the software *first*, and then pair programming (coding in twos) is used to write the product. The code must pass the test, and as the lines of code grow, each new code must pass all previous tests. Even if the code passes the tests, a second look may indicate that there are shorter and cleaner ways to get the same functionality. This is called *refactoring*.

At this point, the functioning part of the system is demonstrated for users, and the cycle starts again. XP advocates timeboxing and short development cycles with frequent releases. Changes in customer requirements are expected.

In XP, story estimates must be small enough to be completed within a 1 to 3 week iteration, and larger stories should be split. Each story should have a single important part so that it can be prioritized as one unit. A story must be testable and the customer should be able to clearly state what acceptance tests will verify that the story is correct and complete. Once the story passes the acceptance tests, it is considered "Done."

When estimating stories, they are given arbitrary units of effort, based on the amount of time it will take to complete them. XP introduces the idea of the **ideal programming week**, *the amount of work you can complete in a week where there* *are no interruptions*, no meetings, you are not pulled off to work on another project, you don't have to help anyone else, no one calls you, you don't answer e-mail, you aren't sick, and all the stars configure to place you in a productivity nirvana.

A release is generally one to three months, and the team cannot promise to complete more work this release than they did in the last release. If this is the first one, they pick an arbitrary velocity they think is reasonable. Usually, the duration of the release is planned, and then the stories are chosen that will fit. As in other Agile practices, the customer gets to decide the content of the project work, but the team provides the estimates. The velocity cannot be "rounded up" or changed.

At the iteration level, stories should not be more that a day or two in "ideal days" in the estimated time to complete them. The customer picks which stories will go into this iteration and agrees not to change them during the duration of this timebox. Plus, he or she defines acceptance tests for each story.

Now the programmers break the stories down even further into tasks, and have a say in the order in which they complete them. The logic of how these tasks need to be done may escape the understanding of any but the most technically skilled customer. The programmers pick their own tasks from the iteration backlog, and no task the team has committed to complete in this iteration can remain unchosen.

As with release and iteration team velocities, no individual can take on stories totaling a personal velocity that exceeds what they completed in the preceding iteration. Note that the delineation of responsibility is well-defined: customers choose stories and define acceptance criteria, programmers create estimates and choose the strategy by which the stories are completed.

In XP, coding is done in pairs that may work together for a few hours, then break up and work with someone else. The social construct is that if you are asked for help, you can't say no. But that entitles you to ask for help, too. In this test based environment a peek at the practices would show you "one test case at a time development." A pair selects a task to work on and designs a *test case* to verify if the software task they create performs as needed to pass the customer's acceptance test. Then, code is written that must pass the test case. As more test cases are written, they form a collective unit test called an *automated test suite* that must be run every time the code is altered.

Individual sections of code that pass unit tests are eventually combined and tested as a group in *integration testing,* to be sure the functionality remains as intact when combined with other pieces as it did when tested originally. Integration testing looks not only at the functionality of the completed code section, it looks at performance metrics and how reliably it performs. Eventually, the code is tested as a whole, and then further tested when it "goes live" and must play nice with the existing legacy software with which it might need to interface.

Just when you think that must be all of the testing information one could be asked to know, there is more. *Big-Bang integration* is where your small team blends in its product with a larger team's work. It is the combination of work from multiple teams, and although all of the previous tests were successful, this is another crossroads where problems can appear for the first time.

With a fuller understanding of software testing processes, you may now be prepared to place the practice of continuous integration, and the value of writing tests before writing code, into a more meaningful frame of reference. Once lines of code are created, if the unit tests have not been written ahead of time, the developer can still write the test and verify that the code works. But the knowledge of what they have already created can subliminally influence the way they construct the test they create—so the test may pass, but not really be a robust verification of working software. If the test is constructed first, then it is created without bias and is based only on the requirements of the user story. This approach tests whether the code actually does the right thing for which it was intended, rather than merely checking that it "works."

Eventually, the software solution being created by your team will need to aggregate all of the individual features into one product. During any one iteration, programmers may each be working on parts of the code. Since **refactoring** (*cleaning up code so that there is no duplication, sloppily written, or unnecessarily complex code*) means that some lines of code may work with multiple features, two or more people might be altering that code at any one time. When working in a team that shares sources, your team will need some form of *source code control (SCC)*. This allows developers to get their own duplicate code copy by "checking out" a file and automatically notifying others that they are going to modify that file.

When the additions are made and tested, the person uploads or "checks in" the file to the server, and it is merged into the older version. There are rules within the SSC software to allow for situations in which developers have made conflicting alterations to the code, but mostly these additions result in a constantly fresh, latest version source, with a version number to allow the team members to distinguish between them. The previous version is also archived in case you need it.

So, continuous integration means that you integrate your new, tested sections of code into the main version as frequently as possible. Usually, this triggers the *test suite* (the collection of user tests written by this team as they go) to run, and if your work has any problems you receive instant feedback. It is preferable to know right this moment that what you just added has issues, rather than burying it in with the work from all of the other team developers day after day and then trying to find the problem at the end of the iteration, or even at the end of the project. Think of it as being akin to the ease with which you can remove ice cubes from your freshly-poured, fizzy, soft drink while they are still frozen, rather than trying to separate out the ice cube water molecules from those of the soft drink molecules after the glass sits on your desk overnight.

There are two main dividends from continuous integration. First, it forces the team to break the work down into small enough pieces that tests can be written. Second, it allows you to find and work to solve small, fixable problems on the spot throughout the iteration timebox rather than being surprised by them at the end when you do your quality testing.

And there's even more. After the source code is tested and found to be acceptable, the code needs to be compiled, or converted into a software artifact that can be run on a computer, also called being converted into *executable code.* This process is referred to as a *software build,* and is done by an automated build tool, which is a program that controls and coordinates other programs. Errors are possible here, too, so if the source code has not changed since the last build, the tool may not recompile it in order to avoid the possibility of introducing errors to clean code. This shortens the build time.

If you do not have a software development background, fortunately being the project manager for an agile team does not require you to perform or oversee these tests or other practices yourself. It is important for you to understand, though, that this is only a portion of the work that the developer does over and above writing the lines of code. This knowledge may keep you from alienating the team and making them view you as totally inept by trying to shorten the time spent on tests and other agile practices, thinking it will speed up the project.

XP Principles

With an understanding of software terms and the ideas behind XP you will see that it has four core values:

- Communication
- Simplicity
- Feedback
- Courage

From those values, there are thirteen practices that work together:

1. **Planning game:** Plan work incrementally.
2. **Small releases:** Release as quickly as possible to decrease the time to market and to get feedback as soon as possible.
3. **Metaphor:** If possible, define a metaphor for the system being developed to help the team have a shared understanding. For example, an online ordering system is often visualized as a shopping cart to allow the team to have common terminology for describing features such as "placing an item in the cart," "removing an item from the cart," "continue shopping," and "checkout."

4. **Simple design**: Use the simplest design that will work for the functionality (user story) being implemented. Do not design for functions that may never actually be used.

5. **Testing:** Test everything, and try to automate the testing if possible.

6. **Refactoring:** Instead of designing an entire system upfront, design as you go, making improvements as needed. Use automated testing to determine the impact of the refactoring.

7. **Pair programming:** Programming in teams of two or three allows for a discussion to occur in real-time that addresses requirement, design, testing, and programming concerns.

8. **Collective code ownership:** Anyone on the team can make a change to any code at any time.

9. **Continuous integration:** The entire code base is constantly being rebuilt, and then retested in an automated fashion.

10. **Sustainable pace:** Ideally, team members do not need to work more than 40 hours per week to meet project deadlines. Racing to perform in a superhuman way to meet deadlines is replaced by consistent, predictable, repeatable delivery.

11. **Whole team**: The team functions as a whole. Members are encouraged to be more generalized rather than specialized. Learning about all technologies and requirements is encouraged.

12. **Coding standards:** In order to maximize communication, coding standards are defined by the team and used to ensure consistent coding practices.

13. **Onsite customer:** Having constant and direct access to the customer allows the team to work at the fastest possible speed.[4]

Ken Auer and Roy Miller, in their book *Extreme Programming Applied,* offer the option that while it is better to start with all thirteen practices, you could begin with only the following six, which they call "essential practices": planning game, small releases, testing, pair programming, refactoring, and continuous integration.[5]

XP Roles

In XP, here are a few of the people who play key roles in the development of successful projects:

- **Customer**—The customer creates and prioritizes the stories that need to be implemented. Because the customer sets the priorities, he or she controls what will be delivered in any given release, and can control the release date by adding or removing stories.

- **Programmers**—Programmers collectively estimate stories, but individually accept responsibility for the tasks that they estimate, write tests, and code.
- **Coach**—The coach, who is probably a team lead or an outside consultant with technical skills in XP, monitors the software development process, mentors the team members on XP processes and techniques, and focuses the team's attention on potential problems or optimizations.
- **Tracker**—The tracker (could this be you as the project manager?) monitors the progress of the team and alerts them when adjustments to the schedule or a rebalancing of tasks might be required.

Dynamic Systems Development Method

Especially popular in Europe, the Dynamic Systems Development Method (DSDM) has its own DSDM® Consortium, which positions itself as the "guardian of DSDM Atern, the Agile Project Framework that provides best practice guidance for on time, in budget delivery of projects—with proven scalability to address projects of all sizes and for any business sector." Much as we are considering how agile practices such as Scrum and XP can be integrated into the traditional or Waterfall approach currently in place in our organizations, DSDM has advertised that it is easily tailored and can be used in conjunction with the traditional processes found in PRINCE2®, a project management process that also enjoys its greatest popularity in Europe.[6]

In addition, the DSDM framework can incorporate other delivery approaches such as XP and Scrum (you can go to the DSDM website at www.dsdm.com and download a copy of the DSDM Atern handbook). Although historically DSDM began as an approach for IT projects, the Atern version has been enhanced to provide clearer support for projects with no software element, as well as a fit for those endeavors that do support IT undertakings. One key difference from Scrum and XP is that DSDM is vendor-independent, i.e., not productized.

When listing the rational for using Atern, the issues sound very familiar: communication problems, late delivery, the delivered solution is not really what the business wanted, there are unused features, the team builds the right thing and then the business changes its mind, there is a delayed or late ROI, or things are over-engineered or "gold plated." What is their solution? A flexible approach that does not freeze time, cost, quality, and features as DSDM proponents suggest happens in traditional projects. Instead, with the Atern approach you freeze time, cost, and quality, and then vary the features delivered as necessary, dropping or deferring lower priority features (called *contingencies*) with the agreement of all of the stakeholders.

In a slightly altered phraseology, the DSDM Consortium says the value of Atern is that it "ensures on-time delivery of a viable solution that can be achieved by protecting the minimum usable subset" (think minimum marketable features), "and dropping or deferring lower priority features, if necessary, in accordance with MoSCoW rules."

The Atern philosophy is that any project must be aligned to clearly defined strategic goals and focus upon early delivery of real benefits to the business. This is best achieved when key stakeholders understand the business objectives, are empowered to an appropriate level, and collaborate in order to deliver the right solution. The solution will be delivered in the agreed timescale, according to the priorities set by the business. The stakeholders must be prepared to deliver a fit-for-purpose solution. They must also be prepared to accept that change is inevitable as they understand more about the solution being developed."

The structure of Atern is that their philosophy (like a roof) is supported by their principles (the pediment) and rests on four pillars: Process, People, Products, and Practices. This could be a useful model for understanding and conveying the substance of any form of agile, not just DSDM.

DSDM Atern Principles

DSDM Atern relies on eight principles. Although there may be a more structured method by which teams work, the eye of the team must always be on fulfilling these principles rather than being lulled into thinking that merely completing process steps will bring the same results as choosing actions based on a belief structure. If you work in a non-IT setting, you may find some DSDM Atern principles are especially useful to you in an agile transition.

Principle 1. Focus on the business need. Given unlimited time and resources, any project can build a larger deliverable with more functionality. However, delivering the "perfect system" that considers every feasible business situation is less crucial than working to develop the critical functionalities that will suffice for the current business need. That is the main criteria for acceptance of a "deliverable".

- Understand the true business priorities.
- Establish a sound business case.
- Seek continuous business sponsorship and commitment.
- Guarantee the minimum usable subset of features.

Principle 2. Deliver on time.

- Timebox the work.
- Focus on business priorities.
- Always hit deadlines.

Principle 3. Collaborate. Collaborative and fast decisions are key to running an efficient and effective project. These decisions must include user involvement. Ideally, users and the product developers share a workplace, either physically or using collaboration tools.

- Involve the right stakeholders, at the right time, throughout the project.
- Ensure that the members of the team are empowered to make decisions on behalf of those they represent.
- Actively involve the business representatives.
- Build a one-team culture.

Principle 4. Never compromise quality.

- Set the level of quality at the outset.
- Ensure that quality does not become a variable.
- Design, document, and test appropriately.
- Build in quality by constant review.
- Test early and continuously.

Principle 5. Build incrementally from firm foundations.

- Strive for early delivery of business benefit where possible.
- Continually confirm the correct solution is being built.
- Formally re-assess priorities and ongoing project viability with each delivered increment.

Principle 6. Develop iteratively. Have a focus on frequent delivery of products, with the assumption that to deliver something "good enough" earlier, is always better than to deliver everything "perfectly" in the end. By delivering product frequently from an early stage of the project, the product can be tested and reviewed, and the test record and review document can be taken into account at the next iteration or phase.

- Do enough design upfront to create strong foundations.
- Take an iterative approach to building all products.
- Build customer feedback into each iteration.
- Accept that most detail emerges later rather than sooner.
- Embrace change—the right solution will not evolve without it.
- Be creative, experiment, learn, evolve.

Principle 7. Communicate continuously and clearly. Communication and cooperation among all project stakeholders is required to be efficient and effective, while poor communication is often cited as the biggest cause of project failure. Atern teams will:

- Run daily team stand-up sessions.
- Use facilitated workshops.
- Use rich communication techniques such as modeling and prototyping.
- Present iterations of the evolving solution early and often.
- Keep documentation lean and timely.
- Manage stakeholder expectations throughout the project.
- Encourage informal, face-to-face communication at all levels.

Principle 8. Demonstrate control.

- Use an appropriate level of formality for tracking and reporting.
- Make plans and progress visible to all.
- Measure progress through focus on delivery of products rather than completed activities.
- Manage proactively.
- Evaluate continuing project viability based on the business objectives.[7]

The Atern Lifecycle Process includes five phases: Feasibility, Foundations, Exploration, Engineering, and Deployment into the business' operational environment, plus pre- and post-project activities. This framework is intended to be both iterative and incremental. The pre-project phase is where projects are selected and assigned, assuring that they are the correct choices for the business and that they are properly set up within the organization.

Lasting only a few weeks, the Feasibility and Foundation phases are sequential, but can be merged in a small project. They are the place where the scope of work is set and the details of the *who, what, when, where,* and *why* of the project are captured. This is the point in the project where it is assessed to see if Atern is the correct set of practices to apply to this work, or if another approach would be more beneficial. It is a unique, but admirable step, as all of the other little agile methodologies assume that their approach is the best one in all situations. To be fair, Scrum and XP are intended to be for software development, so in that sense they know the approach that they espouse is appropriate for the work they are doing.

The Exploration phase is intended to be used to investigate possible problem solutions and perhaps create a partial solution, such as a prototype. The prototype can then be improved upon during the Engineering phase, so that it is sturdy enough for operational use. Finally, in the Deployment phase, it is placed into use in the organization. The post-project phase activities focus on whether or not the solution was successfully deployed, and whether or not performance of the project actually allowed the organization to realize the business value that it expected.

Atern has a unique way of assigning priorities that extends beyond the user story alone to requirements, products, use cases, acceptance criteria, and tests called the **MoSCoW** technique. The concept is that generic terms like high priority, medium priority, and low priority do not convey enough about the item being prioritized. MoSCoW makes the priorities more specific by conveying the reason for their placement on a prioritized list. The capital letters in MoSCoW stand for: **M**ust Have, **S**hould Have, **C**ould Have, and **W**on't Have This Time.

Must Have

If you ask the question, "What happens if this requirement is not met?" and the answer is, "We must cancel the project," it is a Must Have. Must Have examples are:

- Cannot deliver on target date without this.
- No point in delivering on target date without this; if it were not delivered, there would be no point in deploying the solution on the intended date.
- Not legal without it.
- Unsafe without it.
- Cannot deliver the business case without it.

Should Have

Some examples of Should Have are:

- Important, but not vital.
- May be painful to leave out, but the solution is still viable.
- May need some kind of workaround, e.g., management of expectations, some inefficiency, an existing solution, paperwork, etc.

Could Have

Some examples of Could Have are:

- Wanted or desirable, but less important.
- Less impact if left out (compared with Should Have).
- May need some kind of workaround, e.g., management of expectations, some inefficiency, an existing solution.

Won't Have This Time

These are requirements that the project team has agreed they will not deliver. They are recorded in the prioritized requirement list where they help clarify the scope of the project and to avoid them being reintroduced "via the back door" later. This helps to manage stakeholder expectations by clarifying that some requirements will simply not make it into the delivered solution, at least not this time around.

The Atern Iterative Development Cycle follows the path around Identify, Plan, Evolve, and Review. This is similar in concept to the Shewhart/Deming Plan, Do, Check, Act cycle. Regardless, it is an iterative development cycle done within a timebox. If you are in a non-IT organization where the IT focus on other agile methodologies has alienated people, you might want to take a look at the details of DSDM Atern. It could possibly be an Agile approach that would fit into your workspace.

References

[1]"Software development process." *Wikipedia*. Retrieved from http://en.wikipedia.org/wiki/Software_development_process.
[2]Scrum Alliance. Retrieved from www.scrumalliance.com.
[3]Beck, K. & Fowler, M. 2001. *Planning Extreme Programming*. New York: Addison-Wesley Professional.
[4]Newkirk, J. & Martin, R. C. 2001. *Extreme Programming in Practice*. New York: Addison-Wesley Professional.
[5]Auer, K. & Miller, R. 2011. *Extreme Programming Applied*. New York: Addison-Wesley Professional.
[6]DSDM® Consortium. 2012. Retrieved from www.dsdm.org.
[7]*ibid*

18

What Are Lean, Kanban, Crystal, and Other Agile Practices?

Lean Manufacturing

Lean is a manufacturing process evolved from William Edwards Deming's methodology of Total Quality Management (TQM). Sent to work in Japan to help that nation rebuild after World War II, Deming shared American ideas, but brought home important concepts from his Japanese hosts as well. His core ideas were that process is important, and that people are the ones who build and improve the process. As a process, TQM is very metric intensive. However, if you wanted to encapsulate the main concept of Lean into a single sentence, it would be that any activity that does not directly add value to the finished produce is waste, and should be eliminated. The main principles of Lean manufacturing, which should be familiar to you from reading about Agile, are:

1. **Specify value**. This reflects Peter Drucker's thinking and the idea that value is in the eyes of the customer. You need to specify minimum marketable features that show what is being created in the process flow that has value to your customer.
2. **Identify the value stream and eliminate waste**. This concept is reminiscent of Goldratt's Theory of Constraints. Organizations often draw out the process flow of the value stream in a flowchart, so that they can

more easily find the bottlenecks. Think of a cumulative flow diagram. In Lean terminology, you are finding stagnation, or blocking tasks.

3. **Make value flow at the pull of the customer**. Organizations should create the products that provide value for the customer when they request it. The alternative would be to create things as a speculative endeavor, hoping that what you create is something they would want to purchase. The word "pull" comes from the use of the tool *kanban*. As applied to software development, or in non-IT projects, the idea of "pull" is that the customer decides the features that need to be implemented as a part of this project based on what they desire most (brings the most business value), and what they are willing to pay for (or can afford to create) at this point in time. The project team is there to provide what the product owner requests in a prioritized order.

Kanban

Kanban is a tool used in Lean manufacturing. It comes from Toyota's production line practices, and is an actual card that is used to facilitate a "pull" production control system that can be done in a self-directed way by the workers involved. When this idea is moved to the software development arena, it can be translated as sticky notes on a wall chart that show the team when to "pull" and complete additional tasks (particularly if the task is dependent on another team member's task, which must be completed first). You may hear this referred to as "Software Kanban." There are three basic ideas (philosophies) behind kanban:

- Visualize what you do today (workflow).
- Limit the amount of work in progress (WIP).
- Enhance flow.

In addition, here are the nine properties of kanban in a manufacturing environment. It is easy to see where the information radiators of many other agile methodologies have used these positive ideas to enhance both software development and non-IT projects.

1. **Kanban.** A kanban card is a physical card that you move from location to location as a communication signal to others on the project regarding what needs to be done or has been done. The word comes from the Japanese "*kanban*" or "*kamban*," which means signboard, billboard, or shop sign. It probably alludes to the idea of a bar owner's last call for drink orders before taking down the sign, thus "last-minute" or "just-in-time" inventory control.

2. **Limit WIP.** One issue in a manufacturing environment is ensuring smooth flow by making sure that an optimum number of parts are available at the appropriate place in an assembly line at the right time. If too few parts are available at the right time, the speed of the line is diminished. If there are too many parts, there is extra cost for storage, and possible breakage, loss, or damage to the items.

If you saw the *I Love Lucy* TV show episode where the characters Lucy and Ethel got jobs on the production line of a chocolate factory, you might be able to visualize the problems that they satirized. At first things were fine, and Lucy and Ethel were able to take the fresh chocolates from the conveyer belt and box them easily. But when the line sped up, and they had no way to signal that it was too fast, they began to try to eat the excess chocolates, throw them over their shoulders, stuff them into their clothing, and use all other manner of solutions to comic effect to work within the confines of a system that did not provide for worker feedback or adjusting the flow of the line to the needs of the process.

In reality, the Cadbury chocolate factories would never have these situations because, as early as 1917, they were involving their workers in production decisions and any one of them could stop the production line if they saw an issue. A sign hanging in their reception area at the Dunedin, New Zealand manufacturing center has a quote from an employee. It reads, "Cadbury's is a good employer. They listen to our ideas and everyone is responsible for quality control. Staff are really involved in what goes on in the factory. We know it is up to us to keep the business strong."[1]

Issues of flow remain a major consideration for an assembly line. The number of individual parts produced for inclusion in 1,000 finished products, to the mind of a person who does not work in that industry, would be 1,000. In reality, 100% of the small parts produced, or obtained from a third party vendor, can never be used. Obtaining shipments where the quality of the parts received allowed each and every small component to be installed in a finished, shippable piece of merchandise would be cost prohibitive. By the same token, if the parts are manufactured upstream in the production line of the company, they do not know exact counts to produce, either.

In kanban, the intent is to minimize the WIP, or parts inventory being produced upstream, by having the upstream process workers only produce the parts if and when they are needed by the downstream process workers. When new items are needed, the upstream workers produce just enough parts, and at just the right time, to keep the production line flowing smoothly. If upstream falls behind, workers can be shifted temporarily to another place on the line where they are needed to bring the line back into harmony while waiting for new parts.

In software development, prioritizing the user stories and limiting the number of difficulty points each team can commit to complete each iteration is a variation of limiting WIP. If additional help is needed on a user story, cross-functional developers are free to move around to help each other and spend their collective time where it will help the tasks of the project best be completed. More architecture, or software infrastructure, is not created than what is absolutely needed at the moment. Working ahead to try to create a technical or hardware support structure too early is not desirable because, with the flexibility of changing requirements, you might build something that is not actually needed by the final solution.

You can also equate WIP limits to the dedicated agile team, which is limited from working on many different projects at the same time to focus them on only one. The negative effects of constantly changing one's thoughts from project to project in the same day limit a person's ability to have the sub-conscious focused, and inhibits problem solving while you work.

3. **Continuous flow.** The kanban card notifies the "store" where the parts inventory is kept before it runs out of stock.

4. **Pull.** The process where the downstream process workers ask for items created by the upstream process workers.

5. **Self-directing.** By using the kanban card containing all of the pertinent information in writing to indicate inventory needs, the process stands alone. It is not managed by the "central office" nor controlled by a project manager. Another way to think of it is that the team members report to the team, not to a project manager, ScrumMaster, or team lead.

6. **Visual display.** The kanban card, prominently displayed, easily shows the current status and the progress to anyone who is in the area. Again, think of agile team flip chart sheets and whiteboard displays of moveable sticky notes to show the team and other stakeholders a current snapshot of the project at any time. They can pull the information they want, rather than waiting for the project manager to push it to them in a weekly report.

7. **Signal.** The kanban card, through its visual prominence, acts as a signal to indicate the next action needed.

8. **Kaizen.** This Japanese word means "improvement" or "change for the better." Broken down into its parts, "*kai*" means "to change or to

correct", while *"zen"* translates to "good." In a kaizen system, every employee in the organization is encouraged to actively be thinking of and instigating small changes constantly, rather than as a once a quarter or once a year activity. The idea is that productivity, safety, innovation, and other positive movement can happen continuously, and at the same time other innovations can be reducing waste.

Agile methods focus on the rapt involvement and empowerment of every person on the team to make changes that will have positive effects on the project outcome. That is why they are authorized to be the sole role for deciding the degree of difficulty and the way in which the desired outcomes of the project goals will be obtained. The retrospective allows for continuous improvement.

9. **Attached**. The kanban card is physically attached to, and moves with, the physical parts supplied as a result of the request written on this particular card. This closes a feedback loop so that the floor workers who initiated the card can see the results of their request fulfilled in the bin of parts delivered back to their location on the assembly line floor.

Lean believes you should empower the team in the Gemba. *Gemba,* in the Lean environment, literally means, "the real place," the place where all of the activities are happening, because that is where the value is being added. When thinking of a manufacturing environment, it would mean the shop floor, but for a restaurant it would be the kitchen; in a dress boutique it would be the cash register. The concept is that managers (and in our case, project managers) should go to the spot where the work is being done. In other words, get out on the shop floor and see what the issues are first hand. William Glasser, an American psychologist, says:

"We learn....
10% of what we read
20% of what we hear
50% of what we see and hear
70% of what we discuss
80% of what we experience
95% of what we teach others."

This supports the Gemba concept that only by experiencing what is happening in the location where it happens daily, can you really unearth and move forward to solve the roadblocks and issues that are constraining the flow for your employees. Gemba is part of a larger philosophy known as the 3 Reals. You have to go to the:

- Real place (the actual place of work, shop floor, or gemba, pronounced *gem-baah*), to observe the...

- Real thing (the actual product or gembutsu, pronounced *gem-boot-soo*) to get the...
- Real facts and data (jujitsu, pronounced *jew-jeet-soo*).

The idea is that Lean managers should not be secreted in their offices, but be out among the workers. In the 1980s, this was known as "Management by Walking Around (MBWA)," a term coined by the popular business writer, Tom Peters. If there is a problem somewhere, you should get as close to it as possible before proposing a solution. This concept is mirrored for the Agile project manager, in that they should be at the roadmap planning, release planning, iteration planning, daily stand-up, customer demonstration, and retrospective meetings with the core team. The project manager should also be part of meetings to merge output from multiple teams for a single product or service, or for larger projects that will merge into a final organizational program.

Being involved with the team members, company management, and other stakeholders from end-users to vendors, allows the project manager to experience the 3 Reals. Then, you can truly act as a servant-manager to try to remove the obstacles for your team.

The concept of Gemba lends further strength to the idea of a collocated team in a shared space. Even moving team discussions to a conference room is often less productive that having that same exchange is the actual work space with all of the visuals of team rules, progress charts, backlogs, and to-do charts within view.

Continuous Improvement

Pursue perfection, using the Kaizan philosophy. Another tool of the Kanban approach is that there may be smaller teams that are part of a larger undertaking. So, there are portable kanban boards that each sub-team can physically carry to a meeting of the whole group to display their work and coordinate it. Then, changes or new work can be added or rearranged on the spot and carried back to the people working on a specialized part of the project.

As project managers, we are already familiar with this idea. Think of it as a traditional WBS broken down to the work package level and administered in Microsoft Project. The work package can be forwarded to a vendor or another part of the organization electronically, where they break the activities into smaller tasks. Those tasks are tracked within the sub-group who has taken on the commitment to complete them. The fleshed-out details of that portion of the project can be resent and reintegrated into the automated software tool to give a complete picture of the total project statistics.

In an Agile approach, working for lighter documentation, the concept of a portable method of breaking down and then reassembling the project work has some merit. Think simple. It could be a rolling whiteboard that could move to large group status meetings, a folded set of flip chart records, or for a distributed group it could look like a software solution with an interface that allows activity or user stories represented in a sticky note image.

Toyota Production System

The Toyota Production System (TPS) is a specific form of Lean manufacturing used by Toyota Motor Corporation. Their goal is to make "the best quality product at the lowest price as soon as possible." TPS is based on a visual called the TPS House. It has two pillars for support, Just-in-Time and Jidoka. **Just-in-time** is *making what is needed, when it is needed, and in the amount needed.* **Jidoka** means *automation with a human touch.* In practice, it relates to building in quality during the manufacturing process.

Toyota uses the root Japanese term *jido*, which translates as a machine that moves on its own, and enhances the meaning for its purposes to mean a machine that has built-in devices to make judgments on its own, instead of moving and stopping based on the observations and control of an operator. To that end, a machine on the manufacturing line is set to automatically stop when it detects a quality issue. On a shop floor running machines like this, one person can oversee many machines and no resources or time is wasted by a faulty piece of equipment continuing to churn out items of unacceptable quality. When one mechanism stops, workers can to move to another machine while someone else works to identify the problem on the first machine and solve it. This process leads to continuous improvement in the quality of the products produced.

With a single operator responsible for monitoring multiple machines, the ability to have a visual control that displays machines that have stopped is key. Toyota uses a problem display board called an *andon* system to show the production line problems in a single glance. By now, you have already mentally translated this to the display boards of an agile team that allow progress and status updates at a glance.

Lean Software Development

Mary and Tom Poppendieck took the principles of TPS and applied them to software development. They rephrased jidoka as "Stop the Line Culture," in which anyone who sees an issue should be empowered to halt the progress down a path that will lead to time and resources being wasted on work that will not be able to be used.[2] Lean software development also adds the Theory of Constraints (TOC) ideas of Eliyahu Goldratt, which involves identifying constraints and then improving or removing them. Similarly, Lean software development has seven principles:

1. **Eliminate waste**. Eliminate anything that does not add customer value.
2. **Build in quality**. Validate and re-validate all assumptions throughout the process. If a metric or practice no longer has value, discard it. This serves to quicken the learning process. If you consistently find issues, change your process.
3. **Create knowledge**. Use short, iterative cycles to provide quick, constant feedback to ensure the right things are being focused on.
4. **Defer commitment**. Don't make decisions until enough is know to make a decision. A sound understanding of the problems and the tradeoffs of potential solutions is required.
5. **Deliver fast**. Minimize the time it takes to identify a business problem (such as time to market) and deliver a system (or feature) that addresses it. By allowing teams to assign degrees of difficulty to tasks (user stories) and commit to only the amount of work they think they can complete in one timebox, they can establish a reliable delivery rhythm.
6. **Respect people**. Empower the team to succeed. If you encourage self-direction and respect the knowledge of the people who make up the team, you reap engaged, committed team members who will over-perform, compared to the typical team of individuals multitasking on multiple projects at one time.
7. **Optimize the whole**. Use cross-functional teams to keep from missing important, possibly critical aspects of the problem and of the system designed to solve it. But you must also map out business processes, even those at a higher level that your own team, to find bottlenecks that trickle their restrictive poison down to your project level.

Since Lean is a methodology that focuses on the project management aspects of a project and has few technical practices that limit it to software development, it is an easy set of principles to use in a non-software project as well.

Rational Unified Process

Rational Unified Process (RUP) was created in 1996 by Ivar Jacobson, but IBM now owns and markets it though its Rational Software Corporation division, purchased in 2003.[3] This is not a single, mandatory process, but rather a framework that is intended to be tailored to the organization and industry adopting it, and also by software development teams so that the appropriate portions are adopted. There are tools to automate important parts of the process. Technically, RUP is a specific instance of the larger agile category, Unified Process.

To effectively use this approach, which IBM calls a "best practice" because it is taken from practices successfully used in the industry, there are six best practices to follow. Of all of the agile productized varieties, this one is the most complete, complex, and involved. It is not a process that you could gradually integrate on your own, but would require a full contract from IBM to obtain all of the tools and templates. Plus, the intent is that you would hire IBM consultants to guide you through this transition. Here is a high level overview:

1. **Develop software iteratively**. It is almost impossible to develop software sequentially and define the entire problem and the entire solution, build the entire software product, and then test it at the end of the process. RUP focuses on moving risk to the front of every iteration. This is to be sure that risk is moved into a priority position at the first of the project where it is the least costly and least traumatic to the project to deal with it. Progress is demonstrated frequently through executable releases that garner continuous end-user feedback and involvement.

   To be sure that each iteration has a portion of the software that can be released, the team is focused on making sure this small piece of the final product is produced in each iteration. By working in iterations, tactical changes in requirements, features, and schedules are easy to integrate into the project plan.

2. **Manage requirements**. Use case scenarios (we have earlier referred to these as user stories) to capture requirements and make it clear to the development team how the software must be designed, written, and tested to be sure it meets end-user needs.

3. **Use component-based architectures.** This principle involves more detail that we may need or want to know as project managers. Basically, it revolves around the idea of doing some early development (think prototyping) before engaging all of the team resources down a single path. IBM thinks their process can create a flexible, understandable architecture (think substructure) for software that makes future changes to the application easier and allows the reuse of portions of this project in later projects. If the software is broken into smaller components, it is easier to test them before they are integrated into a larger system.

4. **Visually model software.** This phase uses tools to create diagrams of all the major components of the software, the users, and the interactions that take place between the two. It may be created in Unified Modeling Language, which has a series of graphic notations to create "pictures" of the software and how it relates to the needs of the users. If you have seen a network diagram in your project management software, you will be able to imagine icons that represent various processes as applied to software.

5. **Verify software quality.** Software production is subject to many quality reviews built into the process as you go, not just left to be tested at the end of the project. In addition to finding out "does it work," it is checked for reliability, functionality, how it performs as an application, and how it performs on the system as a whole (how fast, how much space it takes, how much electricity to run it, etc.).

6. **Control changes to software code.** The specifics of how to control, track, and monitor changes to the software code are detailed in this process, as is a process to automate integration and build management. If change is to be a constant, there must be a process to be sure that each change is acceptable and that the latest change is quickly made available to the team. Do *not* read this to mean customer feature changes are unwelcome.

The Four Phases of RUP

RUP apportions the development cycle into four phases they call *cycles*. Each cycle consists of four phases, and at any place along the way, the project can be cancelled, re-thought, or fundamentally altered, based on what has been discovered during the time spent on the project:

1. **Inception phase.** This is where the business case is created and project scope is defined.

2. **Elaboration phase.** The business needs are analyzed in greater detail and an architectural prototype is built in an attempt to eliminate the highest risk elements to the project.

3. **Construction phase.** The project development is actually completed, i.e., application design and source code with an emphasis on optimizing costs, schedules, and quality.

4. **Transition phase.** Once the project deliverable is complete and tested, it must be integrated into the user community. At this point, there may be the need to make adjustments, correct problems, or finish items that were postponed during earlier portions of the project.

At the end of each phase, there is a milestone where the work of the iteration must satisfy defined criteria before moving to the next phase. Here, critical decisions must be made as to how the project will move forward, so key goals must have been achieved on which those decisions rest.

Further, unique RUP project process structure uses these four clarifications regarding how projects work:

- Workers are the "who.
- Activities are the "how"
- Artifacts are the "what"
- Workflows are the "when"

RUP is an extensive and finely detailed plan to be implemented through the use of IBM consultants and their detailed process. You can get a glimpse of the general process by considering its best practices.

Crystal Methodologies

Crystal is the collective name given to a family of methodologies started by Alistair Cockburn, one of the original Agile Manifesto signers. They were started in 1992 and pre-date XP, Feature Driven Development, and many other software development approaches. Crystal differs from other types of agile approaches in that it is a family of practices and conventions that work well together, but which can be configured to the specific organization as appropriate.[4] The three defining features of a Crystal method are:

1. **Human-powered**. Other methodologies may focus on process or tools, but this one centers on the belief that the best way to achieve project success is by enhancing the work of the people involved.
2. **Ultralight**. Whatever the size of the project, or whatever the priorities outlined by the organization, there is a method from the Crystal family to reduce the paperwork, overhead, and bureaucracy to the lowest amount that makes sense for the parameters of the project.
3. **Stretch-to-fit**. This concept is that rather than trying to reduce a large, overblown process base and tailor it down, you start with something just slightly smaller than you think you need. Then, you can always expand it enough so that it is appropriate for your project. The idea is that it is easier, safer, and more efficient to stretch it slightly, than to try to cut away the excess after the project has already been defined.

Cockburn stresses that Crystal is a non-jealous method, which means that if there is something, i.e., a tool or a process, that works better and fits better into your current organizational structure, you do not destroy the value of Crystal by making the substitution. Likewise, if you are using another methodology, feel free to borrow useful techniques from Crystal.

If you are in an organizational structure that is locked into firm fixed price contracts, Crystal was developed and tested under this type of contract. Not all projects need to handle rapidly changing requirements, but all kinds of project work need efficiency. Efficiency is the ability to create good quality outcomes with a degree of rapidity. And speed and quality are positive attributes of value, especially in a fixed price situation.

Feature Driven Development

Feature Driven Development (FDD), invented by Jeff De Luca, is one of the lesser known agile processes.[5] Most agile development is predicated on the idea of a small, collocated team of skilled and motivated developers. As acknowledged earlier, many of us manage projects in larger teams to create larger projects for enterprise sized employers.

As the size of the team multiplies, it is unrealistic to assume that you can find a team on which all of the participants are equally skilled and disciplined, so FDD does not always make the same choices that you might use for a Scrum or XP project team. Recall that teams might use the Iteration Zero method to perform enough upfront tasks in a preliminary iteration to determine velocity and arrive at some of the other nebulous decisions that need to be made before the project proper can officially begin.

FDD is organized around five processes, which all revolve around the *features*. The first three processes are parallel to the kinds of activities you might do in an Iteration Zero scenario. While other agile approaches try to steer the team away from creating too much detail at the onset of the project, FDD has a unique approach:

- **Process 1. Develop an overall model**. In order to be sure all of the extended team understands the concepts, relationships, and interactions necessary for this software to work, a modeling tool is used to create a visual plan so that the entire team sees what the end result might look like. It is not broken down into very much detail, but the activity of working together to create it brings out much of the information that teams need from other parts of the project team. Remember, this larger team does not have the cross-functional skills that may be present in a smaller team, i.e., the technical knowledge may be more spread out among the participants and need to be shared during this exercise.

- **Process 2. Build a features list**. Just like Scrum or XP, FDD is driven by customer requirements, which are called *features*. The model does not control what is created, it is just an overview to be sure this expanded team all has a common picture of what is being created. Instead of calling it a backlog, the feature list in FDD is (creatively) named a "feature list." There is more than a vocabulary shift here, as a feature list has a three-level hierarchy. Remember, this is for an enterprise sized undertaking, so there are many more features than would be found in other methodologies. The top, or least detailed level, contains the general subject areas used to create the model. At the middle level, the team identifies business activities, and at the lowest, most defined level, breaks out individual features that are traceable and linked back up to the business activities. With the chief programmers from multiple teams working together, the naming language is more consistent, too.
- **Process 3. Plan by feature**. The planning team will initially sequence the feature sets to be created according to the business value they provide, also considering dependencies and technical risk. Then feature sets are assigned to chief programmers (technical people, not a replacement for the project manager) and each one works with his or her team to complete the subset of the features list they were assigned. This becomes the backlog or "virtual inbox" for each team.

In keeping with the idea not to create too much detail upfront, the last two processes are:

- **Process 4. Design by feature.**
- **Process 5. Build by feature.**

Rather than a traditional team concept of functional requirements that *must* be completed by the project's end, FDD allows the planning team to review and modify the feature set assignments as often as necessary throughout the project. One slightly unique feature of this approach is that there is no shared ownership of code, or other reports, or automated documents that are part of the software development process.

FDD Roles

There are nine main roles in FDD:

1. **Project manager.** Responsible for all administrative aspects of the project, including the financial and reporting ones.
2. **Chief architect.** Responsible for the overall design of the system, including running all design sessions, code reviews, and technology decisions.
3. **Development manager.** On the hook for the daily development activities, coordinating the development team and their activities, and dealing with resource issues.
4. **Chief programmer.** A senior developer involved in ongoing design and development activities, and who is assigned to be responsible for one or more feature sets.
5. **Class owner.** A developer who works under the direction of a chief programmer to design, code, test, and document features as they are implemented.
6. **Domain expert.** Any business related stakeholder who works under the direction of a chief programmer to design, code, test, and document features as they are implemented.
7. **Tester.** Responsible for verifying that each feature performs as defined.
8. **Deployer.** Deals with not only actual deployment of code to various environments, but also the definition and/or conversion of data from one format to another.
9. **Technical writer.** Responsible for creating and maintaining all the online and printed documentation that a user will need for the final system.

Although you might not be working with actual software, many non-IT project managers find things they can borrow from FDD to integrate into their own project practices. This is a simplified explanation, but information is easily available in many books and on the Internet. Throughout your exploration of the various types of methodologies and practices that fall under the Agile umbrella, always keep fresh in your mind that Agile is a collection of principles and is not, in itself, a framework or a methodology.

References

[1]Tour of Cadbury Plant, Dunedin, New Zealand, March 12, 2012.
[2]Poppendieck M. & Poppendieck, T. 2003. *Lean Software Development: An Agile Toolkit*, New York: Addison-Wesley Professional.

[3]Jacobson, I. Rational Unified Process. Retrieved from http://en.wikipedia.org/wiki/ IBM Rational Unified Process.

[4]Crystal methodologies. Retrieved from www.alistair.cockburn.us.

[5]De Luca, J. Feature Driven Development. Retrieved from http://en.wikipedia.org/ wiki/Feature-drivendevelopment.

How Do I Jumpstart Change?

Choosing a Pilot Project

By now you have already started to form your own ideas about how to move some Agile philosophies and practices into your team's processes. You could send your own team to training to give them a firm foundation in the shift you are intending to endorse. Then, you could choose a small, meaningful (but not life or death) internal project, and work for a trusted and supportive manager, or a familiar customer with whom you have a good track record.

Once this pilot program is chosen, you should bring in a skilled Agile coach to lead you through this first project—or, hopefully, through the first few projects that you attempt. If your team is too green and new, or old and hostile, you may want to hire an experienced group that has already had positive results. You might be able to contract with a third-party Agile team provider who specializes in the types of projects where this approach really shines.

Once you have your team intact, you can introduce the overall new philosophies and principles of Agile in general, but then introduce the actual tools and practices a few at a time. The opposite end of the spectrum is to move this team into the whole Agile experience in one smooth and immersive experience. Some software teams have found success by easing in technical practices first, such as writing tests first and testing code as you go. Other teams may first move to iterations and the development cycles that will work for non-IT projects.

You have the prerogative to sneak in by stealth mode to secure concrete numbers and user experiences to reinforce the Agile expansion to other teams and projects. Or, if the organization is already leaning toward moving in this direction and you have management backing, it may be to your advantage to make this a high profile project. Publicity in the company newsletter, high-level executives attending meetings, and the excitement of being out in the open can ramp up the motivation level in your team and encourage them to make this new technique blossom.

Train the Product Owner

We have talked earlier about ways to work with an internal manager or external customer to get them interested in an Agile approach to their next project. One of the most common roadblocks is a product owner who says, "I can't possibly dedicate that much time to the team," or "I can't possibly be available all day." There will never be an organization with one perfect move to Agile so be prepared for compromise while you are showing the benefits of this approach through participation in the actual experience. You may get the product owner to establish "office hours." This is a planned time each day when he or she agrees to be available to the team for questions. As the project progresses, you may be pleasantly surprised to see that the product owner becomes increasingly available as the worth of frequent interactions becomes apparent and useful.

Sell Up, Down, and Sideways

For a truly meaningful penetration of the Agile philosophies in your organization to provide a firm and welcoming platform for your project team, you need to engage people on several fronts. You will need to sell the value of Agile up through the hierarchy to higher levels of management who can influence the company culture far beyond the reach of your single team. Next, you will need to sell to the team that reports to you, or works under your guidance as a project manager, to educate and excite them about the ways this new approach to project work can benefit them. Third, you will want to reach sideways toward internal or external customers who will provide the funding for the project to help them see the mutual benefits of these changes.

Even if you do not fancy yourself a salesperson, or are reluctant to assume this role, this is a hat that you will need to wear if you want to influence your organization to move in an Agile direction. Remove the idea of the plaid jacketed, high-pressure, fast-talking salesman stereotype from your mind and think instead of the honorable and respectful way you influence a friend or spouse in your personal life to open their minds to a new idea.

Marketing professionals often quote the Rule of Seven. Before the customer "buys" or takes action, they need to see or hear a message at least seven times, or even "seven times, seven ways" Here is why one interaction won't suffice:

1. **Too busy**. There is a lot of information flowing to each person in the larger community you want to attract to join your transition process into Agile. They are not just sitting back, waiting for you to come in and revolutionize their lives. Mentioning a success story that you heard about a competitor, vendor, or well-known entity in another industry with Agile can begin to plant the idea. Drop the information casually and let it grow on its own, without adding the hard sell "we should do this, too... tomorrow!" Remember, you are selling the Agile philosophies and principles, not trying to sell a list of process tools and techniques.

2. **Too early**. Often, future customers do not buy something today because they are not ready yet. They don't know that there is a problem, or they might suspect one but aren't ready to admit to it just yet. In your organization, you know there are unfinished and unsuccessful projects. Often an entry into an Agile discussion can be, "You know, I was thinking about the BSTP project. It really did not... (insert issues such as finish on time, solve the problem, sell like we thought, please the customer). I was thinking if we... (insert Agile philosophies or principles such as "focused a little more on involving the customer as we went," or "got a little more collaboration going on between the team members") we could... (insert the benefit such as finish more quickly, have a better result, retain a dissatisfied customer).

3. **Too costly**. You are not the only one going around the organization with great ideas of new things that could be purchased, new benefits that could be distributed, important milestones that could be celebrated, and alternative practices that could "revolutionize" the company. At the same time, your audience may be wondering how they can keep the doors open past the next payday, how they can afford to repair toxic or life-threatening work environments, or how they can respond to a competitive blow in the marketplace.

When resources are tight, as they are everywhere, money is spent to relieve the pain. Your job is to show where the project pain is—from the viewpoint of the organization, not the comfort, preferences, or needs of you or the team. If you can show that there is project pain from lost or dissatisfied customers, loss or dissatisfied employees, lost or lowered company sales, or other pain points that have a dollar amount of loss attached to them, you are in a better position to suggest that some Agile approaches might be a pain-relieving solution. Remember, human nature always leads us to ask WIIFM, "What's In It for Me." Be sure you have embedded the answer to "What's In It for Them" (WIIFT) in the interactions that are intended to sell your ideas.

How do you get Agile ideas in front of your three levels of prospects? Think creatively. Casual conversations and quick meetings you set up to share "solutions" to pain points are a good place to start. Once your ideas are focused on how this will be of value to the organization, not just how much you want to do this yourself, a next step is setting up a Lunch and Learn, or a 15 minute spot at a monthly manager's meeting. Again, you are not trying to "close" or get a commitment from these interactions, but just to get the ideas out there.

Perhaps a local PMI Chapter or Agile Alliance group is having a presentation on the topic. Invite a few key stakeholders to join you at that meeting. Circulate an online white paper or article from your industry, or well-respected new source, with an e-mail or note attached, "Thought you might be interested in this, since we were discussing it last Tuesday."

Ask to attend some Agile training that is appropriate for your types of projects. Perhaps ScrumMaster training if you are going to be working with software and web development teams as part of an upcoming hybrid project, or Agile training for the PMI-ACP might be more valuable to you if you are a more traditional shop. Offer to bring back the information and share it with your team and other interested parties by holding your own training when you return. If training dollars are in short supply, this is often an approach that is desirable. For the price of one training class, the company gets multiple people trained.

Do you have any customers that are using an Agile methodology? Find one that loves it and would find it desirable if teams on your side of the contract were using similar approaches. Set up a meeting with your internal project funders to have the customer share how he came to make the switch, and give concrete examples of how this provided actual dollar returns to him over the old ways he used to use.

Sniff out the perfect pilot project and ask to be allowed to try out this new approach on it to see if it could save money, improve delivery time, or increase end-user productivity—whatever the pain point is in your place of business that could be addressed in this trial. Again, you are not preaching a new religion, merely trying to be active in helping the organization with some burning issues.

Keep careful records of the results of your Agile pilot project so that you can show success, or at least improvement. Once the project is complete and you have positive stories to tell and impressive outcomes to flaunt, this is the time to ask if the team could remain intact and work on a second project. If there was forward momentum, but there are still process issues to work out, now may be the time to ask if an Agile consultant could be brought in to help your team perfect their performance.

Talk the Talk

Any good salesperson knows that you remove your tongue ring, dye the pink streak in your hair, and leave your $1,800 sharkskin suit at home when you set out to sell tractors in a farming community. Good selling involves building a rapport with the potential customer so that they like and trust you. The foundation for that is if they feel you are one of them, they may believe you can truly understand their situation and their needs.

This is also true in project management. If you are talking to your own management, use their vocabulary. Talk in terms of portfolio returns, ROI, present and future value of money, and marketplace competitiveness. Know what your competition is doing. Is this a chance to outpace them in time to market, try to catch up if they are burying you with new innovations in their product line, or increase employee retention and satisfaction at a time when key employees are being stolen? What is a specific problem you know of in your organization that you could address? This is not a sales ploy. Remember, you are retooling your own thinking from just completing a project on time, on budget, and with a high degree of quality to adopting an upper-management type concern for moving the business value of the project through the process flow as efficiently as possible.

Use similar thought processes when preparing conversations with customers and the project team. Customers care about cost, getting exactly what they need, delivery time, and avoiding the "oops" moments of past projects. Teams care about getting out from under heavy documentation and oppressive oversight. They want to use all of their skills and knowledge and feel proud of what they create.

You are not selling Agile; you are selling solutions. You may find your best success by avoiding using the word "Agile" itself. That way, if anyone has a negative attitude or unfounded misconceptions about it, you are merely talking of better ways to meet company goals and you do not alienate them with a buzzword. Dave West, an analyst for Forrester Research says, "A smart Agile project manager does a lot of things the *PMBOK® Guide* talks about without mentioning the *PMBOK® Guide*, and a smart *PMBOK® Guide* project manager does a lot of Agile things without calling them Agile."

One more thing, don't forget your Social Style skills from Chapter 13. They are not a manipulative technique, but rather a way to respectfully communicate with others in the manner that is most familiar and comfortable for them. Use *their* preferred way to interact. Approach Drivers in a succinct manner and get directly to the point. Have support numbers and documents to back your assertions. Do not forget to speak in statements, rather than open-ended questions. Be Task-Directed/Tell-Assertive. For Expressives, paint the vision of what this project could do. Show your excitement and involve the other person with an inclusive statement, "Together we could achieve our goals of… (insert your glorious shared result)." Be People-Directed/Tell-Assertive.

You may recall that Amiables are usually concerned about the effect that any change might have on the people of the organization. Say to them, "Don't you think… (the team, our customers, etc.) would be better served by a more collaborative process?" Be People-Directed/Ask-Assertive. Take in pictures of teams holding a stand-up meeting to show them. Talk about how this new approach you are trying includes everyone from the start, so that they are sure to get what they need. Engage them in thinking through the impact change might have and all of the people who would need to be included in the exchange of information to keep them in the loop.

Details, statistics, and documents are a must-have when you plan a conversation with an Analytical style individual. Be Task-Directed/Ask-Assertive. Pointing to a competitor's annual report statistics chart, ask "Do you think we could match these 47% faster delivery numbers from ABC Corporation if we adopted similar processes here?"

Learn the Change Process

It is naïve to think that you will be able to walk in one day and announce to your team that today you will change to Agile processes. You are changing the way people work, and they don't usually like that. Even unpleasant experiences are familiar. It may be helpful to looks at some ideas about a strategy to manage change. One familiar model of change was created by John Kotter, the professor at Harvard Business School, who described a three-stage, eight-step process:

Stage 1. Creating a Climate for Change. This portion of the change model includes three parts:

- Increasing the urgency.
- Building the guiding team.
- Getting the right vision.

You can recognize that these are the steps that you have the ability to influence through the suggestions you have already read here. The next two stages require that others in your organization catch fire and want to expand the success you are hopefully having with your own transitioned team throughout the whole company.

Stage 2. Engaging and Enabling the Whole Organization. The steps are:

- Communicate for buy-in.
- Empower action.
- Create short-term wins.

While Kotter intends this to be a progression to changes that will permeate the entire enterprise, you can use these steps to guide your personal actions, too. There is always a fear of change, as people wonder if they will be able to measure up to new practice standards. Will they be able to learn and keep up? Will they now have to work harder? Will their job be in jeopardy if efficiencies lead to staff reductions? Do they prefer to coast along and only do what other people tell them to do? Will there be unpleasant conflicts as this new process is implemented?

Clear communication and team involvement in this change process will go a long way toward overcoming many of the fears that change brings to the surface. Ideally, you are involving the team and working together to figure out which Agile ideas are needed, appropriate, and realistic to introduce in your projects. Perhaps you have tried them out in a low-profile way before you moved forward with your extended sales techniques. Once most people on the team see the empowerment and challenge that can revitalize their workdays, and have experienced the change on a trial project, they are fine with moving forward to adopt a tailored version of this on other projects.

Stage 3. Implementing and Sustaining Change. In this third and final stage, the two steps are:

- Don't let up.
- Make it stick.

On the enterprise level, this change now goes beyond the power of an individual project manager. However, the wisdom is appropriate for you at the team level. Do not let the rough edges that occur with any change in team process, some team discouragement or conflict, or a first try that does not garner the eye popping, transformative success for which you had hoped, discourage you. You may have heard the saying, "If change was easy, everyone would be doing it." Let your change process be iterative. Try it, learn, correct your mistakes, and move on to the next project to try it again.[1]

Another pioneer in the arena of change, Kurt Lewin, had a simple, but insightful early change model. He also saw a three-stage process, during which the individual undergoes a psychological transition. First, a person must "Unfreeze" their existing way of thinking. They recognize the need to let go of their old behaviors, and may need time and space to acknowledge their feelings of loss. Next will be the actual "Change." This is a period of transition where the old way is out, but the new way is being learned via trial and error. Think of this as a neutral mindset where new actions, a new purpose, and their new role are being understood and absorbed. Finally, in the third stage, the individual becomes comfortable with the new ways of doing things and the altered way of working will "Freeze." Knowing that these are the phases, you may be better prepared to help your team through the steps of adopting Agile practices.[2]

References

[1]Kotter, J. P. *"The 8-Step Process for Leading Change"*. Kotter International. Retrieved from http://www.kotterinternational.com.

[2]Lewin, K. "Kurt Lewin Change Management Model". Retrieved from http://www.change-management-coach.com/kurt lewin.html.

Who Has Made Agile Work?

CH2M Hill's Rocky Flats Project

When thinking of companies that have not only found success with Agile methods, but who have found it to be the *only* way that a project could be successful, a major engineering and construction company would probably be the last type of company to pop into your mind. However, at the 2010 2do Simposio Nacional de Genercia de Proyectos conference in Panama City, Panama, Mike Kennedy recounted the personal experience of a project manager that led a unique construction and demolition team through that exact experience.[1]

If you are not familiar with CHM2 Hill, they are one of the largest engineering, construction, and consulting companies in the world, and are the group responsible for implementing the Panama Canal expansion project, which adds a third lane to the world-famous landmark. As a construction company, they are heavily invested in the traditional project methods of upfront planning and estimating necessary to be able to win and complete contracts.

In 1995, CH2M Hill won a contract to work on an abandoned government site in Rocky Flats, Colorado, located near the city of Boulder. From 1951 to 1989, this 6,200 acre site was the location of a U.S. Department of Energy facility that produced plutonium triggers for nuclear warheads. After 40 years, the area was a combination of contaminated buildings, foul soil, and polluted groundwater.

Boulder is a community with a laid-back lifestyle whose citizens have a great interest in a clean-living existence centered around an outdoors-oriented, ecology-sensitive belief structure. Having a potentially dangerous, radiation-laden group of empty buildings in close proximity to the town, where healthy living was the dream, was not acceptable. In addition, the abandoned eyesore detracted from the backwoods beauty of the area.

So CH2M Hill came into the Boulder area with a government mandate to remove the buildings, cleanse the soil, and create a wildlife reserve on the renovated land. The detailed scope of the project included demolishing and decontaminating five plutonium production complexes, the razing and removal of 165 chemically contaminated buildings, decimating and hauling away the remains of 555 non-nuclear structures, disposing of any reclaimed nuclear materials, and restoring the befouled soil to a point that the entire area could be used to safely support a protected animal population. As you can imagine, the federal government was a particularly risk-adverse customer.

The project manager had dutifully prepared a Waterfall project plan, probably laying out sequential activities on a week-by-week basis. They probably planned that they would first remove all the structures, and then haul away the debris, fill in the remaining foundations, plant trees, stock the land with wildlife, and submit the bill to the government. The problem was that no one had ever tackled a cleanup project of this magnitude with such copious amounts of radioactive waste.

Kennedy shared in the conference presentation what the project manager told him: "After the first few days, our team knew that the project plan was useless. There was radiation everywhere, and if we proceeded according to our plan, someone was going to die. We pulled back, threw out the plan, and regrouped. All of our high sounding goals went out the window, and our mission statement became, 'No one can die!' Each evening we'd meet to share what we had learned that day, and to plan how we could move forward the next day in a way that there would be no casualties. We practiced change management by the day." He went on to say that they instantly became a culture of safety. The goal was not to work fast, but to work correctly and safely. They became a learning organization, leveraging each day's experiences into tomorrow's approach, so that accelerating results were eventually possible based on doing the work correctly and safely the first time.

They had to work as a collaborative team, regardless of who had the position power, because no one had any experience in a project of this magnitude. There had never been a contractor, government agency, or military unit that had completed the deconstruction of a nuclear facility of this size. Everyone needed to pool their ideas about how to move forward to avoid the real specter of death by radiation poisoning, which was looming over them. The term *Agile* was never mentioned, and the concern was not about which process the team would use. For practical reasons, the project progressed in a way that we might label as Agile, in retrospect.

To support an undertaking of this size in a wasteland removed from towns, CH2M Hill operated 3.6 million square feet of facilities that included radiological facilities, laboratories, medical facilities, and warehouses, as well as a water treatment plant, sewage treatment plant, steam plant, fire station, police station, firing range, cafeterias, vehicle motor pools, information technology data centers, dry cleaners, stores, offices, and other infrastructure needed to provide utilities for the mini-city that housed their team workers.

To give you an idea of the size of the cleanup, the site contained over 21 tons of weapons grade plutonium that was eventually safely stored, packaged, and sent on for resale or reuse. Over 50,000 containers of radioactive wastes were handled and removed, and over 170 areas with soil contamination were revitalized. The Department of Energy (DOE) had estimated the project would take 70 years, finishing in 2065 at a cost of $36 billion dollars. CH2M Hill came up with an aggressive estimate that they could finish this project in only 10 years, projecting a completion date of December 2006.

In October 2005, the Rocky Flats Closure Project was finished. It came in 14 months ahead of the CH2M Hill schedule and 60 years ahead of the DOE's original projection. The cost was $550 million less than the contract budget, and $30 billion less than the Department of Energy's original estimate. There were no fatalities on the project over its 10-year span, despite the precarious nature of the work. While many of the segments of the cleanup were certainly done by relying on traditional project management expertise, there were Agile aspects, too, making this a hybrid approach. If you move beyond looking for Agile practices (tools) and focus on Agile philosophies and principles, you will see that they are clearly seen in this project.

One additional Agile-ish attribute was that this was the first time the Department of Energy had awarded a performance-based contract. In other words, they paid CH2M Hill only for specific units of verifiable work. However, in addition to their fee, the contracting firm received a $170 million bonus for finishing so far ahead of schedule, which still allowed the taxpayers an enormous savings over the original budget.

If you were to go to Rocky Flats today and were allowed on the government lands, you would find a beautiful wildlife preserve that is safe for animals and humans. No software was developed, but Agile processes were key factors in the success of this project where traditional ones could have been literally fatal.

Boeing's 787 Project

Another unlikely guess, if you were asked for a highly Agile manufacturer, might be the Boeing Company, the manufacturer of large commercial airliners based in Everett, WA. Yet, Agile they are. As a production facility, Boeing tends to be more on the Lean side as a philosophy, and it is working well. From observations during a tour of the newest Boeing assembly lines in September 2009, rather than workers standing as planes move slowly by them, a dedicated team of workers actually climbs aboard the partially finished fuselages with all of their parts and tools in hand, and ride along with the plane as they add their contributions to the construction of the aircraft.[2]

The same teams work together day after day to leverage the productivity you get when you develop a pattern or routine with trusted associates. Quality inspectors are part of the same standing team, too, and climb aboard with them, so that each added function is checked before the team disembarks from the aircraft shell moving along the slowly advancing line (a form of continuous integration). Mechanics riding along the moving assembly line with the partially assembled plane in Boeing's largest factory can receive completed parts kits within 20 minutes of alerting the parts room they are needed. Boeing employees created their own speedy parts kit delivery process by using a "pinwheel" sheet that lists the parts destination floor location and other important facts about the kit. Mechanics fill in the sheet to request kits as needed and attach it to a special container. The new kits are returned in the container, with the mechanics original paperwork still attached (a customized, kanban card "pull" system).

Materials management employees have large, plasma screens and *"andon"* lights in their work area to alert them if a coworker needs support from a cross-functionally trained teammate, or if someone is free and available to help others. Any employee can halt the line if need be (cross-functional teams and a "Stop the Line" culture). Special attention is paid to be sure that the knowledge of suppliers, the line workers, customers, and other experts is heard and their ideas are used to leverage the collective knowledge for the good of the project.

In another area, the engineers from Material and Process Technology use Agile development to design solutions to issues presented by workers so that there is no long delay between the need and the fix. Boeing capitalizes on the software development technique of reuse. *Reuse,* or reusability, means small chunks of code are written that can be used again as building blocks, or with slight modifications to add new software functionality. This allows systems to be created more quickly than building them from scratch. They have used this system to create software solutions to production issues literally overnight.[3]

In the job description for a Project Management Specialist listed on the Boeing corporate website, competency headings were broken out into: collaboration, communication, customer focus, managing conflict, and planning and organizing, which specifies a need for skills in identifying more critical and less critical activities (prioritization). After these Agile-sounding soft skills are presented, only then are technical qualifications listed, almost as an afterthought.[4]

When Boeing undertook the production of their latest aircraft, the 787 Dreamliner, they made a conscious choice to alter the process they had used to create past successes in their product line. They moved from a reliance on upfront specifications to a faith in the value of collaboration. Rather than present suppliers with pre-printed sets of technical and functional requirements, they opted to involve the suppliers, vendors, and customers, and leverage their knowledge, expertise, desires, and opinions in the design process. They were betting on the innovation that could result from the collaboration.

Specifications documents for the predecessor aircraft, the Boeing 777, had a page count of over 2,500 pages. Documents for the Boeing 787 were only 20 pages in length. It is not that all specifications have been thrown out the window, but Boeing thinks it is presumptuous to assume that they know everything. Rather, they are relying on suppliers and vendors, who are experts in their own product lines, to become Boeing's partners in creating a new plane together. The old way was, "This is what we want! Build it!" This time around, Boeing invited the suppliers to share their ideas and expertise on the component parts they supply.

Further breaking their own production model mold, rather than purchasing individual parts and assembling them all under the Boeing *aegis*, they opted to allow partners in other countries to assemble entire portions of the aircraft to a finished stage, *sans* paint, and deliver them ready to attach to the final aircraft. This was another vote of trust for the partners. Boeing even had to create and construct the largest cargo plane in existence, the Dreamlifter, to transport those massive pieces to Everett, but their belief in the Agile principles far outweighed the stumbling blocks they needed to overcome.

Subcontractors assemble larger pieces than ever before, and deliver their output to Everett from other U.S. states and other countries: Japan, Italy, South Korea, France, Sweden, and India. The plane was designed so that rather than accepting only engines from one manufacturer, it is wired with a standard interface to allow it to be fitted with either a Rolls-Royce or a General Electric engine. It only takes 800 to 1,200 workers at the plant in Everett to combine the sub-assemblies into the finished tarmac-ready deliverable. Allowing subcontractors a more important role in production made for a quicker turnaround time from start to finish. By 2009, planes were already rolling off the production line bound for Japan's All Nippon Airways.

A funny, but totally off-point, story about the production of the 787 might amuse you. As mentioned earlier, the large, fully-assembled chunks of the plane were flown in from around the world and assembled. Then, the planes needed to be painted, but the paint hangar is not in the same building as the manufacturing line. How do you get the largest plane in the world from one building to another? Answer: you drive it!

The Boeing manufacturing facility is on the south side of huge, multilane Highway 526. In order to get across the highway, there is a bridge that has been reinforced so that it can handle the weight of planes driving across it. This allows

Boeing 787s to be taxied to the paint shop on the North side of the Interstate. Imagine yourself tooling along the highway on a clear blue, sunny day (or even worse, a foggy or cloudy one), and suddenly you round a bend and unexpectedly see the side of a giant 787 stretched across the highway immediately in front of you. Even though you are in no danger, it appears at first glance that a cataclysmic crash is unavoidable. The evasive moves you make to avoid what appears to be an inevitable collision between your tiny vehicle and this behemoth of a machine can only mean disaster for you and the other drivers who are traveling the road right behind you. After several panicky incidents in which, fortunately, no one was hurt, Boeing has wisely decided to only move planes to the shop for painting in the middle of the night, when the possibility of crossing the highway while there are drivers on it is slim.

To be truthful, the 787 experienced some delays in moving from concept to fruition. Some say that is a flaw due to Boeing's new approach, using it as an excuse not to explore Agile in their own situation. However, if the resultant airplane's innovative approach provides larger customer spaces inside, more luggage room, larger windows that can be clicked to a clear state for takeoff (a safety regulation) and then "auto-dimmed" from the cockpit to tint them as a sun block once in the air—maybe the wait was worth it. New, composite hull materials provide a lighter frame that takes less fuel to operate, too, making it the most fuel-efficient airliner in the world. It consumes 20% less fuel than similarly sized aircraft.

If you are working with product-centric projects, you may be interested is a short list of the Agile principles that Boeing followed, as compiled by Robert Bedoll:

- Rapid prototyping, with immediate customer feedback
- Continuous involvement of the customer
- Compress our standard development cycle from three months to releases every week
- Start simple and keep it simple
- Evolve the tool to follow the evolving business process
- Provide a one to three week cycle time for new feature introduction
- Maintain a small development team
- Produce abbreviated versions of our standard design documents[5]

Boeing gave up control for communication, and traded specifications for collaboration.

The Kauffman Performing Arts Center Project

The Kauffman Performing Arts Center is a work designed by Moshe Safdie, who is known for dramatic curves and his use of windows and open spaces. Located in Kansas City, Missouri, it is a double-staged memorial to Muriel Kauffman and houses an acoustical state-of-the-art performance space for the Kansas City Symphony. It is only one of two concert halls in the United States to feature a performance space with the orchestra in the center, surrounded by audience seating on all sides. The second proscenium theater space, created right next to it, features the latest in theater and lighting technology to showcase everything from rock bands to Broadway touring productions.

Esthetically, the Kauffman Performing Arts Center is like nothing you have ever seen before, since it resembles two giant, open clamshells sitting side by side. Each shell houses one of the theaters. As beautiful as it appears now, it was quite a challenge for the construction team from J. E. Dunn Construction during the time it was being built. Once again, when we think "construction," we think of a traditional project process. The design is complete and approved, the time and construction costs are estimated, the bid is let to the winning company, and the rest is just completing the detailed activities of the project plan on a day-to-day basis, right?

This project was unique in that although the creative and unique outside design was finished and approved; when the time came for construction the inside design components still had not been completed by the designer. But time was short, and the building season on the Kansas/Missouri border is somewhat limited, so Kyle McQuiston, the project manager, used a flexible approach to meet the deadlines.[6] He started to build an empty shell with little idea of the rooms that might go into it other than two large theaters.

Fortunately, there was an entire team assembled in Kansas City to create the final space, including an acoustical expert, Yasuhisa Toyota; theater consultant, Richard Pilbrow; and the engineering firm, Arup. While waiting for the designer to finish the interior plans; the rest of the team got together, relying on building information modeling software to try to keep work flowing.

McQuiston worked with the team and his modeling software to try to create the details needed by the construction workers, but anything he did also needed to meet the needs of the acoustical designer in one space and be the appropriate structural backdrop for the theatrical and technological needs of the performance space housed in the other. Trying to work out the specifications for how to house heating and air conditioning in the uniquely shaped space where traditional construction solutions may or may not fit was a test of innovation and creativity. As the designer slowly finished his interior designs, the team was able to install them within the HVAC and insulated exterior shell with only a few reworkings of structural spaces.

Modeling solutions using software, and assembling the team so each person could consider the impact of any construction decisions on their specialty area, finally enabled the project to be completed with stellar success. This may have appeared to be a traditional construction project at the start, but the unique shapes and uneven delivery of interior design plans gave an edge to a flexible, collaborative approach being the best one when tailored to the needs of this project.

AccuRev Agile Sales Team

AccuRev is a company that sells tools that help organizations produce higher quality software faster. Since AccuRev uses Agile processes to create their own software, and sell to customers who are also using similar Agile approaches, they thought that it was important to have consistent principles throughout the entire organization. So, they sent their entire sales team through Certified Scrum Training. Granted, sales is very different from software development, but in addition to giving the salespeople a clearer understanding of what they were selling and how their customers operate (so they can "talk the talk"), AccuRev introduced some Agile practices into the sales department itself.

Frequent, although not daily, stand-up meetings in the sales group help management get feedback as salespeople report about what the customers think of their product, and allows them to get a quick sense of the sales volume that is being generated for that period. While a two, three, or four week iteration is needed in a production environment, AccuRev found a quarterly sprint was enough to report on the sales goals for the time period. At the end of the quarter, a retrospective to discuss territory results (production velocity) and also review how sales processes can be altered for better results in the next quarter (how the team works together with each other and with customers) can be powerful.

AccuRev constructed a to-do backlog with sales goals, and then had individual sales people move them to the "In Progress" or "Done" columns as they were met. The metrics for a sales team would be in dollars, not story points, but if the planned velocity (with sales dollars tracking the measured capacity of the sales team to deliver value) was not achieved, it was an early feedback indicator that the process for targeting customers and closing sales may need to be adjusted.

GVK's Mumbai, India Airport Project

In February 2006, when the Airports Authority of India did not have enough money to finance a redo of the Mumbai Airport, they privatized it and retained a 26% portion. GVK, leader of an Indian consortium, won the bid to manage and operate Mumbai's Chhatrapati Shivaji International Airport. They hired CH2M Hill, known for their international project management and construction skills, to be the contractors on the project.

This project had some challenges that may make you go to work tomorrow feeling like your own project challenges are relatively insignificant. First, the airport was land constrained. People lived right up to the edges of the runways, and there was no room to expand the site in other directions. So, where could they put the second and third runways? Second, the Airports Authority could not shut down the airport in Mumbai, at the time the largest air travel center in India, for the time of the construction. So the project needed to be accomplished around an open, working airport, serving 66,000 passengers a day. It is fair to say that *when* work could be done was tightly constrained.

In reality, the airport owned plenty of space to construct the runways and new terminal they needed. They just owned space that could not be used at the moment—because it was covered with people. In India, the population density is such that any open land, such as land next to a runway, immediately has squatters that not only occupy the space, but who actually construct substantial homes on the government-owned land. Technically, the people needed to move, but politically and socially, it would be poor form for construction teams to come in with dump trucks to cart the families away and then bulldoze their homes. Relocating squatters to open the land for the runways would prove to be an unexpected addition to the time, cost, and scope of the project. Some parts of the occupied land had even taxis on it, with people living in them. At first, the project team tried to move them, but the inhabitants threatened to block the progress of the work if they were moved, so that tactic was temporarily abandoned.

It is almost unbelievable, but the old airport terminal had no shopping, no eating establishments... none of the conveniences modern travelers naturally expect in an airport. So the simple construction project to build two runways, a new terminal, and modernize the existing one to include modern conveniences, which one would initially assume to be primarily a Waterfall project, needed to be creatively rethought.

The Agile approach that CH2M Hill took was to divide this undertaking into 150 small projects. There were projects to little by little find relocation space for the squatters and move them from the runway land. The instant someone was moved out, the construction crew was literally waiting in construction equipment with the motor running, to quickly start to build that small portion of the runway before someone else moved in and the relocation would have been for naught. It was a slow and lengthy process, but little by little the space was cleared and the runways constructed.

The airport terminal also had its challenges. A new terminal was to be constructed, but it took an hour to get from the existing one to the new location because project teams could not go in a straight line as the crow flies. The houses that had filled the unoccupied land necessitated a lengthy detour through busy streets to transport teams of workers to the new building site. Finding contractors with a quality program was also an issue, so resource hiring, training, and managing became an oppressive task.

Incrementally, the second terminal was constructed and the old one was renovated a little at a time, in the midst of serving 22% of India's total air travelers each day. But despite all the hardships, there were some bright spots in the contract. The concessionaire that was awarded the contract to attract and manage the shops and other traveler comforts in the old terminal had a contract that said he had to be up, running, and profitable by a certain date. Despite all the construction delays, and a half-remodeled terminal around him, he met the terms of his contract and got all of the concessions open. The city of Mumbai also got value-added returns on this project as it left them with newly trained workers familiar with quality construction standards. And, CH2M Hill was able to learn new techniques for building on constrained sites that would help them in future projects.[7]

The new terminal, referred to as T2, will be able to handle 40 million passengers annually when it is completed in 2013. To give you an idea of the scope of the T2 project alone, it houses 439,203 square meters, 21,000 square meters of retail space, 5,000 square meters of landscaped area, 188 check-in counters, 60 departure immigration counters, 76 arrival immigration counters, 104 security check posts, 10 baggage carousels, 25 fixed link bridges, 52 passenger boarding bridges, 41 Travelators (moving walkways), 47 escalators, 73 elevators, 101 toilets, parking for 5,000 cars, and a six-lane elevated express way leading to the terminal.[8]

Now, to be fair, the project ran about a year late on its completion date and the cost more than doubled. The international operations at the new terminal are scheduled to open by the end of 2013, with domestic operations in place by the end of 2014.[9] But, because it was broken into smaller projects and done in vertical slices, this project completed pockets of usability along the way. The runways are open and the original, remodeled airport terminal has continued to function throughout the work, with its new customer conveniences. The agility of the project team and the small projects through which they did what they could, when they could, has allowed much greater overall success than could have been achieved by following a traditional plan.

The Sydney Opera House Project

The Sydney Opera House is a common project management story tapped for its lessons. Do we give people what they are already familiar with or do we create new and mind-stretching visions to move the field forward? Does cost and schedule really matter if the ultimate product becomes a signature landmark for the customer? However, the Sydney Opera House construction has seldom been tapped as guidance for those looking to see if flexible approaches are appropriate for traditional types of projects.

When discussing changing project approaches, the attitude is usually "what I am doing now is just fine, so how are you going to convince me to change my ways?" With the Sydney Opera House construction crew, the conversation got reversed to "I don't know how this can be built using my conventional ways, so what else have you got?"

In 1956, the New South Wales government opened a call for designs for a new opera house to sit on the edge of Sydney Harbor. The competition was worldwide in scope, and piles of architectural drawings immediately poured in from known and unknown designers located on every curve of the globe. However, nothing submitted was quite striking enough, or inventive enough to be a clear winner with the selection committee.

Finally, architect Eero Saarinene, a late addition to the selection panel, went back through the pile of rejected designs and happened across an informal sketch, giving only a vague suggestion of the building it could become. In keeping with the intended waterfront site, this design evoked shells, or multiple sails like those already found in the harbor. Saarinene secretly created drawings that appeared more finished to use in convincing the public that Jørn Utzon's idea was truly worthy of a win.

Now came the hard part. The structural engineers could not figure out how to build the roof, which was to be made of 14 outer shells. The technology did not exist to pour such strangely shaped curves in concrete. Many trial and error attempts at constructing these odd shapes failed, until they finally figured it out. If each of the shell shapes was tweaked to become part of a 3-dimensional half circle, its flat side on the ground, the engineering prowess did exist to construct them. Utzon had unwittingly given them a clue when he said early on that he was inspired when peeling an orange. Think of an orange half forming the half circle, and the vertically torn parts of the peel creating the sails. Structurally, it can all be placed back together into the form of an orange half.

The Sydney Opera House became a collaborative effort with multiple protypes. Each portion was build and tested, and then creative solutions were formulated on the spot to make this one-of-a-kind creation structurally sound. The material to cover the shells to create a weatherproof roof posed another challenge, and it was eventually covered with small squares of a specially developed ceramic.[10]

The curve of the roofline was very attractive, but structurally vulnerable to strong winds—like winds found in any ocean harbor—that might come in under a shell and lift it up. To give the shells some "play," they are held at multiple tension points by heavy metal cables that are sunk into the earth. However, there is enough flexibility that the shells can move slightly with the wind without damage, and the cables can be loosened or tightened as needed.

The color was the next hurdle. If too white, it blinded those with homes and buildings on the shore and the occupants of the boats entering the harbor. Multiple shipwrecks were not an intended community goal for the structure. If too dark, the domes looked dingy and gray on a cloudy day, or near evening when residents and tourists wanted to enjoy a spectacular view. Finally, a structural engineer saw a zig-zag pattern on a woman's bathing suit at the beach and adapted it as white and cream tiles in alternating gloss and flat surfaces. The roof now reflected the blue of the sky, the changing colors of the water, or the colors of the sunset, without the blinding glare that came from a single, solid color and surface.

Not only did the outside of the Opera House need an Agile, innovative approach, the acoustics for the main performing area inside were also vexing. Created with an interior of concrete and wood, the hard surfaces were too reflective and bounced back too much sound for the concert hall. The reach for perfection extended to trying to balance the acoustics so that the sound was the same whether the auditorium was full, empty, or somewhere in between.

A creative acoustics team reasoned that the full auditorium audio perfection was due to the sound being absorbed by the soft body tissue of people filling the seats, and also from it bouncing off the hard forehead bone structure of the listeners. So, they custom designed fixed-location chairs for audience seating. The chairs were made of a special type of pine for about four inches at the top, forehead level, but upholstered over on the rest of the chair to approximate the same reverberation bounce from an empty seat as a full one. To this day they continue to test the acoustics as the materials age and the interior wood dries. By cutting grooves in the concrete walls, or hanging curtains, they can absorb more sound and soften it, or make opposite adjustments to get just the right ratio for optimal acoustical performance.

The work on a project that cannot be completed without finding innovative ways to realize the vision of the creator is exactly the type of work that must be done in a flexible way. A collective approach between smart minds looking for new techniques, new materials, and never-before-thought-of engineering and construction questions and answers to realize Utzon's dream created an unparalleled marvel that is one of a kind. That is the essence of Agile.

References

[1]Kennedy, Mike. March 10, 2010 lecture. 2do Simposio Nacional de Genercia de Proyectos.

[2]Davis, Barbee. Boeing Plant Tour. September, 2009.

[3]IT Project Management Specialist. April 20, 2012. Boeing Company. Renton, WA. Retrieved from www.jobs-boeing.com.

[4]Senior Program/Project Manager 4. April 26, 2012. Boeing Company. Renton, WA.

[5]Bedoll, Robert. 2003. "A Tail of Two Projects: How 'Agile' Methods Succeeded After 'Traditional' Methods Had Failed in a Critical System-Development Project". White Paper. Renton, WA: Boeing Company.

[6]McQuiston, Kyle. PMI KC Mid-America Chapter: Professional Development Days 2010, Performing Arts Center, October 4, 2010.

[7]Kennedy, Mike. March 10, 2010 lecture. 2do Simposio Nacional de Genercia de Proyectos.

[8]Chhatrapati Shivaji International Airport website, Mumbai, India. www.csia.in.

[9]Shukla, T. December 14, 2011. "Mumbai airport modernization likely to be delayed to 2014." *The Wall Street Journal*. Retrieved from http://www.livemint .com/2011/12/14231053/Mumbai-airport-modernization-l.html.

[10]Davis, Barbee. Sydney Opera House Tour. April, 2012.

21

Parting Advice

As you try to go Agile, or create a hybrid mix of your organization's traditional processes with the principles and philosophies supporting the addition of Agile practices to your projects, here are some tips:

1. Using a total Agile methodology is not for everyone. Use your Agile Evaluator chart from Chapter 6 to find suitable projects and to see if some of your projects could add more business value by using a more hybrid/Agile approach.

2. Everyone can add *some* Agile practices and philosophies to their projects.

3. It is valuable to have customers, internal or external, who want to work in a collaborative way. But if they don't, try to get them to at least give it a try. Most are quickly converted once they experience the advantages it gives them.

4. Some people claim that Agile methods cannot be used on large projects. However, they can be used if you keep the size of the teams small.

5. Some people advise choosing a project with little business impact to start with. That way, if anything goes wrong, there is less damage. However, an unimportant project makes a poor test since nobody cares much about the outcome. Try taking on a manageable project that won't put your company out of business if you make mistakes, but is a little more critical than you are comfortable with. That will encourage you to work hard to make it successful.

6. Find a good mentor. Find someone who has already made a lot of Agile mistakes, but learned from them, to come into your company to help

you for the first project or two. That way, you can avoid some of the common pitfalls others have experienced in their first attempts.

7. Once you have found a good mentor, actually follow his or her advice. It is easy to second guess new methods and the power of many of these Agile techniques cannot really be understood until you try them.

8. Be patient. Agile is an art, so it will take you and your team time to become artists.

9. Remember the project manager's serenity plea:
   Grant me the serenity to accept the people I cannot change,
   The courage to change the one I can,
   And the wisdom to know it is *me*.

10. You need to *be* Agile, not *do* Agile. Change your own thinking, and it will change your team.

You cannot bury your head in the sand and avoid change while corporate profits plunge, so it is to your advantage to move forward with a clear idea of how to adjust your corporate project culture to prepare for the future and solidify your employment desirability at the same time. Change the way you think, and you will ultimately change the way you do projects. Here are, once again, the thought processes that really matter:

Agile Project Management Principles

1. Customer satisfaction by rapid delivery of useful features or services.
2. Welcome changing requirements, even late in development.
3. Working features or services are delivered frequently (weeks rather than months).
4. Working features or services are the principal measure of progress.
5. Sustainable development; be able to maintain a constant pace.
6. Close, daily cooperation between business people and the developers (team).
7. Face-to-face conversations are the best form of communication (collocation).
8. Projects are built around motivated individuals, who should be trusted.
9. Pay continuous attention to technical excellence and good design.
10. Simplicity—maximize the amount of work not done.
11. Self-organizing teams.
12. Regular adaptation to changing circumstances.

1. Share Vision and create **Goals**
2. Product Owner/Customer and project manager make them into **User Stories**
3. Product Owner/Customer **prioritizes them and ranks them** by value to the business
4. Project Team estimates the **degree of difficulty**, breaking User Stories into smaller chunks, if necessary, and assigns Story Points
5. The Project Team chooses and commits to what the team will **do in this Iteration**
6. Team members **pick which User Stories they want to do**
7. Project teams hold **Daily Stand-up Meetings** to say, "This is what I did yesterday, this is what I will do today, and these are the impediments in my way. Only team members speak.

8. Project Teams **do the work** of the project
9. Hold a **Product Owner/Customer Demo** for quick feedback and approval
10. Hold a **Retrospective** on how well we did on the product and how well we did with our team processes
11. Add changes and In-Progress work that was not completed **back into the Backlog** at the end of each Iteration, and have the Product Owner/Customer reprioritize it
12. Go back to #3 and start the **Second Iteration**

The Agile Project Manager

Figure 21.1 The Agile Project Manager Checklist

Figure 21.1 shows what you and your team might do if you were to become an Agile project manager, regardless of the product, service, or software that your team is tasked to create. It is a quick reference checklist to use to guide your Agile team processes. First, you will share the Vision of the project and create Goals. Next, the Product Owner or Customer, with your help as Project Manager, turns the goals into User Stories.

The User Stories are now prioritized and ranked by the Product Owner/ Customer, according to the business value they provide and the risk they bring to the project. At this point, the Project Team can estimate the User Stories by degree of difficulty, breaking them into smaller chunks if need be, and assign them Story Points.

The Project Team chooses and commits to the User Stories they will do in the upcoming Iteration, and the Team Members each choose the specific stories they each want to do. Once the work of the project begins, Project Teams hold self-led Daily Stand-up Meetings to say, "This is what I did yesterday, this is what I will do today, and these are the impediments in my way." Only team members speak at these meetings.

The Project Team completes the work of the project and at the end of the Iteration, they hold a Product Owner/Customer Demo for quick feedback and approval. Then the Project Team holds a Retrospective to discuss how well they did on creating the product, service, or software, and also how well they did with their team processes.

Any changes and work In Progress that was not completed goes into the Product Backlog to be reprioritized by the Product Owner/Customer. The next working day, the team is ready to have the Product Owner/Customer reprioritize the User Stories. Now the sequence to plan the next Iteration begins the cycle again.

One of the problems that teams are currently having as they attempt to move to Agile is a disconnect within the organization between Agile processes and Waterfall processes. Figure 21.2 is a list of Agile practices that can be used by any department to produce any type of deliverable. If you cannot only change your own team, but begin to spread these ideas to other departments, you will make it easier to collaborate and track work from various teams. The ideas that can work for any place in the organization are:

- Short Iterations or "Small Chunk Planning."
- Daily Stand-up Meetings.
- Work Prioritized by Product Owner/Customer.
- Continuous Integration.

Spreading Agile Flexibility

- Short Iterations or "Small Chunk Planning"
- Daily Stand-up Meetings
- Work Prioritized by Product Owner/Customer
- Continuous Integration
- Customer Demos at the End of Each Iteration
- Retrospectives at the End of Each Iteration
- Test As You Go
- Dedicated, Collocated, Cross-functional Teams
- Collaborative Teams of Knowledge Workers with Authority
- Team Member Self-selection of Tasks
- Lighter, More Visible Documentation
- Measure Useable Products, Services, and Software Delivered
- Measure Meaningful Team Metrics, Not Individual Ones

Figure 21.2 Spreading Agile Flexibility

- Customer Demos at the End of Each Iteration.
- Retrospectives at the End of Each Iteration.
- Test As You Go.
- Dedicated, Collocated, Cross-functional Teams.
- Collaborative Teams of Knowledge Workers with Authority.
- Team Member Self-Selection of Tasks.
- Lighter, More Visible Documentation.
- Measure Useable Products, Services, and Software Delivered.
- Measure Meaningful Team Metrics, Not Individual Ones.

There is a charity group whose slogan is: "We stand on the shoulders of those who came before us. We provide the shoulders for those who follow us." This quote is also quite relevant for us as project managers. As each new architecture, tool, or methodology arises, we tend to get all excited. "This, surely, is the answer to all of our problems." Agile is not a silver bullet to cure all ills. While it may solve today's issues, tomorrow there are always going to be new challenges for us to face. But remember, *Agile is a technique to bring high quality products, services, or software to market more quickly, and get business value or revenue from them faster while protecting and motivating the people on the team.*

This is the reason you may find it advantageous to consider changing your processes to include a more Agile approach as part of your personal and corporate growth and evolution. It provides you with the flexibility to not only address today's challenges, but the ability to adapt to tomorrow's changes, too. Charles Darwin said, "It's not the strongest of the species that survives, nor the most intelligent, but the ones most responsive to change." This is also true for organizations and the project managers they rely on.

There is no magic formula that shows you exactly how to blend Waterfall and Agile methodologies flawlessly to create hybrid projects. It is a custom mix that only you can create with your own team. Every blend will be unique. You are the best person to be able to find a way to mix these philosophies in your own organization, and in doing so you will enhance your own project management practices for building successful projects.

But one reliable way to stay in tune with the profession and enhance your own professional standing as the field of project management shifts and grows and changes, is to be open to the words of wisdom passed along to us by experts who have preceded us in this field, and to be sure we pass along our own knowledge to those who are following in our footsteps.

Glossary Terms

3-D Theory of Management–Created by James Reddin, his premise was that a manager, the team, and the final product are three dimensions of management. If the team produces a good product, the manager did a good job.

Acceptance Criteria–The standards or requirements set out for a User Story in order for it to meet approval. Only when these criteria are met can the User Story be considered "Done".

Actual Cost (AC)–The true dollar amount spent for work performed by a team, and other material resources used, during a set period of time. Also known as Actual Cost of Work Performed (ACWP). In an Agile team, it is ordinarily the payroll costs for the team for the set period of time, however, actual materials can also be included when appropriate.

Affinity Estimates–A method of assigning Story Points to User Stories by arranging them in relative size, rather than estimating how long it will take to do them.

Agile–Agile is a project management technique to bring high quality products to market more quickly, and get business value or revenue from them faster, while protecting and motivating the people on the team. It is a set of philosophies for how we treat customers, team members, functional managers, Product Owners, internal and external customers, end-users, and vendors.

Agile Alliance–A non-profit organization with global membership, committed to advancing Agile development principles and practices.

Agile Manifesto–A belief statement of values written by a group of software developers in February 2001, that forms the basis for Agile principles and supports Agile practices.

Artifact–A tangible by-product produced during the development of Agile projects, such as Backlogs, Team Rules, and Burnup Charts. For example, in software development it might be use cases, models, and design documents.

Assertiveness–The way in which a person is perceived as attempting to influence the thoughts of others. This horizontal scale moves between Ask-Assertive and Tell-Assertive.

Backlog–A group of User Stories describing the features of a project and prioritized by the Product Owner/Customer by their importance, or business value and risk. Those tasks with the highest place on the list will be completed first. (Also called Product Backlog, Release Backlog, or Iteration Backlog.)

Barely Sufficient–The goal of an agile project is to create the maximum business value, or fulfill the business objective for which the project was funded, by doing only the minimum amount of work necessary to have a successful deliverable.

Bugs–A software term for errors, flaws, or some other type of mistake that means the software program does not give the expected results.

Burndown Chart–A visual representation of the amount of work that still needs to be completed before the end of the project. The chart line plots a downward trend to "burn down" the work of the project to zero.

Burnup Chart–A visual representation of the progress of the team toward completing the work of the project. It shows the work of the project as a whole, and the work done toward that goal is plotted on an ascending line.

Business Requirements–A description in business terms of what must be delivered or accomplished by the project to provide value to the organization. Created by upper management or the portfolio team.

Command and Control Management–A managerial style in which the manager is authoritative and controlling.

Continuous Improvement–An Agile practice which means to have a long-term vision and then constantly work in the short term to improve the process to meet your goals.

Continuous Integration–Assembling pieces as you go. Building things in small parts and making sure each new thing works with the others before moving on.

Cumulative Flow Diagram–A visual picture of the work of the project compared to the overall Backlog highlighting work in progress, work completed, or other factors you choose to track to pinpoint problems or bottlenecks in the work flow.

Customer–An internal or external person to the project who knows and understands the project vision and goals, and has some personal interest, involvement, or responsibility for the project outcome, who serves as the management link to the project team. This Agile project role might also be called the Product Owner.

Daily Stand-up–An Agile team meeting in which the team members literally stand. Each person has about 1 minute to say what they completed yesterday, what they intend to complete today, and any constraints or obstacles that are in their way. Only teams members are allowed to speak.

Dedicated Team–A group of people who focus on one project at a time, full-time.

Degree of Difficulty–The basis for Agile team task estimates. Rather than be time-based, it rests on the team's assessment of the amount of effort required to complete the work, and the complexity and amount of concentration it will take to produce it. It is usually translated into Story Points.

Deming, William–A quality guru who popularized the Plan, Do, Check, Act feedback loop cycle for continuous improvement.

Demonstration–An Agile practice in which the Product Owner/Customer and other stakeholders are invited to informally view the completed work of a project at the end of each Iteration. The purpose is to elicit early feedback at a time when it can guide future team performance, allow easy incorporation of changes or adjustments to completed work, and to get sign-offs on the portion of the product or service already completed.

Done–Meets the Acceptance Criteria created by the Project Owner/Customer and has been approved by any necessary internal and external entities.

Drucker, Peter–A business theory guru, known for his concepts of the knowledge worker and outsourcing, respect for the worker as an asset and not a liability, and forwarding the idea that providing value to the customer, not merely earning a profit, should be the goal of a business.

Earned Value (EV)–The value of work performed by a team during a set period of time. Also known as Budgeted Cost of Work Performed (BCWP). In an Agile team, it is the number of difficulty points or Story Points completed in a set period of time.

Earned Value Management (EVM)–A traditional project management methodology for integrating scope, schedule, and resources, and for objectively measuring project performance and progress. Performance is measured by determining the Budgeted Cost of Work Performed (Earned Value) and comparing it to the Planned Cost of Work Performed (Planned Value).

Emotional Intelligence (EI)–The ability to identify, assess, and control the emotions of oneself, others, and groups.

Empirical Process Control–Processes are controlled by inspecting for correct operation and results, and then processes are adapted as needed to be sure the final product is acceptable. Real world results, not estimates, are used to plan and schedule Releases.

Epic–A large umbrella collection or group of related User Stories to describe the work of an Agile project at a high level. Epics are further broken into Features, User Stories, and Tasks.

Explicit Knowledge–The formal information you can write down and share in corporate documents.

Fayol, Henri–Forwarded the thought that there were five primary functions of management: forecast and plan, organize, command, coordinate, and control. His original idea was that a manager would be open to feedback from the employees who were part of the process.

Feature–A chunk of functionality that delivers business value. It can be something new, or an addition or change to existing products, services, or software. Epics are further broken down into Features, User Stories, and Tasks.

Fibonacci Sequence–A mathematical series based on the work of an Italian mathematician who found the series 0 1 1 2 3 5 8 13, etc., in nature. Used to assign Story Points in relative sizes.

Finished Story Points (FSP)–The total number of Story Points moved to the Done column (or Approved column, if applicable) by the team during the Iteration. FSP equates to EV and BCWP.

Fist of Five–A consensus building technique in which team members use 1 through 5 finger signals, or a closed fist, to indicate their agreement or disagreement to a question or statement. This involves everyone in the team decision making process.

Galbraith, Frank–Galbraith was known for doing motion studies in the construction industry to find the most efficient way to do a job. His work was used by the manufacturing industry in their assembly lines.

Galbraith, Lillian–Introduced the idea that psychological factors such as motivation and attitude could affect the throughput of a production line.

Gantt Chart–A horizontal bar chart developed as a production control tool in 1917 by Henry Gantt. Project managers use this graphical illustration of a schedule to plan, coordinate, and track project tasks.

Goldratt, Eliyahu–Known for his Theory of Constraints (TOC) which are present in any project and should either be removed, or the work of the project rearranged to flow around them so that they have minimal effect.

Hardening Release–An Agile Release often added at the end of a project which may include training, operational hand-off, participation in compliance inspections, or other non-production related team activities.

Homeostasis–The process used by the body to maintain a stable environment. "What I have is what I need."

Hybrid Process–A project management approach that uses the best of both a traditional process and an Agile process, tailored to fit the project, company, customer, and team.

Hybrid Product–A product that incorporates hardware or manufactured portions with software portions to create the final result.

Ideal Programming Week–An Extreme Programming idea of the amount of work you can complete in a week where there are no interruptions, meetings, and other non-project interference.

Incremental–Do one piece, or chunk, of the work at a time.

Information Radiator–An Agile term coined by Alistair Cockburn which means a display posted in a place where people can see it as they work, or walk by.

Iteration–A short, regular timebox, typically one to four weeks, during which project work is completed and the team is protected from change.

Iteration Backlog–The User Stories and Tasks that the team has chosen and committed to do during the current Iteration. The list has been prioritized by the Product Owner/Customer by their importance, or business value and risk. Those with the highest place on the list will be completed first.

Iteration Zero–A timeboxed work period ahead of Iteration One. This is time for the team to do some of the prototyping to facilitate better decisions around risk issues, and also to find how quickly the team can produce work.

Iterative–A process you repeat periodically, perhaps every 1 to 2 weeks.

Iterative Relationship–A phase-to-phase relationship approach in which only one phase is planned at any given time, and the planning for the next is carried out as work progresses on the current phase (iteration) deliverables.

Just-In-Time Inventory Control–A method of how items should be requested, produced, and moved in order to arrive "just-in-time" for use on the assembly line. Associated with a "pull" system, or "kanban".

Kaizan–The Japanese term for "improvement" or "change for the better". It refers to practices that focus on continuous improvement.

Kanban–Also know in English as a "pull" system. Associated with the Toyota Production System and Lean manufacturing.

Last Responsible Moment–In Agile, there is value to delaying project decisions as late as possible to take advantage of additional information, internal or external decisions that can alter the project, or results from prototypes.

Lean–The philosophy that anything that is not providing business value to the process flow is an impediment and should be removed. The "art of work not done". Lean includes the ideas of "just-in-time" inventory control, also known as "pull" or "Kanban".

Maslow, Abraham–Know for his Hierarchy of Needs, listing levels of motivators for people. Only when a lower level of needs is met would the next level of needs become a motivator.

McGregor, Douglas–Known for Theory X management (appropriate for managing those with lower order needs) and Theory Y management (appropriate for managing those with higher order needs).

Minimum Marketable Feature (MMF)–The smallest possible set of functionality that, by itself, has value in the marketplace or organization.

MoSCoW Technique–Makes priority placement on the Backlog more specific by conveying the reason for Feature placement, according to **Must** Have, **Should** Have, **Could** Have, and **Won't** Have This Time categories.

Nonaka, Ikujiro–First used the term Scrum in an article, *"The New New Product Development Game,"* written with Hirotaka Takeuchi, in 1986.

Ohno, Taiichi–Originator of *"just-in-time"* inventory control, a part of the Lean approach, with Sakichi Toyoda and Kiichiro Toyoda at Toyota Motor Corporation.

Osmotic Communication–A positive result of teams located in a common space. Information flows in the background hearing of the team so that they pick up relevant information by osmosis, i.e., ideas are gradually, subtly absorbed.

Overlapping Approach–A phase-to-phase relationship approach in which a phase may start before the preceding one is completed.

Pair Programming–A software development practice whereby two programmers work together, typically one at the keyboard and the other sitting next to him to watch and advise. This reduces errors at their source.

Pair Collaboration–An Agile practice adapted for a Waterfall team. Two people work together, one creating and the other watching and advising. It can also be a simple as one person preparing work and asking a team colleague to look it over before it is submitted.

Parkinson's Law–Work expands to fit the time allocated. (Technically, the quote is: Work expands so as to fill the time available for its completion.)

Persona–A specific, detailed description showing an example of the kind of person who would use your product. The team can ask, "Would Ethel be able to replace this battery?"

Plan, Do, Check, Act (PDCA)–An cyclical feedback loop approach to generate continuous improvement in projects. Created by Walter Shewhart and popularized by William Deming.

Planned Value (PV)–The value of work originally scheduled by a team during a set period of time. Also known as Budgeted Cost of Work Scheduled (BCWS). In an Agile team, it is the velocity, or number of difficulty or Story Points, the team commits to complete in a set period of time.

Planning Meeting–A meeting between Product Owner/Customer, Project Manager, and Agile Team to share the vision, review the prioritized backlog, assign difficulty points to tasks, and commit to the work for the upcoming Iteration.

Planning Poker–An Agile technique for estimating how relatively hard it will be to do one task compared to another, rather than how long it will take to do it. Created by Mike Cohn, Mountain Goat Software.

Practices–The concrete, day-to-day things an Agile team does to complete a project which are based on the philosophies and principles in which they believe. Somewhat similar to tools and techniques.

Principles–The bridge between Agile values (philosophies) and daily practices. The values (belief structure) can be listed as principles to follow that further express how people holding those values would behave. Based on those principles, teams can choose daily practices.

Prioritized–Arranged in order. In this usage, the items with the most business value and the highest risk are placed at the top of the Product Backlog to be done first.

Process–A series of actions bringing about a result.

Process Requirements–Activities required by the project organization. They can be specified to map to a particular methodology that must be followed and include any organizational restraints. In an Agile organization, they will be based on Agile philosophies and principles.

Product Backlog–The User Stories for the entire project. They will be prioritized and chosen for an individual Release Backlog and then an Iteration Backlog as time goes on, and planned in more detail in a "just-in-time" process.

Product Owner–Someone who knows and understands the project vision and goals, and has some personal interest, involvement, or responsibility for the project outcome who serves as the management link to the project team. This Agile project role might also be called the Customer.

Product Requirements–A description of the properties of a system or product (or one of several ways to accomplish a set of business requirements). In Agile, product requirements are expressed in User Stories and are the responsibility of the Product Owner. The team is responsible for choosing the way in which the business requirements are accomplished.

Productized Processes–Specific little agile methodologies that may include books, classes, certifications, and other supporting materials that are sold as a for-profit product or service.

Progressive Elaboration–A planning process in which the work of the project is planned in broad strokes far out in the future. More detail is added just before doing the work, to lower the risk to the project and lower the cost of change.

Project Roadmap–The highest level look at an entire Agile project which may show multiple Releases broken into multiple Iterations.

Pull–A Lean manufacturing system process in which the workers signal when they are going to need more parts by using a Kanban card. Know in Japanese as "Kanban".

Reddin, James–Known for his doctrine of the 3-D Theory of management. If the 3 dimensions of a project: manager, team, and final product, all produce the desired results, the manager did a good job.

Retrospective–A team meeting at the end of each Iteration to consider the team's performance on creating the product or service and also the performance of the team in working together. The idea is to make any adjustments immediately (at the start of the next Iteration) to incorporate continuous improvement into the project.

Release–A portion of an Agile project structure which contains Iterations. The Release length is the total of all of the Iterations it contains. A Project Roadmap may contain several Releases.

Release Planning–A meeting to break high-level Agile Roadmaps into smaller Releases and plan the most eminent one in further detail.

Responsiveness–A vertical evaluation scale attribute comparing the way a person prefers to place their initial focus when communicating with others: Task-Directed or People-Directed. It can also measure the way in which a person is perceived as preferring to control or express their feelings and emotions.

Return on Investment (ROI)–A performance measure used to evaluate the efficiency of an investment, or to compare the efficiency of a number of different investments. If an investment does not have does not have a positive ROI predicted, or if there are other opportunities that have a higher ROI, then the investment—possibly a project—should not be done.

Roadmap Planning–The overview of an Agile project to show the project in its entirety. It is further broken down into Releases and Iterations.

Rolling Wave Planning–A form of Progressive Elaboration used in Waterfall methods and also in Agile methods. Planning where the work is to be accomplished in the near term is planned in detail, and future work is left less planned at a higher level. Each wave (or Iteration) is planned just before it starts.

Royce, Winston–A leader in software development in the second half of the 20th century who described the Waterfall model for software development in a 1970 paper, but didn't use the term "Waterfall" or recommend this approach.

Scope Creep–The uncontrolled expansion of the agreed upon work of the project as a result of delays, additions, customer changes, or poorly defined work. This usually occurs without a corresponding increase in project time or budget to complete the unexpected additional work.

Scrum–A specific methodology for creating software and web-based projects using Agile philosophies and principles along with a standardized set of practices.

Scrum of Scrums–A meeting where ScrumMasters meet to coordinate the work of multiple teams.

Sequential Approach–A phase-to-phase relationship approach in which one phase must finish before the next one can start.

Servant-Leader–A newer type of management style in which the manager acts as a servant to remove constraints from the team, and leads them by showing respect for the worker.

Shewhart, Walter–Creator of the Plan, Do, Check, Act cycle which provides a feedback loop for continuous improvement. Popularized by quality guru William Deming.

Social Loafing–The fear by management that people in a group have a tendency to "slack off", or not work as hard in a group as they would if they were alone.

Sprint Backlog–The User Stories and Tasks that the team has chosen and committed to do during the current sprint (Iteration). The list has been prioritized by the Certified Scrum Product Owner by each item's importance, or business value, and risk. Those with the highest place on the list will be completed in the first sprint.

Start-Finish Rule–Agile teams use the 0-100% method. A Task has 0 value until is done, accepted, approved by the Product Owner or Customer, and approved by any other outside compliance inspections, if necessary. Only then is the Task assigned a value of 100%.

Story Points–A unit of measure for expressing the overall size of a User Story, Feature, Task, or other piece of work in relationship to other items, either in terms of size or complexity. There is no direct correlation between Story Points and the hours needed to complete them.

Strategic Objectives–Statements of specific outcomes to be achieved, used to operationalize the Mission Statement and provide specifics on how the organization can turn the their Mission and Vision into reality in a well-defined timeframe. They may be focused on greater profits, rate of growth, new products, productivity, or social responsibility, for example.

Tacit Knowledge–The knowledge embedded in a person's individual experience. Knowledge that is unwritten, but can be transmitted between team members in a group setting.

Takeuchi, Hirotaka–First used the term Scrum in an article, *"The New New Product Development Game,"* written with Ikujiro Nonaka, in 1986.

Tasks–The lowest decomposition of Agile project work to create a piece small enough for the team to assign Story Points based on difficulty, and to complete in one Iteration. The levels from top to bottom are Epic, Feature, User Story, and Task.

Taylor, Frederick–The Father of Scientific Management who is know for time studies. Taylor studied workers to find the most efficient movements to do a job quickly. This technique was then used to create the best assembly lines.

Test Driven Development (TDD)–A little agile methodology in which automated tests are created first, then they are used to test the actual lines of code written to create a software feature or function.

Theory of Constraints (TOC)–Created by Eliyahu Goldratt, this theory says constraints are present in any project and should either be removed or the work of the project rearranged to flow around them so that they have minimal effect.

Theory X–A type of command and control management based on the theory of human motivation that frames workers as people who dislike work, are inherently lazy, and will avoid work if they can.

Theory Y–A type of management based on the theory of human motivation that frames workers as people who are self-motivated and self-controlled, have the talent for creative problem solving, and want to do well at work. Managers should be open, trusting, and share decision making.

Timebox–A short period of time, typically one to four weeks, also called a sprint or an Iteration. All timeboxes in a single project should, ideally, be equal in length.

Toyoda, Kiichiro–Originator of *just-in-time* inventory control, a part of the Lean approach, with Sakichi Toyoda and Taiichi Ohno at Toyota Motor Corporation.

Toyoda, Sakichi–Originator of *just-in-time* inventory control, a part of the Lean approach, with Kiichiro Toyoda and Taiichi Ohno at Toyota Motor Corporation.

Transparency–The processes that affect the outcome of a process must be visible to those controlling the processes, i.e., the project team.

User Stories–A descriptive, short explanation of a feature created by the Product Owner/Customer with the help of the Project Manager. Used in Agile projects to replace lengthy technical and functional requirement documents. User Stories are further broken into Tasks.

Velocity–The measured capacity of the team to deliver value. The number of Story Points a team can complete during an Iteration. This shows the rate at which the team can produce work.

Versatility–The ability to adapt one's behavior to the concerns and expectations of others in order to create productive relationships.

Vertical Slice–A small portion of the final product or service that was created so that it contains all the necessary elements to make it usable. This term comes from the concept of a slice of cake, which would include a cross-section of frosting, cake, filling, and bottom layer.

Waterfall–A sequential process for project work in which progress flows downward through various project phases, each of which is typically completed before the next one begins.

Index

A

AccuRev Agile sales team, 308
adaptability, 259
advice for, Agile projects
    Charles Darwin's view, 319
    checklist of, 317
    ideas, 318
    project management principles, 316
    spreading Agile flexibility, 318
    teams, 317–8
    tips for, 315–6
Agile candidates, 75
Agile complexity amplifier, 56
Agile Earned Value, 165–9
Agile evaluator, 77
    checklist, 78f
    pinpoint issues, 77
    sample results, 79f
Agile model, 57
Agile practices, 1, 2, 9, 233, 257
    Corporate Change and Performance, 2–3
    culture, 3
    information technology, 6
    management issues, 4

    methodology, 3
    process selection criteria, 76f
    vs. Waterfall
        sequential approach, 49
        Waterfall Phases, 48f
Analytical Engine (Charles Babbage), 80
andon system, 283
Applied Research and Consulting (ARC), 226–7
Assembler language, 81
    complier, 81
    object, 81
Atern Iterative Development Cycle, 275
Atern Lifecycle Process, 273
Atern philosophy, 271
automated test suite, 266

B

Bicycle Wheel Flange Project, 44f
big Agile, 11
    philosophy, 12
big-bang integration, 267
Boeing's 787 Project, 303
    Agile principles, 305–6

manufacturing facility, 306
materials management employees,
304–5
modeling software, 307–8
product-centric projects, 306
specifications documents, 305
subcontractors, 305
teams work, 304
Budgeted Cost of Work Scheduled
(BCWS), 165
building information modeling
software, 307
burndown chart, 264
with scope changes, 172f
additional iterations, 173
business and economic
development, 171
traditional team, 171
voluntary scope, 173
burnup chart, 174f
finish line, 174
industry metrics, 174
business, shifts in, 221
Agile manifesto, 231f
inventory control, 221
team workspaces, 222–4
business skill sets, 201
Agile budgeting, 212
anointed, 201
authorizes travel, 219
competitor, 211
cost of failure, 203
balance sheet, 205
failure rate, 204
strategic objectives, 205, 206f
customer involvement, 202
embrace, 201
fixers, 202
forecasting, 212
maintenance rate, 206
market share, 206

maximizing revenue, 208
measurement system, 209
milestones, 207
MMF, 209
project charter, 202
quicker return on investment, 210f
return on investment (ROI), 203
smarter utilization, 202
team recognition, 219
Waterfall model, 210
business value, 4

C

Canticle for Leibowitz (Walter Miller),
32
capability maturity model (CMM),
130
case studies, Agile projects
AccuRev Agile sales team, 308
Boeing's 787 Project, 303–6
CH2M Hill's Rocky flats project,
301–3
GVK's Mumbai, India airport
project, 308–10
The Kauffman performing arts
center project, 307–8
The Sydney Opera house project,
310–12
cathode ray tube (CRT), 81
Certified Associate in Project
Management (CAPM®), 5
Certified ScrumMaster (CSM), 261
Certified Scrum Product Owner
(CSPO), 261–2
Certified Scrum Professional (CSP)
certification, 261
Certified Scrum Trainers (CSTs), 261
change for free, 243
change process, 14–6, 298–9
being timeboxed, 16
Control Boards inspection, 14

obsolescence, 15
overriding obsession, 15
stakeholders, 14
CH2M Hill's Rocky flats project,
 301–3
 department of energy (DOE), 303
Chrysler C3 project, 264
coding standards, 269
collaborating, 230–1
collective code ownership, 269
committed story points (CSP), 168
communications tools, 158–60
 collaboration technology, 158
 3D telecommunications, 159
 Cisco Corporation, 159
 TeleHuman, 159
 instant messaging (IM), 158–9
 video teleconferencing and web
 conferencing, 158
 web cams, 159
continuous integration, 269
Corporate Change and Performance
 (James L. Heskett and John P.
 Kotter), 2
cost plus award fee (CPAF), 239
cost plus fixed fee (CPFF), 239
cost plus incentive fee (CPIF), 239
cost plus percentage of costs (CPPC),
 239
credit card, 16
critical path method, 24
crystal methodologies, 116, 287–8
cumulative flow diagram, 175*f*
 burnup chart, 174*f*
 Iteration Zero, 175
 project statistics, 176
customer relationship management
 (CRM), 81

D

daily burndown chart, 165, 166*f*

daily scrum, 264
demonstration, 68
deployment phase, 273
Design That Matters, 225
development team, 263
digital video recorder (DVR), 132
distributed teams
 Agile development survey, 153
 casual conversations
 oneness, 154
 cross-functional, 151
 divided, 152*f*
 economic crises, 153
 inhibiting communication, 154
 language, 156
 cultural idioms, 157
 one-on-one coaching, 157
 overkill, 157
 lone expert, 161–2
 remote daily stand-ups, 160
 team dysfunction, 154
 travel, 161
 work tracking tools, 160
documentation, in Agile, 259
 burndown chart with scope
 changes, 171–3
 burnup chart, 174
 earned value method (*see* earned
 value management [EVM]
 method)
 software documents (*see* software
 documents)
dramatic impact, 233
Drucker, Peter, 25–6
 Burger King, 26
 business guru, 25
 knowledge workers, 26
 mainstream business philosophy,
 26
DSDM Atern principles, 271–5
dumb terminals, 81

dynamic systems development
method (DSDM), 12, 34
Agile project framework, 270
Atern principles
business need, 271
collaborative and fast decisions,
272
communication and
cooperation, 272–3
control, 273
delivery, 271
foundations, 272
iteration, 272
lifecycle process, 273
MoSCoW technique, 274
quality, 272
contingencies, 270–1
DSDM® Consortium, 270–1
examples, 274–5
in PRINCE2®, 270

E
early customer involvement, 45–8
Agile methodology, 46
corporate management software,
46
earned value management (EVM)
method, 164
actual cost, 167
BCWS, 165
committed story points (CSP), 168
grey dotted line, 165
planned value, 164
PMOs, 163, 168
schedule variance, 164
start-finish rule, 168
timeboxed period, 164
traditional project, 165
velocity, 164
Waterfall team, 165
empirical process control, 261

engineering phase, 273
enterprise level, 141
collocated teams, 147
project puzzle, 147
cooperating teams, 146
Drucker, Peter, 142
interest teams, 148
iteration switch, 149
Agile experts, 150
methodologies, 141
multiple, independent product
backlogs, 145f
one backlog—many teams, 145
one backlog—mixed teams, 143
software-centric team, 144
one backlog—one team
project manager/ScrumMaster,
143
reserve mornings, 148
special skill, 149
team switch, 149
errors, 41
continuous integration, 42
fail early, fail fast, 41
last responsible moment, 41
pair programming, 42
TDD, 42
escape velocity, 213
dealing with Darwin, 213
risk adverse, 213
"essential practices," 269
explicit knowledge, 228
exploration phase, 273
Extreme Programming Applied (Ken
Auer and Roy Miller), 269
Extreme Programming (XP), 12, 34
automated test suite, 266
big-bang integration, 267
defination of, 265
executable code, 268
ideal programming week, 265–6

methodology, 265
practices, 264
principles of
    core values, 268
    practices, 268–9
refactoring, 265, 267
roles of
    coach, 270
    customer, 269
    programmers, 270
    tracker, 270
SCC, 267
software build, 268
values, 264

F

Fayol, Henri, 22–3
    command and control, 23
    *General and Industrial
        Management,* 22
    Project Management Institute
        (PMI®), 23
    servant leader, 23
feasibility and foundation phases, 273
feature driven development (FDD), 12
    Agile processes, 288
    Iteration Zero, 288
    process of, 288–9
    roles in, 290
Fibonacci sequence, 108
    consecutive numbers, 111
    criticizing Fibonacci's, 110
    index finger, 110
    offspring, 109
    rabbit question, 109*f*
financial foundation, 233
firm fixed price (FFP), 238
first Agile practices to introduce, 134*f*
fixed price economic price adjustment
        (FPEPA), 238
fixed price incentive fee (FPIF), 238

fixed Waterfall and Agile project
        parameters, 260*f*
focusing, 229
Ford, Henry, 23–4
    Ford Motor Company, 23
    Model Ts, 23
    Tin Lizzie, 23
    traditional methodology, 24

G

Galbraith, Frank, 21–2
    Cheaper by Dozen, 21
    motion studies, 21
Galbraith, Lillian, 22
Gantt, Henry, 24
    bar chart, 24
    critical path method, 24
    Gantt chart, 24
    Program Evaluation and Review
        Technique (PERT), 24
    Project Management Institute
        (PMI), 24
Gemba concept, 281–2
globalization, 2
Goldratt, Eliyahu
    The Goal, 26
    TOC, 26
Goldratt's Theory of Constraints,
        277–8
Google car, 83–5
    artificial intelligence software, 84
    GPS system, 84
    hybrid product, 83
    hybrid project, 84*f*
Google Maps, 85
GVK's Mumbai, India airport project,
        309

Agile approach, 309
challenges, 309–10

H
hardening release, 73*f*
high-level involvement, 244
history of business theory, 20*f*
homeostasis, 9
hybrid medical devices, 85
    ophthalmologist, 86
    PASCAL photocoagulator, 86
    TOPCON Medical Laser Systems,
      86
    Tumor treatment, 86
hybrid products, 80
    analytical engine, 80
    Bjarne Stroustrup, 80
    Charles Babbage, 80
    hybrid sweet spot, 77*f*
    IBM, 80
    iPhone®, 80
    smartphone, 80
hybrid project, 91
hybrid team, 91

I
ideas, in Agile
    slow-moving assembly, 19
    traditional project processes, 19
information security, 259
Information Technology (IT), 165
Insights on Leadership (Stephen
    Covey), 193
instant messaging (IM), 158
integration testing, 266
Iron triangle, 259–60
"Iron Triangle," 259–60
iteration, 16
    time breakdown
      Customer Demo, 137–8
      PMBOK® Guide, 137

two-week iteration time
    breakdown, 136*f*
Iteration Zero method, 288
iterative and incremental
    development, 13
    dedicated team, 14
    incremental, 13
    iterative, 13
    WBS, 14

J
Johnson, Stephen
    adjacent possible, 178
    cross-pollination, 178
    Where Good Ideas Come From, 178
Junkyard Incubators, 225–6
just-in-time inventory control, 30–1

K
Kaizan philosophy, 282–3
kanban, 278
    philosophies of, 278
    as physical card, 278
    pull production control system, 278
    uses of, 278–81
The Kauffman performing arts center
    project, 307–8

L
LabVIEW FPGA software, 86
last responsible moment, 41
lean manufacturing process
    Gemba, 281–282
    kanban, 278
    principles of
      customer, 278
      value, 277
    TQM, 277
    WIP limits, 280
lean software development
    principles of, 284

Theory of Constraints (TOC), 284
learning, 229
lighter documentation, 163
little agile, 11–17, 257-275
local area network (LAN), 81

M

Machine Design magazine, 43
maintainability, 258
"Management by Walking Around
  (MBWA)," 282
managers, 263
*Manifesto for Agile Software
  Development,* 39
manifesto, in Agile, 35*f*
Maslow, Abraham
  concept of motivation, 27
  Hierarchy of Needs, 27
  prediction, 28
McGregor, Douglas, 27–9
  piggy-backing, 27
  PMP exam, 28
  Theory X and Theory Y, 27, 28*f*
metaphor, 268
*Microsoft Project 2010 Scrum
  Solution,* 171
Mike Vizdos, 120
Minecraft, 198
minimum marketable feature (MMF),
  209
money for nothing, 243
MoSCoW technique, 274

N

need for change, 8–10
  Apple, 8
  economic downturn, 8
  Facebook, 9
  freeze in fear, 10
  Hewlett-Packard Company (HP), 8
  homeostasis, 9–10

more flexible, 9
  paradigm learning, 10
  speed-driven economy, 8
  Twitter, 9
new marketing strategy, 82
  global positioning satellite (GPS),
    83
  product-centric selling model, 82
new product or service measurements
    of quality, 88
  adaptability, 89
  performance, 88
  security, 89
non-IT projects, 13
non-software Agile process, 59
  product owner, 61
  complexity, 55
  complex products, 56
  feature-rich, 55
  Scott Davis, 55
  speedcook, 56

O

onsite customer, 269
organizational changes, 233
  authorization
    antithesis of, 234
    Iteration Zero, 234
    mid-level position, 234
    unrealistic number, 234
  communications, 236
    cube farm, 236
    face-to-face communication,
      236
  contracts, 237
    lump sum, 238
    partnership, 237
  cost accounting, 245
    Agile opportunities, 246
  cost reimbursable contract, 238
    CPAF, 239

CPFF, 239
CPIF, 239
CPPC, 239
human resources (HR), 252
intangible assets, 249
lump sum contracts, 238
  FFP, 238
  FPEPA, 238
  FPIF, 238
metrics, 236
PMO refocusing, 249
  erroneous, 252
  quality software management,
    250
    systems thinking, 250
  sloppy, 251
radical management shifts, 247
  dramatic shifts, 247
  principles of radical
    management, 248
resource management, 235
rolling contracts, 242
  vertical slice, 242
team member reactions, 247
time and materials (T&M), 240
  Agile alliance, 240
  Agile contracts, 241
osmotic communication, 222

P
pair programming, 42, 269
Panama canal expansion project, 301
Parkinson's Law principle, 121
PASCAL photocoagulator, 86
Personal Knowledge (Michael
    Polanyi), 228
phase-to-phase relationships, 58
  iterative, 59
  overlapping, 59
  PMI, 58
  sequential, 59

pilot project, 293
  change process
    steps, 298–9
  PMBOK® Guide, 297
  product owner, training, 294
  rule of seven, 295
  sell up and down, 294
  and sideways, 294
  talks, 297
  WIIFM, 295–6
plan-driven approach, 260
Planning Poker, 111
  brad, 113
  cards, 112*f*
  Cohn, Mike, 111
  quality metrics, 113
  quality speak, 112
  wideband, 111
  Wideband Delphi, 111
PMBOK® Guide, 58, 164
practices, 264–5
predictability, 259
principles, in Agile, 37
  enhances agility, 38
  environment, 41
  Goldratt's Theory of Constraints, 37
  manifesto, 38–9
  McGregor concept, 37
  position-power-driven, 41
  practices and work, 37
  Reddin's idea, 37
  traditional and modern
    organizational hierarchies, 40*f*
  traditional representations, 41
  upstairs, 39
12 Principles of Agile Software, 39
3D printers, 217
  larger machines, 217
  pencil printer, 217
  RITI Coffee, 217
processes, defined, 261

product
  backlog, 261, 264
  owner, 263
productized processes, 11–2
Professional Development Units
    (PDUs), 6
program evaluation and review
    technique (PERT), 24
Program Management Professional
    (PgMP®), 5
progressive elaboration, 67
  Agile roadmap, 70*f*
  demo, not memo, 68
  demonstration, 68
  product owner, 69
  project roadmap, 69, 70*f*
  retrospective, 68
  rolling wave planning, 68
project management, 5
  CAPM®, 5
  Egyptian project, 7
  genesis of, 6–8
  Government Extension, 5
  PDUs, 6
  PgMP®, 5
  pharaoh, 7
  PMI-ACP®, 5
  PMI Construction Standard, 5
  PMI-RMP®, 5
  PMI-SP®, 5
  PMOs, 7
  PMP®, 5
  Project and Portfolio Standard, 5
  Project Management
      Certifications, 5
  scrum advocates, 6
*Project Management Body of
    Knowledge—Fifth Edition,* 5
Project Management Institute Agile
    Certified Practitioner
    (PMI-ACP)®, 5

Project Management Institute (PMI),
    24
Project Management Institute Risk
    Management Professional
    (PMI-RMP®), 5
Project Management Institute
    Scheduling Professional
    (PMI-SP®), 5
project management level, 233
project management offices (PMOs),
    7, 47, 163, 208-210, 249-252
Project Management Professional
    (PMP®), 5
project managers, 1
  skills, 1–3
  work ethic, 2
project questions, 3–5
prototyping
  hub flange, 45
  Iteration Zero scenario, 44
  Machine Design magazine, 43
  shorter spokes, 43
  sporting goods, 43
  wheel hub, 43
  wider spoke, 43
pull system, 30–1

Q
QSM Associates, 5
quality risks, 76

R
Raisin Personal Monitor system, 87
Rational Unified Process (RUP)
  overview, 12
    component-based architectures,
        284–6
    iteration, 285
    requirements, 285
    software code, 286
    software quality, 286

visually model software, 286
phases of, 286–7
project process structure, 287
Reddin, James, 29
3-D Theory of Management, 29
refactoring, 265, 267, 269
retrospective, 68–9
return on investment (ROI), 203
rolling wave planning, 68
Royce, Winston
    Lockheed Software Technology, 25
    rigid methodology, 25
    spacecraft missions, 25
    Walker Royce, 25
    Waterfall, 25

S
scalability, 258
ScrumMaster, 261–3
scrum process, 257
    adaptability, 259
    Agile developments methods, 259
    Alliance
        training and certification, 261
        website, 262
    Bugs, 263
    core artifacts, 264
    core ceremonies, 264
    core roles, 263
    CSD, 261
    CSM and CSP, 261
    CSPO and CSTs, 261
    empirical process control, 261
    fixed Waterfall and Agile project
        parameters, 260
    iron triangle, 259–60
    knowledge acquisition, 263
    plan-driven approach, 260
    predictability, 259
    product backlog, 262
    scrum of scrums, 263

    sprint backlog, 262
    sprint goal, 263
    transparency, 261
    value-driven approach, 260
    waterfall/traditional practices, 259
seldom used features, 57f
Servant Leadership Learning
    Community in 2000, 193
The Seven Qualities of Wildly
    Desirable Software (Mike
    Gualtieri), 88
Shewhart Cycle
    Agile act cycle process, 52f
    Check phase, 50
    Do and Check processes for Agile
        teams, 51f
    Do and Test, 50
    Do part, 50
    Plan, 49–50
        Agile project cycle, 49
        collocated, 49
        Evans, Jeffrey, 49
        Meyer, David, 49
        plan cycle process for Agile
            teams, 50f
        Rubinstein, Joshua, 49
Shewhart/Deming Plan, 275
skill set, changes, 177
    amiable style, 188
    analytical style, 188
    assertiveness, 187
    collaboration skills, 181–2
        conflict, 182
    collocated and dedicated teams,
        178
    conflict resolution skills, 182–4
    coordination skills, 181
    driver style, 187
    expressive style, 188
    facilitation skills, 179
        demonstrations, 179

iteration planning, 179
release planning, 179
roadmap planning, 179
group decision making skills, 184
millennium management skills
baby boomers, 194, 197
echo boomers, 194
millennials, 194
Tech-savvy, 194
tech-trained, 195
process tailoring skills, 199
lockstep approach, 200
sales skills, 180
piece-by-piece, 181
self-managed teams
self-directed, 177
worker bee, 178
servant-leader skills
Greenleaf, R. K., 192
Insights on Leadership, 193
social styles model, 185*f*
social styles skills
communications styles, 186
managerial grid, 186
Social Style Model™, 185
versatility, 186
team building skills
learn-on-the-job, 182
tell-assertive, 190
training skills, 184
Skype, 227–8
socializing, 229–30
social loafing, 129
best grade, 128
CMM, 130
stop-gap, 127
software build, 268
software development life cycle
(SDLC)
HIPAA, 259
Sarbanes-Oxley, 259

scalability, 258
scrum process, 257
technical performance metrics, 258
test driven development (TDD),
258
software documents. *see also*
documentation, in Agile
barely sufficient, 171
Microsoft Project, completed
Iteration in, 170*f*
project culture, 171
vendor solutions, 169
Waterfall project, 169
Source Code Control (SCC), 267
space design, 226
sprint
backlog, 261
planning, 261, 264
reviews and retrospectives, 264
stakeholders, 263
Standish Group, 56
start-finish rule, 168
State of Agile Survey from
VersionOne (2011), 12–13
Steelcase, 226–7
Stephen Johnson, 15
stock market adjustments, 12
story cards, 155
last responsible minute, 155
primarily tool, 155
Street View mapping service, 85
survey, 12
sustainable pace, 269
The Sydney Opera house project, 311
Agile approaches, 312
multiple protypes, 311
project approaches, 311
structural engineers, 311

T

tacit knowledge, 228

Takeuchi, Hirotaka and Nonaka,
   Lkujiro, 29–30
   Harvard Business Review, 29
   Scrum, 29
Taylor, Frederick, 19–21
   scientific management, father of,
      21
   time studies, 19
team, in Agile, 107, 269
   degree of difficulty, 108
   dog estimates, 115
   empirical data, 108
   estimation game, 113, 114*f*
      Bockman, Steve, 113
   framing team, 107
   header, 107
   Planning Poker, 111
   selecting tasks, 115
   story points, 108
   stretcher, 107
   teams estimates, 108
   tracking Agile progress, 116
      approved, 118
      daily stand-up meeting, 119
      to do chart, 117*f*
      guesstimate, 119
      information radiator, 116
      iteration backlog, 117
      product backlog, 117
      transparency, 116
   T-shirt sizes, 115
team operating rules, 91
   conflict resolution, 93
   motivation, 93
   PMBOK® Guide, 93
technical performance metrics, 258
techniques, 93
   closed fist, 94
   fist of five technique, 93, 94*f*
   scissors, 94

test driven development (TDD), 42,
   258
testing, 269
theory of constraints (TOC), 26
3-D Theory of Management, 29
time zones, gap, 156
tools, in Agile, 123
   Ambysoft Agile Practices survey,
      133
   continuous integration, 133
   crystal, 12
   digital video recorder (DVR), 132
      phase, 133
      release, 133
   DSDM, 12
   end-of-iteration, 123
   Extreme Programming (XP), 12
   FDD, 12
   kanban, 12
   lean manufacturing, 12
   lean software development, 12
   philosophies, 123
   planning project length using
      velocity, 126*f*
   practices introduce, 134*f*
      iteration planning, 135
   retrospective, 133
   roadmap planning, 136
   RUP, 12
   SCRUM, 12
   social loafing (*see* social loafing)
   TPS, 12
   two-week iteration time
      breakdown, 136*f*
   velocity, 124–6
TOPCON Medical Laser Systems of
   Santa Clara, 86
total quality management (TQM), 277
Toyoda, Sakichi, Toyoda, Kiichiro and
   Ohno, Taiichi, 30–4
   adaptive software development, 34

Canticle for Leibowitz, 32
crystal, 34
DSDM, 34
Extreme Programming, 34
FDD, 34
just-in-time inventory control, 30
just-in-time production, 30
Kaizen, 31
PMBOK® Guide, 32
Pragmatic Programming, 34
pull system, 31
Toyota principles, 31
Toyota's Lean approach, 30
TPS, 30
Toyota production system (TPS)
    andon system, 283
    jidoka, 283
    just-in-time, 283
traditional bookends, 72*f*
traditional processes moving to Agile
    processes, 58*f*
traditional teams, 132–3
trajectories, 13
transparency, 261

U
unemployment rates, 2
usability, 258
user stories, 16, 62
    acceptance criteria, 63
    epic story, 64
    ISO standards, 63–4
    persona, 63
    planning meeting, 67
    process flow, 67*f*
    product backlog, 64
    sample, 62*f*
    sample bank project, 65
    sticky notes, 66
    WBS approach, 66

V
value-driven approach, 260
values, 264–5
velocity, 124. *see also* tools, in Agile
    death by PowerPoint, 124
    demonstration, 124
    difficulty points, 126
    team velocity, 124
Visica 2™ Cryoablation Treatment
    System, 86
vision planning, 72
voice biometrics, 214

W
Waterfall project, 3
    and Agile project structures, 60*f*
    candidates, 74
    organization, 95
        Iteration Zero, 96
        work breakdown structure
            (WBS), 95
    phases, 48*f*
    proponents, 3
    selection criteria, 75*f*
    Waterfall/traditional practices, 259
Where Good Ideas Come From
    (Stephen Johnson), 15, 34–5,
    223
work breakdown structure (WBS), 14
    Agile-ish, 98
        build website, 100
        coffee, 99
        contact growers, 100
        equipment, 99
        philanthropic mission, 98
        philanthropic outreach
            program, 98
        scope creep, 100
        transportation, 99
Uganda coffee project, 99*f*
Uganda coffee website, 102*f*

demonstrations, 106
games database, 104
mission statement, 105
planning, 106
prototype, 106
retrospectives, 106
work planning in Agile, 96
    citing specifics, 97

cost of change, 97, 98*f*
cost overruns, 97
iterative development, 97
plummet, 97
risk, 97
working closely with customer,
    16–7